PAKISTAN
PAST AND PRESENT

PAKISTAN
PAST AND PRESENT

Prakash Chander

A P H PUBLISHING CORPORATION
5 ANSARI ROAD, DARYA GANJ
NEW DELHI-110 002

Published by
S.B. Nangia
A P H Publishing Corporation
5 Ansari Road, Darya Ganj
New Delhi-110002
☎ 3274050
Email : aph@mantraonline.com

ISBN 81-7648-447-4

2003

Printed in India at
Efficient Offset Printers
New Delhi-110 035

PREFACE

Pakistan, a nation for only fifty five years, has had a turbulent history. Ruled by the military for half its existence, it has seen three wars with India and the loss of much of its territory. The combination of political instability, deep-seated economic and social problems, and access to nuclear weapons has made it one of the most strategically sensitive countries in the world. The recent war in neighbouring Afghanistan has placed it at the very centre of global attention and projected its military ruler, General Pervez Musharraf, onto the world stage. Musharraf has become the first Pakistani leader in thirty years to dare to confront the country's Islamic extremists.

In this riveting history of Pakistan from 1947 to the present the author describes many fault lines in Pakistani Society. While most Pakistanis have a moderate, tolerant vision of Islam, the country's central institutions are so weak that the military region may prove incapable of rescuing the "failed State" of Pakistan.

The book therefore, merits attention of experts on Asia, diplomats and policy makers of the developed countries.

Editor

CONTENTS

Contents

CHAPTER 1

INTRODUCTION

Nation building remains a difficult process in Pakistan. But although the country has undergone a succession of traumatic socio-political experiences since achieving independence in 1947, it continues to demonstrate its resilience and its capacity to survive and adapt to changing circumstances. Joining the community of nations as a bifurcated state, with its two wings separated by 1,600 kilometers of foreign soil, Pakistan was faced with the immediate task of absorbing large numbers of refugees from India in the months immediately following partition. The new nation struggled with severe economic disadvantages made acutely painful by a shortage of both administrative personnel and the material assets necessary to establish and sustain its fledgling government. With the death of Mohammad Ali Jinnah—the revered Quaid-i- Azam (Great Leader)—only thirteen months after independence, the nation was dealt another severe blow.

Created to provide a homeland for the Muslims of the Indian subcontinent, Pakistan was heir to a government structure and a political tradition that were essentially Western and secular. From its inception, Pakistan has worked to synthesize Islamic principles with the needs of a modern state. The young nation was immediately challenged by a host of other factors affecting national development, including ethnic and provincial tensions, political rivalries, and security considerations. The country subsequently survived civil war and the resultant loss of its East Wing, or East Pakistan, which became the independent nation of Bangladesh in December 1971, and has accommodated an influx of refugees resulting from the

Soviet occupation of Afghanistan (December 1979–February 1989), which over the course of the conflict exceeded 3.2 million people.

India's relations with Pakistan are influenced by the centuries-old rivalry between Hindus and Muslims which led to partition of British India in 1947. The principal source of contention has been Kashmir, whose Hindu Maharaja chose in 1947 to join India, although a majority of his subjects were Muslim. India maintains that his decision and the subsequent elections in Kashmir have made it an integral part of India. Pakistan asserts Kashmiris' rights to self-determination through a plebiscite in accordance with an earlier Indian pledge and a UN resolution. This dispute triggered wars between the two countries in 1947 and 1965.

In December 1971, following a political crisis in what was then East Pakistan and the flight of millions of Bengali refugees to India, Pakistan and India again went to war. The brief conflict left the situation largely unchanged in the west, where the two armies reached an impasse, but a decisive Indian victory in the east resulted in the creation of Bangladesh.

Since the 1971 war, Pakistan and India have made only slow progress toward normalization of relations. In July 1972, Indian Prime Minister Indira Gandhi and Pakistani President Zulfikar Ali Bhutto met in the Indian hill station of Simla. They signed an agreement by which India would return all personnel and captured territory in the west and the two countries would "settle their differences by peaceful means through bilateral negotiations." Diplomatic and trade relations were re-established in 1976.

After the 1979 Soviet invasion of Afghanistan, new strains appeared in India-Pakistan relations; Pakistan supported the Afghan resistance, while India implicitly supported Soviet occupation. In the following eight years, India voiced increasing concern over Pakistani arms purchases, U.S. military aid to Pakistan, and Pakistan's nuclear weapons program. In an effort to curtail tensions, the two countries formed a joint commission. In December 1988, Prime Ministers Rajiv Gandhi and Benazir Bhutto concluded a pact not to attack each other's nuclear facilities. Agreements on cultural exchanges and civil aviation also were initiated.

In 1997, high-level Indo-Pakistani talks resumed after a 3-year pause. The Prime Ministers of India and Pakistan met twice and the foreign secretaries conducted three rounds of talks, in June 1997, the foreign secretaries identified eight "outstanding issues" around which continuing talks would be focused. The dispute over the status of Jammu and Kashmir, an issue since partition, remains the major stumbling block in their dialogue. India maintains that the entire former princely state is an integral part of the Indian union, while Pakistan insists that UN resolutions calling for self-determination of the people of the state must be taken into account.

In September 1997, the talks broke down over the structure of how to deal with the issues of Kashmir and peace and security. Pakistan advocated that the issues be treated by separate working groups. India responded that the two issues be taken up along with six others on a simultaneous basis, in May 1998 India, and then Pakistan, conducted nuclear tests. Attempts to restart dialogue between the two nations were given a major boost by the February 1999 meeting of both Prime Ministers in Lahore and their signing of three agreements. These efforts have since been stalled by the intrusion of Pakistani-backed forces into Indian-held territory near Kargil in May 1999, and by the military coup in Pakistan that overturned the Nawaz Sharif government in October the same year.

Pakistan has had difficulty in establishing stable, effective political institutions. The country has experimented with a variety of political systems, has endured periods of martial law, and has had five constitutions, one inherited from the British and four indigenous creations since independence. Its political parties have suffered from regionalism, factionalism, and lack of vision. Power has shifted between the politicians and the civil-military establishment, and regional and ethnic forces have threatened national unity. However, the impulse toward cohesion has been stronger than the impetus toward division, and the process of nation building has continued. The return to democracy in 1988, and the peaceful, constitutional transfer of power to new governments in 1990 and 1993 testify to Pakistan's progress in the quest for political stability.

In November 1996, President Leghari dismissed the Bhutto government, charging it with corruption, mismanagement of the economy, and implication in extra-judicial killings in Karachi. Elections in February 1997 resulted in an overwhelming victory for the PML/Nawaz, and President Leghari called upon Nawaz Sharif to form a government. In March 1997, with the unanimous support of the National Assembly, Sharif amended the constitution, stripping the President of the power to dismiss the government and making his power to appoint military service chiefs and provincial governors contingent on the "advice" of the Prime Minister. Another amendment prohibited elected members from "floor crossing" or voting against party lines. The Sharif government engaged in a protracted dispute with the judiciary, culminating in the storming of the Supreme Court by ruling party loyalists and the engineered dismissal of the Chief Justice and the resignation of President Leghari in December 1997. The new President elected by Parliament, Rafiq Tarar, was a close associate of the Prime Minister. A one-sided accountability campaign was used to target opposition politicians and critics of the regime. Similarly, the government moved to restrict press criticism and ordered the arrest and beating of prominent journalists. As domestic criticism of Sharif's administration intensified, Sharif attempted to replace Chief of Army Staff General Pervez Musharraf on October 12, 1999, with a family loyalist, Director General ISI Lt. Gen. Ziauddin. Although General Musharraf was out of the country at the time, the Army moved quickly to depose Sharif.

On October 14, 1999, General Musharraf declared a state of emergency and issued the Provisional Constitutional Order (PCO), which suspended the federal and provincial parliaments, held the constitution in abeyance, and designated Musharraf as Chief Executive. While delivering an ambitious seven-point reform agenda, Musharraf has not yet provided a time-line for a return to civilian, democratic rule, although local elections are anticipated at the end of calendar year 2000. Musharraf has appointed a National Security Council, with mixed military/civilian appointees, a civilian Cabinet, and a National Reconstruction Bureau (think tank) to formulate structural reforms. A National Accountability Bureau (NAB), headed by an active duty military officer, is prosecuting those accused of willful default on bank loans and corrupt practices, whose conviction can result in disqualification from political office for twenty-one years. The NAB Ordinance has attracted criticism for holding the accused without charge and, in some instances, access to legal counsel. While military trial courts were not established, on January 26, 2000, the government stipulated that Supreme, High, and Shari'a Court justices should swear allegiance to the Provisional Constitutional Order and the Chief Executive. Approximately 85 per cent of justices acquiesced, but a handful of justices were not invited to take the oath and were forcibly retired. Political parties have not been banned, but a couple of dozen ruling party members remain detained, with Sharif and five colleagues facing charges of attempted hijacking.

CHAPTER 2

HISTORICAL SETTING

HISTORICAL SETTING

When British archaeologist Sir Mortimer Wheeler was commissioned in 1947 by the government of Pakistan to give a historical account of the then new country, he entitled his work *Five Thousand Years of Pakistan*. Indeed, Pakistan has a history that can be dated back to the Indus Valley civilization (ca. 2500-1600 B.C.), the principal sites of which lay in present-day Sindh and Punjab provinces. Pakistan was later the entryway for the migrating pastoral tribes known as Indo-Aryans, or simply Aryans, who brought with them and developed the rudiments of the religio-philosophical system of what later evolved into Hinduism. They also brought an early version of Sanskrit, the base of Urdu, Punjabi, and Sindhi languages that are spoken in much of Pakistan today.

Hindu rulers were eventually displaced by Muslim invaders, who, in the tenth, eleventh, and twelfth centuries, entered northwestern India through the same passes in the mountains used earlier by the Indo-Aryans. The culmination of Muslim rule in the Mughal Empire (1526–1858, with effective rule between 1560 and 1707) encompassed much of the area that is today Pakistan. Sikhism, another religious movement that arose partially on the soil of present-day Pakistan, was briefly dominant in Punjab and in the northwest in the early nineteenth century. All of these regimes subsequently fell to the expanding power of the British, whose empire lasted from the eighteenth century to the mid-twentieth century, until they too left the scene, yielding power to the successor states of India and Pakistan.

The departure of the British was also a goal of the Muslim movement championed by the All-India Muslim League (created in 1906 to counter the Hindu-dominated Indian National Congress), which in turn wanted both political independence and cultural separation from the Hindu-majority regions of British India. These objectives were reached in 1947, when British India received its independence as two new sovereign states. The Muslim-majority areas in northwestern and eastern India were separated and became Pakistan, divided into the West Wing and East Wing, respectively. The placement of two widely separated regions within a single state did not last, and in 1971 the East Wing broke away and achieved independence as Bangladesh.

The pride that Pakistan displayed after independence in its long and multicultural history has disappeared in many of its officially sponsored textbooks and other material used for teaching history (although the Indus Valley sites remain high on the list of the directors of tourism). As noted anthropologist Akbar S. Ahmed has written in History Today, "in Pakistan the Hindu past simply does not exist. History only begins in the seventh century after the advent of Islam and the Muslim invasion of Sindh."

INDEPENDENCE

Pakistan became an independent state in 1947, the realization of a yearning by India's Muslims, who feared domination by the Hindu majority in a post-colonial India. As the British made their final plans to surrender the "Jewel in the Crown" of their empire, the earlier, elite "Two Nations Theory," premised on the notion of a separate homeland for the, subcontinent's Muslim minority, had broadened its popular appeal and evolved into a collective vision championed by Muslims of all backgrounds. After independence, a debate commenced among contending groups over further refinement of that vision. Agreement on what system of government the new nation should adopt—a critical aspect of the debate—was never fully reached. Indeed, few nations have in so short a period undergone as many successive political and constitutional experiments as has Pakistan. This irresolution contributed, in the decades following independence, to a recurrent pattern of crisis: repeated coups and extended periods in which martial law replaced civilian government, violent deaths of several national leaders, periodic strife among ethnic groups, and, most traumatically, a civil war that divided the country in two.

The struggle over the character and soul of Pakistan continues. Although democracy returned to Pakistan in 1988 after a long lapse, it is on trial daily, its continuation by no means certain. Definition of the vision of what Pakistan represents is still being contested from many opposing quarters.

The partition plan that led to the separate states of India and Pakistan was drawn up in an atmosphere of urgency as a swell of religious and ethnic unrest shook India. Under guidelines established with the help of Britain's last viceroy in India, Lord Louis Mountbatten, the perplexing task of establishing the new boundaries of Pakistan was accomplished. Most Indian Muslims lived either on the dusty plains of Punjab or in the humid delta of Bengal. Contiguous Muslim-majority districts in Punjab and Bengal were awarded to Pakistan under the plan's guidelines. The additional task of deciding the status of the more than 500 semi-autonomous princely states of India still remained. All but three of these quickly acceded to either Pakistan or India. But the two largest princely states, Jammu and Kashmir (usually just called Kashmir) and Hyderabad, and one small state, Junagadh, posed special problems. Hyderabad and Junagadh were located within territory awarded to India but were both Hindu majority states ruled by a Muslim leader. These states hesitated but were quickly incorporated by force into India. The status of the third state, Kashmir, which had borders with both India and Pakistan, proved especially problematic.

Unlike Hyderabad and Junagadh, Kashmir had a Muslim majority and was ruled by a Hindu. Kashmir's maharaja was reluctant to accede to either Pakistan or India, but when threatened by a Muslim uprising (with outside support from Pakistani tribesmen) against his unpopular rule, he hurriedly signed the documents of accession, in October 1947, required by India before it would provide aid. Pakistan then launched an active military and diplomatic campaign to undo the accession, which it maintained was secured by fraud. Kashmir was subsequently divided by the occupying armies of both nations, the Indians holding two-thirds of the state, including the Muslim-dominated Vale of Kashmir and the Hindu-majority region of Jammu to the south, while the Pakistanis controlled the western third (PoK). India and Pakistan would fight two major wars to maintain or seize control over this state: in 1947-48 and in 1965. Kashmir's contested and indeterminate status continues dangerously to complicate relations between South Asia's two most powerful states.

The bifurcated Pakistan that existed from August 1947 to December 1971 was composed of two parts, or wings, known as East Pakistan and West Pakistan, separated by 1,600 kilometers of Indian territory. Observers pointed out, however, that the people of the two wings were estranged from each other in language and cultural traditions: that the Bengali "monsoon Islam" of the East Wing was alien to the "desert Islam" of the West Wing. The East Wing, notable for its Bengali ethnic homogeneity and its collective Bangla cultural and linguistic heritage, contained over half of the population of Pakistan and sharply contrasted with the ethnic and linguistic diversity of the West Wing. The West Wing consisted of four major ethnic groups—Punjabis, Pakhtuns, Sindhis, and Baloch. The muhajirs constituted a fifth important group. The political leaders of Pakistan, however—particularly those of West Pakistan—asserted that the Islamic faith and a shared fear of "Hindu India" provided an indestructible bond joining the two societies into one nation. This assertion proved flawed, however. A culture of distrust grew between the two wings, fueled by imbalances of representation in the government and military. Furthermore, Bengali politicians argued that the economic "underdevelopment" of East Pakistan was a result of the "internal colonialism" of the rapacious capitalist class of West Pakistan. In the final analysis, real and perceived iniquities would fray this "indestructible" bond holding the country together. Less than a quarter century after the country's founding, Pakistan would fission, the eastern wing becoming the independent nation of Bangladesh.

It was not Pakistan's precarious security nor even its cultural and ethnic diversity, but rather characteristics deeply rooted in the nation's polity that most impeded its early democratic development. The essentials for such a process—disciplined political parties and a participatory mass electorate—were missing in Pakistan's first years as an independent state. The All-India Muslim League, the party that led the struggle for Pakistan, failed to mature into a stable democratic party with a national following capable of holding together the nation's diverse ethnic and cultural groups. Instead, it disintegrated into rival factions soon after independence. Lack of a consensus over prospective Islamic provisions for the nation's governance, Bengali resentment over the West Pakistanis' initial imposition of Urdu as the national language, and the reluctance of West Pakistani politicians to share power with politicians of the East Wing—all were factors that delayed the acceptance of Pakistan's first constitution until nine years after independence. The nation was also dealt a severe psychological blow when in September 1948, only thirteen months after independence, Mohammad Ali Jinnah—known reverentially as the Quaid-i-Azam (Great Leader)—died. Jinnah's role in the creation of Pakistan had been so dominant that it has been observed that he had neither peers nor associates, only lieutenants and aides. Jinnah's primary lieutenant, Liaquat Ali Khan, the nation's first prime minister, was assassinated in October 1951.

Jinnah's and Liaquat's leadership, so critical to the nation in its infancy, was replaced in the early and mid-1950s by the generally lackluster, often inept performances of the nation's politicians. Those few politicians who were effective were all too willing to play upon the emotions of an electorate as yet unaccustomed to open democratic debate. The ethnic and provincial causes championed by these politicians too often took precedence over national concerns. The government was weak and unable to quell the violence and ethnic unrest that distracted it from building strong parliamentary institutions.

COLLAPSE OF THE PARLIAMENTARY SYSTEM

Believing that Pakistan's first attempt at establishing a parliamentary system of government failed, in the late 1950s the military ousted the "inefficient and rascally" politicians. During this period, however, the belief that democracy was the "natural state" of Pakistan and an important political goal was not entirely abandoned. Mohammad Ayub Khan, Pakistan's first "soldier-statesman," regarded himself as more of a reformer than an autocrat and, as chief martial law administrator, early on acknowledged the need to relinquish some military control. In his unique governmental system called the "Basic Democracies,"

Ayub Khan became the "civilian" head of a military regime. Ayub Khan's "democracy from above" allowed for controlled participation of the electorate and was supposed to capture the peculiar "genius" of Pakistan. To his critics, however, Ayub Khan's political system was better characterized as a form of "representational dictatorship." In 1969 an ailing Ayub Khan was forced to resign following nationwide rioting against his regime's perceived corruption, spent economic policies, and responsibility for Pakistan's defeat in the 1965 Indo-Pakistani War over Kashmir. Ayub Khan was briefly succeeded by his army commander in chief. General Mohammad Yahya Khan, who would best be remembered for presiding over the two most traumatic and psychologically devastating events in the country's history: the humiliating defeat of Pakistan's armed forces by India and the secession of East Pakistan.

REVOLT OF EAST PAKISTAN

The East Wing of Pakistan had not benefited greatly from Ayub Khan's "Decade of Progress," with its gains in agricultural production and trade. Bengali politicians wanted to improve what they considered to be the second-class political and economic status of their province vis-a-vis West Pakistan, just as they had earlier agitated for greater cultural and linguistic recognition. The country's first nationwide direct elections were held in December 1970. The East Pakistan-based Awami League, campaigning on a platform calling for almost total provincial autonomy, won virtually all the seats allotted to the East Wing and was thereby assured a majority in the national legislature.

The results of Pakistan's first nationwide experiment in democracy were not honored. Fearing Bengali dominance in the nation's political affairs, West Pakistani politicians, led by Pakistan People's Party (PPP) leader Zulfiqar Ali Bhutto and supported by senior army officers, most of whom were Punjabis, pressured Yahya Khan to postpone the convening of the National Assembly. When the Bengalis of East Pakistan revolted openly at this turn of events, the Pakistani military banned the Awami League, arrested its leader, Sheikh Mujibur Rahman, and began a massive military crackdown. In the savage civil war that followed, tens of thousands of Bengalis were killed, and an estimated 10 million people took refuge in India, in early December 1971, India entered the war and within weeks decisively defeated the Pakistan military. From the aftermath of the war and the dismemberment of Pakistan came the birth of a new nation: Bangladesh.

To most Pakistanis, the news of Pakistan's defeat came as a numbing shock—their military was disgraced and condemned for its brutal crackdown in East Pakistan. Literally overnight, the country had lost its status as the largest Muslim nation in the world. Gone, too, were any illusions of military parity with India.

PAKISTAN UNDER ZULFIQAR ALI BHUTTO

Pakistan soon recovered under the charismatic leadership of Zulfiqar Ali Bhutto, who launched a forceful campaign to restore the people's self-confidence and to repair Pakistan's tarnished image abroad. Initially, Bhutto was sworn in as president and chief martial law administrator, the two positions he took over from Yahya Khan. Although he soon revoked formal martial law, he governed autocratically until he was overthrown in 1977.

A man of contradictions, a product of a privileged feudal background, the Western- educated Bhutto nonetheless expounded populist themes of shared wealth, national unity, and the need to restore political democracy under the slogan "Islam our Faith, Democracy our Polity, Socialism our Economy." Bhutto nationalized a large number of the most important manufacturing, insurance, and domestically owned banking industries—actions that substantially slowed economic growth.

MILITARY RULE

By the mid-1970s, Bhutto's autocratic tendencies were interfering with his ability to govern. His determination to crush any and all potential opposition had become obsessive. Bhutto purged his party of real or imagined opponents, created a praetorian security force answerable only to himself, brought the prestigious civil service under his personal control, and sacked military officers who possessed what he described as "Bonapartist tendencies." Fatefully, Bhutto then named General Mohammad Zia ul-Haq—a relatively junior and obscure general—to hold the top army post. Most observers had predicted that Bhutto's PPP would retain control of the National Assembly in the elections of March 1977, but the margin of the PPP's victory was so overwhelming that charges of fraud were immediately made, and riots erupted throughout the country. General Zia was well positioned to act against Bhutto. He abruptly informed the nation that he had taken over as the chief martial law administrator but assured the people that the military desired only to supervise fair elections, which he said would be held in ninety days. This was the first of many promises Zia did not keep. As election time approached, Zia announced that criminal charges were being brought against Bhutto and postponed the elections until after Bhutto had been tried in court. Bhutto was found guilty of complicity in murder of a political opponent, and later hanged. The memory of Bhutto and the circumstances surrounding his fall became a rallying cry for his daughter, Benazir, who, during the 1980s, embraced the politics of revenge as she began her political ascent in steadfast opposition to Zia and martial law.

Zia ul-Haq's eleven years of rule left a profound—and controversial—legacy on Pakistani society. Zia's military junta differed in important aspects from the earlier military regime of Ayub Khan. Like Zia, Ayub Khan had been contemptuous of politicians: his style of governing was autocratic in the tradition of the British Raj and its Mughal predecessors. Nevertheless, Ayub Khan welcomed Western influences in his quest for economic development, and he introduced various reform measures, such as the Muslim Family Laws Ordinance, which provided protection for women within their families. Moreover, early in his rule, Ayub Khan isolated the army from the governmental decision-making process and instead relied heavily on senior civil servants and a few conservative politicians.

Zia's rule, by contrast, was notable for the high visibility of a small number of army officers and for his fervent advocacy of a more stringent version of Islamic orthodoxy. Zia made clear his desire to supplant the prevailing legal system with Islamic law, the sharia, and championed a role for Islam that was more state directed and less a matter of personal choice. He proclaimed that all laws had to conform with Islamic tenets and values and charged the military with protecting the nation's ideology as well as its territorial integrity. His establishment of the Federal Shariat Court to examine laws in light of the injunctions of Islam further involved the state in religious affairs.

The crucial and perplexing question of the role Islam should play in Pakistan existed before the creation of the nation and remains unresolved today. Jinnah, himself, supplied a historical reference to the dilemma, stating in his inaugural address, "You will find that in course of time Hindus would cease to be Hindus and Muslims would cease to be Muslims, not in the religious sense, because that is the personal faith of each individual, but in the political sense as citizens of the State." Although each of Pakistan's indigenous constitutions has defined Pakistan as an Islamic state, determining what this means in practice has usually been left open to individual preference. Zia elevated the tempo of the debate over the role of Islam in Pakistani society by directly involving the state with religion.

WAR IN AFGHANISTAN

The Soviet invasion of Afghanistan in December 1979 and its nine-year occupation of that country not only had a direct impact on Pakistani society in general but also held vital importance for Zia's leadership, influencing his domestic and international image as well as the survivability of his regime. From the beginning of his rule, Zia was regarded by much of the world community as a usurper of power and as something of an international pariah. He furthered his isolation by deciding, early in his regime, to pursue the development of nuclear weapons, a program begun earlier by Bhutto. Building on the long and close relationship between the United States and Pakistan dating from the early years of the Cold War, United States president Jimmy Carter and his administration worked energetically but unsuccessfully to discourage Pakistan's nuclear program, and finally suspending all economic and military aid on April 6, 1979. The execution of Bhutto two days earlier that month had added to United States displeasure with the Zia regime and Pakistan. Relations with the United States soured further when a Pakistani mob burned down the United States Embassy in November 1979.

The Soviet invasion of Afghanistan abruptly ended Pakistan's estrangement from the United States. Within days, Pakistan once again became Washington's indispensable frontline ally against Soviet expansionism. Massive military and economic assistance flowed into Pakistan despite Zia's continued pursuit of nuclear weapons technology. Pakistan's nuclear program made major advances in the 1980s. Moreover, the change in geo-strategic circumstances following the occupation of neighboring Afghanistan allowed Zia to postpone the promised elections repeatedly while he consolidated his position. Foreign assistance provided a stimulus to the economy and became an important means by which Zia neutralized his opponents. The war, depicted by Zia and the Afghan resistance as a holy war of believers versus non-believers, facilitated Zia's efforts to transform Pakistan into a state governed by Islamic law.

The war in Afghanistan had many profound and disturbing residual effects on Pakistani society. Pakistan absorbed more than 3.2 million Afghan refugees into its North-West Frontier Province and Balochistan. The influx of so many displaced people threatened to overwhelm the local economies as refugees competed with Pakistanis for resources. With the refugees came an arsenal of weapons. Domestic violence increased dramatically during the war years, and observers spoke dismally of a "Kalashnikov culture" asserting itself in Pakistani society.

END OF MILITARY RULE

By the time of Zia's death in an airplane explosion in August 1988, an agreement had been signed signaling the end of Soviet military intervention in Afghanistan, and the Soviet pullout had already begun. Domestic politics in Pakistan were surprisingly tranquil as Pakistan prepared for a transition of power and elections for the National Assembly, which Zia had earlier dissolved. An era seemed to have ended and a new, more promising one to have begun. The prospect for genuine democracy in Pakistan appeared to have dramatically improved, and Pakistan appeared to have reached a watershed in its political development.

After her party won a plurality of seats in the parliamentary elections of November 1988, Benazir Bhutto formed a fragile coalition government and assumed the position of prime minister. She became the first freely elected leader in Pakistan since her father was deposed and the first woman to hold such a high position in a Muslim country. Confronted by severe disadvantages from the start, Benazir soon discovered that the art of governance was considerably more difficult than orchestrating opposition politics. An experienced politician but an inexperienced head of government, she was outmaneuvered by her political opposition, intimidated by the military, and diverted from her reform program. Benazir was also frustrated by her inability to control the spreading social disorder, the widespread banditry, and the mounting ethnic violence between Sindhis and muhajirs in her home province of Sindh. A prolonged struggle between Bhutto and the provincial government of Mian Nawaz Sharif in Punjab culminated in bureaucrat-turned- president Ghulam Ishaq Khan's siding with Nawaz Sharif against Benazir. Empowered by the Eighth Amendment provisions of the constitution—a direct legacy *of* the Zia ul-Haq regime, which strengthened the powers of the president at the expense of the prime minister— Ishaq Khan dismissed Benazir in August 1990 for alleged corruption and her inability to maintain law and order. He also dismissed her cabinet and dissolved the National Assembly as well as the Sindh North-West Frontier Province provincial assemblies and ordered new elections for October.

The elections brought Nawaz Sharif's Islamic Democratic Alliance (Islami Jamhoori Ittehad—IJI) coalition to power, and for a brief period there appeared to be a workable relationship between the new prime minister and the president. Yet this alliance soon unraveled over policy differences, specifically over the question of who had the power to appoint the top army commander. In charges similar to those Ishaq Khan had before brought against Benazir, Nawaz Sharif was accused in early 1993 of "corruption and mismanagement." Nawaz Sharif, like Benazir before him, was dismissed and the Parliament dissolved—without a vote of confidence ever having been taken in the legislature. This time, however, the Supreme Court overturned the president's action, declaring it unconstitutional. The court restored both the prime minister and the parliament. The Supreme Court's ruling, which served as a stunning rebuke to Ishaq Khan, succeeded in defusing his presidentially engineered crisis and, more important, allowed Ishaq Khan's opponents to boldly challenge the legitimacy of the civil-military bureaucracy that had so often interrupted the process of democratic nation building.

The crisis in government continued as Ishaq Khan, still resolved to undermine the prime minister, brazenly manipulated provincial politics, dissolving the provincial assemblies in Punjab and the North-West Frontier Province. Pears of military intervention and the reimposition of martial law loomed as the ongoing feud between the president and prime minister threatened to bring effective government to a standstill. Although the army ultimately intervened in mid-1993 to break the stalemate and convinced both men to step down, fears of a military takeover were unfounded. The army proved sensitive to the spirit of the times and exercised admirable restraint as it assumed a new and benign role as arbiter rather than manipulator of the nation's politics.

A caretaker government led by World Bank official Moeen Qureshi was installed in July 1993, with the mandate to preside over new elections for the national and provincial assemblies. The caretaker government surprised everyone by its vigor and impressed Pakistanis and international observers alike. During his three-month tenure, Qureshi earned the accolade "Mr. Clean" by initiating an impressive number of reform measures. Qureshi published lists of unpaid debts and prevented debtor-politicians from running for office. He also devalued the currency and cut farm subsidies and public-service expenditures. Because the Qureshi caretaker government was temporary and not much constrained by the realpolitik of Pakistani society, observers doubted that any succeeding government would be able to match its record and boldness of action.

In October 1993, Qureshi fulfilled his primary mandate of holding new elections for the national and provincial assemblies. The contest was now between two staunch adversaries—Nawaz Sharif and Benazir Bhutto—and their respective parties. Although Benazir's PPP received less of the popular vote than Nawaz Sharif's Pakistan Muslim League (PML-N), it won a narrow plurality of seats in the National Assembly, enabling Benazir to form a government. Presidential elections were held in November and Farooq Leghari, a member of Benazir's party, won, thereby strengthening her position.

In a political culture that traditionally placed great emphasis on the personal characteristics of its leaders and considerably less on the development of its democratic institutions, the personality of these leaders has always been of paramount, and many would argue exaggerated, importance. The case of Benazir Bhutto, Pakistan's prime minister in mid-1995, is no exception. Benazir's return to the pinnacle of Pakistani politics in October 1993 was portrayed with great theater as a redemptive second coming for the country's self-proclaimed "Daughter of Destiny." Benazir pledged this time to fulfill some of the promises she had failed to keep during her first tenure as prime minister. These included calming the potentially explosive ethnic problems in the country, strengthening a treasury overburdened with debt, reconstructing a financial system weakened by corruption, managing a burgeoning population with inadequate access to social services and one making heavy demands on the country's fragile ecology, enforcing women's rights in a decidedly male-dominated society, and forging a consensus on the role of Islam in contemporary Pakistani society. Above all, Benazir promised to steer Pakistan further along the road to democracy—a difficult and sensitive task in a country whose power structure has traditionally been authoritarian and whose politics has been socially divisive and confrontational.

As before, Benazir faces a continual challenge from Nawaz Sharif's Punjab-based PML-N, which appears to be pursuing the same strategy of zero-sum politics that succeeded in paralyzing her first government. For a short while, following Benazir's return to power, her public rhetoric and that of her opponent seemed less confrontational than before and tended to stress themes of political stability, cooperation, and accommodation. This period of détente was short-lived, however, as a familiar pattern in Pakistani politics soon reasserted itself, with vigorous opposition attempts to bring down the Benazir government. Unrestrained and sometimes chimerical criticism fueled opposition-orchestrated general strikes, which continued unabated throughout 1994 and into 1995. In response, Benazir branded her opposition as traitorous and "antistate." By the end of the first half of 1995, relations had become so vitriolic between Benazir and Nawaz Sharif that in June, Nawaz Sharif accused Benazir of being "part of the problem" of the escalating violence in Karachi, and Benazir, for her part, leveled an accusation of treason against the former prime minister and chief rival, only months after her government had arrested Nawaz Sharif's father for alleged Financial crimes.

Promising to be true to her reform agenda, Benazir unveiled a government budget in June 1994 that called for lowering import duties, making the rupee convertible on the current account, broadening the tax base, and holding down defense spending. These measures will be strengthened by Pakistan's receipt of most of the US$2.5 billion in aid that it requested at a meeting of international donors in 1994. In order to receive US$1.4 billion in preferential International Monetary Fund credits, Pakistan agreed to a three-year structural adjustment program of fiscal austerity and deficit cutting. Under guidelines set by the IMF, Pakistan hopes to raise its gross domestic product growth to an average of 6.5 per cent per year while eventually bringing down inflation to 5 per cent. Whether this goal can be reached depends largely on raising Pakistan's export earnings, which suffered in the past few years primarily as a result of a drought, a major flood, and a plant virus "leaf curl" that has devastated cotton production.

Most observers believe that Pakistan's greatest economic advantage is its people: the country possesses the reservoir of entrepreneurial and technical skills necessary for rapid economic growth and development. The textile industry is especially critical to Pakistan's development. This dynamic sector in the economy— a major producer of cotton cloth and yarn—should benefit from the phaseout of textile import quotas under the General Agreement on Tariffs and Trade (GATT). By late 1994, Pakistan's official foreign-exchange reserves had risen from below US$300 million the previous year to more than US$3 billion. The government's continuing strategy of privatizing state-owned enterprises appears to be invigorating the economy and attracting substantial foreign investment in the country's stock exchanges. An optimistic Benazir stated that "Pakistan is poised for an economic takeoff "and noted that in the "new world of today, trade had replaced aid."

Benazir will also need to address Pakistan's most pressing social problems if her reform program is to have a lasting effect. Many of these problems are caused by the skewed distribution of resources in Pakistan. Although the middle class is growing, wealth has remained largely in the control of the nation's elite. Agitation caused by the unfulfilled promise of rising expectations is fueled by sophisticated media, which extend a glimpse of a better life to every village and basti (barrio).

Pakistan must also work to protect its international image, in mid-1995 human rights violations continued to be widely reported, including arbitrary arrest and detention, torture of prisoners, and incidents of extra-judicial killings by overzealous police, most often in connection with government efforts to restore law and order to troubled Sindh. The government, faced with unprecedented levels of societal violence, has been forced to take strong action. Prime Minister Benazir Bhutto pledged to use "ruthlessness" where necessary to confront and to root out ethnic and religious militants. Pakistan is also challenged by pervasive narcotics syndicates, which wield great influence in Karachi, as well as in Peshawar in the North-West Frontier Province. Pakistan has, along with Afghanistan, become one of the world's leading producers of heroin, supplying a reported 20 to 40 per cent of the heroin consumed in the United States and 70 per cent of that consumed in Europe. Pakistan also has an expanding domestic market for illicit drugs—a scourge that is having a devastating effect on Pakistani society. The Pakistan government estimates that there are 2.5 million drug addicts in the country—1.7 million of them addicted to heroin.

A particularly worrisome problem is Pakistan's unwanted role as a base for Islamic militants. These militants come from a wide range of Arab countries, including Algeria, Tunisia, Egypt, Iraq, Jordan, Saudi Arabia, and Sudan, as well as nations in Central Asia and the Far East, and are mostly based in the North-West Frontier Province. Many of these militants participated in the war in Afghanistan but now serve other, often extremist, causes. An attack that killed two American employees of the United States consulate in Karachi in March 1995 has drawn international attention to the growing terrorist activity in Pakistan.

The rebellion, which is centred in the Vale of Kashmir, a scenic intermontane valley with a Muslim majority, has claimed 20,000 lives since 1990. Pakistan claims only to have lent moral and political support to Muslim and Sikh separatist sentiments in Kashmir and the Indian state of Punjab, respectively, while it accuses India of creating dissension in Pakistan's province of Sindh. The Kashmir issue has now broadened in scope and has taken on a new and ominous dimension. In February 1993, then

Central Intelligence Agency Director James Woolsey testified before Congress that the arms race between India and Pakistan represented the "most probable prospect" for the future use of nuclear weapons. These sentiments were echoed the following year by United Nations Secretary General Boutros-Ghali, who cautioned that an escalation of hostilities between Pakistan and India could lead to an accident, with "disastrous repercussions."

CHAPTER 3

HISTORY

PREHISTORY

ADVENT OF ISLAM IN THE SUB-CONTINENT

The last Prophet of Islam, Prophet Muhammad (SAW), completely changed the intellectual outlook of Arabia. Within a span of 23 years, he transformed the barbarous and impious Arabs into a civilized and religious nation. On the demise of the Prophet, the expansion of Islam was not stopped.

The Muslim conquest of Persia including the provinces of Kirman and Makran brought the Arabs face to face with the then ruler of Sindh, who had made common cause with the ruler of Makran against the Muslims. But, it was not until the sea-borne trade of the Arabs in the Indian ocean was jeopardized that serious attempts were made to subjugate Sindh.

Trade relations between Arabia and the sub-continent of Pakistan and India date back to antiquity. Long before the advent of Islam to Arabia, the Arabs used to visit the coast of southern India which then provided the link between the ports of South and South East Asia.

CAUSES OF THE INVASION OF SINDH

The commercial activities of Arabs intensified after the Arabs had been converted to Islam. The Umayyad Khalifah, al Walid I appointed Hajjaj bin Yousaf as the governor of the Eastern provinces. It was during the governorship of Hajjaj bin Yousaf, that pirates plundered eight ships near Diabul, a seaport in Sindh. The ships were carrying the orphan daughters of the Arab merchants, who had died in Ceylon and many valuable presents sent by the King of Ceylon for the Khalifah and the governor.

Hajjaj demanded from Dahir, the ruler of Sindh, adequate compensation, to which Dahir replied that he had no control over the pirates and was, therefore, powerless to chastise them. On this Hajjaj decided to invade Sindh. Two smaller expeditions having failed, he sent his son in-law Imaduddin Muhammad bin Qasim, a youth of seventeen to invade Sindh.

EXPEDITION UNDER MUHAMMAD BIN QASIM

Muhammad bin Qasim invaded Sindh with 6,000 picked Syrian and Iraqi soldiers, a camel corps of equal strength and a baggage train of 3000 camels. His siege engines included a manjaniq worked by 500 men. Proceeding through Makran, Muhammad bin Qasim appeared before Daibul in 712. On his way he was joined by the governor of Makran who gave him additional force. In addition, a good number of Jats and Meds, who had suffered at the hands of native rulers, joined the Arab forces.

After the fall of Daibul, Muhammad bin Qasim turned towards Nirun, near modem Hyderabad and obtained the submission of it's inhabitants. Dahir decided to oppose the Arabs at Raor. After a fierce struggle, Dahir was overpowered and killed. Raor fell into the hands of the Muslims.

Muhammad bin Qasim then occupied Alor and proceeded towards Multan. On the way a fortress called Sikka (Uch) situated on the bank of the Ravi was occupied. Multan offered resistance for two months after which the Hindus were overpowered and defeated. Prior to this, Muhammad bin Qasim had taken Brahmanabad and a few other important towns of Sind.

DEATH OF MUHAMMAD BIN QASIM

The new Khalifah Sulayman was an arch enemy of Hajjaj bin Yousaf, as a result, Muhammad bin Qasim fell victim to party politics and put to prison, where he died prematurely.

ADMINISTRATION OF SIND

In conformity with Muslim practice Muhammad bin Qasim guaranteed to the conquered people the security of life and property and freedom of worship. Meaning, that the people of Sind were treated as Zimmis, a protected people.

CONQUESTS OF MAHMUD GHAZNAVI

The Arab conquest of Sind belongs to the first phase of Islamic expansion under the Umayyad Caliphs. It was after nearly three centuries that the second phase of the conquest of the sub-continent began under the Turks. The Turkish rulers of Ghazni and later those of Ghur carried Muslim arms across Pakistan and into northern India.

Sultan Mahmud obtained formal recognition of his sovereignty from the Abbasid Khalifah, al-Qadir Billah, who also conferred upon him the titles of Yamin-ud-Dawlah and Amin-ul-Millah. He undertook an expedition every year to Hind and according to Sir Henry Elliot, led as many as seventeen expeditions. The only permanent result of his expeditions was the conquest of the Punjab. However, along with Muslim warriors came Muslim saints and Sufis, who promulgated Islam in India.

Shaikh Ali Hujweri, popularly known as Data Ganj Baksh, renowned sufi who settled in Lahore, wrote the first authentic book on sufism in Persian titled "Kashaful-Mehjub".

SUFIS AND THE SPREAD OF ISLAM

The spread of Islam in the sub-continent is the story of the untiring efforts of the numerous saints and sufis who dedicated their lives to the cause of service to humanity. By the time the Muslim empire was established at Delhi, the Sufi fraternities had come into being and the sufi influence was far more powerful than in the earlier days under the Arabs in Sind.

The two great fraternities that established themselves very early in Muslim India were the Suhrawardiyah and the Chishtiyah. The Suhrawardiyah order was founded by Shaikh Ab-al-Najib Suhrawardi (1097–1162) and was introduced into Muslim India by Shaikh Baha-ud-din Zakariya (1182–1267-68), of Multan. With Multan as it's center the silsilah became dominant in the areas which now constitute Pakistan.

The Chishtiyah silsilah was introduced in the sub-continent by Hadrat Khawaja Muin-ud- din. He settled at Ajmer. As he established in the Indian sub-continent the first sufi silsilah, he is often referred to as Hind-al-Wali. Khawaja Muin-ud-din Ajmeri's chief disciple, Khawaja Qutb-ud-din Bakhtiyar Kaki, who lived at Delhi, was held in high esteem by Iltutmish. Baba Farid who was the disciple of Khawaja Qutb-ud-din Bakhtiyar Kaki, decided to settle in Punjab. The Chishtiyah order remained the most popular order during the Sultanate period.

Baba Farid appointed Shaikh Nizamuddin Auliya (1238–1325) as his Khalifah. It was Nizamuddin Auliya who trained a band of sufis for the propagation of Islam in Gujarat, the Deccan and Bengal. Earlier, Shaikh Ali Hujweri popularly known as Data Ganj Baksh came from Ghazni to Lahore a few days after the death of Sultan Mahmud. He is mainly responsible for the propagation of Islam in the Punjab.

The disciple of Shaikh Baha-ud-din Zakariya, Sayyid Jalaluddin Bukhari, popularly known as Mukhdum Jahanian Jahangasht was one of the most important saints of the Suhrawardiyah order. He played an important part in the propagation of Islam in Sind.

Shah Jalal came from Turkey and was a great Suhrawardi saint of Bengal. He came to the sub-continent in the reign of Iltutmish. Due to his missionary activities, Islam gained a good ground in Sylhet. Shaikh Ala-ul-Haq and his son Nur Qutb Alam established new orders after their names in Bengal, and are responsible for large scale conversions in Sylhet, Bengal.

ESTABLISHMENT OF MUSLIM EMPIRE

The establishment of Muslim rule in the sub-continent is a significant event in the history of Islam and of the sub-continent. Islam gained it's first foothold. The Muslim empire in Sind continued to exist until the decline of the Umayyads. In the field of learning, decimal numerals were learned from the Indians. The Arabs learnt chess from the Hindus. Indian books on Astronomy such as Siddharta, were translated into Arabic as were books on Ayuverdic medicine.

During the reign of Harun ar Rashid, the Barmakids invited Hindu scholars to Baghdad to translate into Arabic Sanskrit works on medicine, philosophy, astronomy and other subjects.

The establishment of Muslim rule in Sind prepared the way for future propagation of Islam in Sind and the adjoining regions. The people were so impressed with the justice and leniency of the Muslims that when Muhammad bin Qasim and later Umayyad Caliph Umar bin Abdul Aziz invited the people to accept Islam, the response was good. Sind and Multan attracted Arab travelers, writers and missionaries. They spread their activities into Punjab, Baluchistan, and the tribes of the mountains in the northwest.

Later Sind attracted Ismaili missionaries who were so successful that Sind passed under Ismaili rule. With the conquest of Lahore by Mahmud of Ghazni, missionary activity began again under the aegis of Sufis who were the main agents in the Islamization of the entire region of West Pakistan.

Muhammad Ghuri

Muhammad Ghuri played a significant role in expanding Muslim rule in northern India. His vigorous and systematic campaigns for the first time roused the Rajput confederacy into concerted action and a real trial of strength ensued resulting in the triumph of Muslim arms.

His important victories remain at the battles of Taraori (1191-92), in which he defeated Prithvi Raj Chauhan, ruler of Delhi and Ajmer. After the second battle of Taroari, Muhammad Ghuri returned to Ghazni and entrusted the charge of his conquered territories to his lieutenant, Qutbuddin Aibak. He soon extended the conquests of his master and made Delhi the capital of the empire (1194).

Muhammad Ghuri was killed by an Ismaili fanatic, while he was on his way to Ghazni from Lahore. He is remembered as an empire builder and is justly called the founder of the Muslim empire in Indo-Pakistan.

On his death, Qutbuddin Aibak was elected Sultan by Turkish Amirs. He, thus became the first Sultan of the newly established Sultanate of Delhi.

The Ancient Empires of the Sub-Continent

Some of the earliest relics of Stone Age man were found in the Soan valley near Rawalpindi, dating back to atleast 50,000

years. Predominantly an agricultural region, its ancestors learned
to tame and husband animals and to cultivate crops some 9,000
years ago. Farming villages dating from 6,000 BC have been
excavated in Baluchistan, the North-West Frontier Province and
Punjab.

The Indus Valley Civilization is considered to have evolved
around 2600 BC. Built on the ruins of fortified towns near Kot
Diji, it is now believed to have emerged from farming communities
of the area. The Civilization boasted immense cities like
Mohenjodaro and Harappa. These towns were well planned, with
paved main roads, multi-storied houses, watchtowers, food
warehouses, and assembly halls. Their people developed an
advanced script which still remains undeciphered. The Indus
Civilization's decline around 1700 BC is attributed to foreign
invaders, who at some sites, violently destroyed the cities.

Aryans, who were rough cattle breeders, came from Central
Asia around 1700 BC, seeking grazing land for their herds. Their
religion was well developed, with gods identified from elements
of nature. They followed a strict caste system, which later became
Hinduism. They wrote the first book of Hindu scripture, the Rig
Veda, which was a collection of hymns remembered through
several generations. In the sixth century BC, the people of the
region were getting increasingly dissatisfied with the Hindu
explanation of the caste system. When Buddha, son of a kshatriya
king preached equality in men, his teachings were quickly accepted
throughout the northern part of the Sub-continent. Around the
same time, Gandhara being the easternmost province of the
Achaemenid Empire of Persia, became a major power in the
region. Its two cities—Pushkalavati, or present day Charsadda near
Peshawar, and the capital Taxila, were the center of civilization
and culture.

Alexander the Great invaded the Sub-continent in 327 BC.
Conquering the Kalash valley, he crossed the mighty Indus at
Ohind, sixteen miles north of Attock. He then defeated the mighty
elephant army of Porus at Jhelum, and began his march towards
the long Ganges plain. However, he was forced to plan for
homeward sailing when his war-wary troops refused to advance
further. On his way back, a serious wound, received while battling
the Malloi people at Multan, finally took its toll, and Alexander

died in 323 BC, leaving his conquests for grab among his own officers.

Chandragupta Maurya was an exiled member of the royal family of Magadha, a kingdom flourishing since 700 BC on the bank of river Ganges. After Alexander's death, Chandragupta captured Punjab with his allies, and later overthrew the king of Magadha in 321 BC, to form the Mauryan Empire. After twenty four years of kingship, Chandragupta was succeeded by his son, Bindusara, who added Deccan to the Mauryan rule.

Ashoka, son of Bindusara, was one of the greatest rulers the world has ever known. Not only did he rule a vast empire, he also tried to rule it compassionately. After initially causing thousands of lives during his conquest of Kalinga, he decided to rule by the law of piety. He was instrumental in spreading Buddhism within and outside the Sub-continent by building Buddhist monasteries and stupas, and sending out missionaries to foreign lands.

The Greek king of Bactria, Demetrius, conquered the Kabul River Valley around 195 BC. The Greeks re-built Taxila and Pushkalavati as their twin capital cities in Gandhara. They were followed in 75 BC by the Scythians, Iranian nomads from Central Asia, and in about 50 BC by the powerful Parthians, from east of the Caspian Sea.

After defeating the Greeks in 53 BC, the Parthians ruled the northern Pakistan area. During their era of trade and economic prosperity, the Parthians promoted art and religion. The Gandhara school of art developed, which reflected the glory of Greek, Syrian, Persian and Indian art traditions.

The Kushana king, Kujula, ruler of nomad tribes from Central Asia, overthrew the Parthians in 64 AD and took over Gandhara. The Kushans further extended their rule into northwest India and Bay of Bengal, south into Bahawalpur and short of Gujarat, and north till Kashghar and Yarkand, into the Chinese frontier. They made their winter capital at Purushapura, the City of Flowers, now called Peshawar, and their summer capital north of Kabul.

Kanishka, the greatest of Kushans, ruled from 128 to 151 AD. Trade flourished during his rule, with the Romans trading in gold for jewelry, perfumes, dyes, spices and textiles. Progress was made in medicine and literature. Thousands of Buddhist monasteries and stupas were built and the best pieces of sculpture in the Gandhara school of art were produced. He was killed in his sleep when his unending expansionist pursuits were resisted by his own people.

The Kushans empire was usurped both from the North, where the Sassanian Empire of Persia eroded their rule, and the South where the Gupta Empire took hold. In the fourth century, due to decline in prosperity and trade, the Kushans empire was reduced to a new dynasty of Kidar (Little) Kushans, with the capital now at Peshawar. Coming from Central Asia, the White Huns, originally the horse-riding nomads from China, invaded Gandhara during the fifth century. With declining prosperity, and the sun and fire-worshipping Huns ruling the land. Buddhism gradually disappeared from northern Pakistan, taking the glory of the Gandhara school of art with it.

After the defeat of Huns by Sassanians and Turks in 565 AD, the area was mostly left to be ruled by small Hindu kingdoms, with the Turki Shahi rulers controlling the area till Gandhara from Afghanistan, and the raja of Kashmir ruling northern Punjab, and the areas east of the Indus. Buddhism's decline continued as more people were converted to Brahman Hindus.

Overthrowing the Turki Shahis, the Central Asian Hindu Shahis ruled from 870 AD till the year 1008 AD. With their capital established at Hund on the Indus, their rule extended from Jalalabad in Afghanistan to Multan, and covered as far north as Kashmir.

1206—1526

ESTABLISHMENT OF DELHI SULTANATE BY ILBARI DYNASTY

Muizuddin Muhammad Ghuri, the last Turkish conqueror of North India, had no sons. He had bought a large number of slaves, whom he had appointed as his officers, but he did not nominate any particular one as his successor. At the time of Muhammad Ghuri's death in 1206, Qutbuddin Aibak was in Lahore, where he assumed the sovereign powers as he was elected Sultan by the

Amirs. The assumption of sovereign powers by Qutbuddin Aibak in 1206 is regarded as the foundation of the Sultanate of Delhi.

The Sultanate of Delhi (1206–1526) had five ruling dynasties:

1. The Ilbari or slaves (1206-90)
2. The Khaljis (1290–1320)
3. The Tughluqs (1320–1413)
4. The Saiyads (1414–51)
5. The Lodhis (1451–1526)

Of these five dynasties, the first three were of Turkish origin and the Lodhis were Afghans.

Qutbuddin [1206—10]

He was a Turk of the Aibak tribe. During his brief rule of four years, he did not make any fresh conquests. Lahore and later Delhi were his capitals. He died in 1210 from fall from a horse while playing Polo in Lahore. For his generosity he is known as lakh-baksh (giver of lakhs). He laid the foundation of Qutb Minar, which was completed by his son-in-law and successor Iltutmish.

Iltutmish [1210—36]

Shamsuddin Iltutmish was the real founder of the Sultanate. He secured his position in 1217 by defeating his rivals. By his diplomatic skill, Iltutmish saved his infant kingdom from the fury of the Mongol invasion. After a series of conquests, he received a deed of investiture from the Abassid Caliph of Baghdad.

But Iltutmish failed to deal conclusively with a resurgent Rajput threat early in the 1220s and his position was undermined in the 1230s by Mongol invaders who won the northern Punjab. The Turkish nobles were reasserting themselves by the time of his death and, after a period of chaos, one of them, Balban, seized the throne in 1265.

Balban [1266—86]

Ghiasuddin Balban organized a strong army to face the Mongol threat and made military reforms. His views about kingship were that kingship was second only to prophethood. He dealt severely with the Turkish nobility to which he had previously belonged and gave a centralized system of administration. With his death ended the Ilbari dynasty.

Khalji Dynasty [1290—1320]

The coming of Khaljis to power was more than a dynastic change. Their ascending is known as the Khalji revolution, because it marked the end of the monopolization of power by the Turkish nobility and racial dictatorship. The Khaljis initiated a higher imperialism and gave political homogeneity to the Turkish state.

Among the Khaljis, Alauddin Khalji (1296—1316) reign is marked by innovative revenue reforms, market control regulations and a whirlwind period of conquests.

The Lodhis [1451—1526]

After thirty-seven years of chaotic rule, Bahlol Lodhi recognized as primus interpares by his compatriots, acquired control of Delhi and laid the foundation of the Lodhi dynasty. The Lodhis ruled for seventy-five years, were Afghans by race. The last Lodhi Sultan, Ibrahim Lodhi (1517—26) was defeated and killed by Babur in the first battle of Panipat in 1526. With the fall of the Lodhis, the Sultanate of Delhi also ended.

The Saiyids [1414—51]

Khizr Khan, the founder of the Saiyid dynasty had collaborated with Timur and as a reward he was given the governorship of Lahore, Multan and Dipalpur. In 1414, he invaded Delhi and became it's master. Alauddin Alam Shah was the last ruler of the Saiyid dynasty and hardly did more than sustain the Sultanate in Delhi until 1451.

Tughluq Dynasty [1320—1412]

Ghazi Malik ascended the throne as Sultan Ghiyasuddin Tughluq Shah and founded the third dynasty of the Sultanate. The Tughluqs belonged to the "Qarauna Turk" tribe.

Among the Tughluq dynasty, Muhammad Tughluq and Firuz Tughluq stand out. Muhammad Tughluq has been grossly misunderstood and is assessed on account of his five ambitious projects. These projects were:

(a) transfer of capital from Delhi to Devagiri (1327),
(b) introduction of token currency,
(c) expedition for the conquest of Khurasan and Iraq,

(d)   conquest of Qarachil scheme,

(e)   increase in land revenue in the Doab.

The failure of all these schemes made him very unpopular. Denounced by the clergy and increasingly deranged, Muhammad died campaigning in Sind in 1351. The clergy elevated his tractable cousin Firuz Shah in return for concessions that left the sultan without adequate material or moral resources to meet any real challenge to his authority.

Firuz Shah Tughluq [1351—88]

Firuz Shah Tughluq's rule is marked by his promotion of agriculture through the construction of canals and his interest in civil works. He founded a number of new cities and towns, three most famous being Hissar Firuza, Jaunpur and Firuzabad.

During Nasiruddin Mahmud's reign Timur, the Mongol leader of Central Asia, invaded India and completely ransacked Delhi in 1398. In the fifteenth century, the Sultanate completely disintegrated and the Sultanate of Delhi under the succeeding two dynasties—the Saiyids and the Lodhis—was like any other provincial kingdom.

1527—1857

BABUR—THE FIRST MUGHAL EMPEROR
[1526—30]

Zahiruddin Muhammad Babur, who defeated Ibrahim Lodhi at Panipat in 1526, founded the Mughal empire in India. Babur was a descendant of Timur on his father's side and of Chengiz Khan on his mother's. On the death of his father Umar Shaikh Mirza, Babur inherited the ancestral kingdom of Farghana in 1494. On account of his precarious position in Central Asia, he after crossing the Indus, invaded India five times. The fifth expedition resulted in the death of Ibrahim Lodhi in the first battle of Panipat in April 1526.

Panipat was merely the beginning of the Mughal rule, it's real foundation was laid by Akbar in 1556. At the time of the battle of Panipat, the political power in India was shared by the Afghans and the Rajputs. Consequently, a decisive battle took place on

March 16, 1527 at Kanwaha, near Agra between the forces of
Babur and Rana Sanga of Mewar, who was the most powerful
Rajput prince. In this battle, the latter was decisively defeated and
Kanwaha confirmed and completed Babur's victory at Panipat.

HUMAYUN'S RULE [1530—40,1555]

Babur was succeeded by his eldest son Humayun, who failed
in asserting strong monarchical authority. The Mughal empire
received a setback, when Sher Shah Suri defeated Humayun in
the battles of Chausa and Kanauj in 1540. For nearly fifteen year;
(1540—55), Humayun had to stay in exile. But shortly after regaining
the empire Humayun died in 1556 after falling down his library
stairs (the 'Sher Mandil'). The foundation of Mughal painting was
laid by Humayun who during the years of his exile in Persia and
Afghanistan secured the services of Persia's two greatest masters,
Mir Sayyid Ali and Abdus Samad. During the reign of Akbar,
there was a fusion of Persian and Indian style of painting.

SURI DYNASTY [1540—55]

Sher Khan, known as Sher Shah Suri was an Afghan leader
and took over the Mughal empire after defeating Humayun in
1540. He was successful in formulating a sound imperial
administration, which was inspired by the Safavid regime in Iran.
Sher Shah died in 1545 and his heir succumbed to old Afghan
rivalries.

Sher Shah commissioned the construction of tombs for his
father, Hasan Khan Sur and himself. A third was begun for his
son Islam, but remained unfinished at the Dynasty's fall.

AKBAR'S REIGN [1556—1605]

Humayun's heir, Akbar was born in exile and was only
thirteen years old when his father died. He survived to demonstrate
his worth, thanks to his exceptionally capable guardian, Bairam
Khan.

Akbar's reign is prominent due to the fact that he was the
first Mughal ruler to firmly lay the foundation of the Mughal
empire. After a series of conquests, area under the empire was
increased and conciliatory policy towards the Rajputs reduced
any threat from them. As a potent gesture of good faith, Akbar
took a Rajput bride who bore him his heir.

Akbar's rule also stands out due to his liberal policies towards the non-Muslims, his religious reforms, and Mansabdari system. Akbar's Mansabdari system became the basis of Mughal military organization and civil administration, with changes made by later Mughals.

The reign of Akbar was a period of renaissance of Persian literature. The Ain-i-Akbari gives the names of fifty-nine great Persian poets of Akbar's court. History was the most important branch of Persian prose literature. Abul-Fazl's "Akbarnama" and "Ain-i-Akbari" are complementary works.

Akbar and his successors, Jehangir and Shah Jehan greatly contributed to the development of Indian music. Tansen was the most accomplished musician of the age. Ain-i-Akbari gives the names of thirty-six first rate musicians of Akbar's court where Hindu and Muslim systems of music mingled freely.

The history of Mughal architecture begins with Babur. He, however, did not usher in any new style or movement. The adverse political circumstances did not afford much opportunity to Humayun to undertake any significant architectural activity. The Mughal architectural style began as a definite movement under Akbar. In spirit, the structure of Humayun's tomb stands as an example of synthesis of two great building traditions of Asia, namely the Persian and the Indian.

Akbar's most ambitious and magnificent architectural undertaking was the new capital city that he built on the ridge at Sikri near Agra. To commemorate Akbar's conquest of Gujarat in 1572, the city was named Fatehpur. The most impressive creation of this new capital is the grand Jamia Masjid. The southern entrance to the Jamia Masjid is an impressive gateway known as "Buland Darwaza". The total height of this gateway is 53 meters. Like most other buildings at Fatehpur Sikri, the fabric of this impressive gateway is of red sandstone which is relieved by carving and discreet inlaying of white marble.

MUJADDID ALF-THANI [1564—1624]

In the 16th century, during the reign of Akbar, Islam was facing overwhelming threats. Akbar's Din-i Ilahi had literally made the orthodox Muslims outcasts in the affairs of the state. The Infallibility Decree in 1579 and Din-i Ilahi in 1581 were considered to be grave threat to the religion of Islam. Din-i Ilahi, as propounded by Akbar, was a mixture of various religions. The new religion combined mysticism, philosophy and nature worship, it recognized no gods or prophets and the emperor was its chief exponent. Also, to believe in revelation was considered as taqlid or following authority blindly—a low kind of morality, fit only for the uneducated and the illiterate.

Akbar was influenced by Bhakti Movement started during the sultanate period, which propounded Hindu-Muslim unity. Many sufis of Akbar's time condemned his religious innovations. Qazi Mulla Muhammad of Jaunpur, Qazi Mir Yaqoob of Bengal, opposed the new religion. However, the man who took upon himself to revive Islam by purification from within was Sheikh Ahmad of Sirhind, commonly known as Mujaddid Alf-Thani, or "the reformer of second millennium".

Sheikh Ahmad was born in Sirhind on June 26, 1564. He joined the Naqshbandiya Silsilah under the discipleship of Khawaja Baqi Billah. Then he dedicated his sincerity of purpose to purify and to rid Islam of the accretions of Hindu Pantheism as well as the philosophy of Wahdat-ul Wujud. He gave the philosophy of Wahdat-ush-Shuhud.

Mujaddid Alf-Thani wrote Ithbata-al-Nubuwwah. In this pamphlet, he quoted Imam Ghazali justifying the need for prophethood and explaining the inadequacies of human intellect. Through the medium of oral preaching and discussions and his maktubat addressed to important nobles and leaders of religious thought, he spread his message amongst the elite in particular.

He boldly opposed all plans to bring Islam and Hinduism together on the religious level, which could not but loosen the Muslim grip on the sources of imperial strength. Due to these letters, and partly due to atmosphere in the country, he contributed largely to the swing from Akbar's heterodoxy to Aurangzeb's vigorous orthodoxy rather than a return to Babur's and Humayun's policy of laissez faire. Iqbal rightly regarded him as the "spiritual guardian of the Muslims" of the subcontinent and one whom God had alerted to the dangers inherent in the syncretism of Akbar and one of the sufis.

BRITISH ARRIVE IN INDIA

In 1583, Queen Elizabeth I despatched the ship Tyger to the sub-continent to exploit opportunities for trade. Sixteen years after the Tyger sailed to India, Queen Elizabeth granted trading rights to a group of London entrepreneurs. In 1614, the British East India Company opened its first office in Bombay.

The British continued to seek concessions from the Mughal rulers and enjoyed unique trading monopoly. By the middle of the 18th century, the British in the guise of East India Company, had become deeply enmeshed in the politics of India and, after the battle of Plassey in 1757, began the systematic conquest of the subcontinent.

JEHANGIR'S REIGN [1605-1628]

Akbar was succeeded by his son, Salim, who took the title of Jehangir—Conqueror of the world. He enlarged the empire through the addition of Kangra. Jehangir is renowned for administering impartial justice to his people, irrespective of their religious faith Mughal rule reached it's climax during Jehangir's reign. In the history of Mughal architecture Jehangir's reign marks the period of transition between it's two grand phases, namely the phase of Akbar and that of his grandson Shah Jehan. The most important feature of this period is the substitution of red sandstone with white marble. During Jehangir's reign, due to his love for color, the system of pietra dura, i.e. the inlaid mosaic work of precious stones of various shades, began towards the end of his reign. He was also fond of laying gardens. One of the most famous gardens laid by him was the Shalimar Bagh in Kashmir.

Mughal painting reached a logical culmination during the reign of Jehangir. The most important feature of the paintings in his reign is the decline of Persian influence and rise of Indian touch.

Mughal painting lost much of it's glamour and refinement after Jehangir's death. During the late seventeenth and eighteenth centuries it migrated to regional centers where it prospered under different styles, such as Rajput and Jaipur styles.

SHAH JEHAN'S RULE [1628—58]

Jehangir was succeeded by his second son, Khurram in 1628. Khurram took the name of Shah Jehan—meaning Emperor of the World. He further expanded his Empire to Kandahar in the North and conquered most of Southern India. The Mughal Empire was at its zenith during Shah Jehan's rule. This was due to almost a hundred years of unparalleled prosperity and peace. As a result, cultural sphere during Shah Jehan's reign witnessed a unique glory.

During the reign of Shah Jehan Mughal architecture reached it's supreme exuberance. He chose marble as the chief medium for all his architectural undertakings.

Elaborate ornamentation, pietra dura and creation of exclusive landscape setting are some important features of the buildings of the period.

Shah Jehan built marble edifices at Agra such as the Diwan-e-Aam, the Diwan-e-Khas, the Shish Mahal, the Moti Masjid which have been described as the most elegant buildings of their class to be found anywhere.

But all other architectural creations of Shah Jehan are nothing when compared to the exquisite conception of the mausoleum of his wife, Arjumand Banu Begum (Mumtaz Mahal) at Agra. The Taj Mahal is the crowning glory and culmination of Mughal architecture. It was commenced in 1631 and completed sometime around 1653. Gulbadan Begum's "Humayun Namah", Jehangir's autobiography "Tuzuk-i-Jahangir", Abdul Hamid Lahori's "Padshahnama", Inayat Khan's "Shah Jahannama" are some of the examples of Mughal literature in the later period.

AURANGZEB ALAMGIR'S REIGN [1658—1707]

Aurangzeb ruled longer than any of his predecessors, yet he could not stop the decline of the Mughal empire, which was hastened after his demise, and finally in 1858 India came directly under the control of British government.

DECLINE OF MUGHAL RULE AND THE BATTLE OF PLASSEY

The death of Alamgir in 1707 is generally regarded as the beginning of the gradual decline and ultimate fall of the once extensive, prosperous and powerful Mughal Empires. Although it took nearly 150 years before the House of Babur finally disappeared from the scene, the cracks which appeared at Alamgir's death widened. Aurangzeb Alamgir was succeeded by his son, Bahadur Shah Zafar (1707–1712), who momentarily revived the Mughal Empire. But the Marahattas power increased and they became the unchallenged rulers of the Deccan. In the province of Punjab, Sikh power under Guru Govind Singh become a force to reckon with. One of the reasons for springing up of power centers apart from Delhi was quick change in the succession of Empires. That is from 1707 to 1857, nearly seventeen kings were throned and dethroned The weakening Mughal Empire invited havoc in the form of Nadir Shah, a Persian King in 1738-39. On his orders a general massacre of the citizens of Delhi was carried out resulting in the death of 30,000 people. Another threat to the Mughal Empire came from Afghans of Rohilkhand, lying Northeast of Delhi. By the middle of 18th century the Rohillas become independent of the Mughal rule. At the same time the Jats also raised their heads against the central rule.

Taking advantage of this chaotic situation, East India Company began strengthening its military capabilities and along with Hindu traders and money lenders conspired against Nawab Siraj-ud Daulah of Bengal to take over his principality. The battle of Plassey of 1757 is considered a major breakthrough for the British in the Sub-continent.

It paved the way for the company's rule in Bengal and from there later on whole of India came under company's rule.

In the 19th century, Muslims like Sayyed Ahmed and Shah Ismail carried out jihad against the Sikhs, and Haider Ali and Tipu Sultan in the Deccan against the British, however, they failed in their efforts to stop the downfall of the Muslim rule. The final crunch came after the war of 1857, when the Mughal rule officially came to an end and India came under the direct rule of the British crown.

SHAH WALI ULLAH'S REFORM MOVEMENT
[1707—1762]

In the eighteenth century, Islam in the sub-continent was faced with menacing problems, such as sectarian conflict, the low moral tone of society, poor understanding of the Holy Quran, and general ignorance of Islam. These were valid grounds for fearing that political disintegration would be accompanied by religious collapse. This did not happen, rather an era of religious regeneration was inaugurated, which was due more than anything else, to the activities of one man, Shah Wali Ullah.

Shah Wali Ullah was born on February 21, 1703 at Delhi. His father, Shah Abdul Rahim was a sufi and theologian of great repute. Shah Wali Ullah received his academic and spiritual education at the hands of his father, and later he taught at his father's Madrassah-i-Rahimiyah for twelve years. He left for Arabia in 1730 for higher studies where he obtained his Sanad in Hadith. At that time, Muslims in India were divided into Hanafi, Sufi, Shia, Sunni and Mullah sects. While in Hijaz he decided to:

(a)   reinterpret Islam,
(b)   popularize Islamic values amongst the Muslims,
(c)   present Islam in a rational manner.

Shah Wali Ullah's single most important act was his translation of the Holy Quran into simple Persian, language of the land, to be understood by the people in the sub-continent. He studied writings of all schools of thought to understand their viewpoint, then wrote comprehensive volumes about what is fair and just and worked out a system of thought, belief and values on which all but the extremists could agree. Thus providing a spiritual basis for national cohesion.

Shah Wali Ullah trained students in different branches of Islamic knowledge and entrusted them with the teaching of students. He recommended the application of Ijtihad against blind Taqlid. He also interpreted Quran and Hadith in the context of times.

Shah Wali Ullah directed his teachings towards reorienting the Muslim society on the basis of social justice and removing inequalities and iniquitous distribution of wealth. He established several branches of his school at Delhi for effective dissemination of his ideas. In his book, "Hujjat-ullah-il-Balighah" pinpointed the causes of chaos and disintegration of the Muslim society. These were:

(a)   Pressure on Public treasury, the emoluments given to various people without doing any service to the State.

(b) Heavy taxation on peasants, merchants, workers and as a result tax evasion was rampant. According to Shah Wali Ullah, a state can prosper only if there were light and reasonable taxes.

He wrote open letters to:

(a) Mughal rulers to give up their corrupt and inefficient practices.
(b) Soldiers for forgetting to inculcate within themselves the spirit of Jihad.
(c) Artisans, workers and peasants and reminded them that on their labors the economic prosperity of the state depends.
(d) The Emperor to teach a lesson to the Jats threatening the Mughal empire and also wrote to him not to give jagirs to mansabdars who were not loyal to the state.
(e) Masses to be conscious of their duties and not to indulge in the accumulation of wealth.

Shah Wali Ullah tried to reconcile the basic differences amongst the different sections of the Muslims and considered the government as an essential means and agency for the regeneration of his community. He wrote to Ahmad Shah Abdali "to give up the life of ease and draw the sword and not to sheath it till the distinction is established between true faith and infidelity...". His efforts resulted in Maratha debacle at the hands of Ahmad Shah Abdali and Najibud Daula in the third battle of Panipat in 1761.

Shah Wali Ullah's teachings created a new awareness of the present dangers and what the future had in store for the Muslims of the sub-continent. This was a psychological preparation for the revolution of 1857-58, a revolution which in some ways was perhaps the most fortunate thing to have happened from the Muslim point of view, because in spite of their great sufferings, it turned their mind to new remedies.

FARAIZI MOVEMENT [1830—57]

The first half of the 19th century witnessed a movement known as Faraizi movement in East Bengal. The founder of this movement was Haji Shariatullah. At that time the condition of the Bengali Muslims in the sub-continent was very miserable. The British policy of distrust and oppression towards the Muslims rendered them economically and educationally crippled, and the oppression of the Zamindars made their lives unbearable.

Haji Shariatullah went to Makkah on the Pilgrimage. After 20 years he came back to his country and started his reform movement known as Faraizi movement. He asked the most depressed classes of Muslims to give up un-Islamic customs and practices and to act upon the commandments of religion called Faraiz or duties. Hence his followers came to be known as Faraiz. He forbade Tazia on the occasion of Muharram and singing and dancing at the time of wedding ceremonies. His movement was also directed against the oppression of the Zamindars. He declared the country as Dar-ul-Harb where Eid and Friday prayers could not be offered.

The movement infused a new life and brought a greater agitation among the Bengal Muslims—specially among the peasants who were imbued with his doctrines. Thus, he sowed the seeds of independence in Bengal. He died in 1840.

Haji Shariatullah was succeeded by his son Muhammad Mohsin, known as Dadhu Mian. Dadhu Mian made the movement of his father strong and popular by organizing it in a systematic way. He acquired a greater influence among the Muslim peasants and craftsman of Bakerganj, Dhaka, Faridpur and Pabna districts. He divided the whole place under Khalifas who kept him informed on all occurrences in the jurisdictions. Dadhu Mian vehemently opposed the cusses imposed by the landlords on the Muslim peasants for the decoration of the image of Durgah.

He asked his followers to settle in lands managed by the government. During the revolt of 1857, he was put under arrest for organizing the peasants of Faridpur districts against the British government. He died in 1860.

Mir Nasir Ali, known as Titu Mir, is another important figure who was moved by the sufferings of the Muslim of Bengal. After returning from pilgrimage, Titu Mir, devoted himself to the cause of his country. Narkelbaria, a village near Calcutta was made center of his activities. Many oppressed Muslim peasants gathered under Titu Mir in their resistance against the Hindu landlord, Krishna Deva Raj. Titu Mir, was able to defeat Krishna Deva, and set up his government. The British aiding the Hindu landlords sent an army of 100 English Soldiers and 300 sepoys to Narkelbaria. In 1831, Titu Mir died fighting the British forces.

The death of Titu Mir did not dishearten his followers, rather his example became a source of inspiration to them in the years to come.

WAR OF INDEPENDENCE

By 1845, the British empire had grown from Bengal to Sind, and all that remained free was the Punjab. The Sikhs were ruling over Punjab and after the second Sikh war in 1848, the British gained control over the Indus. The Koh-i-Noor Diamond that Ranjit Singh had worn in his headdress, now became a part of the crown jewels at Westminster.

The British army recruited local Indians in their force. They used cartridges which were greased with fat from tabooed animals and had to be bitten before use. In 1857, these Indian soldiers began a mutiny against the British, which started from the British Army in Bengal, but spread swiftly across the sub-continent. This war of Independence, or the Mutiny of the Sepoys, as it is termed by the British, was not successful because the Muslims and Hindus were unable to work together.

After the War of Independence in 1857, the British government assumed sovereignty over the lands of the British East India Company. The British control over the sub-continent grew in the next 50 years and culminated in the British Raj. Queen Victoria's Indian realm continued to expand, until Hunza, the remote kingdom bordering China, fell into British hands in 1891, bringing the expansion to an end.

The frontier separating British India from Afghanistan was delineated by the British in 1893. The resulting Durand Line cut straight through the tribal area of the Pathans. The British left the tribal areas to govern themselves under the supervision of British political agents.

British became masters of India, where for nearly 800 years Muslims had ruled. However, their attitude towards the Muslims was of antipathy. According to Hunter, "The Muslims of India are, and have been for many years, a source of chronic danger to the British power in India". The British also attributed the war of 1857 to the Muslims alone. As a result properties of the Muslims were confiscated, employment opportunities in the army, in revenue department, and the judiciary were closed for the Muslims.

A policy of discrimination against the Muslims was deliberately followed by the British administrators, even in filling minor jobs. Advertisements inviting applications for government jobs specifically mentioned that Muslims would not be appointed. Hunter admits that the exclusion of the Muslims was so complete that in the government offices in Calcutta they could not accept a post higher than that of a porter, messenger, filler of ink-pots and mender of pens.

By a series of revenue and financial measures, the British smashed the political and social position of the Muslims. In the Province of Bombay, the government appointed "Inam Commission" to inquire into the land grants of the Muslim times. The Commission took away 20,000 estates from the Muslims and thus ruined many families and institution of the community.

The company's commercial policy eliminated the Muslims from internal and foreign trade. With the coming of the Europeans in the Sub-continent the Muslim merchants lost much of their commerce with foreign countries. Still they maintained their hold on internal trade and their commercial activities extended to the Persian Gulf and the coastal territories of the Arabian Sea. During the company's rule the Muslim traders were pushed out of this area by the competition of the company's traders who enjoyed many special concessions.

The newly introduced English system of education had many drawbacks for the Muslims, mainly because it made no provision for religious education. So they stayed aloof from this education. Thus within a few years of the loss of their political power, the Muslims lost all avenues of employment, were dispossessed of their estates and deprived of the benefits of the education. A highly cultured community turned into a backward and poor people. And in their place English educated Hindus began to occupy positions in governments offices formerly held by the Muslims.

1858—1902

ALIGARH MOVEMENT [1858—98]

The War of Independence 1857 ended in a disaster for the Muslims. The British believed that the Muslims were responsible for the anti-British uprising of 1857 and therefore, they were subjected to ruthless punishment and merciless vengeance. The British had always looked upon the Muslims as their adversaries because they had ousted them from power. With the rebellion of 1857 this feeling was intensified and every attempt was made to ruin and suppress the Muslims forever. Thus the Mughal rule was liquidated and the sub-continent went directly under the British crown.

After dislodging the Muslim rulers from the throne, the new rulers—the British implemented a new educational policy with drastic changes. The policy restricted Arabic, Persian and religious education in schools and made English as the only medium of instruction as well as the official language in 1835. A wrong attitude of everything modem and western, and disinclination to make use of the opportunities opening under the new regime was created among the Muslims. This tendency, had it continued long, would have proved disastrous for the Muslim community.

Such were the days of despair and despondency when Sir Syed appeared on the horizon of Muslim India to rescue them. Sir Syed had the conviction that regeneration of the Indian Muslims had not at all visualized that mankind had entered a very important phase of it's existence, i.e. an era of science and learning which was the source of progress and prosperity for the British. Therefore, modem education became the pivot of his movement for the regeneration of the Indian Muslims, which brought a complete orientation in their lives. He tried to transform Muslim minds from medieval outlook to a modern one.

Sir Syed's first and foremost objective was to acquaint the British with the Indian mind; his next anxiety was to open the minds of his countrymen to European literature, science and technology.

Therefore, in order to fulfill this desire he started the Aligarh movement of which Aligarh was the center. He had two immediate objectives in view: to remove the state of misunderstanding and tension between the Muslims and the new British Government, and to induce them to go in for advancements available under the new dispensation without in any way deviation from the fundamentals of their faith.

Keeping education and social reform as the two planks of his program, he launched the Aligarh movement with the following objectives:

1. Create an atmosphere of mutual understanding between the British government and the Muslims.
2. Persuade Muslims to learn English education.
3. Persuade Muslims to abstain from agitational politics.
4. To produce an intellectual class of Muslims.

Fortunately, Syed Ahmad Khan was able to attract to his orbit a number of sincere friends who shared his views and helped him. Among them were well-known figures like Nawab Mohsin ul Mulk, Nawab Viqar ul Mulk, Hali, Shibli, Nazir Ahmad, Chiragh Ali, Mohammad Hayat, and Zakaullah. Above all his gifted son Syed Mahmud, a renowned scholar, jurist and educationalist was great help to him.

Syed Ahmad also succeeded in enlisting the services of a number of distinguished English professors like Bech, Morison, Raleigh and Arnold who gave their best in building up the Aligarh college into a first rate institution.

Syed Ahmad launched his educational movement by setting up Gulshan school at Muradabaad—1859; Victoria school at Gazipur in 1863; Scientific Society for the translation of English works in the native language at Aligarh in 1864; Aligarh Institute Gazette imparting information on history—ancient and modern, science of agriculture, natural sciences, physical sciences and Advanced Mathematics in 1866; Committee Striving for the Educational Progress of Muslims - 1870; Mohammadan Anglo-Oriental school (MAO) at the pattern of English public schools at Aligarh in 1875 and later raised to the level of college in 1877 and university in 1913; Mohammadan Educational Conference - 1886, which met every year to take stock of the educational problems of the Muslims and to persuade them to get modern education and abstain from politics, it later became a political mouthpiece of the Indian Muslims and the forerunner of the Muslim League.

Besides his prominent role in the educational uplift of the Muslims, Syed Ahmad Khan's writings played important role in popularizing the ideals for which the Aligarh stood. His "Essay on the Causes of Indian Revolt" in 1858; and other writings as "Loyal Mohammadans of India"; Tabyin-ul-Kalam and "A series of essays on the life of Muhammad and subjects subsidiary therein" helped to create a cordial relation between the British Government and the Indian Muslims and also helped to remove the misunderstanding about Islam and Christianity.

It was this platform from where Syed Ahmad Khan strongly forbade the Muslims to join the Congress. He stood for reserved seats for Muslims and also promoted the idea that Hindus and Muslims are two distinct nations which led to the Two Nation Theory.

Syed Ahmad Khan's Aligarh Movement played a significant role to bring about an intellectual revolution among the Indian Muslims. Thus Aligarh Movement succeeded in achieving it's major objectives, i.e. educational progress and social reform and earned for Sir Syed the title "Prophet of Education".

ANJUMAN HIMAYAT-I-LSLAM, LAHORE
[1884—1947]

For the last 1,000 years, Lahore has been a great Muslim cultural and intellectual center. Under the Mughals, also, Lahore could once again boast of rapid progress in the domain of education and learning. But it was toward the end of Muslim rule in India that the Sikhs devastated large areas of the Punjab province. The annexation of Punjab brought peace to the region but failed to create conditions conducive to the growth of intellectual and academic activities. The War of Independence of 1857 added to the woes and worries of the Indian Muslims. The Muslims refused to get modern education.

Towards the close of 19th century, the impact of Sir Syed's Aligarh Movement was felt all over the sub-continent and Punjab was no exception. It was in March 1884 that Maulana Qazi Hamid-ud-Din invited his pupil Maulvi Ghulamullah Qasuri and a number of other public-spirited persons to a small gathering and set up the Anjuman Himayat-i-Islam.

On September 22, 1884, the establishment of the Anjuman was formally announced and Qazi Hamid-ud-Din was elected its first president. The Anjuman decided to work for the following aims and objectives:

(a)   To arrange for the religious and general education of Muslim boys and girls;

(b)   To propagate and defend Islam against the Christian missionaries and Hindu revivalists;

(c)   To counteract the propaganda against Islam through speeches and publications.

Fortunately, a team of selfless workers associated themselves for the cause of the Anjuman. Among them were Nawab Sir Fateh Ali Khan Qazilbash, Mian Sir Mohammad Shafi, Sir Mohammad Iqbal, Sir Abdul Qadir, Dr. Khalifa Shuja'-ud-Din and a host of others.

The Anjuman established educational institutions in arts, sciences and technology for men and women; orphanages for helpless Muslim to which widows home was added. The Moplah orphans, victims of Bihar and Quetta earthquakes and later the destitute children and widows of 1947 holocaust found shelter at these orphanages.

In 1885, Risala-i-Anjuman Himayat-i-Islam made its appearance, publishing the principles of Islam. In 1892, it started a college - Islamia College - at Lahore and was elevated to Degree level in 1903. The contribution of the college to general Muslim awakening has been great. Its students played an important role in the Muslim national movement in Punjab. In 1939, the Anjuman established another Islamia College for Girls.

Of these services in the field of education, the Anjuman had the greatest impact on Muslim society and politics. In 1928, the Anjuman expanded its Press and published standard works on religious and literary themes and modern subjects like geography, physical sciences and economics. A landmark in the history of the Anjuman publication was the production of an absolutely correct text of the Quran.

ESTABLISHMENT OF INDIAN NATIONAL CONGRESS [1885]

In 1885, a retired British civil servant, Allan Octavian Hume established the Indian National Congress in Simla.

Sir Syed Ahmad Khan urged the Muslims to abstain from politics and thus the Indian National Congress was initially dominated by Hindus, but there were some Muslim leaders, including Muhammad Ali Jinnah who joined the Congress in 1913. Later, when the Muslims realized that the Congress was indifferent to their goals and aspirations, they withdrew their support for the Congress and gave it to the All India Muslim League.

NADVA-TUL-'ULAMA OF LUCKNOW [1894—1947]

This institution came into existence in 1894 as a result of the efforts of some religious minded government officials, Ulama and Sufis, who wished to bring the Ulama together and remove sectarian differences. The main work of the organization was the establishment of a Dar-ul-Uloom at Lucknow. For some time Shibli Nomani, Syed's co-worker for many years, was associated with the institution. Under his influence it gained importance, but in 1914 he was forced to resign.

Shibli Nomani wrote extensively on Islam, highlighting those periods and personalities which offered guidance and provided inspiration to the present day Muslim, enabling them to take their proper place in the world of today. His writing include "Heroes of Islam". The first book of the series was Al-Mamun, a biography of Mamoon-ur-Rasheed. Other books in the series included biography of Imam Abu Hanifa, Imam Ghazali and Maulana Rumi.

Shibli tried, through his writings, to refute western allegations against Islam and Muslims. His Tarajum, gave fairly full account of the steps taken by the Muslims in the hey day of their glory, and to incorporate into Arabic, the fruits of the learning of Greece, Iran, India etc. He took great pains to pick out and train the promising youths, who could carry on his work and spread his message. His basic purpose remained to train and educate Muslim youths so that they may get together and lead their nation out of despondency.

A magnificent building was constructed for the Dar-ul-Uloom with a grant from Bahawalpur state. The tradition of training in literary craftsmanship and style of modern Arabic which Shibli introduced is maintained and the "Academy of Authors" (Dar-ul-Musannifin) at Azamgarh manned by the former students of the Nadvah is also a by-product of the institution.

1903—1927

PARTITION OF BENGAL [1905—11]

In 1905, the English finding Bengal Presidency too large for one Governor to administer, decided to redraw it's boundaries and divided it into two parts.

The province of Bengal and Assam were reconstituted so as to form the two provinces of manageable size: Western Bengal, with a population of 54 million, of which 42 million would be Hindus and 9 million Muslims; and Eastern Bengal and Assam with a population of 31 million of which 18 million would be Muslims and 12 million Hindus. The territory to be transferred from Bengal to the new province consisted of the districts of Chittagong and Dacca divisions, those of Rajshahi division except Darjeeling and the district of Malda.

The scheme was sent to London by Curzon in February 1905. It was sanctioned by the Secretary of State for India, St. John Brodrich, in June, and the proclamation of the formation of the new province was issued in September. The province of Bengal and Assam came into being on October 16, 1905.

Incidentally, the partition went in favor of the Muslims. As before the partition the Western Bengal, being the first area to come under the western influence, was developed and industrialized, a striking contrast to the Eastern part where the Muslim peasantry was crushed under the Hindu landlords; river system was infested with pirates; a very few funds were allocated for education and was dreaded as a place of banishment. But the partition helped to boost Bengali literature and language; efforts were also made towards social, economic and educational uplift of the Muslims.

The Muslims outnumbered the Hindus in Eastern Bengal and thus alleviated the Bengali Muslims politically and economically. Thus this modification of boundaries was made an occasion for unprecedented agitation by the Hindus. They alleged that Lord Curzon deliberately tried to divide the Hindus and the Muslims by drawing the line between the Hindu and the Muslim halves of Bengal; he had favored the Muslims by giving them a new province in which they were in a clear majority; he had struck a deadly blow at Bengali nationality and that he was the upholder of the devilish official policy of divide and rule.

Whereas the partition of Bengal was welcomed by the Muslims of India, the Hindu community strongly opposed it and started a gigantic mass movement celebrating October 16, as the day of mourning in Calcutta. The Swadeshi movement influenced by the Chinese boycott of American goods was started by Hindus against the British. In the meantime, the sectarian cry of Band-e-Matram was raised as the national cry protecting worship of Shivaji as national hero. This organized anarchist movement took a terrorist turn resulting in political sabotage and communal riots.

In 1911, keeping in view the fluid political situation in India and the cult of Hindu revivalism, the British decided to undo the earlier decision to please the Hindus and they reunited the province in 1911—which saddened the Muslims. Thus the minds were divided long before the territory were divided.

SIMLA DEPUTATION [1906]

In 1905, with Viceroy Minto a new installment of reforms was indicated in which the elected principle would be extended. The anti-partition agitation had convinced the Muslims of the futility of expecting any fairplay from the Hindu majority. Therefore, to safeguard their interests, the Muslim leaders drew up a plan for separate electorates for their community and presented it to Viceroy Lord Minto at Simla on October 1, 1906,

The Simla Deputation consisting of seventy representatives of all shades of opinion and led by Sir Aga Khan who read the address, written by Mr. Bilgrami. The long address said, among other things, that the position of the Muslim community should not be estimated on it's numerical strength alone, but in terms of it's political importance and the service rendered to the Empire. He also pointed out that the representative institutions of the West were inappropriate and inadequate for India and their application raised difficult problems and that it was necessary to proceed in this unchartered field with utmost care and in whatever sphere (municipal or provincial) it was intended to introduce or extend the electoral system.

The Muslims should be represented as a community

The Viceroy in his reply to the Simla Deputation address reassured the Muslims that their political rights and interests as a community shall be safeguarded by any administrative reorganization under him.

The acceptance of the Deputation's demand proved to be a turning point in the history of the sub-continent. For the first time, the Hindu-Muslim conflict was lifted to the constitutional plane. The Muslims made it clear that they had no confidence in the Hindu majority and that they were not prepared to put their future in the hands of assembly elected on the assumed basis of a homogenous Indian nation. It is in this sense that the beginning of separate electorate may be seen as glimmerings of the two nation theory—it's final and inevitable consequence being the partition of British India in 1947.

The Simla Deputation was successful because the Muslims were strongly urged to protect their separate identity, whereas the British responded to their demand as Lord Minto was anxious to pull them out of their political discontent.

Separate electorates were given statutory recognition in the Indian Councils Act of 1909. Muslims were accorded not only the right to elect their representatives by separate electorates, but also the right to vote in general constituencies. In addition, they were also given weightage in representation.

ESTABLISHMENT OF ALL INDIA MUSLIM LEAGUE [1906]

On December 30, 1906, the annual meeting of Mohammadan Educational Conference was held at Dacca under the chairmanship of Nawab Viqar ul Mulk. Almost three thousand delegates attended the session making it the most representative ever gathering of Muslim India. For the first time the conference lifted it's ban on political discussion, when Nawab Salim ullah Khan presented a proposal to establish a political party to safeguard the interests of the Muslims—All India Muslim League.

So far three factors had kept the Muslims away from the Congress—Sir Syed's advice to the Muslims to give it a wide berth, the Hindu agitation against the partition of Bengal and the Hindu religious revivalism's hostility towards the Muslims. The Muslims remained loyal to Sir Syed's advice but events were fast changing the Indian scene and politics was being thrust on all sections of the population.

Besides these, the motivating factors were that the Muslim intellectual class wanted representation; the masses needed to unite at one platform and it was through the dissemination of western thought of John Locke, Milton, Thomas Paine, etc. at the MAO College that initiated the emergence of Muslim nationalism.

With the establishment of All India Muslim League with it's headquarters at Lucknow, it elected Sir Aga Khan as it's President. It also elected six vice presidents, a secretary and two joint secretaries for a term of three years. It's initial membership was four hundred in fixed proportions of the provinces. The constitution of the League known as the "Green Book" was written by Maulana Muhammad Ali Johar. It's branches were also setup in other provinces. Syed Ameer Ali established a branch of the League in London in 1908, supporting the same objectives.

The Muslim League was established with the following objectives:

1. To inculcate among Muslims a feeling of loyalty to the Government and to disabuse their minds of misunderstandings and misconceptions out of it's actions and intentions.
2. To protect and advance the political rights and interests of the Muslims of India and to represent to the Government from time to time, their needs and aspirations.
3. To prevent the growth of ill-will between Muslims and other nationalities without prejudice to it's own purposes.

Many Hindu historians and several British writers have alleged that the Muslim League was founded at official instigation. They argue that Lord Minto who inspired the establishment of a Muslim organization so as to break the Congress and to minimize the strength of Indian Freedom movement. But these statements are not supported by evidence. Contrary to this, the widely accepted view is that the Muslim League was basically established to protect and advance the Muslim interests and to combat the growing influence of the Indian National Congress.

THE LUCKNOW PACT [1916]

In the aftermath of World War I, Lord Chelmsford, the Viceroy began to think out a scheme of post-war reforms and for this purpose, invited practical suggestions from the Indian politicians. In October, 1916—nineteen elected members of the Imperial Legislative Council addressed a memorandum to the Viceroy on the subject of reforms. But their suggestions did not become news in the British circle but were discussed, amended and accepted at a subsequent meeting of the Congress and the Muslim League.

With the beginning of World War I and the previous fluid situation prevailing in India as annulment of partition of Bengal; merciless massacre in Kanpur; casualties in the Balkan war; growing anti-British thought continued unabated among Muslim orthodox religious circles which called for a shift in Muslim alliance with the Hindus rather than the British.

Finally, in December 1916, Congress and the Muslim League held a joint session at Lucknow in which a scheme of reforms was unanimously adapted as the irreducible minimum of political freedom for India. The Congress League scheme came to be known as the Lucknow Pact. Jinnah was the principal architect of the Lucknow Pact and was hailed as an ambassador of Hindu-Muslim unity.

The following scheme of reforms was agreed upon:

1. The Muslim League and Congress should jointly demand for self-government in India.
2. Seats should be reserved for the Muslims in the Legislatures with the right of separate electorate.

3. Muslims should elect one-third of the elected members to the Central Legislature through separate electorates.
4. Any private resolution effecting a particular community, should require three-fourth majority of the members of that community for the advancement of that resolution in the council.
5. Fourth-Fifth of the total members of the provincial and legislative councils should be properly elected and the rest should be nominated.
6. Elections should be held on Adult Franchise basis.
7. Half of the members of the Central and the Provincial Government should be elected by the members of their respective Legislative Councils.
8. The Governor General or the Governor would be bound by the resolutions passed by their respective legislative councils. The Governor General would be authorized to put such resolutions off for a period of not more than a year.
9. The Secretary of State should be given the same powers as were enjoyed by the Secretary of State for other colonies.
10. The Executive and the Judiciary should remain separate from each other.

The Lucknow Pact was an experiment of integration of Congress and the Muslim League on political grounds. It showed that it was possible for educated middle-class Muslims and Hindus to arrive at an amicable settlement of Hindu-Muslim constitutional and political problems. It is also significant because the constitutional features of the Lucknow Pact were incorporated in the 1919 Act.

In the dismissal history of Hindu-Muslim relations in the sub-continent, Lucknow Pact was the only bright spot.

KHILAFAT MOVEMENT [1919—1924]

The Lucknow pact showed that it was possible for middle-class, English-educated Muslims and Hindus to arrive at an amicable settlement of Hindu-Muslim constitutional and political problems. The Hindu-Muslim unity reached its climax during the Khilafat and the Non-cooperation Movements.

The Muslims of South Asia, under the leadership of the Ali Brothers, Maulana Muhammad Ali and Maulana Shaukat Ali launched the historic Khilafat Movement after the First World War to protect the Ottoman Empire from dismemberment, Mohandas Karam Chand Gandhi linked the issue of Swaraj with the Khilafat issue to associate the Hindus with the Movement. The ensuing movement was the first country-wide popular movement.

The Muslims of India, for many reasons had a strong feeling of identity with the world community of Islam. They had seen the decline in the political fortunes of Islam as the Europeans powers conquered the Muslim land one after the other. The Anglo-Russian convention of 1908 had reduced their next door neighbor Iran to a mere dependency. Afghanistan also suffered as it was a bone of contention between Russia and Great Britain, and was now under the latter's sphere of influence.

The general impression among the Muslims of India was that the Western power were waging a war against Islam throughout the world to rob it of all its power and influence. The Ottoman Empire was the only Muslim power which had maintained a semblance of authority and the Muslims of India wanted to save the Islamic political power from extinction.

The Indian Muslims had affiliation with the Turkish Caliphate. As an institution the Khilafat had a checkered past. Originally migrated from Medina to Damascus and from Damascus to Baghdad. For sometime it was located in Egypt, then it fell to the lot of Turkey, very much as a prize.

The Turkish sultans had claimed to be the caliphs of the Muslims world. Their claim had not been recognized by the Muslims of India so long as the Mughal Empire had been in existence. Tipu Sultan was the first Indian Muslim who having been frustrated in his attempts to gain recognition from Mughal bast turned to the Sultan of Turkey to establish a legal right to his throne.

At this critical juncture also, when the Muslims of the sub-continent had no sovereign of their own, they began to see the necessity of recognizing the Sultan of Turkey as their caliph. When Turkey chose to fight on the side of Germany against the Allied powers, to avenge the European powers which played a leading role to reduce Turkey in Europe to Eastern Thrace, Constantinople and the straits in the Balkan Wars (1912-13), the sympathies of the Indian Muslims were with the Turks.

The British hoped to neutralize the status of the caliph and the right of the Turks to their homeland. But there was a wide gap between the promise and performance. The peace settlement and the Treaty of Serves broke off the Ottoman Empire and reduced Sultan to the status of a vassal prince.

The peace treaty placed the Muslim holy places under the Allied powers. Thus, it had also become important for the Muslims of the sub-continent to abide by the command of their Holy Prophet (may peace be upon him), who with dying breath had bidden them never to surrender the Jazirat-ul-Arab (Arabia, Iraq, Syria and Palestine) to any non-Muslim government.

Mohammad Ali argued that for Muslims to accept mandates over Iraq, Syria and Palestine would amount to a total disregard of the wishes of the Prophet (may peace be upon him). Thus with the objectives:

(a) to maintain the Turkish caliphate;
(b) to protect the holy places of the Muslims; and
(c) to maintain the unity of the Ottoman empire

the Muslims of India launched the Tehrik-i-Khilafat. There was absolute unanimity among the Indian Muslims. Though separated from Turkey by thousands of miles, they were determined to fight Turkey's battle from India.

Rioting started in Amritsar on April 10, 1919, followed by the Jalianwala Bagh tragedy on April 13, 1919 when Sir Michael O'Duiyer opened fire on a crowd, assembled at the Jalianwala Bagh and unfamiliar with the ban imposed on public meetings by martial law administrators. The incident caused 379 innocent lives and left 1200 wounded.

In the meantime, when the terms of the Treaty of Serves were announced in 1920, it caused deep resentment among the Muslims. They felt as if they were betrayed. Thus in June, 90 influential Muslims wrote to Lord Chelmsford, the Viceroy, that they would start non-cooperation with the government from August, until the terms of treaty with Turkey were revised.

But that was to no avail as the British Prime Minister, Lloyd George was an implacable enemy of Turkey and by implication, of the Indian Khilafat Movement. When in 1920, the Indian Khilafat deputation visited England to put their views before the British Government, he gave them a cold shoulder and the deputation met a failure.

A tragic off shoot of the Khilafat was the Hijrat Movement. When a land is not safe for Islam, a Muslim has two options—Jehad or Hijrat. This was proposed by Jamiyat al Ulama-i-Hind, a fatwa signed by 925 eminent Muslims. According to one version, the idea of Hijrat was originated by Maulana Abul Kalam Azad.

In NWFP province and Sind, hundreds of families sold their land and property and departed in the direction of the Khyber pass, to migrate to Afghanistan, a brotherly independent Muslim State. Only in the month of August, some 18,000 Indian Muslims migrated to Afghanistan. Afghanistan, a poor country, was unable to absorb so large an influx of population and sealed its borders. It is difficult to establish who was responsible for misleading such a large number of Muslims.

Another tragic event was the Moplah Uprising. In mid-August 1921, agrarian riots broke out in Nilambur. The Moplah peasants revolted against the Hindu landlord's oppressive policies in alliance with the British. The Hindu landlords redistributed their lands and the Moplahs, who had been suffering, rose in revolt. A pitched battle between the British regiment and the Moplahs killed several Europeans. The Moplahs were also injured in tens of thousands and 4,000 were killed in action.

Then there was the notorious Moplah Train Tragedy. A hundred prisoners confined in a close and almost air-tight goods van were transported by rail. When the door was opened 66 Moplahs were found suffocated to death and the remaining 34 were on the verge of collapse.

This was followed by Hindu-Muslim communal clashes, particularly in Multan and Bengal in September 1922. The Sanghattan and Shuddi movements were the offshoots of these communal rioting, which were anti-Muslim and aimed at Hindu revivalism.

Besides other events, the arrest of the Ali brothers in September 1921 gave a severe blow to the Khilafat Movement. Gandhi, who was using this movement to accelerate India's advance towards Swaraj, also withdrew his support for the Muslim cause in the aftermath of the Chauri Chaura incident in February, 1922. Making an excuse that the national volunteers were responsible for the murder of 21 policeman, thus leading to violence, he called off the whole movement.

In 1924, Turks, who under Mustafa Kamal were consolidating their position in Turkey, announced an end to the Khilafat. It was a great blow to Indian Khilafatists who had been campaigning on behalf of Turkey and Khilafat. Gradually the enthusiasm of the people died down and the Khilafat Conference and Committee developed new interests and in a short time nothing but their name remained.

Although the Khilafat Movement failed to achieve its declared objectives, it carried political awakening to large masses of Muslims. It was during the Khilafat days that representatives of Indian Muslims came into contact with eminent personages from other Muslim countries to save the semblance of unity in the world of Islam.

The Khilafat Movement was an asset for struggle of Pakistan. It made clear to the Indian Muslims neither to trust the British nor the Hindus but to look to their own strength for their self-preservation.

DELHI MUSLIM PROPOSALS [1927]

Considering that separate electorates posed the main hindrance to improving Hindu-Muslim relations, Quaid-i-Azam proposed that if the Hindus agreed to providing certain safeguards, the Muslims would give up this demand. Consequently, the proposals were formally approved at a conference held by the Muslims in 1927 at Delhi, and are now called "The Delhi Proposals":

1. The formation of a separate province of Sind.
2. Introduction of reforms in the NWFP and in Baluchistan on the same footing as in other provinces.
3. Unless and until the above proposals were implemented, the Muslims would never surrender the right of their representation through separate electorates. Muslims would be willing to

abandon separate electorates in favor of joint electorates with reservation of seats fixed in proportion to the population of different communities, if the above two proposals were implemented to the full satisfaction of Muslims and also if the following proposals were accepted.

4.　Hindu minorities in Sind, Baluchistan and the NWFP would be accorded the same concessions in the form of reservation of seats over and above the proportion of their population as Muslims would get in Hindu majority provinces.

5.　Muslim representation in the Central Legislature would not be less than one third.

6.　In addition to provisions like religious freedom, there was to be a further guarantee in the constitution that on communal matters no bill or resolution would be considered or passed if a three-fourths majority of the members of the community concerned were opposed to it.

These proposals were to be accepted or rejected in toto. So, in effect, the Muslims agreed to give up the separate electorates in form of the reservation of seats. Unfortunately, the Congress first accepted but later rejected the proposals.

SIMON COMMISSION [1927]

The government of India Act of 1919 was essentially transitional in character. Under section 84 of the said Act, a statutory commission was to be appointed at the end of the ten years to determine the next stage in the realization of self rule in India.

The British government appointed a commission under Sir John Simon in November 1927. The commission which had no Indian members on it was being sent to investigate India's constitutional problems and make recommendations to the government on the future constitution of India.

The Congress decided to boycott the Simon Commission and to challenge Lord Birkenhead, Secretary of State for India, to produce a constitution acceptable to the various elements in India.

There was a clear split in the Muslim League. Sir Muhammad Shafi, wanted to cooperate with the commission, decided to hold Muslim League session in Lahore in December, 1927.

The other faction, led by Jinnah stood for the boycott of the commission, held the Muslim League session at Calcutta and decided to form a sub-committee to confer with the working committee of Indian National Congress and other organizations with a view to draft a constitution for India.

1928—1947

ALLAHABAD ADDRESS [1930]

Several Muslim leaders and thinkers having insight into the Hindu-Muslim question proposed separation of Muslim India.

However, the most lucid explanation of the inner feelings of the Muslim community was given by Allama Muhammad Iqbal in his presidential address to the All-India Muslim League at Allahabad in 1930. Allama Muhammad Iqbal was a poet, philosopher and thinker who had gained country-wide fame and recognition by 1930.

Political events took an ominous turn. There was a two-pronged attack on the Muslim interests. On one hand, the Hindus offered a tough opposition by proposing the Nehru report as the ultimate constitution for India. On the other, the British government in India in the course of observations on the Simon Commission report ignored the Muslim demands.

At this critical juncture, Iqbal realized that the peculiar problems of the Muslims in North-West India could only be understood by people belonging to this region and that in order to survive they would have to chalk out their own line of action.

Allama Iqbal explained in his address that Islam was the major formative factor in the life history of Indian Muslims. It furnished those basic emotions and loyalties which gradually unify scattered individuals and groups and finally transform them into a well-defined people, possessing a moral consciousness of their own.

Allama Iqbal defined the Muslims of India as a nation and suggested that there could be no possibility of peace in the country unless and until they were recognized as a nation and under a federal system the Muslim majority units were given the same privileges which were to be given to the Hindu majority units. It was the only way in which both the Muslims and the Hindus could prosper in accordance with their respective cultural values.

As a permanent solution to the Hindu-Muslim problem. Allama Iqbal proposed that the Punjab, North-West Frontier Province, Baluchistan and Sind should be converted into one province and declared that the North-West part of the country was destined to unite, self government within the British empire or without the British empire. This he suggested was the only way to do away with the communal riots and bring peace in the sub-continent.

The greatest historical significance of Allama Iqbal's Allahabad address was that it washed all political confusions from the minds of the Muslims thus enabling them to determine their new destination.

The national spirit which Iqbal fused among the Muslims of India later on developed into an ideological base of Pakistan.

CABINET MISSION PLAN [1946]

All attempts so far of the British government at bringing about peace between the Congress and the Muslim League had failed. The results of the general elections held in 1945-46 had made the British government feel the urgency to finding out a solution to the political deadlock which was in result of non-cooperation between the two major parties—the Congress and the Muslim League. Therefore, the British government decided to send to India a special mission of cabinet ministers.

The mission consisted of Lord Pethic Lawrence, the Secretary of State for India, Sir Stafford Cripps, President of the Board of Trade, and A. V. Alexander, the first Lord of the Admiralty.

The purpose of the mission was:

1. Preparatory discussions with elected representatives of British India and the Indian states in order to secure agreement as to the method of framing the constitution.
2. The setting up of a constitution body.
3. The bringing into being of an Executive Council having the support of the main Indian parties.

The mission arrived on March 24, 1946. After extensive discussions with Congress and the Muslim League, Cabinet Mission put forward it's own proposals on May 16, 1946.

The main principles of the plan were:

1. There would be a union of India comprising both British India and the Indian States, which would deal with Foreign Affairs, Defense and Communications. The union would have an Executive and a Legislature.
2. All residuary powers would belong to the provinces.
3. All provinces would be divided into three sections. Provinces could opt out of any group after the first general elections.
4. There would also be an interim government having the support of the major political parties.

Muslim League accepted the plan on June 6, 1946. Earlier Congress had accepted the plan on May 24, 1946, without accepting the interim setup.

The Viceroy should now have invited the Muslim League to form Government, as it had accepted the interim setup, but he did not do so. Jawaharlal Nehru, meanwhile, addressing a press conference on July 10, said that the Congress had agreed to join the constituent assembly, but it would be free to make changes in the Cabinet Mission Plan.

Muslim League accepted the plan on June 6, 1946. Earlier Congress had accepted the plan on May 24, 1946, without accepting the interim setup.

The Viceroy should now have invited the Muslim League to form Government, as it had accepted the interim setup, but he did not do so. Jawaharlal Nehru, meanwhile, addressing a press conference on July 10, said that the Congress had agreed to join the constituent assembly, but it would be free to make changes in the Cabinet Mission Plan.

Under these circumstances, Muslim League disassociated itself from the Cabinet Plan and resorted to "Direct Action" to achieve Pakistan.

As a result, Viceroy Wavell invited the Congress to join the interim government, although it had practically rejected the plan.

However, the Viceroy soon realized the futility of the scheme without the participation of the League. An invitation was, therefore, extended to the League and on October 14, 1946 Jinnah nominated Liaquat Ali Khan, I.I. Chundrigar, Sardar Abdur-Rab-Nishtar, Ghazanfar Ali Khan and Jogandra Nath Mandal to the Cabinet.

Congress allocated the Finance Ministry to the League. The budget which Liaquat Ali Khan presented as finance minister, was called a "poor man's budget" and it adversely affected the Hindu capitalists.

Moreover, the whole governmental setup came under the Muslim League due to holding of Finance Minister's portfolio by Liaquat Ali Khan. The deadlock between the Congress and the League further worsened in this setup.

On March 22, 1947, Lord Mountbatten arrived as the last Viceroy and it was announced that power would be transferred from British to Indian hands by June 1948.

Lord Mountbatten entered into a series of talks with the Congress and the Muslim League leaders. Quaid-i-Azam made it clear that the demand for Pakistan had the support of all the Muslims of India and that he could not withdraw from this. With staunch extremists as Patel agreeing to the Muslim demand for a separate homeland, Mountbatten now prepared for the partition of the sub-continent and announced it on June 3, 1947.

CRIPPS MISSION [1942]

The British government wanted to get the cooperation of Indian people in order to deal with the war situation. The divergence between the two major representative parties of the country harassed the British government because it was difficult to make the war a success without the cooperation of both the Hindus and the Muslims.

On March 22, 1942, Britain sent Sir Stafford Cripps with constitutional proposals.

The important points of the declaration were as follows:

(a) General elections in the provinces would be arranged as soon as the war ended.

(b) A new Indian dominion, associated with the United Kingdom would be created.

(c)   Those provinces not joining the dominion could form their own separate union.

(d)   Minorities were to be protected.

However, both Congress and Muslim League rejected these proposals. Jinnah opposed the plan as it did not concede Pakistan. Thus the plan came to nothing.

FOURTEEN POINTS OF M.A. JINNAH [1929]

It was on March 28, 1929, that Quaid-i-Azam invited members of the Delhi Muslim Conference to a meeting of the council of All-India Muslim League. It was at this meeting, in which Shafi group also participated, that Quaid gave a more cogent presentation to the Muslim demands in his famous Fourteen Points, as counter proposals to Hindu demands as expressed in the Nehru Report.

According to this resolution, no scheme for the future constitution of the Government of India would be acceptable to Muslims unless and until the following basic principles were incorporated in it :

1.   The form of the future constitution should be federal with the residuary powers vested in the provinces.

2.   A uniform measure of autonomy shall be granted to all provinces.

3.   All legislatures in the country and other elected bodies shall be constituted on the definite principle of adequate and effective representation of minorities in every province without reducing the majority in any province to a minority or even equality.

4.   In the Central Legislative, Muslim representation shall not be less than cne-third.

5.   Representation of communal groups shall continue to be by means of separate electorates as at present, provided it shall be open to any community at any time to abandon its separate electorate in favor of a joint electorate

6.   Any territorial distribution that might at any time be necessary shall not in any way affect the Muslim majority in the Punjab, Bengal and the North-West Frontier Province.

7.   Full religious liberty, i.e. liberty of belief, worship and observance, propaganda, association and education, shall be guaranteed to all communities.

8. No bill or any resolution or any part thereof shall be passed
    in any legislature or any other elected body if three-fourths
    of the members of any community in that particular body
    oppose such a bill resolution or part thereof on the ground
    that it would be injurious to the interests of that community
    or in the alternative, such other method is devised as may
    be found feasible and practicable to deal with such cases.
9. Sind should be separated from Bombay Presidency.
10. Reforms should be introduced in the North-West Frontier
    Province and Baluchistan on the same footing as in the other
    provinces.
11. Provision should be made in the constitution giving Muslims
    an adequate share, along with the other Indians, in all the
    services of the state and in local self-governing bodies having
    due regard to the requirements of efficiency.
12. The constitution should embody adequate safeguards for the
    protection of Muslim culture and for the protection and
    promotion of Muslim education, language, religion, personal
    laws and Muslim charitable institutions and for their due
    share in the grants-in aid given by the state and by local self-
    governing bodies.
13. No cabinet, either Central or Provincial, should be formed
    without there being a proportion of at least one-third Muslim
    ministers.
14. No change shall be made in the constitution by the Central
    Legislature except with the concurrence of the State's
    contribution of the Indian Federation.

GANDHI-JINNAH TALKS [1944]

Gandhi-Jinnah Talks occupy an eminent significance with
regard to the political problems of India and Pakistan movement.
The talks between the two great leaders of the sub-continent
began in response to a general public desire for a settlement of
Hindu-Muslim differences.

Gandhi wrote to Quaid-i-Azam on July 17, 1944 in which he
expressed his desire of meeting Quaid-i-Azam. Quaid-i-Azam
asked for permission of meeting Mr. Gandhi from the Muslim
League which was duly accorded.

Gandhi-Jinnah talks began on September 19, 1944 in Bombay
and lasted upto September 24, 1944. The talks were held directly

and through correspondence. Gandhi told Quaid-i-Azam that he had come in his personal capacity and was not representing the Hindus or Congress.

Gandhi's real concern was to extract from Jinnah's mouth that the whole proposition of Pakistan was absurd. Quaid-i-Azam painstakingly explained the basis for the demand of Pakistan. "We maintain" he wrote to Gandhi, "that Muslims and Hindus are two major nations by any definition or test of a nation. We are a nation of hundred million. We have our distinctive outlook on life and of life. By all the cannons of international law, we are a nation". He added that he was, "convinced that the true welfare not only of the Muslims but of the rest of India lies in the division of India as proposed in the Lahore Resolution".

Gandhi on the other hand maintained that India was one nation and saw in the Pakistan Resolution "Nothing but ruin for the whole of India". "If, however, Pakistan had to be conceded, the areas in which the Muslims are in an absolute majority should be demarcated by a Commission approved by both the Congress and the Muslim League. The wishes of the people of these areas will be obtained through Referendum. These areas shall form a separate state as soon as possible after India is free from foreign domination. There shall be a treaty of separation which should also provide for the efficient and satisfactory administration of foreign affairs, defense, internal communication, custom and the like which must necessarily continue to be the matters of common interest between the contracting countries".

This meant, in effect, that power over whole of India should first be transferred to Congress, which thereafter would allow Muslim majority areas that voted for separation to be constituted, not as independent sovereign state but as part of an Indian Federation.

Gandhi contended that his offer gave the substance of the Lahore resolution. Quaid-i-Azam did not agree to the proposal and the talks finished.

GOVERNMENT OF INDIA ACT, 1935

The deliberations of the round table conference resulted in the Government of India Act, 1935.

The main features of the Act were:

1. A Federation of India was promised for, comprising both provinces and states. The provisions of the Act establishing the federal central government were not to go into operation until a specified number of rulers of states had signed Instruments of Accession. Since, this did not happen, the central government continued to function in accordance with the 1919 Act and only the part of the 1935 Act dealing with the provincial governments went into operation.

2. The provinces were given autonomy with respect to subjects delegated to them.

3. Dyarchy came to an end, and the provincial governments now had full responsibility.

4. Sind was made a separate province.

5. Separate electorates were continued.

6. One-third Muslim representation in the Central Legislature was guaranteed.

7. Autonomous provincial governments in eleven provinces under ministries responsible to legislatures would be setup. The Act came into force on April 1, 1937.

JUNE 3RD PLAN [1947]

According to the June 3rd plan, power would be handed over to two separate governments in August 1947, and Punjab and Bengal would be divided by demarcating the Muslim majority districts. The demarcation was to be done by the Demarcation Commission.

Referendum was to be held in the NWFP. British Baluchistan was also to be given an opportunity to decide whether it would join the existing constituent assembly. Fate of Sylhet was also to be decided by a referendum.

Both League and the Congress accepted the plan.

NEHRU REPORT [1928]

Towards the end of the All-Parties Conference, which had been convened by the Congress to protest against the composition and terms of reference of the statutory commission, was now asked by the Congress leaders to prepare a constitution for India to confound the British Government. The Conference appointed a committee of jurists with Motilal Nehru as chairman, to study the problem and draft a constitution.

The committee worked for three months at Allahabad and its memorandum was called the "Nehru Report". The chairman joined hands with the Hindu Mahasabha and unceremoniously quashed the recent Congress acceptance of the Delhi Proposals.

The Nehru Report recommended that a Declaration of Rights should be inserted in the constitution assuring the fullest liberty on conscience and religion.

The following are the recommendations advanced by the Nehru Report:

1. India should be given the status of a Dominion on a unitary basis with parliamentary powers of seat.
2. Residuary powers should vested in the center.
3. India should have a parliamentary form of government headed by Prime Minister and six ministers appointed by Governor General.
4. There should be no separate electorate or weightage for minorities.
5. Reservation of Muslim seats could be possible in the provinces where Muslim population was at least 10%, but this was to be in strict proportion to the size of the community.
6. Muslims should enjoy one-fourth representation in the Central Legislature.
7. The N.W.F.P. should be given full provincial status and Sind should be taken away from Bombay and made a separate province.
8. A new Canarese-Speaking province "Karnatak" be established in South India.
9. Hindi should be made the official language of India.

The recommendations of the Nehru Report went against the interest of the Muslim community. It was an attempt to serve Hindu predominance over Muslims. A Muslim member of the Nehru Committee, Shoaib Qureshi disagreed with the proposals, but his pleadings were simply rejected.

The immediate result of the publication of the report was that Muslims of all shades of opinion united in opposition to it. The two wings into which the Muslim League had been split since 1924 came closer.

On January 21, 1929, nearly every shade of opinion was represented in the All India Muslim Conference which met at Delhi under the Aga Khan and laid down the demands of the Muslims in India in the clearest possible terms:

1. The only form of Government suitable to Indian conditions was a federal system with complete autonomy and residuary powers vested in the constituent states.
2. Muslims should not be deprived of the right to elect their representatives through separate electorates without their consent.
3. Muslims should continue to have weightage in the Hindu majority provinces and they were willing to accord the same privilege to non-Muslim minorities in Sind, the N.W.F.P. and Baluchistan.
4. Muslims should have their due share in the central and provincial cabinets.
5. Muslim majority in all Muslim majority provinces (with particular reference to Bengal and Punjab) should in no way be disturbed.

This resolution was the Muslim reply to the Nehru Report. The rejection of the Congress-inspired constitution was completely unanimous and clear. On two points the Muslims were adamant: separate electorates must continue and India must have a federal form of government. The Nehru Report was primarily repudiated because it denied these conditions.

At this critical juncture, Jinnah made the last move to unite the Hindus and the Muslims by suggesting certain modifications to be made in the recommendations of the Nehru Report, at All Parties Convention at Calcutta in 1929.

They were as follows:

1. One-third of the elected representatives of both the houses of the central legislature should be Mussalmans;
2. In the Punjab and Bengal, in the event of adult suffrage not being established, there should be reservations of seats for the Mussalmans on the population basis for ten years, subject

to a re-examination after that period, but they shall have no right to contest additional seats;

3. Residuary powers should be left to the provinces and should not rest with the central legislature.

The committee rejected these suggestions. Thus in March 1929, Quaid-i-Azam drew up greatly influenced Muslim thinking for the better part of the next decade.

PAKISTAN RESOLUTION [1940]

Muslim League had been trying for the last 25 years, to reach an honorable agreement with Congress on the following two principles:

1. Congress rule should recognize Muslim League as the representative body of the Muslims of India.
2. The Muslims of India should not be taken as a mere minor community; on the other hand they should be recognized as a nation.

However, the recent two years of Congress rule proved that it worked on the basis of hostility against Muslims.

A resolution adopting the "Two Nation Theory" had already been passed by the provincial Muslim League at Karachi in October 1938. The Two Nation theory stated that the Hindus and the Muslims were two distinct nations.

It was finally at it's annual meeting held at Lahore on March 23, 1940, that the Muslim League for the first time categorically adopted the idea of partition of India as it's final destination. The resolution that came to be known as the Pakistan Resolution was moved by the Bengal's Chief minister, A. K. Faziul Haq.

Jinnah's address on this occasion gave clear expression to the basic concept underlying the resolution. He said:

"Hindus and the Muslims belong to two different religions, philosophies, social customs and literature. They neither inter-marry nor inter-dine and, indeed they belong to two different civilizations which are based mainly on conflicting ideas and conceptions. Their concepts on life and of life are different. It is quite clear that Hindu and Muslims derive their inspiration from different sources of history. They have different epics, different heroes and different episodes. Very often the hero of one is a foe of the other, and likewise, their victories and defeats overlap. To yoke together two such nations under a single state, one as a numerical minority and the other as a majority, must lead to growing discontent and final destruction of any fabric that may be so built up for the government of such a state."

"Mussalmans are a nation according to any definition of nation. We wish our people to develop to the fullest spiritual, cultural, economic, social and political life in a way that we think best and in consonance with our own ideals and according to the genius of our people."

On the basis of the above mentioned two nation theory, the resolution which was moved declared:

"No constitutional plan would be workable or acceptable to the Muslims unless geographical contiguous units are demarcated into regions which should be so constituted with such territorial readjustments as may be necessary, that the areas in which the Muslims are numerically in majority as in the North-Western and Eastern zones of India should be grouped to constitute independent states in which the constituent units shall be autonomous and sovereign.

That adequate, effective and mandatory safeguards shall be specifically provided in the constitution for minorities in the units and in the regions for the protection of their religious, cultural, economic, political, administrative and other rights of the minorities, with their consultation. Arrangements thus should be made for the security of Muslims where they were in a minority."

Congress reaction was hostile to the resolution. However, with the coining of the word "PAKISTAN" by Choudhary Rahmat Ali, as the name of the country which was to be formed by this resolution, it soon became a household word.

From then onwards, the Muslims of India, instead of seeking alliance with the Hindu community, set on the way leading to the destination of complete independence of the Muslims of India.

PROVINCIAL AND GENERAL ELECTIONS
[1945—46]

With the failure of the Simla Conference, Lord Wavell announced that the elections of central and provincial legislature would be held in the winter of 1945 and after the elections a constitution making body would be set up. He also announced that after the elections Viceroy would set an Executive Council, which would have the support of the main Indian Political Parties. The proposal was opposed by both Muslim League and Congress. Quaid-i-Azam declared that Muslims were not ready to accept any settlement less than a separate homeland for them and the All India Congress Committee characterized the proposal as vague, inadequate and unsatisfactory because it was not talking about independence. Yet the two parties launched huge election campaigns. They knew that the elections would be crucial for the future of India, as the results were to play an important role in determining their standing. The League wanted to sweep the Muslim constituencies so as to prove that they were the sole representatives of the Muslims of Sub-continent, while Congress wanted to prove that, irrespective of religion, they represent all the Indians. Both Muslim League and Congress rose opposite slogans during their campaign. Muslim League presented one point manifesto; if you want Pakistan vote for Muslim League. Congress on the other hand stood for United India. Quaid-i-Azam himself toured the length and breadth of India and tried to bridge up all the factions of the Muslim community under the banner of Muslim League.

To counter his move Congress press abused the Quaid and termed his demand for Pakistan as 'vivisection of Mother India', 'reactionary primitivism' and 'religious barbarism'. Congress tried to brand Muslim League as an ultra-conservative clique of Knights, Khan Bahadurs, toadies and Government pensioners. Congress also tried to get the support of all the provincial and central Muslim parties who had some differences with the League, and backed them in the elections. Elections for the Central Legislature were held in December 1945. Though the franchise was limited, the turnover was extraordinary.

Congress was able to sweep the pools for the non-Muslim seats as they managed to win more then 80 per cent of the general seats and about 91.3 per cent of the total general votes. However, Leagues performance was even more impressive as it managed to win all the 30 seats reserved for the Muslims. The results of the provincial election held in early 1946 were not different. Congress won most of the non-Muslim seats while Muslim League captured approximately 95 per cent of the Muslim seats. The Central Election Board of the Congress in a bulletin issued on January 6, 1946 claimed that the election results have vindicated the party as the biggest, strongest and the most representative organization in the country. On the other hand League celebrated January 11, 1946 as the Day of victory and declared that the election results were enough to prove that Muslim League under the leadership of Quaid-i-Azam was the sole representative of the Muslims of the region.

ROUND TABLE CONFERENCES [1930—33]

The report of the Simon Commission issued in June 1930— was received with great resentment and the Indian political parties reacted in different ways. In resentment, the Congress started a Civil Disobedience Movement under Gandhi's command.

The Muslims reserved their opinion on the Simon Report and declared that this report was not final and the matters would be finally decided after consultations with the leaders representing all communities in India.

The Indian political situation seemed deadlocked. The British government refused to contemplate any form of self-government for the people of India who were frustrated and often expressed their anger in violent clashes.

However, in 1931, Labour government returned to power in Britain, and a glimmer of hope ran through Indian hearts. Labour leaders had always been sympathetic to the Indian cause. The Labour Government decided to hold a Round Table Conference in London, to consider new constitutional reforms. All the Indian politicians, Hindus, Muslims, Sikhs and Christians were summoned to London for the conference.

Gandhi immediately insisted at the conference that he alone spoke for all Indians, and that the Congress was the party of the people of India. He argued that the other parties only represented sectarian viewpoints.

First Round Table Conference

The first session of the conference opened in London on November 12, 1930. All parties were present except for the Congress, whose leaders were in jail due to the Civil Disobedience Movement. Congress leaders stated that they had nothing to do with further constitutional discussion unless the Nehru Report was enforced in it's entirety as the constitution of India.

Almost eighty-nine members attended the conference, out of which fifty-eight were chosen from various communities and interests in British India, and the rest from princely states and other political parties. The prominent among the Muslim delegates invited by the British government were Sir Aga Khan, Quaid-i-Azam, Maulana Mohammad Ali Johar, Sir Mohammad Shafi and Maulvi Fazl-i-Haq. Sir Tej Bahadur Sapru, Mr. Jaikar and Dr. Moonje were outstanding among the Hindu leaders.

The Hindu-Muslim differences overcast the conference as the Hindus were for a powerful Central government while the Muslims stood for a loose federation of completely autonomous province. The Muslims demanded maintenance of weightage and separate electorates, the Hindus their abolition. The Muslims claimed statutory majority in Punjab and Bengal, while Hindus resisted their imposition. In Punjab, the situation was complicated by inflated Sikh claims.

The Conference dealt with the details through eight sub-committees on federal structure, provincial constitution, franchise, Sind, the North-West Frontier Province, defense services and minorities.

The conference broke up on January 19, 1931, and what emerged from it was a general agreement to write safeguards for minorities into the constitution and a vague desire to devise a federal system for the country.

Gandhi-Irwin Pact

After the conclusion of the First Round Table Conference, the British government realized that the cooperation of the Indian National Congress was necessary for further advancement in the making of Indian constitution. Thus, Lord Irwin, the Viceroy, extended invitation to Gandhi for talks. Gandhi agreed to finish the civil disobedience movement without laying down any pre-conditions.

The agreement between Gandhi and Irwin was signed on March 5, 1931, with the following salient proposals:

1. The Congress would discontinue it's civil disobedience movement.
2. The Congress would participate in the Round Table Conference.
3. The Government would withdraw all ordinances issued to curb the Congress.
4. The Government would withdraw all prosecutions relating to offenses not involving violence.
5. The Government would release all persons undergoing sentences of imprisonment for their activities in the civil disobedience movement.

The pact shows that the British Government was anxious to bring the Congress to the conference table.

Second Round Table Conference

The second session of the conference opened in London on September 7, 1931. The main task of the conference was done through the two committees on federal structure and minorities. Gandhi was a member of both but he adopted a very unreasonable attitude. He claimed that he represented all India and dismissed all other Indian delegates as non-representative because they did not belong to the Congress.

The communal problem represented the most difficult issue to the delegates. Gandhi again tabled the Congress scheme for a settlement, a mere reproduction of the Nehru Report, but it was rejected by all the minorities.

As a counter to the Congress scheme the Muslims, the depressed classes, the Indian Christians, the Anglo-Indians and the European presented a joint statement of claims which they said must stand as an interdependent whole. As their main demands were not acceptable to Gandhi, the communal issue was postponed for future discussion.

On the concluding day, the British Prime Minister, Ramsay Macdonald appealed to the Indian leaders to reach a communal settlement. Failing to do so, the British government would take a unilateral decision.

Quaid-i-Azam did not participate in the session of the Second Round Table Conference as he decided to keep himself aloof from the Indian politics and to practice as a professional lawyer in England.

On his return to India, Gandhi once again started civil disobedience movement and was duly arrested. Three important committees drafted their reports: The Franchise Committee, the Federal Finance Committee and States Inquiry Committee.

Third Round Table Conference

The third session began on November 17, 1932, was short and unimportant. The Congress was once again absent, so was the Labour opposition in the British parliament. Reports of the various committees were scrutinized and ended on December 25, 1932.

The recommendations of the Round Table Conferences were embodied in a White Paper. It was published in March 1933, and debated in Parliament directly afterwards, analyzed by the Joint Select Committee and after the final reading and the loyal assent, the Bill reached the Statute Book on July 24, 1935.

RULE OF CONGRESS MINISTRIES [1937—1939]

For the discussion of the constitutional problem, the British government convened the three Round Table Conferences at London from 1930 to 1932. The deliberations of the Round Table Conferences resulted in the Government of India Act, 1935.

Both the Congress and the Muslim League were critical of the Government of India Act, 1935, but decided to participate in the elections, which were held under it during the first weeks of 1937. After the elections, Congress was able to form ministries in eight out of eleven provinces.

The Muslim League did not do so well. The reason for this was that for a number of years it had been divided into factions. When Jinnah toured India in 1936, he found that local Muslim leaders who had entrenched themselves in the provinces were extremely reluctant to follow on All India Muslim League policy. As a result, All India Muslim League lost in the elections.

Congress rule from 1937–39 is often termed as a "Hindu Rule" due to a number of steps which Congress took during power.

One of the first controversies to arise was the singing of Congress Anthem, Band e-Mataram with which opened each day's proceedings in Legislative Assemblies in the Congress run provinces. The schools also made singing of Bande Mataram a permanent feature of school curriculum. The song appeared in Bankim Chandra Chatterji's novel Ananda Matha. It's theme was a sanyasi rebellion against the Muslim conqueror.

Another issue was of Warda Education scheme or Vidya Mandar scheme started in Central province and Bihar. The purpose of the scheme was to obliterate the cultural traditions of the Muslims and to inculcate into the minds of Muslim children the superiority of the Hindu culture.

As a result, Muslim League formed, under the chairmanship of Raja Syed Muhammad Mahdi of Pirpur, the "Pirpur Report", to investigate Muslim grievances. Other reports concerning Muslim grievances in Congress run provinces were A. K. Faziul Haque's "Muslim sufferings under Congress rule", and "The Shareef Report".

The allegation that Congress was representing Hindus only was voiced also by eminent British personalities, e.g. The Marquees of Lothian in April 1938 termed the Congress rule as a "rising tide of Hindu rule". Sir William Barton writing in "National Review" in June 1939 also termed the Congress rule as "the rising tide of political Hinduism".

At the outbreak of the Second World War, the Viceroy proclaimed India's entry into it without prior consultations with the main political parties. When Congress demanded an immediate transfer of power in return for cooperation of the war efforts, the British government refused, as a result Congress resigned from power.

Jinnah declared December 22, 1939, as a Day of Deliverance and thanks-giving in token of relief from the tyranny and oppression of the Congress rule.

Thus came an end to Congress rule, which was an eye opener for the Muslims of India, who realized that the only option left for them was independence. Consequently, only three months later, the demand for the partition of India was formally put forward by the Muslim League.

The stage was set for the struggle that culminated in the birth of Pakistan.

SIMLA TALKS [1945]

Viceroy Wavell called a conference of representatives of major parties at Simla for discussing reconstitution of Viceroy's council.

However, Simla Conference failed on account of the refusal of the British government as well as the Congress party to recognize the Muslim League as the only representative party of the Muslims.

THE BIRTH OF PAKISTAN [AUGUST 14, 1947]

Indian Independence Act

British parliament on July 18, 1947 passed the Indian Independence Act. The Act created two dominions: Indian Union and Pakistan. It also provided for the complete end of British control over Indian affairs from August 15, 1947.

Indian Independence Act

The Muslims of the sub-continent finally achieved an independent state for themselves, but only after a long and relentless struggle under the single-minded guidance of the Quaid. The Muslims faced a gamut of problems immediately after independence, however, keeping true to their traditions, they overcame them after a while. Quaid-i-Azam Muhammad Ali Jinnah was appointed the first Governor General of Pakistan and Liaquat Ali Khan became it's first Prime Minister. Pakistan became a Dominion within the British Commonwealth of nations.

Ideology of Pakistan

The boundaries of Pakistan emerged out of the sub-continent on the map of the world in 1947. This was accomplished on the basis of Two Nation Theory, which held that there were two nations—Hindus and Muslims—living in the territory of the subcontinent.

Sir Syed Ahmad Khan was the first exponent of the Two-Nation theory. He believed that India was a continent and not a country, and that among the vast population of different races and different creeds, Hindus and Muslims were the two major nations on the basis of nationality, religion, ways of living, customs, mores, culture and historical condition.

The politicization of the Muslim community came about as a consequence of three developments:

(a) Various efforts at Islamic reform and revival during the late 19th and early 20th centuries,
(b) the impact of Hindu-based nationalism and,
(c) the democratization of the government of British India.

Ideology of Pakistan

While the antecedents of the Muslim nationalism in India go back to the early Islamic conquers of the sub-continent, organizationally it stems from the demands presented by the Simla Deputation to Lord Minto, the Governor General of India, in October 1906, proposing separate electorates for the Indian Muslims. The principal reason behind this demand was the maintenance of separate identity of the Muslim nationhood.

In the same year, the founding of the All-India Muslim League—a separate political organization for Muslims explained that the Muslims of India had lost trust in the Hindu-dominated Indian National Congress. Besides being a Hindu-dominated body, the Congress leaders, in order to win grass-roots support for their political movements used Hindu religious symbols and slogans thereby arousing Muslim suspicions regarding the secular character of the Indian National Congress.

But after the collapse of the Khilafat Movement, the Hindu-Muslim antagonism was in the air. The proposals forwarded by the Nehru Report were rejected by the Muslim League and they chose a separate path for themselves. The idea for a separate homeland for the Muslims of Northern India as proposed by Allama Iqbal in his famous Allahabad Address showed that the creation of two separate states for the Muslims and Hindus was the only solution. The idea was reiterated during the Sind provincial meeting of the League and finally adopted as the official League position in Lahore Declaration of March 23, 1940.

Thus, these historical, cultural, religious and social differences between the two nations accelerated the pace of political developments, finally leading to the division of British India into two states—India and Pakistan—on August 14, 1947, on the basis of the Two-Nation Theory.

THE COMMUNAL AWARD [1932]

When the Indian leadership failed to settle down the communal issue of the country through a Constitutional solution, British Prime Minister, Ramsay MacDonald announced his own formula of solving the communal problem of India. He said that he was not only a Prime Minister of Britain but was also a friend of the Indian and thus wanted to solve the problems of his friends. After the failure of the Second Round Table conference, Mr. MacDonald announced 'Communal Award' on August 16, 1932. According to the Award, right of Separate Electorate was not only given to the Muslims of India but was also given to all the minority communities in the country. The Award also declared untouchables as a minority and thus the Hindu Depressed Classes were given a number of special seats to be filled from special Depressed Class electorates in the area where the voters were concentrated. Under the Communal Awards principle of weightage was also maintained with some modifications in the Muslim-minority Provinces. Principle of Weightage was also applied for Europeans in Bengal and Assam, Sikhs in the Punjab and North-Western Frontier Province, and Hindus in Sind and North-Western Frontier Province. Though the Muslims constituted almost 56% of the total population of the Punjab but they were given only 86 out of 175 seats in the Punjab Assembly. Likewise, the Muslim majority of 54.8% in the Punjab was also reduced to the minority. This formula favored the Sikhs of the Punjab and Europeans of the Bengal the most.

The Award was not popular with any Indian party. Muslims were not happy with the Communal Award as it has reduced their majority in Punjab and Bengal to minority. Yet they were prepared to accept it. All India Muslim League in its Annual Session in

November 1933 passed a resolution that reads, 'Though the decision falls far short of the Muslim demands, the Muslims have accepted it in the best interest of the country reserving to themselves the right to press for the acceptance of all their demands'. On the other hand Hindus refused to accept the awards and decided to launch a campaign against it. For them it was not possible to accept Untouchables as a minority. They organized Allahabad Unity Conference in which, they demanded for the replacement of Separate Electorates by the Joint Electorates. Many Nationalist Muslims and Sikhs also participated in the conference. The Congress also rejected the Award in toto. Gandhi protested against the declaration of Untouchables as a minority and undertook a fast unto death. He also hold meetings with the Untouchable leadership for the first time and try to convince them that they were very much part of the main stream Hindu society. He also managed to sign Poona pact with Dr. B. R. Ambedker, the leader of Untouchables and in the pact many demands of the Untouchables were met by Gandhi.

1948—1957

POST INDEPENDENCE PROBLEMS

Pakistan was carved out in desperate urgency. It came into existence with horrible loss of life and property, and the migration of millions of dazed and destitute men, women, and children. The cost was heavy in terms of human suffering. But this is what the Muslims wanted and this is what they achieved—a homeland of their own. They could now worship, practice their religious faith and develop their culture in freedom. Moreover, independence had opened up a bright future for the Muslims, who hoped for a better standard of living, economic development, prosperity and a fuller life.

But it seemed in those early years (1947-58) that the immense sacrifices might have been in vain. For Pakistan had struggled from one major crisis to another, fighting to ward-off the problems which threatened the nation.

These problems were:

1. Refugees
2. Indus Water
3. Accession of Princely States

Refugees

It was agreed between Jinnah and Nehru that a Boundary Commission should be setup to define the borders between India and Pakistan. The British Government immediately appointed a Boundary Commission under Sir Cyril Radcliffe to demarcate permanent borders.

The boundaries had to be fixed in such a manner that provinces, districts, and villages which were predominantly Muslim went to Pakistan, while Hindu areas went to India. Provinces like Baluchistan, Sind, NWFP and East Bengal provided little difficulty. But deep problem arose when boundaries in Punjab had to be fixed as their was also a substantial number of Hindus and Sikhs besides the Muslims. However, the province was partitioned.

When the boundaries were drawn between India and Pakistan, it resulted in many tragic events. In an almost frantic, cruel hurry the commission divide districts, villages, farmlands, water and property. Thousands of innocent men, women and children were caught unaware. The result was that many hastened across the border, leaving their homes, land and personal property to seek refuge. Panic, fear, revenge and reprisals followed. Both India and Pakistan were soaked in blood. It left on Pakistan's doorstep, seven million refugees. These seven million refugees had to be rehabilitated, clothed, fed and sheltered.

Partition also involved dividing of the assets of the subcontinent. India, being the larger country, got the lion's share in all the transactions leaving Pakistan with minimal resources either to survive or build on.

Equally disastrous was the economic situation. There were not sufficient skilled personnel to run the railways, hospitals and offices. There were not even enough chairs, tables or even stationery for administrative purposes. Food was scarce. Pakistan had no industry.

At the time of partition, the cash balances of undivided India stood at about 4,000 million Rupees. At the beginning of December 1947, however, India and Pakistan mutually came to an agreement that Pakistan would get Rs. 750 million as her share, out of which Rs. 200 million had been paid to Pakistan as interim installment and Rs. 550 million remained outstanding.

Soon afterwards, Sardar Patel threatened that the implementation of the agreement would depend upon the settlement of the Kashmir issue. But, it was upon Gandhi's request that the Reserved Bank of India paid Pakistan Rs. 500 million, retaining the balance of Rs. 50 million to adjust some claim against Pakistan.

The Indus Water

The most explosive of Indo-Pakistan disputes was the question of sharing the waters of the Indus basin.

On April 1, 1948, India cut off the supply of water from the two headworks under her control. Fortunately, Eugene Black, President of the International Bank for Reconstruction and Development, offered the good offices of the Bank for the solution of the water problem, which both governments accepted in 1952, and finally signed as 'Indus Water Treaty', at the Indus Basin Development Fund Agreement at Karachi.

The treaty allowed for a transitional period of ten to thirteen years, after which the three eastern rivers would fall exclusively to India's share and the three Western rivers to Pakistan. During the transitional period, Pakistan would construct a system of replacement works consisting of two dams, five barrages and seven link canals financed by the Indus Development Fund.

Accession of Princely States

Prior to Partition, there existed in British India many semi-autonomous Princely states whose future had to be settled before Britain withdrew from India.

There were some 560 such states all over the sub-continent. Some fell within the area of India, others in Pakistan.

On July 25, 1947, Lord Louis Mountbatten (the last Viceroy of India) in his address to the Chamber of Princes advised them that in deciding on the question of accession, they should take into consideration communal composition and the geographical location of their states. Nearly all the states accepted the reality of the situation and opted either for Pakistan or India accordingly. But there were four states, Junagadh, Hyderabad, Jodhpur and Kashmir who defied the principle of partition.

I. *Junagadh*

Junagadh ruler was a Muslim but his subjects were 80 per cent Hindu. On September 15, 1947, the Nawab acceded to Pakistan, despite the fact that his state did not fall within the geographical grouping of Pakistan. India protested, rushed in her troops and forcibly reversed the Nawab's decision and Junagadh become a part of India.

II. *Hyderabad*

Hyderabad, the second of defiant states was the largest and richest in India. Its population was 85 % Hindu but the ruler (Nizam) was a Muslim. He was reluctant either to accede to India or Pakistan but was dismissed by Mountbatten from adopting this course. The Nizam was forced by Indian government and Lord Mountbatten to join India. A standstill agreement was concluded between India and Hyderabad. The Hindu subjects were incited to revolt against the Nizam's desire to be independent. The whole province plunged into violence. Hyderabad filed a complaint with the Security Council of the UNO. Before the hearing could be heard Indian troops entered Hyderabad. The Indian army went in to restore order and under the pretext of "police action" India annexed Hyderabad. The Hyderabad army finally surrendered on September 17, 1948 and was annexed in to the Indian union.

III. *Jodhpur*

Yet another prince, the Maharaja of Jodhpur, expressed a wish to join Pakistan but Mountbatten warned him that his subjects were mostly Hindus and his accession to Pakistan would create problems. As a result Jodhpur, too, acceded to India.

IV. *Kashmir*

Please see Kashmir Crisis.

KASHMIR CRISIS [1948]

Kashmir the last of the defiant states, was the reverse of Hyderabad. It had a Hindu ruler Maharaja Hari Singh but his subjects were Muslims, accounting to 78% of the total population. The Mahraja was reluctant either to join India or Pakistan. But Lord Mountbatten urged him to take a decision to join either states before August 15, 1947.

The Maharaja asked for more time to consider his decision. In the meantime he asked the Indian and the Pakistani government to sign a "standstill agreement" with him. Pakistan consented but India refused.

The local population of Poonch began to press the Maharaja to accede to Pakistan. In August, 1947 they held a massive demonstration to protest against the Maharaja's indecisiveness. The Maharaja panicked. He asked his Hindu paratroops to shoot, within a matter of seconds several hundreds Muslims were killed.

By October 1947, the war of Kashmir had began in earnest. The Pathans tribesmen from the North West Frontier Province wanted to avenge the deaths of their brothers. Thousands of Pathans warriors invaded the valley and on reaching the valley of Kashmir, they routed the Maharaja's troops and reached the gates of Srinagar, the capital.

The Maharaja sensing defeat took refuge in Jammu. From there he appealed to India to send troops to halt the relentless onslaught of the tribesmen. India agreed on the condition that Kashmir would accede to India. On October 26, 1947 the Maharaja acceded to India. Lord Mountbatten accepted the accession on behalf of India.

On October 27, 1947 India began to airlift her troops to Srinagar, and launched a full-scale attack on the tribesmen. Pakistan was stunned. Despite Pakistan's slender military resources, Pakistan was prepared to send in her troops but the British General, Gracey, Commander in Chief of the Pakistan Army advised against it. Jinnah also proposed an immediate cease-fire and later that a plebiscite should be held.

In January, 1948 India took the dispute to the Security Council. There it accused Pakistan of aggression and demanded that Pakistan withdraw her tribesmen. But Pakistan held that accession of Kashmir had been brought about by force and requested the Security Council to arrange a cease-fire and ask both the tribesmen and the Indian troops to withdraw so that a free and impartial plebiscite could be held to ascertain the wishes of the people of Kashmir.

While the Kashmir issue was still at the table, the Indian troops launched a full scale attack and drove the tribesmen right back to the Pakistani border.

Pakistan, rushed her regular troops into Kashmir and had a full-scale war with India. She took control of PoK Army. But the Security Council on August 13, 1948 called for an immediate cease-fire, the withdrawal of all Pakistani and Indian troops and holding of plebiscite under the UN supervision. Both the Indian and Pakistani governments accepted the resolution.

In January, 1949, the resolution began to be implemented. In July, 1949 the cease-fire line was demarcated. Pakistan's side of Kashmir consisted of some parts of Jammu, Poonch, some areas of Western Kashmir, Gilgit and in the North a great chunk of Ladakh territory near the Chinese border. India kept the valley of Kashmir, Jammu and the remainder of Ladakh territory near the Tibet border.

The cease-fire has remained in existence since 1949. No plebiscite has been held and thus the Kashmir issue remains unresolved to-date.

JINNAH DIES AND KHAWAJA NAZIMUDDIN BECOMES GOVERNOR GENERAL [1948]

It was on September 11, 1948, that the Quaid-i-Azam passed away after a protracted illness. He was buried in Karachi amidst the entire nation mourning over this irreparable loss.

Khawaja Nazimuddin took over as the second Governor General of Pakistan.

OBJECTIVES RESOLUTION IS PASSED [1949]

History of Pakistan's constitution making begins with the Lahore Resolution of 1940, which first outlined the idea of a separate homeland for the Muslims of India, to be called Pakistan. It came to be called the Pakistan Resolution.

On June 3, 1947, the British Government accepted the principal of partition of India in order to create two independent dominions of Pakistan and India. In view of this, the British Parliament passed the Indian Independence Act on July 18, 1947.

Accordingly, the new state of Pakistan came into being on August 14, 1947, consisting of East Bengal, a part of Assam (Sylhet), West Punjab, Sind, NWFP and Baluchistan provinces of undivided India.

Under Section 8 of the Indian Independence Act, 1947, the Government of India Act, 1935, became with certain adaptations, the working constitution of Pakistan.

However, establishment of a truly Islamic society was the aim of Quaid. As a result, a Constituent Assembly was provided for the new dominion of Pakistan under the Independence Act. The Constituent Assembly had a dual purpose, to make a constitution for Pakistan and also to act as a legislative body till the new constitution is passed and enforced.

Objectives Resolution

On March 12, 1949, the Constituent Assembly adopted a resolution moved by Liaquat Ali Khan, the then Prime Minister of Pakistan, called the Objectives Resolution. It proclaimed that the future constitution of Pakistan would not be modeled on European pattern, but on the ideology and democratic faith of Islam.

Objectives Resolution, which is considered to be the "Magna Carta" in Pakistan's constitutional history, proclaimed the following principles:

1.   Sovereignty belongs to Allah alone; but he has delegated it to the State of Pakistan through it's people for being exercised within the limits prescribed by Him as a sacred trust;
2.   The State shall exercise it's powers and authority through the chosen representatives of the people;
3.   The principles of Democracy, freedom, equality, tolerance and social justice as enunciated by Islam shall be fully observed;
4.   The Muslims shall be enabled to order their lives in the individual and collective spheres in accordance with the teachings of Islam as set out in the Holy Qur'an and Sunnah.
5.   Adequate provision shall be made for the minorities to freely profess and practice their religions and develop their cultures;

6. Pakistan shall be a Federation;
7. Fundamental Rights shall be guaranteed;
8. Judiciary shall be independent.

Objectives Resolution is one of the most important and illuminating documents in the constitutional history of Pakistan. At the time it was passed, Mr. Liaquat Ali Khan called it "the most important occasion in the life of this country, next in importance, only to the achievement of independence."

The importance of this document lies in the fact that it combines the good features of the Western and Islamic democracy. Also, it is a happy blend of modernism and Islam. Objectives Resolution became a part of the constitution of Pakistan in 1985 under the Eighth Amendment.

KHAWAJA NAZIMUDDIN BECOMES PRIME MINISTER [1951]

Under Quaid-i-Azam's constitutional framework, the executive powers lay with the Prime Minister, Liaquat Ali Khan. When Liaquat Ali Khan was assassinated in October 1951, in Rawalpindi, Khawaja Nazimuddin who was the Governor General at that time took over as the second Prime Minister of Pakistan.

Ghulam Muhammad, who had been Finance Minister from the earliest days of inception of Pakistan, was selected as the Governor General. It was under Prime Minister Nazimuddin that the second draft of the Basic Principle Committee was presented to the Constituent Assembly on December 22, 1952. The Basic Principle Committee was set up to determine the basic principles for further development of the constitution of Pakistan. Khawaja Nazimuddin remained in power till April 1953 when he was removed from office by Ghulam Muhammad. Khawaja Nazimuddin's downfall was not only due to his nobility of character but also due to the struggle among leaders for power. The movement for Tahafuz-i-Khatam-i-Nabuwwat in Punjab and the worsening food condition in Punjab further caused trouble for Khawaja Nazimuddin.

The Anti Ahmediya movement was started in Punjab by the Ahrar and had the support of Mian Mumtaz Daultana, the Chief Minister of Punjab. This movement soon spread to other parts of the country. There was wide spread disturbance and the situation in the country soon worsened to the brink of anarchy and civil war. Imposition of martial law became imminent. Khawaja Nijimuddin was summoned by the Governor General along with his Cabinet and was ordered to resign. Khawaja Nazimuddin declined and was dismissed by Malik Ghulam Muhammad on April 17, 1953. After the dismissal of Khawaja Nazimuddin the Governor General appointed a not well-known leader of East Pakistan Muhammad Ali Bogra as the Prime Minister.

The removal of Khawaja Nazimuddin was improper, undemocratic and objectionable because the Prime Minister still enjoyed the confidence of the parliament. This act of Ghulam Muhammad set an unhealthy tradition and precedent of Presidents removing elected governments. This tradition was later carried on by various Presidents, creating a continuous instability in the country.

GHULAM MUHAMMAD BECOMES GOVERNOR GENERAL [1951]

When Khawaja Nazimuddin took over as Prime Minister in 1951, Ghulam Muhammad became the Governor General.

He wanted to change the status quo of executive powers, and dismissed the Prime Minister, Khawaja Nazimuddin in April 1953.

MUHAMMAD ALI BOGRA BECOMES PRIME MINISTER [1953]

Khawaja Nazimuddin was dismissed by the Governor General, Malik Ghulam Muhammad on April 17, 1953, and replaced by Muhammad Ali Bogra.

Bogra was then the Pakistani Ambassador to United States. He realized the insecurity of his office, and passed an Act stripping the Governor General of his overriding powers at a time when Malik Ghulam Muhammad was out of the then capital, Karachi.

ISKANDER MIRZA BECOMES GOVERNOR GENERAL [1955]

Malik Ghulam Muhammad was succeeded by Iskander Mirza in 1955. When the 1956 Constitution was adopted, he was elected the first President of Pakistan.

CHAUDHARY MUHAMMAD ALI BECOMES PRIME MINISTER [1955]

On October 24, 1954, Malik Ghulam Muhammad dissolved the Constituent Assembly of Muhammad Ali Bogra on the grounds that it had 'lost the confidence of the people', and declared a state of emergency in the country. Chaudhary Muhammad Ali was appointed the new Prime Minister on August 11, 1955.

Under his leadership the Constituent Assembly adopted the constitution of the Islamic Republic of Pakistan in 1956.

THE CONSTITUTION OF 1956

After assuming charge as Prime Minister, Chaudhary Muhammad Ali, along with his team, worked day and night in order to give Pakistan a constitution. Due to his efforts, Pakistan's status as a dominion finished and the country was declared an Islamic Republic on March 23, 1956, when the first constitution was enforced in the country. With this the Constituent Assembly of Pakistan became interim National Assembly and Governor General Iskandar Mirza was sworn in as the first President of Pakistan.

The Constitution of 1956 consisted of 234 articles, which were divided into 13 parts and 6 schedules. According to this Constitution Pakistan was named as Islamic Republic of Pakistan and one of the main features of the Constitution was its Islamic character. The Islamic provisions were contained in the directive principles of the State policy. Along with other Islamic provisions in the Constitution, the president, who was required to be a Muslim with age not less than 40 years, was to set up an organization for Islamic research with the aim to establish a true Islamic society. However, Objectives Resolution was only made the preamble of the Constitution and was not included in its main text.

The constitution vested the executive authority of the president in the Federation. The President had the discretionary powers to make the appointment of the chairman and members of the Election Commission, Delimitation Commission and Public Service Commission. He also had the power to appoint Prime Minister from amongst the members of the National Assembly. However his appointee has to take the vote of confidence from the assembly within two months. The President also had the power to remove the Prime Minister if he feels that the Prime Minister had lost the confidence of the majority members of the National Assembly.

The Constitution of 1956 provided for the parliamentary form of government with unicameral legislature. The only house of the parliament. National Assembly, was to consist of 300 members. As the concept of one unit was there in the Constitution, the seats were divided equally between both the wings of the country. Thus the principle of parity was introduced. For the first ten years five additional seats were reserved for women from each of the wings. National Assembly was to meet at least twice a year with at least one session at Dhaka. The Constitution offered direct elections under adult franchise. Every citizen of Pakistan with minimum age of 21 was allowed to vote in the elections.

The Constitution provided for the federal form of government in the country. The provincial structure was similar to that at the center. Pattern for the center-province relations was the same as it was in the Government of India Act 1935. There were federal, provincial and concurrent list of subjects. There were thirty items in the federal list, ninety-four items in the provincial list and nineteen items in the concurrent list. The federal legislation was to get precedence over provincial legislation regarding concurrent list. Residuary powers were vested in the provinces. In case of a conflict between center and provinces or between the two provinces. Chief Justice of the Supreme Court was to act as the mediator.

The Constitution of 1956 was a written and flexible Constitution. It advocated for the fundamental rights of the individuals. However, the President had the power to suspend these rights in case of emergency. Judiciary was to remain independent. Urdu and Bengali both were accepted as State languages while English was to remain official language for the first twenty-five years. After ten years of the passage of the Constitution, the President was to appoint a commission with the task to make recommendation for the replacement of English as the official language.

The Constitution of 1956 proved to be a short-lived one. On October 7, 1958, Marital Law was proclaimed and the constitution was abrogated.

ISKANDER MIRZA BECOMES PRESIDENT
[1956]

The Constitution of 1956 changed the status of Pakistan from that of Dominion within the British Commonwealth to that of Republic within the Commonwealth. Iskander Mirza was elected as the first President of the Islamic Republic of Pakistan in 1956.

During his tenure from 1955 to 1958, he brought about various cabinet changes and advocated a controlled democracy for Pakistan.

H. S. SUHRAWARDY BECOMES PRIME MINISTER [1956]

Soon after the adoption of the 1956 Constitution, Chaudhary Muhammad Ali was replaced by Huseyn Shaheed Suhrawardy as Prime Minister on September 12, 1956.

During his tenure, Suhrawardy tried to remove economic disparity between the East and West wings of Pakistan.

I.I. CHUNDRIGAR BECOMES PRIME MINISTER
[1957]

After merely a year in office, Suhrawardy resigned from premiership in October 1957, due to President's refusal to convene a meeting of the parliament to seek a vote of confidence.

I.I. Chundrigar was appointed interim Prime Minister by the President, Iskander Mirza II.

MALIK FEROZ KHAN NOON BECOMES PRIME MINISTER [1957]

On December 16, 1957, Malik Feroz Khan Noon took over the office of Prime Minister from Chundrigar. But his term lasted for less than a year and Martial law was declared in 1958.

1958—1977

OUSTER OF PRESIDENT ISKANDER MIRZA—1958

On October 7 1958, President Iskander Mirza abrogated the Constitution and declared martial law in the country. General

Muhammad Ayub Khan, the then Commander-in-Chief of the Armed Forces became the Chief Martial Law Administrator (CMLA).

Iskander Mirza and Ayub Khan had begun the new era with apparent unanimity, jointly describing it as a two-man regime. However, although the two were responsible for bringing about the change, they had different views on dealing with the new situation. Iskander Mirza wanted to assume the premarital role where he had the power to maneuver things according to his own whim. Thing however had changed as CMLA Ayub Khan knew that the power rested with the army and was determined to assert himself. Within a week of the proclamation of Martial Law Iskander Mirza realized the delicate position in which he had gotten himself. He regretted his decision and said, "I did not mean to do it", and assured that the Martial Law would be for the shortest possible duration.

The sharing of power soon led to the intensification of the power struggle between the two men. President Mirza tried to rationalize the power structure by appointing Ayub Khan as Prime Minister on October 24, 1958. He set up a Cabinet consisting entirely of non-Political personalities. This did not satisfy Ayub Khan who had more powers as the Chief Martial Administrator. President Iskander Mirza, in order to secure himself, tried to get the support of Ayub Khan's rivals within the army and the air force. He was however unsuccessful in this attempt.

On October 27, 1958 Ayub Khan after consulting the Military Generals decided to get rid of Iskander Mirza. Iskander Mirza was arrested and exiled to Great Britain where he later died, a sad end to an ambitious man who ultimately fell pray to his own intrigues. General Ayub Khan, after the ouster of Iskander Mirza became the all in all. He, in addition to being the Martial Law Administrator (CMLA) later also declared himself as the President of Pakistan.

MARTIAL LAW UNDER FIELD MARSHAL AYUB KHAN [1958—62]

On October 7, 1958, President Iskander Mirza abrogated the Constitution and declared martial law in the country. This was the first of the many martial laws to mar Pakistan's history. With this step the Constitution of 1956 was abrogated, ministers were dismissed, Central and Provincial Assemblies were dissolved and all sort of political activities were banned. General Muhammad Ayub Khan, the then Commander-in-Chief of the Armed Forces became the Chief Martial Law Administrator (CMLA). Thus the parliamentary system in Pakistan came to end. Within three weeks of assuming charge on October 27,1958 Iskander Mirza was ousted by General Ayub Khan, who declared himself as President.

General Ayub Khan gave himself the rank of 'Field Marshal". Corruption had become so endemic within the national and civic systems of administration that Ayub Khan was welcomed as a national hero by the people. The new military government soon after coming to power promised that they would carry out reforms in the entire government structure and would cleanse the administration from malpractices. The Ayub's government started a thorough screening process against all government servants by conducting a close scrutiny of their service records. Public servants were tried for misconduct by tribunals consisting of retired judges of Supreme Court or High Court. On proving of charges disciplinary actions such as dismissal, compulsory retirement of the public servant could take place. A public servant could also be disqualified from holding any public office for more than 15 years. About three thousand officials were dismissed and many others were reduced in rank. Due to these steps rest of the government servants were provided with incentive for working hard. Like the public servants a law called the Elective Bodies Disqualification Order (popularly known as EBDO) was promulgated for the disqualification of politicians. Under this law a person could be disqualified for being a member of any elective body until December 31, 1966. Under this harsh law several politicians like, Suhrawardy and Qayyum Khan were disqualified. This law, particularly its application, was severely criticized in the legal and political circles throughout Pakistan.

Ayub Khan soon after taking over the country focused on the long-standing question of land reforms in West Pakistan. The land reforms included the reduction of land ceiling to 1000 acres for un-irrigated land and 500 acres for irrigated land and with ownership rights granted to the tenants. The land in excess to these limits was taken over by the government to be distributed amongst the deserving persons. Ayub Khan also introduced a comprehensive scheme of local-government popularly known as Basic Democracies. This scheme was enforced through the Basic Democracies Order on October 27, 1959. Basic Democracies was a pyramidal plan enabling the people to elect directly to local council men they knew, who would in turn elect the upper tier of the administration. There were altogether 80,000 Basic Democrats elected. Ayub Khan in order to find legitimacy for his rule used the Basic Democrats as an electoral college, holding a referendum to seek a mandate to continue in office as President and to have the authority to frame the future Constitution of Pakistan.

The Basic Democrats were to vote by a secret ballot on the question: Do you have confidence in President Field Marshal Muhammad Ayub Khan, Hilal-i-Jurat?'. The referendum was held on February 14, 1960 as a result of which Ayub Khan was elected not only the President of Pakistan for five years but also got the mandate to give Pakistan a Constitution of his choice.

For the purpose of forming the future Constitution Ayub Khan set up a Constitution Commission which was not only given the responsibility to make recommendations on the future Constitution but also to examine the causes of failure of parliamentary government in Pakistan. The report of the Constitution Commission was presented to Ayub Khan on May 6, 1961. The report however was not up to the demands of Ayub Khan and thus the 1962 Constitution was very different from the recommendation of the Constitution Commission, as Ayub Khan favored a presidential form of government. The 1962 Constitution was promulgated on March 1, with which the three and a half year martial law era of Ayub Khan came to an end and a civilian constitutional government under Ayub Khan replaced his previous military regime.

THE CONSTITUTION OF 1962

With the aim to investigate the reasons for the failure of the parliamentary system in Pakistan and to make recommendations for a new constitution, Ayub Khan appointed a Constitution Commission under the supervision of Justice Shahabuddin. The Commission after a number of considerations submitted its report on May 6, 1961. The report was not up to the demands of Ayub

Khan and thus was processed through various committees. The Constitution, which was promulgated on March 1, and was enforced on June 8, 1962 was entirely different from the one recommended by Shahabuddin Commission.

The Constitution of 1962 consisted of 250 Articles, which were divided into twelve Parts and three Schedules. It advocated Presidential form of Government with absolute powers for the President, who was supposed to be a Muslim and was not be less than thirty-five years in age. The term of the President was for five years and nobody could hold the post for more than two consecutive terms. The President was the Head of the State as well as the Head of the Government. He had the power to appoint Provincial Governors, Federal Ministers, Advocate General, Auditor General and Chairmen and Members of various Administrative Commissions. As the Supreme Commander of the Armed Forces of Pakistan the appointment of the Chiefs of the Forces was also his duty.

The Constitution of 1962 provided for the Unicameral Legislature. The National Assembly was to consist of 156 members, including six women. Later on, Eighth Amendment in the Constitution increased the number of the members of the central legislature to 218. Principle of Parity was retained and seats were distributed equally between the two wings of the country. Principle of Basic Democracy was introduced for the first time in the country and system of indirect elections was presented. Only eighty thousand basic democrats were given the right to vote for the Presidential elections. Eighth Amendment increased the number of Electoral College to 120,000. Half of them were to be from the Eastern, the rest from the Western wing of the country.

According to the Constitution of 1962, the Executive was not separated from the Legislature. The President exercised veto power in the legislative affairs and could even turn down a bill passed by the National Assembly even with a two-third majority. He had the power to issue Ordinances when the Assembly was not in session. The Ordinance needed the approval of the National Assembly within forty-eight days of its first meeting or 108 days after its promulgation. However, if the President enforced emergency in the country, which according to the constitution was within his jurisdictions, then the Ordinances needed no approval from the Legislative body. The President had the power to dissolve the National Assembly. Federal form of Government was introduced in the country with most of the powers reserved for the Central Government. There was just Federal List of subjects and provinces were entitled only to look into the subjects, which were not mentioned in the Federal List. Principle of One Unit for West Pakistan was maintained and numbers of seats, for the Punjab, were curtailed to 40% in the Western wing for the initial five years. Provincial Governors were to enjoy the same position in the provinces, which the President was to enjoy in the center.

According to the Constitution of 1962, almost all the Islamic clauses were included in the part of the Constitution, which could not be challenged in court of law. The state was named as the Republic of Pakistan, but with the first amendment in the Constitution word Islamic was added to the name. Word 'Islam' and not 'Quran and Sunnah' was used in the Islamic clauses to give liberal touch to the constitution. However, Advisory Council of Islamic Ideology was introduced, with the aim to recommend to the government ways and means to enable Muslims to live their lives according to the teachings of Islam, was introduced.

The Constitution of 1962 was a written Constitution upholding the Fundamental Rights of the citizens. Under the Constitution, the Judiciary had little independence and the appointment of the Chief Justices and Judges of the Supreme and High Courts was in the hands of the President. The President also had the power to remove a judge after an inquiry on misconduct or on the basis of mental or physical illness.

Both Urdu and Bengali were made the National Languages of Pakistan and English was declared as the Official language of the country for the first 10 years. The Constitution was flexible in nature and could be amended by the 2/3rd members of the National Assembly and with the approval of the President. In its short life of seven years, eight amendments were made in the Constitution.

With the handing over of power by Ayub Khan to Yahya Khan, Martial Law was enforced in the country and the Constitution was terminated on March 25, 1969.

FIELD MARSHAL AYUB KHAN BECOMES PRESIDENT [1962—69]

In March 1962, Ayub Khan suspended Martial Law and proclaimed the Constitution of 1962. Presidential elections were held in January 1965, and Ayub Khan defeated Miss Fatima Jinnah, Jinnah's sister, to once again become the President of Pakistan.

During his term, the "Great Decade" was celebrated, which highlighted the development plans executed during ten years of Ayub's rule. The 1965 war was fought during Ayub's term and Ayub Khan represented Pakistan in the subsequent Tashkent talks.

Ayub Khan moved the capital of Pakistan from Karachi to Islamabad in 1965, but could not complete his term due to public pressure.

He handed over power to General Muhammad Yahya Khan on March 25, 1969.

PRESIDENTIAL ELECTION (1965)

Miss Fatima Jinnah popularly acclaimed as the 'Madar-e-Millat' (the Mother of the Nation) for her role in the Freedom Movement contested the 1965 elections at the age of seventy-one. Since independence she had not participated in politics, except for her brief tour to East Pakistan in 1954, where she received a warm welcome. After the imposition of Martial Law by Ayub Khan, she once wished the regime well. But after the lifting of the Martial Law her sympathies went out with the opposition, as she had a strong favour for democratic ideals. Since she was the Quaid's sister, she was held in high esteem, and came to symbolize the democratic aspirations of the people. The electoral landscape was changed for women, when Miss Fatima Jinnah decided to contest the elections for the President's office in 1965. She was challenging the incumbent President Ayub Khan in the indirect election, which Ayub Khan had instituted.

The Presidential candidates for the elections of 1965 were announced before the commencement of the Basic Democracy (BD) elections, which was to constitute the Electoral College for the Presidential and Assembly elections. There were two major parties contesting the election. The Convention Muslim League (ConML) and the Combined Opposition Parties (COP). The COP consisted of five major opposition parties. COP had a 9-point program, which included restoration of direct elections, adult franchise, democratization of 1962 Constitution. The opposition parties of COP were not united and did not possess any unity of thought and action. They were unable to select a Presidential candidate from among themselves, therefore they selected Miss Fatima Jinnah as there Presidential candidate.

The elections were held on January 2, 1965. There were four candidates to the election—Ayub Khan, Miss Fatima Jinnah and two obscure persons with no party affiliation. There was a short campaigning period of one month which was further restricted to nine projection meetings which were organized by the Election Commission and were attended only by the members of the electoral college and members of the press. The public was barred from attending the projection meeting which would have enhanced Miss Fatima Jinnah's image.

Ayub Khan was in a more advantageous position than the other candidates: the constitution (second amendment) act confirmed him the president until the election of his successor, and armed with all the wide ranging constitutional powers of a president, he exercised complete control over all governmental machinery during elections. He utilized the state facilities as head of state, not as the president of the Convention Muslim League (ConML) or as the Presidential candidate, and did not even hesitate to legislate on electoral matters. Bureaucracy and business, the two beneficiary of the Ayub Khan regime helped him in his election campaign. Ayub Khan being a political opportunist brought all the discontented elements together to support him, the students were assured the revision of the University Ordinance, the journalists the scrutiny of the press laws. Ayub Khan also gathered the support of the Ulema who considered that Islam does not permit a women to be the head of an Islamic state.

Miss Jinnah's great advantage was that she was the sister of the founder of Pakistan and had been detached from the political conflicts that had plagued Pakistan after the founder's death. The sight of this dynamic lady moving in the streets of big cities, and even in the rural areas of a Muslim country, was both moving and unique. She proclaimed Ayub Khan, to be a dictator. Miss Jinnah's line of attack was that by coming to terms with India on the Indus Water dispute, Ayub had surrendered control of the rivers over to India. Her campaign generated tremendous public enthusiasm. She drew enormous crowds in all the cities of East and West Pakistan. The COP Campaign, however, suffered from a number of drawbacks. Unfair and unequal election campaign, poor financial position of COP, and the indirect elections through the Basic Democracy System were some of the basic problems faced by COP. Miss Fatima Jinnah lost the election of 1965 and Ayub Khan was elected the President of Pakistan.

In all probability Fatima Jinnah would have won the elections if the contest was by direct election, but the Electoral College consisted of only 80,000 Basic Democrats, who were easily manipulated. The importance of this election, which was rigged otherwise, lay in the fact that a woman was contesting the highest political office of the country. It is widely held that if the elections had been honest she would have won them. The orthodox religious political parties, including the Jamaat-e-Islami led by Maulana Maudoodi, which had repeatedly declared that a woman could not hold the highest office of a Muslim country, then modified their stand and supported the candidature of Miss Fatima Jinnah. The election showed that there was no prejudice among the people against women holding high offices of the country, and women, indeed, could be key players in politics of the country.

INDO-PAK WAR [SEPTEMBER, 1965]

In September, 1965, the long standing border disputes, communal tensions and conflict over the question of Kashmir flared up in a full-scale war between India and Pakistan.

The War of Rann of Kutch

Skirmishes at the Rann of Kutch flared up almost accidentally in the spring of 1965, and India and Pakistan found themselves drawn into the first of their two undeclared wars.

The dispute goes back to the days of the British rule in India. The Rann was the bone of contention between the princely state Kutch and British Indian province of Sind.

When British India was partitioned, the issue was inherited by India, to whom Kutch acceded, and Pakistan, whom Sind joined, involving some 3,500 miles of territory leading to frequent border incidents, from January 1965 onwards.

By all accounts the Indian forces were badly mashed in the Kutch area by the Pakistan army.

It was at the Commonwealth conference at Britain, that the British Prime Minister Harold Wilson successfully persuaded both India and Pakistan to sign an agreement on June 30 to resolve the dispute. Failing to do so bilaterally, a tribunal was set up which announced its verdict on February 19, 1965 by giving 350 sq. miles in Northern part to Pakistan and the rest of Rann area to India.

The War in Kashmir

Events in Kashmir were also moving towards a climax. The Indian Prime Minister Lal Bahadur Shastri added more fuel to the fire by taking steps to absorb Kashmir further into the body politic of India and said Kashmir problem occupied a secondary place to successful relations between India and Pakistan.

The application of articles 356 and 357 of the Indian constitution to the Kashmir state, which enabled the President of India to establish President rule in Kashmir and legislate there, were efforts to amalgamate Kashmir completely into the Indian union.

Sheikh Abdullah, the Kashmiri leader took extensive foreign tours to enlist international support for the Kashmiri cause.

But he was arrested and the Kashmir legislative assembly adopted the constitutional amendments bill on March 30, providing:

(a)   the Sardar-i-Riyasat would henceforth be known as Governor and would be appointed by President of India instead of being elected by the local assembly.

(b)   the Prime Minister would be styled as Chief Minister, as in the states of the Indian union.

The Lahore Offensive

The domestic Indo-Pak conflict transformed into an international conflict and raised super power concerns.

The U.S. suspended military supplies to both sides during the Indo-Pak war. Both the Soviet Union and the United States took a united stand to curtail the conflict within the boundaries of Indo-Pakistan from escalating into a global conflict. China had threatened to intervene and offered military support on behalf of Pakistan. It was this fear that both the Soviet Union and the United States pressured the UN to arrange for an immediate cease-fire, to keep China away from this conflict.

The main diplomatic effort to stop the fighting was conducted under the United Nations auspices and a cease-fire came into effect on September 23, 1965.

The Soviet Union which remained neutral when India and Pakistan went to war in September 1965, played the broker afterward at Tashkent.

A Soviet Government communique, formally announced on December 8 that the Indian Prime Minister Shastri and the Pakistani President Ayub would meet at Tashkent on January 4, 1966.

The Tashkent conference lasted from January 4 to January 10. The Soviet Premier Kosygin earned the praise as a peace maker. The main achievement of the conference was to withdraw, not later than February 25, 1966, all armed personal to the position held before August 5, 1964.

AWAMI LEAGUE SIX-POINT PROGRAM

The Awami League Party led by Sheikh Mujibur Rehman, fought the 1970 election of the Pakistan National Assembly on the basis of its Six-point Program of regional autonomy in a federal Pakistan. Mujibur Rehman had given the Six-point program as the constitutional solution of East Pakistan's problems vis-a-vis those of West Pakistan. First enunciated on February 12, 1966 the Six-points are:

1. The Constitution should provide for a Federation of Pakistan in the true sense on the basis of the Lahore Resolution and for a parliamentary form of government based on the supremacy of a directly elected legislature on the basis of universal adult franchise.

2.   The Federal Government shall deal with only two subjects—
     defense and foreign affairs—with all residuary subjects vested
     in the federating states.
3.   There should be either two separate freely convertible
     currencies for the two wings or one currency with two
     separate reserve banks to prevent inter-wing flight of capital.
4.   The power of taxation and revenue collection shall be vested
     in the federating units. The Federal Government will receive
     a share to meet its financial obligations.
5.   Economic disparities between the two wings shall disappear
     through a series of economic, fiscal, and legal reforms.
6.   A militia or para-military force must be created in East
     Pakistan, which at present has no defense of it own.

After the elections of 1970 difference arouse between the
government and the Awami League on the transfer of power on
the bases of the Six-point formula.

There was a political deadlock with talks ending in a failure
and the postponement of the first session of the National Assembly.
The postponement of the National Assembly session triggered a
chain of events, which eventually led to the separation of East
Pakistan.

MARTIAL LAW UNDER GENERAL YAHYA KHAN [1969—71]

The Tashkent Declaration signed by the Indian Prime Minister,
Shastri and his Pakistani counterpart, Ayub Khan was regarded
by many Pakistanis as submission to India. The then Foreign
Minister, Zulfikar All Bhutto resigned from office and formed a
party of his own, called the Pakistan People's Party with the
agenda to 'defeat the great dictator with the power of the people'.
As a result, he and others were arrested. Meanwhile, Mujib-ur-
Rehman's popularity grew in East Pakistan.

Ayub Khan tried to handle the situation by releasing a
number of political prisoners and holding a round table conference
in Rawalpindi in March 1969. The conference was a stalemate and
Ayub Khan handed over power to General Muhammad Yahya

Khan on March 25, 1969. Pakistan was now under it's second martial law era.

Being deeply aware of the explosive political situation in the country, General Yahya Khan, set in motion moves to transfer power to the elected representatives of the people and announced that the general elections would be held on October 5, 1970.

LEGAL FRAMEWORK ORDER [1970]

After the abrogation of the Constitution of 1962, Yahya Khan needed a legal framework to hold elections. In order to know the opinion of the politicians, Yahya Khan had two rounds of discussions with the leaders of all-important political parties on individual basis, during April and July 1969. Most of them asked for the revival of the Constitution of 1956 on the ground that its abrogation was unlawful and thus the country should return to the constitutional position prevailing on the eve of the 1958 coup. Initially Yahya Khan agreed with the plan but due to the opposition of Awami League, later he had to change his mind. Yahya Khan himself was not well versed in the constitutional affairs, thus he appointed a team to draft a new constitutional formula. Though Yahya Khan voiced his ideas about decision on constitution issue in his broadcast address to the nation on November 28, 1970, yet the formula was officially issued on March 30, 1970 and is known in history as Legal Framework Order 1970. According to Legal Framework Order, One Unit was dissolved in West Pakistan and the principle of parity was replaced by rule of one-man one vote.

The National Assembly was to constitute of 313 seats, including 13 seats reserved for women. The women were also allowed to contest the elections from general seats. 162 general and 7 women seats were reserved for East Bengal, 82 general and 3 women seats for Punjab, 27 general and one women seat for Sindh, 18 general and 1 women seat for North Western Frontier Province, 4 general and one women for Baluchistan and 7 general seats for Centrally Administered Tribal Areas.

LFO also laid down the qualifications of the persons, who could contest for the elections. The Constituent Assembly was to stand dissolved if it was unable to frame the Constitution within

120 days. Actually Legal Framework Order was to act as an interim constitution.

The primary function of LFO was to provide a setup on which elections could be conducted and then it was the duty of elected Constituent Assembly to draft a constitution of Pakistan. However, LFO defined the directive principles of the state policy and made it clear that the future Constitution should not violate these basic principles. The directive principles demanded an Islamic way of life, observation of Islamic moral standards, teaching of the Quran and Sunnah to the Muslims.

Legal Framework Order also demanded from the Constituent Assembly to frame a Constitution in which Pakistan was to be a Federal Republic and should be named as Islamic Republic of Pakistan. It also demanded for the preservation of the Islamic Ideology and the democratic values so that the elections should be held in the country on the basis of population and adult franchise. The Constituent Assembly was also supposed to frame a Constitution in which all the citizens of Pakistan were to enjoy fundamental human rights. Judiciary should remain independent from the executive and the provincial autonomy be protected. President was given the power to reject any Constitution framed by the Constituent Assembly, if the document does not match with the above-mentioned requirements. The President also had the power to interpret and amend the Constitution, and his decision was not supposed to be challenged in the court of law.

ZULFIKAR ALI BHUTTO BECOMES PRESIDENT
[1971]

Zulfikar Ali Bhutto launched Pakistan People's Party (PPP) following the Tashkent Pact. In December 1970, PPP won a large majority in West Pakistan. Following the 1971 war and the separation of East Pakistan, Yahya Khan resigned and Bhutto took over as President and Chief Martial Law Administrator on December 20, 1971.

In early 1972, Bhutto nationalized ten categories of major industries, withdrew Pakistan from Commonwealth of nations and SEATO. On March 1, he introduced land reforms. On July 2, 1972, he signed the Simla Agreement with India allowing exchange of occupied territories and POWs of the 1971 war.

THE SEPARATION OF EAST PAKISTAN [1971]

The separation of East Pakistan was a great setback to Pakistan. By 1970 sentiments for national unity had weakened so much in East Pakistan and the constant conflict among East and West Pakistanis dramatically erupted into mass civil disorder, resulting tragically in the most brutal and violent amputation of Pakistan's Eastern wing.

The fact of physical separation of one thousands miles between the two wings, without a common border, surrounded by Indian territory and influences led to constant political, economic and social conflicts between the two wings thus embittering the relations and bringing the country on the verge of collapse.

As a result of the separation of Eastern wing, the Pakistani's international credit was depleted; its most powerful institution— the military suffered. Even the idea of Pakistan as the homeland for the Muslims in South Asia no longer appeared valid.

Trouble started right at the inception of Pakistan in 1947. Almost immediately. East Pakistan's claimed that as their population (55% as opposed to 45 per cent in the West) was greater, they were in a majority. Democratically, therefore, the Federal Capital should have been in Dacca and not in Karachi.

Since Karachi was the seat of the National Government, ministers, government officials and industrialists, exerted immense influence on national and regional affairs which brought them many benefits. But the East Pakistanis were enable to extract the same kind of advantages as they were a good thousand miles away from the Capital. Moreover, the Capital, attracted initially the wealthy industrialists, businessman, administrators, doctors etc. who had fled from India.

The location of the Capital, it was said, created great economic imbalance, uneven distribution of national wealth and privileges, and better jobs for Westerners because they were able to sway decisions in their own favor.

Secondly, Bengalis resented to the way vast sums of foreign exchange, earned from the sale of jute from the East, were being spent on defense. They were unable to see how this expenditure for the Kashmir cause, which otherwise could have been productively used to build dams, barriers to control floods, eradication of poverty, illiteracy and supply of food for the ever-growing population.

Thirdly, the people of the East believed that it was sheer regional prejudice that all the white-collar jobs were taken by the West Pakistanis.

There is no doubt that many mistakes were made early in the short history of Pakistan, but many of these grievances, though genuine enough, were often exaggerated to foster anti-Western Pakistani feelings which would eventually create a kind of Bengali nationalism or a separatist tendency.

It must not be forgotten that there lived in East Pakistan about 15 million Hindus who, with the help of their fellow West Bengali Indians from across the border, were able to exploit the East-West regional differences. Some political leaders went around depicting the Central Government and West Pakistan as hostile and exploiters.

No effective effort was made to check the anti-national trends.

In 1970 elections, the Awami League (formed in 1951 in East Pakistan) was headed by Sheikh Mujibur Rehman. He had always been an ardent Bengali nationalist and began to attract attention of the oppressed Bengalis in the East.

Sheikh Mujibur Rehman put forward his "Six Points" which demanded autonomy for East Pakistan.

Mujib gained wide publicity for his "Six Points" plan for East Pakistan in Dacca. But he was arrested in April, 1966, soon released, only to be re-arrested and imprisoned in June, 1966 and languished in prison until February, 1969.

Being deeply aware of the explosive political situation in the country, the then President Yahya Khan, set in motion moves to transfer power to the elected representatives of the people and announced that the general elections would be held on October 5, 1970.

In all his election speeches. Sheikh Mujibur Rehman stepped up his demand for the "Six Points" and provincial autonomy plans.

In September, 1970, elections were postponed, from October to December, due to heavy floods which caused immense destruction and havoc in the province of East Pakistan. The sheer enormity of the disaster attracted world-wide attention. This gave Sheikh Mujibur Rehman a golden opportunity to hammer home for the benefit of the foreigners his anti-western feelings. He accused West Pakistan of brutal callousness.

The Awami League gained much sympathy and benefit out of this suffering and Sheikh Mujibur Rehman and his people arrived on the international scene as the victims of West Pakistan's indifference.

However, the general elections were held for the National and the Provincial Assemblies in December, 1970. The result was an overwhelming victory in the East for the Awami League, which captured 167 seats. In the West, the Pakistan's People Party had won 85 seats. The way was now open to draw up a new constitution.

The Awami League, now overwhelmingly a victor, stood firm on its "Six Points" plans. It refused to compromise an inch on that issue. The People's Party in the West maintained that the "Six Points" did not really permit a genuine federation. It was, in fact, a unique constitutional proposal which proposed a federation which had power only over defense and foreign policy.

Efforts were made to start a constitutional dialogue and narrow the differences between the two wings, but all in vain. The adamant stand of Sheikh Mujibur Rehman in support of his "Six Points", and his proposal that East Bengal should have sovereign status independent of Pakistan, further aggravated the situation.

The Awami League leader, Mujib launched a non-cooperation movement. The civil administration was totally paralyzed. All government and educational institutions were closed. People were asked not to pay the taxes. The transport system came to a standstill. Factories and shops were shut. All government activities between both the wings ceased.

In fact, the Awami League had setup a parallel government. Gangs of local Awami League freedom fighters known as Mukti Bahini led violent demonstrations, howled racial and anti-West

Pakistani feelings and slogans, and thereby inciting the people to more violence.

Amongst these disturbances, President Yahya decided to convene the National Assembly in March, 1971. But Sheikh Mujibur Rehman unexpectedly put forward other demands as lifting of martial law immediately and power transfer to the elected representatives of the people, prior to the National Assembly session.

Unfortunately, on March 23, the Republic Day of Pakistan, the Awami League declared a Resistance Day and Bangladesh flags flew all over the province. There was great massacre. East Pakistan had reached a point of no return.

To prevent the armed rebellion of the Awami League militants, the Pakistan Army struck their first blow on March 27, 1971. President Yahya Khan used force to bring law and order in the country. The real force of the Army was directed against the millions of Hindus living in East Pakistan and the Indian infiltrations who had crossed the border to cause trouble in the cities.

India, exploited to the full Pakistan's dilemma. It sought to wring the full propaganda value out of Bengali suffering and misery.

In the meantime, India launched their attack on East Pakistan on November 22,1971. The help of modern Soviet missiles, the local Army, Mukti Bahini and the Indian Army—made Pakistan's military defeat in the East almost certain.

On December 10, 1971, the first feeler for surrender in East Pakistan was conveyed to the United Nations. On December 17, 1971, a formal surrender was submitted and accepted.

Forty-five thousand troops and an almost equal number of civilians of West Pakistan were taken prisoners of war.

Though the Pakistan Army suffered a defeat in East Pakistan but it was not because of want of courage but because of lack of supply and re-enforcement, and the geographical separation by 1000 miles lying across the hostile Indian territory.

The surrender lead to the disintegration of East and West Pakistan and the establishment of Bangladesh.

After 25 years, the East Pakistanis declared themselves independent and renamed their province Bangladesh.

Pakistan finally recognized Bangladesh at the Islamic Conference in Lahore on February 22, 1974.

THE SIMLA AGREEMENT [1972]

In consequence of the 1971 war between India and Pakistan more than 93 thousand personnel of Pakistan Army were arrested by India. In Pakistan there was a growing demand for getting these prisoners released. As a result of this growing demand, a summit conference between Pakistani President Zulfiqar Ali Bhutto and the Indian leader Mrs. Gandhi was held at Simla from June 28 to July 2, 1972. An agreement between both the countries was finally arrived at on July 2. The agreement contained the elements of earlier Indian draft, but the wording was considerably modified. In particular the clause referring to the cease-fire line in Kashmir was rephrased to make it acceptable to Pakistan.

The broad features of this pact included that the principle and purpose of the charter of United Nations would govern the relations between the two countries. The two countries resolved to settle their differences by peaceful means through bilateral negotiations or by any other peaceful means mutually agreed upon by them. The foremost condition for understanding, good neighborly relations and stable and lasting peace would be that no country would interfere with the other country's internal matters on the basis of mutual respect for peace, security, territorial sovereignty, and mutual friendship and equality. It was reiterated again in the agreement that efforts would be made to put to end as far as possible all such disputes and differences, which have been the cause of dissension between the two countries for the last 25 or 26 years. Both governments also agreed to take all steps within their power to prevent hostile propaganda directed against each other.

In order to progressively restore and normalize relations between the two countries, it was agreed that steps would be taken to resume communications, postal service, and travel by sea, land

and air routes and to promote travel facilities. Trade and cooperation in economic and other agreed fields would also be resumed. In order to initiate the process of durable peace, both the governments agreed that Indian and Pakistani forces should be withdrawn to their sides of the international border. The control line between Jammu and Kashmir would be the same as was on December 17, 1971. Both the countries would respect, the international border and the return of the armies would be completed within thirty days of the implementation of the agreement. The agreement was to be approved by the respective countries through constitutional methods and it would come into force from the date of exchange of documents of approval.

Leaders of both the countries agreed at Simla to meet again at a mutually agreed time. So that representatives of both the countries could discuss more arrangements for durable peace including matters relating to prisoners of war, local prisoners, final settlement of Jammu and Kashmir dispute and diplomatic relations. The effect of the clauses relating to the withdrawal of forces and the ceasefire line in Kashmir was that Indian troops withdrew from 5139 square miles of Pakistani territory in Punjab and Sindh occupied during the war, and Pakistani troops from 69 square miles of territory in Punjab and Rajasthan. In Kashmir, India retained 480 square miles and Pakistan 52 square miles.

The Simla Agreement was ratified by Pakistan on July 15 and by India on August 3, after which the agreement came into effect on August 4, 1972.

THE CONSTITUTION OF 1973

The first achievement of Bhutto's government was to prepare a constitution for the country. The most prominent characteristic of this constitution was that it was accepted by almost all the big political parties of the country and the proposal of the opposition Parties were also accommodated in it. The 1973 Constitution was approved by the National Assembly on April 10, 1973 as a result of which the constitution came into effect from August 14, 1973. On August, 14 Bhutto took over as the Prime Minister of Pakistan and Chaudhary Fazal Illahi was appointed the President of Pakistan.

The Constitution of 1973 opens with a preamble, which is the preliminary part of the Constitution in which the broad features of the constitution have been explained. The first Article of the Constitution declares Pakistan as a Federal Republic to be known as the Islamic Republic of Pakistan. Islam was declared as the state religion of Pakistan. Pakistan was to be a Federation of four federating Units—Punjab, Sindh, N.W.F.P and Baluchistan. The 1973 Constitution of Pakistan was Parliamentary in nature. Article 41 of the Constitution laid down that the President was to be the Head of the State. The President was to be a Muslim above 45 years of age and was to be elected by a joint sitting of members of the parliament for 5 years. He could be reelected but could not hold office for more than two terms. The President was to act on the advice of the Prime Minister of Pakistan. The President could be removed on the grounds of physical or mental incapacity or on charges of violating the constitution or gross misconduct. The President was to appoint the Attorney-General, Judges of Supreme Court and High Courts and the Chief Election commissioners. The Prime Minister of Pakistan according to the constitution would be elected by a majority vote of the total members of the National Assembly. The Prime Minister was to appoint Federal Ministers and Ministers of the State from amongst the members of the Parliament.

The 1973 Constitution set up a bicameral legislature at the Center consisting of two Houses—the National Assembly and the Senate. The National Assembly consisted of 200 seats elected directly for duration of 5 years. The National Assembly could be dissolved by the President on the advice of the Prime Minister, The Senate was to consist of 63 members, each province was to elect 14 members. In the Provincial Government each province had a Governor appointed by the President. The Provincial Assembly for each province consisted of 240 seats for the Punjab, 100 seats for NWFP, and 40 seats for Balochistan.

The 1973 Constitution provided a free and independent judiciary. The Constitution guaranteed a right to the Citizens, that is, to be protected by law, and imposed two duties on them, loyalty to the Republic and obedience to the law. Any person who was found to abrogate or attempt or conspire to abrogate or subvert the Constitution was to be treated guilty of high treason. The Constitution conferred several kinds of Fundamental rights to the people such as the Right to life, liberty, equality and Freedom of speech, trade and association. The Constitution also declared laws inconsistent with or in derogation of fundamental rights to be void.

In the light of the past experience the Constitution of 1973 was more Islamic in character than the previous constitutions. Emphasis was made to establish a real Islamic system in all aspects of social life, keeping this objective in mind more Islamic provisions were laid down in the Constitution of 1973. The Constitution recognized Islam as the religion of the country and enjoined upon the state to serve the cause of Islam and to bring all existing laws in conformity with Islam. The Islamic Advisory Council was set up to recommend ways and means to bring existing laws of the country in conformity with the Islamic principles.

The constitution of 1973 remained in force for nearly four years. It was however suspended by General Muhammad Zia-ul-Haq, who imposed Martial Law in the country on July 5, 1979. However General Mohammad Zia-ul-Haq did not put to an end the Constitution of 1973 in all, and ran the country with the constitution and .martial law. In 1985 General Zia-ul-Haq passed the 8th Amendment in the Constitution. This Amendment empowered the President to dissolve the National Assembly under Article 58(2) b. This Article was later removed by Nawaz Sharif's 13th Amendment introduced on April 1, 1997.

FAZAL ILAHI BECOMES PRESIDENT [1973]

After the promulgation of 1973 Constitution, Zulfiqar Ali Bhutto was sworn in as the Prime Minister of the country, and Fazal Ilahi Choudhary became the President of Pakistan on August 14, 1973 for five years. On July 5,1977 the army took over the reigns of power in the country. Fazal Ilahi however continued his tenure as President of Pakistan. He resigned on September 16, 1978.

ZULFIKAR ALI BHUTTO BECOMES PRIME MINISTER [1973]

After the promulgation of 1973 Constitution, the elections for the President, Prime Minister, Chairman of Senate, Speaker and Deputy Speaker of the National Assembly were to be undertaken. The 1973 Constitution had given a federal parliamentary system to the country in which the President was only a figurehead and the real power lay with the Prime Minister.

Z.A. Bhutto was sworn in as the Prime Minister of the country on August 14, 1973 by securing 108 votes in a house of 146 members. Choudhary Fazal Ilahi was elected the President under the new constitution.

Mr. Bhutto carried out the first six amendments in the 1973 constitution. The First Amendment led to Pakistan's recognition of Bangladesh and the Second Amendment in the constitution declared the Ahmedis as non-Muslims. The rights of the detained were curtailed under the Third Amendment and the powers and jurisdiction of the courts in providing relief to political opponents were curtailed under the Fourth Amendment. The Fifth Amendment passed under Prime Minister Bhutto on September 15, 1976 focused on curtailing the power and jurisdiction of judiciary. This amendment was greatly criticized by lawyers and political leaders. The main provision of the Sixth Amendment extended the term of the Chief Justices of the Supreme Court and the High Courts beyond the age of retirement. This amendment was made in the constitution to favour the then Chief Justice of the Supreme Court who was a friend of Mr. Bhutto. The bottom line being that the Constitution was amended to accommodate a friend.

The government of Z.A. Bhutto carried out a number of reforms in the industrial sector. His reforms were two-pronged: nationalization and the rights of the workers. The nationalization program was carried out in two phases. The first step for the first phase of nationalization was that basic industries like steel, chemical and cement were nationalized. This was done in 1972. The next major step in nationalization took place on January 1, 1974, when Mr. Bhutto nationalized all banks. The Last step in the series of assets that were being nationalized was the most shocking, it was the nationalization of all flour, rice mills and cotton ginning mills throughout the country. This nationalization process was not successful as was expected by Mr. Bhutto.

The factories or nationalized units were all small businesses, which could not be described as industrial units hence making no sense for the step that was taken. A large number of small businessmen and traders were ruined, displaced and rendered unemployed.

In the concluding analysis, nationalization caused colossal loss not only to the national treasury but also to the people of Pakistan. During his period as the Prime Minister, a number of land reforms were also introduced. The important land reforms included the reduction of land ceilings and introducing the security of tenancy to tenant farmers. The land ceiling was fixed to 150 acres of irrigated land and 300 acres of non-irrigated land. Another step that Mr. Bhutto took was to democratize Pakistan's Civil Service.

1978—1990

MARTIAL LAW UNDER GENERAL ZIA-UL-HAQ [1977—85]

On March 7, 1977, elections were held. Pakistan People's Party (PPP) was accused of rigging the elections. Pakistan National Alliance (PNA) started a country-wide movement against the Bhutto government on March 14, 1977. Talks between PNA and the Bhutto government were held in June 1977 and an agreement was reached but could not be implemented.

On July 5, 1977, the Chief of Army Staff, General Muhammad Zia-ul-Haq imposed Martial Law and the previously announced elections of October 15, 1977, were postponed. General Zia-ul-Haq announced holding of elections within 90 days.

A conference of political leaders was held in February 1978, but a year later, in 1979, General Zia-ul-Haq declared political parties to be defunct and certain political leaders were disqualified.

Under Zia's martial law, there was steady economic growth favoring the private sector, and efforts were made to Islamise the political, legal and economic structures. Pakistan gained the status of the Most Favored Nation from the United States following the Soviet invasion of Afghanistan in December 1979. Vast amounts of military equipment and aid were donated to Pakistan to help the four million Afghan refugees who crossed into Baluchistan and North-West Frontier Province (NWFP).

On February 6, 1981, Movement for Restoration of Democracy (MRD) was established to return democracy to Pakistan. A provisional Constitution was enforced on March 23, 1981, after the Constitution of 1973 was suspended with the imposition of Martial Law.

GENERAL ZIA-UL-HAQ BECOMES PRESIDENT
[1984]

General Zia wanted to establish a Pseudo democracy in Pakistan, with a continuation of him as the President under a civilian setup. Zia took a number of steps in this direction; the first was the establishment of Majlis-e-Shoora. Majlis-e-Shoora was to take the part of the National Assembly, but was to be without any legislative powers at all. General Zia's second step was to ask the public to endorse his rule. The appeal was in the form of a referendum, which was so worded that a 'Yes' meant that Zia himself would be further endorsed, even though the referendum did not refer to this directly. The Referendum Order, 1984 put forward a complex question to the citizens, but in essence, seeking endorsement of the process of Islamization initiated by General Zia. The question read as follows:

'Whether the people of Pakistan endorse the process initiated by General Muhammad Zia-ul-Haq, the President of Pakistan, for bringing the laws of Pakistan in conformity with the injunctions of Islam as laid down in the Holy Quran and Sunnah of the Holy Prophet (PBUH) and for the preservation of the Islamic ideology of Pakistan, for the continuation and consolidation of that process, and for the smooth and orderly transfer of power to the elected representatives of the people.'

The question by all standards, was a very complicated and complex one, particularly for the simple-minded people of Pakistan. It was a loaded, one single question which had just asked—'Do you wish Pakistan to be an Islamic state? '. The answer, of which of course, could not be given in negative. An affirmative vote in the referendum was to result in a five-year term for Zia as a President of Pakistan.

The referendum was held on December 19, 1984, The Movement for the Restoration of Democracy (MRD) boycotted the elections. Very few people voted in the elections but such minor, inconvenient details were simply overlooked by Zia who claimed he had been given public support to continue as President of Pakistan for the next five years. As a result of the referendum the Chief Martial Law Administrator (CMLA), General Muhammad Zia-ul-Haq became the President of Pakistan. After the referendum,

General Zia announced that the elections for the National and Provincial Assemblies would be held in February 1985 on a non-party basis.

GENERAL ELECTIONS, FEBRUARY 1985

After the referendum. General Zia announced elections to the National Assembly and Provincial Assemblies in February 1985. The elections were to be held on a party less basis, which was legalized through an amendment to the 1973 constitution. Each candidate was to be supported by at least fifty people to be able to contest in the elections. In a nation-wide speech on January 12, 1985 General Zia also announced various other conditions for the elections. Amendments were made in the Political Parties Act of 1962. These amendments effected all the Political Parties.The opposition parties (the MRD) boycotted the elections for the reason that their demand for party based elections and restoration of the 1973 Constitution were not met.

The elections were held on the 25th and 28th of February, 1985 for the National and Provincial Assemblies. The successful boycotting of the referendum of December 1984 led MRD to miscalculate. They being confident of public support boycotted the elections. The voters, faced, with the prospect of voting in the elections after seven years, turned to the polls in large numbers. Surprisingly, many of the political leaders who had seemed strong in their appeals, including former minister, MNAs, MPAs and advisors, could not win from their constituencies. Many new faces were returned by the people. The MRD soon realized that it had miscalculated badly, that it should have fought the elections on Zia's terms. An alternative leadership was in place with many of the old political leaders routed out.

The general elections to the National and Provincial Assemblies were held peacefully and with a large participation of the people. Total turnout of the voter for the National Assembly was 53.69%. In the Provincial Assemblies elections, where the constituencies were smaller and the contest harder, the turnout of the voters was even better. It was 57.37% nationwide. The newly elected National Assembly was to replace the Majlis-e-Shoora and was to have legislative powers as well. Mr. Junejo was appointed the Prime Minister and formed the government. It was this newly elected Assembly which set the tone for later years by the incorporation of the controversial Eighth Amendment in the constitution of Pakistan.

HISTORIC 8TH AMENDMENT IS PASSED [1985]

The 1973 Constitution of Pakistan envisaged a parliamentary system of government, with the balance of power tilted favorably towards the Prime Minister. The President could not exercise his powers without the concurrence of the Prime Minister. The 8th Constitutional Amendment, however, altered the form of the Constitution drastically. Passed by the Senate on November 14, 1985, the 8th Amendment tampered with almost 19 clauses of the Constitution and brought the office of the President of Pakistan almost at par with that of the Prime Minister.

The President was given the right to nominate the Prime Minister, governors of the provinces, judges of the High and Supreme Courts including the Chief Justice. Thus, the democratically elected Prime Minister became subservient to the President.

The President was to act on the advice of the Prime Minister. He was empowered to use his unlimited constitutional powers and was liable to be counseled by the Premier. The President had the power to be informed about the decisions relating to the administrative affairs of the federation and proposals of legislation. The President could ask the Prime Minister to get a vote of confidence from the Assembly, issue ordinances, set date for the elections for the National Assembly and appoint caretaker government. The President had power of appointing service chiefs and other important federal officers. He could also call a referendum on an issue of great importance.

However, the most controversial power awarded to the office of the President was under the Article 58(2) b, which was the power of the dissolution of the National Assembly on his own discretion.

According to the proponents of this clause, due to Post-Constitutional deadlocks in the country, it was necessary to vest this authority in the President so that in case of a political crisis the Assembly could be dissolved and new elections could be held and a Martial Law could be avoided. The Article 58(2) b changed the entire complexion of the constitution. The constitution was transformed from a Parliamentary system into a Presidential one. This amendment was like the proverbial sword of Damocles for the successive governments. On four occasions since the passing of 58(2) b the National Assemblies were dissolved. However, the dissolution of the Assembly by President Zia-ul-Haq in 1988, President Ghulam Ishaq Khan in 1990 and in 1993, and President Farooq Leghari in 1996, are subject to a lot of speculation. Other clauses amended by the 8th Amendment dealt with the office of the Prime Minister, Senate, and Governors. The Article 51 increased the number of the National Assembly seats to 207 from 200. The number of the Senate seats were increased to 87 from 63 under Article 59. The 8th Amendment also indemnified the entire President's orders, ordinances, martial law regulations, martial law orders, including the referendum orders made between July 5, 1977 and September 13, 1985.

Eighth Amendment is considered as a landmark in the Constitutional history of Pakistan. It had not only altered the very form of the Constitution, from purely Parliamentary to semi-Presidential but has also changed the constitutional and political history of the country.

MUHAMMAD KHAN JUNEJO BECOMES PRIME MINISTER [1985—88]

After the Presidential referendum of December 1984, elections for the National and Provincial Assemblies were held in February 1985 on a non-party basis. President Zia-ul-Haq nominated Muhammad Khan Junejo as the Prime Minister of Pakistan on March 20, 1985.

Muhammad Khan Junejo on being nominated the Prime Minister promised the nation that he would lift the Martial Law and would restore a civilian government at the earliest. Junejo's position was weak and vulnerable under the constitutional amendments made by Zia, which made the position of the President paramount and that of the Prime Minister subordinate. Despite his weak position Junejo after being sworn in as the Prime Minister carried out his promise of lifting the Martial Law and the restoration of the fundamental rights, but at the price of the eighth Amendment and validating the Revival of the Constitutional Order (RCO).

Muhammad Khan Junejo after coming to power introduced a five-point program in December 1985. The program was multi dimensional in nature. The main objective was to induct a new and progressive civilian order, establish institutions of social justice, introduce an egalitarian economy, increase employment opportunities, strike hard at corruption and other social evils, liberate at least fifty per cent of the people from illiteracy, and to start socio-economic development of the country.

After the lifting of Martial Law, Junejo tried to take a course independent of Zia. He annoyed military generals by withdrawing big staff cars from them and replacing them with small cars. He tried to conduct an independent foreign policy, particularly on Afghanistan, by taking into confidence and consulting leaders of the political parties, including Benazir, the leader of the PPP. His government even tried to probe into the military fiasco at the Ojheri Camp near Islamabad on April 10, 1988, which resulted in the death and serious injuries to a large number of civilians. This probe perhaps became the immediate cause for the dismissal of his government.

It was after the visit of South Korea, Junejo's regime met its end with a sudden and unexpected announcement by the President General Muhammad Zia-ul-Haq on May 29,1988. General Zia dismissed Junejo's government using the controversial power under Article 58(2) b. According to General Zia, Junejo's government was dismissed because the law and order situation had broken down to an alarming extent and the government could not be run in accordance with the Constitution. Not only was the Junejo government dismissed but also the Federal and Provincial Assemblies and the Provincial Cabinets with their Chief Ministers were also dismissed. General Zia installed a new caretaker government in the center and provinces. Fresh elections were said to be held after 90 days but were eventually held on November 16, 1988 after some delay.

Although Junejo had no claim of his own to power as Zia appointed him Prime Minister, but his performance was commendable. With limited options, he did what was possible for him. He restored the fundamental rights of citizens under the Constitution that had been denied to them for a very long time. He tried to put the country on the course of development and some progress was made, particularly in the area of construction of roads in rural areas and the electrification of villages. He was honest, polite and had a low-key political personality, traits which are not easy to find in political leaders today.

BENAZIR BHUTTO BECOMES PRIME MINISTER [1988]

Elections were held as scheduled in November 1988. Pakistan People's Party won 94 seats in the National Assembly without forming any alliance. With the cooperation of 8 MQM members and 13 members of the Federally Administered tribal Area, the PPP showed clear majority in the National Assembly. Benazir Bhutto, daughter of Zulfikar All Bhutto was sworn in as the Prime Minister—the first woman to govern an Islamic state.

After becoming Prime Minister Benazir Bhutto announced that the ban on student unions and trade unions would be ended. The PPP government hosted the fourth SAARC Summit Conference in December 1988. As a result of the Conference Pakistan and India finalized three peace agreements. Benazir's government started facing problem on the political front. ANP deserted the Pakistan People Party and on November 1, 1989, a no confidence motion was moved against the Prime Minister by the opposition. Benazir was barely able to pull through with 12 votes to her advantage. MQM who had formed an alliance with the PPP also broke away and started creating trouble in Sindh.

Serious conceptual differences arouse between PPP government and the Establishment. And less than two years later, on August 6, 1990, her government was accused of corruption and dismissed by the President, Ghulam Ishaq Khan, who exercised his power through the controversial 8th Amendment of the constitution.

DEATH OF GENERAL ZIA-UL-HAQ [1988]

General Muhammad Zia-ul-Haq was killed in an air crash on August 17, 1988. He had gone to Bahawalpur to see a demonstration of tanks where he was accompanied by a number of Generals, including the Chairman Joint Chiefs of Staff Committee, Chief of General Staff, high Military Attache as well as the American Ambassador. On his return journey his military aircraft C-130, crashed a few minutes after take off from Bahawalpur airport, killing the entire passengers aboard, including the President. This tragic air disaster was the worst in Pakistan's history and was unprecedented in the history of military aircraft. The cause of the crash was not known and as usual, the enquiry report was never made public.

General Zia's remains were buried in the ground of Faisal mosque in Islamabad. With the death of General Zia the eleven-year military rule came to an end. And the country set forward on the road to democracy. This transition from dictatorship to democracy took place constitutionally.

After the crash, a high level meeting was held in Islamabad to decide the question of succession. Some of the participants in the meeting were in favour of the imposition of Martial Law. However the military chief present did not support the idea. Under the constitution whenever the office of President becomes vacant by reason of death or resignation, or removal of the President, the Chairman of Senate acts as President until a new President is elected under the constitution. As a result Ghulam Ishaq Khan, Chairman of the Senate, became the next acting President of Pakistan.

GHULAM ISHAQ KHAN BECOMES PRESIDENT [1989—93]

In 1988, President Zia-ul-Haq dissolved the Junejo government and announced that fresh elections would be held in November 1988. But on August 17, 1988, he was killed in a C-130 plane crash in Bahawalpur, along with five senior generals and the American Ambassador. The cause of the crash has never been ascertained.

After the death of General Zia, Ghulam Ishaq Khan, Chairman of the Senate, took over as acting President. Elections to the National and Provincial Assemblies were held on 16 and 19, November 1988 respectively. The RCO (Revival of the Constitutional Order) had amended the constitution, which empowered the President to appoint, at his discretion, any member of the National Assembly as Prime Minister. Ghulam Ishaq Khan appointed Benazir Bhutto, as Prime Minister of Pakistan on a condition that she would offer full support to Ghulam Ishaq Khan in the forthcoming Presidential elections.

According to the deal between Ghulam Ishaq Khan and Benazir Bhutto, Pakistan's Peoples Party (PPP) voted for Ghulam Ishaq Khan. Ghulam Ishaq Khan was also the consensus candidate of IJI (Islami Jamuhri Itehad). Ghulam Ishaq Khan won the election with an overwhelming majority. Four candidates took part in the election, with Ghulam Ishaq Khan winning and securing the highest 608 votes in the election. The Constitutional amendments made by the RCO and the Eight Amendment had led to the ascendancy of the President. Unforeseen by both this inevitably led the President and the Prime Minister into Conflict. The conflict between the President and the Prime Minister arose in two areas: the appointment of the military chiefs and the superior court judges.

The conflict between the President and the Prime Minister had its drop scene on August 6,1990 when the President dissolved the National Assembly and Benazir Bhutto lost her Prime Ministership. The dissolution of the National Assembly was soon followed by the dissolution of the Provincial Assembly. Fresh elections were scheduled to be held on October 24, 1990. President Ghulam Ishaq Khan appointed Mustafa Jatoi as the caretaker (interim) Prime Minister.

Elections for the National and Provincial assemblies were again held on October 24 and 27, 1990 respectively, Mian Muhammad Nawaz Sharif was elected as the Prime Minister on November 1, 1990. Nawaz Sharif's government remained in power till April 19, 1993. President Ghulam Ishaq Khan dissolved the National Assembly once again exercising his power through the 8th Amendment and appointed Mir Balakh Sher Khan Mazari as the caretaker Prime Minister. General Elections were scheduled to be held on July 14, 1993 but were canceled when the Supreme Court quashed the Presidential order and reinstated Nawaz Sharif as the Prime Minister.

Differences between Nawaz Sharif and Ghulam Ishaq Khan arouse once again, this time to deepen to an extent that it led to the resignation of the President, Ghulam Ishaq Khan and the Prime Minister, Mian Muhammad Nawaz Sharif on July 19, 1993, thus dissolving all the Central and Provincial assemblies. Moin Qureshi was appointed the caretaker Prime Minister, and Ghulam

Ishaq Khan was appointed the caretaker President. Fresh elections for the National and Provincial Assemblies were held. Benazir Bhutto returned to power a second time and Farooq Ahmed Khan Leghari was elected the new President of Pakistan.

This brought to an end the Presidentship of Ghulam Ishaq Khan, which oversaw the dismissal of two popularly elected governments. It set an unhealthy tradition of Presidents removing elected governments by the use of the controversial Eighth Amendment. This tradition was also carried out by the later Presidents creating a continuous instability in the country.

THE AFGHAN WAR SETTLEMENT

In 1979, the Russian forces invaded Afghanistan. Communism came to the thresh hold of Pakistan when the government of Afghanistan was overthrown by forces led by Babrak Karmel. Some 1,20,000 Russian troops entered Afghanistan. The Afghan people organized a resistance force against the blatant aggression. The Soviet forces had to suffer greatly in terms of men and material. The Afghan war proved expensive even for a world power like the Soviet Union. In the beginning the Soviet army was successful in occupying and controlling Afghanistan. It has always been said about Afghanistan that it can be invaded and occupied easily but it is very difficult to hold and control it. Afghans have a history of resisting foreign invaders. The British imperial power failed in all three attempts to occupy and control Afghanistan. The Soviets were to learn the same lesson. General Zia stood against the spread of Communism. The solution to Afghanistan according to him was reiterated in 1983 at New Delhi, he said that Pakistan has given political Asylum to millions of Afghans. He demanded the expulsion of Russian forces from Afghanistan. America responded to the call of Pakistan and flooded Pakistan with monetary help to finance the anti-communist regime in Afghanistan and to equip the freedom fighters in Afghanistan. The freedom fighters "the mujahideen" put forward a strong resistance to the Russian invasion. Although the Afghans suffered enormous causalities in the beginning of the war but the turning point in the war came when the US supplied the Stinger missiles to the Afghans.

General Zia's gamble in supporting the Russian invasion in Afghanistan paid him huge dividends. On the domestic front his policy of Islamization became more relevant as it was seen that in the neighboring Afghanistan Islam was in danger. As Pakistan was a frontline state huge amount of money, military equipment and aid arrived in Pakistan. The huge amounts of aid that poured in propped up Zia's government. With the Afghan problem a new phase of modernization of the military stared. The arms provided to Afghanistan freedom fighters were also provided to Pakistan army. As a result the Pakistan army became better equipped.

Other than the problems faced due to the Afghan war efforts, the Soviet Empire was breaking apart at the seams. This led the Soviet empire to seek peace in Afghanistan. Negotiations on Afghanistan were carried out under Zia's government, the Geneva Accord was signed on April 14, 1988 under which the Soviet Union agreed to withdraw its forces in two installments. The Soviet government lived up to its commitment of withdrawal of forces according to the agreed timetable.

The victory in Afghanistan was achieved at a great cost to Pakistan. It had to look after and feed more than three million Afghan refugees that had crossed over to Pakistan. The refugees were a great economic burden on Pakistan not only this but, they also caused the problem of drugs and guns running in the country.

Long after the Soviet forces had left Afghanistan, fighting continued between the various factions of the mujahideen and even still today peace has yet to return to the country. Pakistan continues to suffer numerous problems from the legacy of the Afghan war such as refugees, drugs, guns, crime, and terrorism.

ISLAMIZATION UNDER GENERAL MUHAMMAD ZIA-UL-HAQ

Islam has always been the motivating force for the Muslims of the subcontinent. Pakistan was created in the name of Islam. Quaid-e-Azam had wanted Pakistan to be a democratic state based on the Islamic principles of social justice. The Objectives Resolution of 1949 was the first constitutional document, which laid down the Islamic principles on which the Constitution of Pakistan would be framed.

In 1974, the 1973 Constitution was amended and a clause incorporated which stated that non-believers in the Finality of Prophethood were non-Muslims. Islamisation was given a new boost when General Zia-ul-Haq took over as the Chief Martial Law Administrator on July 5, 1977. General Zia-ul-Haq was a practicing Muslim who raised the slogan of Islam. The Islamic sentiment has always been fully alive in Pakistan. Various governments have used this to their benefits. The reason why General Zia raised the slogan of Islam is not sure; whether it was for political purposes to counter balance Bhutto's appeal or was it to enforce Islam in its true sense is not known for sure.

In his first address to the nation, he declared that Islamic laws would be enforced and that earnest attention would be devoted towards establishing the Islamic society for which Pakistan had been created. General Zia wanted to bring the legal, social, economic and political institution of the country in conformity with the Islamic principles, values and tradition in the light of Quran and Sunnah to enable the people of Pakistan to lead their lives in accordance to Islam.

The Government of Zia-ul-Haq took number of steps to eradicate un-Islamic practices from the country. He introduced the Zakat, Ushr, Islamic Hadood and Penal code in the country. Islam is a complete code of life containing specific teachings about all matters. All governments should be based on a proper financial system. The government of General Zia for this purpose invited eminent scholars to compile laws about Islamic financing. The Zakat and Ushr Ordinance to Islamise the economic system was promulgated on June 20, 1980. It covered only Islamic organizations, associations and institutions. Zakat was to be deducted from the account of every Muslim lying in the bank at the rate of 2 % annually above the balance of Rs. 3000. Ushr was levied on the yield of agricultural land in cash or kind at the rate of 10% of the agricultural yield, annually.

Government appointed Central, Provincial, District and Tehsil Zakat Committees to distribute Zakat funds to the needy, poor, orphans and widows. The Shias were exempted from Zakat deduction from their accounts. The Zakat tax was to be deducted by the banks on the 1st day of Ramzan.

A Federal Shariat Court was established to decide cases according to the teaching of the Holy Quran and Sunnah. Appeals against the Lower and High Courts were to be presented before the Shariat Court for hearing. It changed the sentence from, life imprisonment to execution in the case of blasphemy of the Holy Prophet (Peace Be Upon him).

The President Muhammad Zia-ul-Haq selected his Majlis-e-Shoora in 1980, the Islamic Parliament to act as the Parliament of Pakistan in place of the National Assembly. Most of the members of the Shoora were intellectuals, scholars, ulema, journalists, economists and professionals belonging to different fields of life. The Shoora was to act as a board of advisors for the President.

A number of other Islamisation programs were carried out including the teaching of Islamiat and Arabic, which were made compulsory. Pakistan Studies and Islamiat were compulsorily taught to BA, B.Sc., Engineering, M.B.B.S, Commerce, Law students and Nursing students. For professional studies extra marks were given to people who were 'Hafiz-e-Quran'. The first Ombudsman was appointed to rectify the misadministration of the Federal Government, officials and agencies.

A Shariat Council consisting of ulema was established to look into the constitutional and legal matters of the State in order to bring them into line with Islamic thought. Since Islam does not allow interest. On January 1, 1980 Muhammad Zia-ul-Haq introduced in the country 'Profit and Loss sharing system'. According to which an account holder was to share the loss and profit of the bank. The media was also targeted, especially the T.V was brought under the Islamisation campaign, News in Arabic were to be read on both T.V and radio, female TV announcers were forced to cover their heads with 'dopattas', the call for prayers, the Azan, was relayed on radio and television.

In the armed forces, the status of the religious teachers was raised to that of a commissioned officer. This was done to attract highly qualified individuals from the universities and religious institutions to serve on such assignments.

As the government grew further in its Islamic leanings, the numbers of mosques were increased. Ordinance for the sanctity of Ramzan-Ul-Mubarik was introduced to pay reverence to the holy month of Ramzan. The Ordinance forbade drinking and eating during the holy month of Ramzan. A three months imprisonment and a fine of 500 rupees were imposed for violating the ordinance. A program to ensure the regularity of prayers called the Nizam-e-Salaat was launched by General Zia himself.

Zia's Government introduced "Hadood Ordinance" for the first time in Pakistan, which meant the punishments ordained by the Holy Quran or Sunnah on the use of liquor, theft, zina and qazf. Under this Ordinance, a culprit could be sentenced to lashing, life imprisonment and in some cases, death by stoning.

The Islamic laws of Zia also included the laws for the women. Zia put forward the theory of 'chadar ur chaar devari' and this was to be applied to women. Thus, for the first time, a woman could be flogged for adultery; if a rape was reported, 4 witnesses were to be provided; otherwise, legally the rape could be termed adultery. Another law, 'the law of evidence' under the Shariah laws proposed that the testimony of a woman was not equal to that man: in legal matters, two women would have to stand witness against the testimony of one man. The status of women was thus arbitrarily cut in half by Zia. There was little consensus amongst Muslim authorities over this law. The lack of consensus among the religious authorities combined with countrywide protests forced Zia to hold back on making the Shariah law the law of the country.

The most important achievement of Zia's Government was the implementation of reforms to introduce the Islamic system in the country. General Zia-ul-Haq wanted to make Pakistan the citadel of Islam so that it could play an honorable and prominent role for the Islamic world. The steps taken by General Zia were in the right direction and had long-term impacts, the Zakat tax introduced by General Zia still holds and so do many the other laws. General Zia set Pakistan on the right track of Islamisation.

NAWAZ SHARIF BECOMES PRIME MINISTER [1990]

On October 24 and 27, 1990, respectively, elections were held for the National and Provincial assemblies. Mian Muhammad Nawaz Sharif, the ex-Chief Minister of Punjab was elected the Prime Minister on November 1, 1990.

During his tenure as the Prime Minister, Nawaz Sharif made efforts to strengthen the industrial sector with the help of private sector. Projects like Ghazi Brodha, Gawadar Mini port, were initiated. Land was distributed among landless haris in Sind. A massive uplift of Murree and Kahuta was done during his term as Chief Minister Punjab. Relations with the Central Asian Muslim republics were strengthened and ECO was given a boast.

To end the Afghan crisis, "Islamabad Accord" was reached between various Afghan factions. His most important contribution was economic progress despite American sanctions on Pakistan through Pressler amendment.

Nawaz Sharif's government remained in power till April 19, 1993, when President Ghulam Ishaq Khan dissolved the National Assembly once again exercising his power through the 8th Amendment.

GHULAM MUSTAFA JATOI BECOMES CARETAKER PRIME MINISTER [1990]

President Ghulam Ishaq Khan dissolved the National and Provincial Assemblies on August 6, 1990 and declared a state of emergency in the country. The President had the power to appoint a caretaker Prime Minister and a caretaker Cabinet at the federal as well at the provincial level as a result of the changes made in the constitution by the RCO and the Eighth Amendment.

Elections were scheduled to be held on October 24, 1990. Ghulam Ishaq Khan did not appoint neutral or non-partisan caretaker Cabinet. The leader of the opposition in the erstwhile National Assembly, Ghulam Mustafa Jatoi was appointed as the caretaker (interim) Prime Minister.

1991—2000

BENAZIR BHUTTO BECOMES PRIME MINISTER [1993]

Benazir Bhutto returned to power a second time in 1993 after the resignation of both the President Ghulam Ishaq Khan and the Prime Minister Nawaz Sharif on 18th July 1993. The resignation led to the announcement of fresh elections for the National and Provincial Assemblies. The elections were held on 6th October and 9th October 1993, respectively.

The elections were boycotted by the MQM. No party emerged with an absolute majority in the elections. As a result the PPP formed the new government with the help of alliances. Benazir Bhutto took oath as Prime Minister on 19th October 1993. Presidential election was held on November 13. Farooq Ahmed Khan Leghari the PPP candidate won by 274 to 168 votes against, the then acting President Wasim Sajjad. During her second tenure Benazir again faced trouble from the opposition, in autumn of 1994, Nawaz Sharif led a 'train march' from Karachi to Peshawar. This was followed by general strike on the 20th September. Two weeks later Nawaz Sharif called a 'Wheel-jam' strike on 11th October. The second tenure of Benazir Bhutto was however high-lightened by the visit of the US first Lady Hillary Clinton and her daughter Chelsea in 1995. Hillary's visit considerably changed Pakistan's perceptions and highlighted Pakistan as a liberal, modern and forward-looking country. In April 1994 Benazir visited the US, and projected Pakistan's stance on the US F-16 fighter planes. Her visit resulted in passing of the Brown Amendment by the US Senate, easing the restrictions on Pakistan on 21st September 1995. It also helped in attracting foreign investors. On the domestic front she continued facing problems with MQM. In spite of all her political endeavors, a smooth relationship could not be established between the government and MQM.

Benazir Bhutto's brother Mir Murtaza Bhutto was assassinated under mysterious circumstances on 20th September, 1996. The high-profile killing of her brother harmed her the most.

Things were not going on well, between the President and Benazir's government. Differences had started appearing, the government felt that there was interference in the political matters of the government by the President. President Farooq Leghari dismissed Benazir Bhutto's government on Charges of corruption and mismanagement on 5th November, 1996 under the Article 58(2) b of the Eighth Amendment.

BALAKH SHER MAZARI BECOMES CARETAKER PRIME MINISTER [1993]

President Ghulam Ishaq Khan dissolved the National and Provincial Assemblies on April 19, 1993, and appointed Mir Balakh Sher Khan Mazari as the caretaker Prime Minister.

General Elections were scheduled to be held on July 14, 1993.

Balakh Sher Mazari's tenure as caretaker Prime Minister ended in May 1993, when the Supreme Court quashed the presidential order and reinstated Nawaz Sharif as the Prime Minister.

MOIN QURESHI BECOMES CARETAKER PRIME MINISTER [1993]

On May 26, 1993, the Supreme Court of Pakistan declared the presidential order of assemblies' dissolution as ultra-vires and ruled for restoring the Nawaz government and the National Assembly. On July 19, 1993, the President, Ghulam Ishaq Khan and the Prime Minister, Mian Muhammad Nawaz Sharif resigned, thus dissolving all the Central and Provincial Assemblies.

Moin Qureshi, a top World Bank official was appointed the caretaker Prime Minister, and Ghulam Ishaq Khan was appointed the caretaker President. Moin Qureshi at the time of his appointment was totally unknown in Pakistan; it was therefore felt that as he was a political outsider he would remain neutral.

Despite the fact the Moin Qureshi was new to the economic and political problems of Pakistan, he made his presence felt during his short tenure of ninety days. During this short period of time he undertook numerous steps, which were appreciated by the general public. One of such steps included his effort to expose the misdeeds of the previous governments by publishing the lists of defaulters of bank loans and taxpayers. These lists exposed a number of affluent persons who were involved in abusing the banking system and dodging the tax collectors. Moin Qureshi made the State Bank of Pakistan an autonomous body with an effort to keep out political interference in the working of the bank. He took numerous other steps including the imposition of a nominal tax on agriculture, making Pakistan Television and Radio Pakistan autonomous, downsizing of the administrative machinery and abolishing the discretionary power of the Prime Minister and the Chief Minister's of allotting residential plots. It goes to his credit that he undertook various endeavors in a short period of time and made a serious effort to recover government dues. The only blotch on Moin Qureshi's tenure as PM was in his last days when he was accused of making a large number of promotions and other administrative decisions in favor of his relatives.

MALIK MERAJ KHALID BECOMES
CARETAKER PRIME MINISTER [1996]

President Farooq Leghari, exercising his power through the 8th Amendment, dismissed Benazir Bhutto's government in November, 1996 on charges of corruption and extra-judicial killings.

Malik Meraj Khalid, rector of the International Islamic University, was appointed caretaker Prime Minister by the President. Elections were scheduled to be held in February 1997.

FOURTEENTH AMENDMENT IS PASSED [1997]

Horse-trading and defection was on a rise in the past and was causing problems to various governments. The overthrow of Wyne's government by Wattoo's defection, the defection of MNAs from the opposition against the no confidence motion to support Benazir in 1989 are some of the examples of this problem.

The Nawaz Sharif's government on coming to power took step to do away with this ever-increasing problem. It was under Nawaz's government that the National Assembly unanimously adopted the Constitution Bill (14th Amendment) on July 1, 1997.

The Anti-defection Bill that was earlier passed by the Senate and later by the National Assembly with a large majority is a structural reform to end the practice of switching party loyalties. As a result of this Bill, blackmailing party leadership for ministerial slots, bank loans and other concessions will lead to unseating of such parliamentarians.

EIGHTH AMENDMENT IS REPEALED [1997]

Soon after being elected to office, Prime Minister Nawaz Sharif moved to repeal the controversial Eighth Amendment. The discretionary powers of the President under the Eighth Amendment were done away with the passage of the Thirteenth Amendment. The Thirteenth Amendment Act was passed on April 4, 1997. The National Assembly confirmed it unanimously. The most significant amendment was the end of the article 58(2) b of the Constitution, which empowered the President of Pakistan to dismiss the Government and the National Assembly. The power of the governor to dissolve the Provincial Assemblies under article 112(2) b was also done away with. The discretionary power of the President to appoint the chiefs of the armed forces was also taken away.

The discretionary power of the President to dissolve the National Assembly under the Eighth Amendment had led to the removal of governments elected in 1985, 1988, 1990 and 1993.

The Thirteenth Amendment proved to be the end of the Eighth Amendment. Once again, the powers of the President were bought back to those as envisaged in the Constitution.

MUHAMMAD RAFIQ TARAR ELECTED AS PRESIDENT [1997]

Muhammad Rafiq Tarar a former Judge of the Supreme Court and a Senator was elected as the ninth President of Pakistan and took oath to his office on January 1, 1998.

The office of President had become vacant due to a serious constitutional crisis prevailing in the country in December of 1997. The crisis resulted due to insurmountable differences between the President, Prime Minister and the Judiciary. This crisis ended with the resignation of President Leghari on December 2, 1997. His resignation cut short the normal term of the office of President from five year by nearly one year thus clearing the way for Mr. Nawaz Sharif to go down in history as the strongest ever premier who successfully ousted two Presidents, an Army Chief and a Chief Justice of Pakistan.

The Pakistan Muslim League had a two-thirds majority in the parliament and some provincial assemblies and therefore was in a position to have its candidate elected as the head of state. The Nawaz government nominated Muhammad Rafiq Tarar, a 68 year former Judge of the Supreme Court and a Senator as their presidential candidate. The nomination of Muhammad Rafiq Tarar was however criticized by the opposition parties and newspapers because the nominated President was from the Punjab province, which was also the home province of the Prime Minister. It was felt by many that since the Prime Minister was from Punjab, the President should be from a smaller province to prevent the possibility of a sense of deprivation among the smaller federating units and to avoid the concentration of the main government offices in one province. The election of the President was held on December 31, 1997.

The President was to be indirectly elected by the two houses of Parliament—the National Assembly and the Senate—and the four provincial governments. As Prime Minister Nawaz Sharif's ruling party Pakistan Muslim League dominated most of the six voting groups, Mr. Tarar was elected President comfortably by securing 374 out of 457 votes of the Electoral College. His rivals— PPP's Aftab Shahban Mirani and JUI's Maulana Muhammad Khan Shirani - ended up only with 31 and 22 votes, respectively. No one before President Rafiq Tarar received such overwhelming support from the elected representatives of the people of Pakistan.

Unlike the former presidents, Rafiq Tarar was a very unassuming, low profile and ceremonial President who remained loyal to the governments in power. He delivered in parliament only those speeches, which were provided to him by the government and also kept away from the press. Immediately after taking over, he declared that from now on the presidency would not work in conspiring against the elected government. He said he would confine himself to powers available to him under the Constitution and would not aspire for anything more. He honored his word and remained loyal to his political benefactors, the Sharif's even after their ouster on October 12, 1999. Making a departure from the precedent set by his predecessors, he never criticized any government policy.

After the overthrow of the Nawaz government, the military authorities retained Mr. Tarar as President, mainly to show to the outside world that since an elected President was in place and since the assemblies had not been dissolved, the new system could not be regarded as martial law. The President term was till December 31, 2002 but he was however removed by Chief Executive General Pervez Musharraf who him self took over the office of President of Pakistan on June 20, 2001.

Muhammad Rafiq Tarar was not a politician of standing nor had been a distinguished Judge. The office of President being a symbol of state should have gone to someone well acquainted with statesmanship. Despite this President Tarar was noted for his honesty, loyalty, devotion to justice and a firm personal religious faith. Coming from a relatively humble background, he was the first elected President to have made it to the top.

NAWAZ SHARIF BECOMES PRIME MINISTER
[1997]

As scheduled, elections were held in February 1997. Pakistan Muslim League won with an overwhelming majority with no strong opposition. The Muslim League was able to obtain a two-third majority in the National Assembly and Mian Nawaz Sharif was re-elected as Prime Minister. He obtained a vote of confidence from the National Assembly on February 18, 1997.

A number of very important constitutional changes were introduced during Nawaz Sharif's second term, which include the end of the Eighth Amendment, passing of the Thirteenth Amendment and the Ehtesab Act, 1997. Nawaz Sharif also faced a confrontation with the judiciary and the executive, which eventually brought about the resignation of President Leghari on December 2, 1997.

It was during the second term of Nawaz Sharif that Pakistan carried out its nuclear tests on May 28, 1998 in response to Indian detonation of its three nuclear devices. It had become imperative for Pakistan to carry out these nuclear tests in order to provide an effective defense and to deter Indian adventurism.

The Nawaz government proclaimed an emergency on May 28, 1998, on the day the nuclear tests were conducted. All fundamental rights were suspended and all the foreign currency accounts with banks in Pakistan were frozen. In August 1998, Nawaz regime introduced the Fifteenth Amendment on August 28, 1998. The bill generated heated debate throughout the country but was passed on October 9, 1998 by the members of the National Assembly. The bill however was not put before the Senate within 90 days as was required by the constitution. The bill was held back, as Nawaz Sharif did not have the required two-third majority in the Senate.

The Fifteenth Amendment was an effort by Nawaz Sharif to acquire more powers for himself. This soon brought him into serious confrontation with the leadership of the Armed forces. This confrontation led to the resignation of General Jehangir Karamat on October 7, 1998. General Pervez Musharraf replaced General Jehangir Karamat. The Kargil crisis in its aftermath led to tense relationship between Nawaz Sharif and the Armed forces. It was this tense relationship, which culminated in the removal of the Nawaz government by General Pervez Musharraf on October 12, 1999 thus bringing to an end the second term of Nawaz Sharif's government.

PAKISTAN: A NUCLEAR POWER
[MAY 28, 1998]

On May 28, 1998, Pakistan became a nuclear power when it successfully carried out six nuclear tests at Chaghi, in the province of Balochistan. This was in direct response to five nuclear explosions by India, just two weeks earlier.

Widely criticized by the international community, Pakistan maintains that its nuclear program is for self-defense, and to act as deterrence against nuclear India. A former Prime Minister of Pakistan, Zulfiqar Ali Bhutto, offered justification for Pakistan's nuclear program in 1965, when he said that if India were to produce a bomb, Pakistanis would eat grass to get one of their own. It has always been clear to Pakistan that a nuclear threat posed to its security can neither be met with conventional means of defense, nor by external security guarantees.

India had maintained a nuclear threat against Pakistan since it tested a nuclear device in May 1974. At that time Pakistan had no nuclear weapons. India maintained that its nuclear program was based on their requirement to have a minimum nuclear deterrent, and that it was not against any specific country.

After the tit-for-tat nuclear explosions, the United Nations Security Council unanimously passed a resolution urging India and Pakistan to halt their nuclear weapons programs. The United States and other Western states imposed economic sanctions against both the countries. The UN Secretary General, Kofi Annan, urged both the countries to sign the Comprehensive Test Ban Treaty (CTBT).

After the tests, both sides said that they had completed their series of nuclear testing and both announced a moratorium on future testing. Pakistan announced the moratorium on June 11, 1998 and offered to join in new peace talks with India. Pakistan has time and again proposed for a nuclear-weapon-free zone in South Asia. It has opted to be a signatory to the CTBT, provided India also opts for the same simultaneously.

PASSAGE TO INDIA: THE HAMOOD-UR-RAHMAN COMMISSION REPORT

The Hamood-ur-Rahman Commission was formed by Z. A, Bhutto in December, 1971, within a week after replacing General Yahya as the President of Pakistan. The Commission was headed by Justice Hamood-ur-Rahman, Chief Justice of the Supreme Court, to find the facts of the 1971 debacle and to determine the causes of the military defeat in Pakistan. The Commission after interviewing 213 persons including General Yahya, Z. A. Bhutto, Chief of the Pakistan Air Force, Chief of Navy, Senior Commanders, and political leaders completed its first report and submitted the same in July, 1972. The inquiry was reopened in 1974 to further look into the 1971 surrender of the Pakistan military in East Pakistan. The Commission again interviewed 73 bureaucrats and top military officers and submitted its supplementary report in November 1974. It is this supplementary report which is presumed to have been published by an Indian magazine.

Originally 12 copies of the report were and then destroyed. Only one copy was handed over to Z. A. Bhutto, which was taken back during the 1977 military take-over. The report was not made public.

Though the proceedings of the inquiry commission and its recommendation remained a classified document, but it has been presumed from various writings and memoirs of the military officers narrating their side of the story what the Hamood-ur-Rahman Inquiry Commission had to say. The report recommended public trials of the concerned officers responsible for the 1971 debacle.

The Hamood-ur-Rahman Commission report is a valuable document. The writings and Memoirs disclose that far apart from its inquiry into the events of the 1971 crises, it also makes thoughtful recommendations about the defense of the country as a whole.

Publicizing the report by the Indian media has not offered any surprise. The report has come out at a time when there is increasing international pressure on India to resolve the Kashmir dispute and when immense human rights violations are being reported by international organizations, such as Amnesty International, Asia Watch etc. with reference to role of Indian Security Forces in the Indian-held Kashmir. The effort is to dissuade world attention from its inhumane actions in Kashmir.

The Government of Pakistan should ascertain if the report was doctored. It is also being proposed to hold an inquiry to ascertain if the published report is the supplementary report. If it is then how did it made its passage to India?

SARDAR FAROOQ LEGHARI BECOMES PRESIDENT [1993]

As a result of the general elections in 1993, PPP came to power by forming an alliance with PML (J), some independent members and some small parties. After the formation of the governments at the center and in the provinces, the next step was the election of the president. Initially, a number of candidates filed their nomination papers. Later on, however there were only two candidates left in the field. The two candidates included the acting President Wasim Sajjad, a nominee of the PML (N), and Farooq Ahmed Leghari, a nominee of the PPP. As a result of the voting Leghari got 274 votes in his favour against 168 votes for Wasim Sajjad. On November 13, 1993, Sardar Farooq Legahri was appointed as the President of Pakistan for a term of five years.

Leghari began his term with a clean reputation, but this was soon to change with the Mehran Bank scandal and the inappropriate appointments made by him to the judiciary. In his first speech, Leghari had said that the Eighth Amendment would be removed but during the term of Benazir, no bill was ever presented to do away with this article of the constitution.

Differences appeared between Benazir and Legahri, which eventually resulted in the President using the Eighth Amendment for the dissolution of the National Assembly and the removal of Benazir. After dismissing the Benazir government Leghari helped Nawaz to come to power. However differences arose between Nawaz, Legahri and the judiciary.

As a result of the constitutional crisis Legahri resigned on December 2, 1997. His resignation brought to an end the high drama of conflict between the judiciary, the executive, and the legislature. His resignation cut short the normal term of his office of the president of five year by nearly one year.

THIRTEENTH AMENDMENT

The National Assembly unanimously adopted the Constitution Bill (13th Amendment) on April 1, 1997 by a two-thirds majority. The Thirteenth Amendment was put before the National Assembly on April 1 empowering the Prime Minister to repeal 58(2) b, give advise to the President for the appointment of three forces chiefs and JCSC Chairman and the Governors. In the proposed Amendment bill, clauses to restore the women parliamentarian seats and to convert the ordinance into the act of the parliament were also incorporated.

The Thirteenth Amendment was an effort to do away with the controversial Eighth Amendment and to deprive the President of several of his discretionary powers in order to restore the supremacy of the Parliament.

The infamous Amendment was inserted in the Constitution in 1985 by the party less parliament when General Zia ul Haq was the chief martial law administrator and President of Pakistan. Its most notorious provision, 58(2) b had empowered the President to sack the Prime Minister and the government and dissolve the National Assembly.

The provision has since been used by three successive Presidents since 1985 and four Prime Ministers along with their Cabinets and the National Assembly have been dismissed.

The Prime Minister Nawaz Sharif on announcing the Amendment said that the Amendment was introduced to revive the democratic concept as envisaged by the Quaid- e-Azam and Allama Iqbal.

The passing of the Thirteenth Amendment started a new era of democratic freedom and political stability. It was the first time in Pakistan's history that a complicated and sensitive constitutional issue was solved in an amicable way through consensus.

THE KARGIL OPERATION [1999]

One dispute that remains unresolved at the tables of the United Nations is the 52-year-old Kashmir dispute between India and Pakistan. This disputed State of Jammu and Kashmir has been a continuous flash point and the cause of two wars (1948 and 1965) between the two countries. The last few years, and particularly during the 1990s, the issue of Kashmir has been brought to the forefront of world agenda by the freedom struggle of Kashmiri fighters, fighting in the Kashmir. This freedom struggle against this brute Indian force, now in excess of 700,000 troops, demands the fulfillment of UN Resolutions and of Indian commitments to give them the opportunity to decide their political future through a fair and free plebiscite. This plebiscite to be held under UN auspices, is mandated by the UN Security Council Resolutions of August 13, 1948 and January 5,1949.

The freedom struggle gained further momentum in 1999 when the freedom fighters, in probably the most brilliant and courageous maneuver in modern military history, made high-altitude conquests, and captured a high ground of 140 kilometers stretch of 4,500 meters high mountain ridges near the strategic Indian-held garrison towns of Kargil and Drass. These towns lie on the only usable road between Srinagar, capital of Kashmir, and to the East. This threatened India's main supply route to its forces on the Chinese border.

The occupation by the Kashmiri freedom fighters came as a "Spring Surprise" to the Indian patrols. During the winter freeze the area is abandoned by Indian patrols and isolated from the rest of Kashmir. In the beginning of May 1999, when the Indian forces returned to the mountains, they were surprised to find around 600 Kashmiri freedom fighters, occupying a territory 5 km inside Kashmir. India alleged that these "militants" were sponsored by Pakistan, and that these militants crossed the provisional borderline, the "line of control", in an attempt to alter the de facto border by force. The Government of Pakistan stated that it was not involved in any way and clarified that it is only the moral, diplomatic and political support that the Government of Pakistan continues to extend to Kashmiri freedom fighters for their cause of self-determination. It further clarified that the heights near Kargil were occupied by indigenous Kashmiri freedom fighters. On May 26, 1999, India resorted to air strikes to drive out the freedom fighters. During this episode, two Indian aircrafts entered the territory of Pakistan, one of which was shot down.

The situation across the line of control became tense and several innocent civilians became the target of indiscriminate Indian shelling. The conflict posed a threat to the region of South Asia.

International community was concerned about the escalation of the conflict between the two newly declared nuclear powers, India and Pakistan. Talks, however, resumed between India and Pakistan in summers 1999 and efforts were made to resolve the crises. International intervention, most notably from the President of United States, Bill Clinton, persuaded Pakistan to use its influence on the freedom fighters to avert a full-scale war with India.

The freedom fighters vacated the captured territory by July-August, 1999.

2001—PRESENT

CHINESE PRIME MINISTER ZHU RONGJI VISITS PAKISTAN

Chinese Prime Minister Zhu Rongji arrived in Pakistan on 11th May, 2001 for a four-day visit. This was against the backdrop of the U.S spy-plane issue. He held a one-to-one meeting with the Chief Executive General Pervez Musharraf. The focus of their discussions was the current international, political and strategic scenario.

A number of economic agreements were signed between the two countries. China agreed to extend assistance worth over 1 billion dollars for various projects in Pakistan. The major projects include the Makran Coastal project, Gawader port, Sandak copper mine project and modernization of Pakistan Railways.

China's assistance in the above-mentioned projects is very crucial for the social uplift of the people of Balochistan and also has great strategic significance for the rest of Pakistan in general. China also agreed to provide $200 million credit for the modernization of Pakistan Railways. Credit was also to be provided for new equipment for the Pakistan Telecommunication Company Limited, for oil pipelines, and development of coal mines.

The visit of the Chinese Prime Minister boosted the friendly relations and bilateral cooperation established between the two countries. The visit also opened a new chapter in the history of trade and economic relations of the two nations.

AGRA SUMMIT

A historic summit meeting was held between Pakistan's President Pervez Musharraf and the Indian Prime Minister Atal Behari Vajpayee in Agra, from 14th to 16th of July, 2001. The summit started amid high hopes of resolving various disputes between the two countries including the decade old Kashmir issue. Both sides started the summit with optimism, President Musharraf used the phrases "cautious optimism", "flexibility" and "open mind" to describe his state of mind for the summit. The Indian President also promised to take "bold and innovative" measures and to discuss the "core issue" between the two countries.

Various rounds of one-to-one positive talks were held between President Musharraf and Prime Minister Vajpayee. On the first day, a 90-minute one-on-one session of talks was held between the two leaders. The Kashmir issue, cross-border terrorism, nuclear risk reduction, release of prisoners of war (PoWs) and commercial ties were the issues discussed in these talks. The talks went in the right direction and were declared by both the leaders as "positive, frank and constructive". Hopes were aroused that an agreement would be reached and a joint statement or declaration would be made at the end of the summit as the two leaders plunged into serious talks.

President Musharraf during his visit also held face-to-face meetings with the top Kashmiri leadership represented by the APHC. During his stay in India, he also visited his ancestral home, the Naharwali Haveli in the walled city. President Pervez Musharraf also visited the Taj Mahal, the 17th century architectural marvel. During the 40-minute visit, Musharraf and his wife Sehba sat on the "lovers platform"—a marble bench in front of the Taj Mahal, which is no stranger to national leaders and celebrities. Asking questions and pointing to various features of the white marble edifice, President Musharraf spent considerable time studying the intricate carvings on the walls of the Taj Mahal. The two day Agra summit between President Pervez Musharraf and Prime Minister Atal Behari Vajpayee however collapsed and no formal agreement could be reached as the two sides remained inflexible on the core issue of Kashmir, despite five long and arduous one-to-one rounds between the two leaders and hours of discussion between the two delegations. Despite the failure of the talks General Pervez Musharraf on his part to improve the atmosphere, joined Vajpayee to call on the two countries to bury their past. He also invited the Indian Prime Minister to visit Pakistan as he felt that the issues between Pakistan and India were much more complicated and could not be resolved in a short time.

Although the Agra summit ended in failure, but it was the first step in the right direction. The Agra Summit opened the path of dialogue between the two countries and it was hoped that in the future the two heads of the governments would pick up from the threads of understanding reached during discussions at Agra and would find a lasting solution to their long standing disputes.

SAARC SUMMIT [JANUARY, 2002]

The South Asian Association for Regional Cooperation (SAARC) was established in 1985 at the first SAARC Summit held in Dhaka, Bangladesh. SAARC comprises of seven countries of South Asia, i.e. Bangladesh, Bhutan, India, the Maldives, Nepal, Pakistan and Sri Lanka. SAARC is a manifestation of the determination of the peoples of South Asia to work together towards finding solutions to their common problems in a spirit of friendship, trust and understanding and to create an order based on mutual respect, equality and shared benefits. SAARC's main goal is to accelerate economic and social development in member states through joint action in certain agreed areas of cooperation.

The eleventh South Asian Association for Regional co-operation (SAARC) Summit was held at Kathmandu after a delay of three years. The summit was attended by Indian Prime Minister Atal Behari Vajpayee and Pakistani President Pervez Musharraf as well as by leader of Bangladesh, Sri Lanka, Nepal, Bhutan and the Maldives. The inaugural session was postponed due to President Musharraf's delayed arrival at Kathmandu due to bad weather. Musharraf during the visit called on Nepal's King Gayanendra Bir Bikram Shah and on Nepalese Prime Minister Sher Bahadur Deuba.

The world's attention was focused keenly on the SAARC Summit held at Kathmandu in Nepal to see if whether this summit would reduce the tension between Pakistan and India. The Indian government blamed Pakistan-based militants for the December 13 attack on Indian Parliament. India put a ban on over flights from Pakistan, which was reciprocated by Pakistan. India also cancelled the Samjhota Express and the Delhi-Lahore bus service. Terrorism and the India-Pakistan face-off overshadowed all other issues during the three-day SAARC session. The present session however did endorse conventions on human trafficking for prostitution in South Asian countries, and on child welfare, and on discussion in general of the issue of terrorism in the region and a possible South Asia free trade agreement. The SAARC leaders agreed to remove step by step tariff and non-tariff barriers to create a free trade area in South Asia and agreed to finalize the draft treaty by the end of 2002.

In the midst the thickening of war clouds on the Indo-Pak horizon, the SAARC summit offered a ray of hope and opportunity for peace. It was hoped that the summit would provide opportunity to the leaders of the two nuclear rivals—India and Pakistan—to meet and diffuse the current tension. No bilateral meeting however could take place between the two leaders except for two informal interactions. Indians called these meetings as mere courtesy calls.

But despite Indian view the SAARC Summit was very significant as it brought the two leaders together on one forum. President Musharraf very rightly used this forum to de-escalate tension with India by extending a hand of friendship to Prime Minister Atal Behari Vajpayee at the inaugural session of the summit.

The SAARC Summit led to some melting of ice between both the countries. The risk of immediate war between India and Pakistan was to some extent pushed back. There is now hope that the present tense situation between the two countries would improve and de-escalation would take place. On the economic and political front the Kathmandu SAARC Summit ended on an upbeat note with all the members agreeing to forge a multilateral cooperation in a wide range of fields to realize their full potential.

PERVEZ MUSHARRAF BECOMES PRESIDENT [JUNE, 2001]

Chief Executive General Pervez Musharraf took over the office of President of Pakistan on June 20th, 2001 under the Provincial Constitutional Order (PCO). He immediately dissolved the senate, national and provincial assemblies and sacked the chairman of the senate and speaker of the national assembly. President Musharraf however continued to hold the offices of the Chief Executive, Chief of the Army Staff, and Chiefs of the Staff Committee. General Musharraf took over the office by removing Rafiq Tarar who was due to complete his five-year tenure early next year. The General was sworn in by an oath taking ceremony held at the Darbar Hall of the President house in Islamabad. Chief Justice Irshad Hasan Khan administered the oath to the new President, who took more than 600 days to assume power since the army seized power in October 1999. Cabinet members, senior civil and military officers, diplomats, some family members attended the oath taking ceremony.

General Pervez Musharraf issued the Chief Executive Order No. 3 under which the Chief Executive was to hold office as President until his successors entered upon the office. President Pervez Musharraf however promised to hold parliamentary elections as mandated by the Supreme Court in 2002. The Chief Executive also issued an Order called the President's Succession Order 2001, which was to have effect with standing any thing in the constitution or any other law. It clearly defined as to who was to be the President, and in case of his absence from Pakistan or any other cause, was unable to perform his functions, the Chief Justice of Pakistan or, if the Chief Justice of Pakistan was also absent from Pakistan, the most senior Judge of the Supreme Court was to perform the functions of President until the President returns to Pakistan or resumes his functions.

President Musharraf after assuming the new office announced, "The change will augur well for the future of Pakistan". In a speech at the swearing -in-ceremony he said: "I think I have a role to play; I have a job to do here; I cannot and will not let this nation down." He gave three reasons for taking over as the President of Pakistan: constitutional, political, and economic considerations.

General Musharraf assumed the office of the President, just a few weeks before his travel to India for peace talks with the Indian Prime Minister Vajpayee on the 14th of July. The assumption of the office of President provided General Musharraf a chance to talk with the Indian Prime Minister as an equal in terms of civilian and constitutional authority.

TONY BLAIR VISITS PAKISTAN [JANUARY, 2002]

Tony Blair arrived in Pakistan on a two-day tour on January 7, 2001 during his South Asian tour. The British Prime Minister was not scheduled to visit Pakistan. In a bid to ease tension in the sub-continent he also included Islamabad in his itinerary that had earlier included India and Bangladesh. Mr. Blair, during the last leg of his visit to South Asia in Islamabad, laid emphasis at easing military tensions between India and Pakistan and on the initiation of dialogue process between Pakistan and India for resolving the Kashmir dispute and addressing the issue of terrorism. Both the leaders held one and a half-hour talks through their aides and later a twenty minute one-to-one meeting was held between both the leaders followed by a joint press conference at Aiwan-i-Sadar. Pakistan-India tension, Kashmir and other issues including Afghanistan and matters of bilateral cooperation between both Britain and Pakistan were discussed. Tony Blair called for rejection of terrorism and initiation of political dialogue between Islamabad and New Delhi for resolving of all outstanding issues including Kashmir. "I hope and believe that both countries in these difficult times would understand the need to defeat terrorism and to resolve difficult issues through dialogue", he said, adding that it was in the interest of not just the two countries and its people but also the whole region and the wider world.

With regard to Kashmir issue he said that the issue should be solved by dialogue and no matter how strongly people felt about the issue of Kashmir and although they were entitled to their struggle, there could be no place for acts of terrorism. He cited the example of Northern Ireland, which eventually realized that the issue could be resolved only through dialogue. Prime Minister Tony Blair condemned the terrorist acts and welcomed the actions taken by the Musharraf government against the terrorist organizations such as Jaish-i-Muhammad and Lashkar-e-Taiba.

The British Prime Minister was also informed of the comprehensive plan that had been hammered out by Musharraf's government to address the issue of terrorism which he planed to unveil in a televised address to the nation within the next few days. President Musharraf also assured the British Prime Minister Tony Blair that Pakistan was ready to take steps necessary for the de-escalation of tension with India.

Talks between President Musharraf and British Prime Minister Tony Blair were termed by both the sides as useful. Tony Blair's visit was significant in the sense that it was part of the international community's effort to stop the two nuclear countries from engaging into armed conflict. Tony Blair's visit in the backdrop of Indo-Pak tension hopefully would make things move in the right direction and would enhance the chances of initiation of a dialogue process between India and Pakistan in the future.

CHAPTER 4

FATHER OF PAKISTAN : MUHAMMAD ALI JINNAH

BRITISH RULE AND MUSLIM LEAGUE

The British ruled the Indian subcontinent for nearly 200 years—from 1756 to 1947. After the Indian Mutiny of 1857, the British government abolished the powers of the British East India Company, which had ruled the subcontinent on behalf of the British Crown, and took on direct powers of governance. Political reforms were initiated, allowing the formation of political parties. The Indian National Congress, representing the overwhelming majority of Hindus, was created in 1885. The Muslim League was formed in 1906 to represent and protect the position of the Muslim minority. When the British introduced constitutional reforms in 1909, the Muslims demanded and acquired separate electoral rolls. This guaranteed Muslims representation in the provincial as well as national legislatures until the dawn of independence in 1947.

The idea of a separate Muslim state in south Asia was raised in 1930 by the poet and philosopher Sir Muhammad Iqbal. He suggested that the north-western provinces of British India and the native state of Jammu and Kashmir should be joined into such a state. The name "Pakistan", which came to be used to describe this grouping, is thought to have originated as a compound abbreviation made up of letters of the names of the provinces involved, as follows: Punjab, Afghania (North West Frontier Province), Kashmir, Indus-Sindh, and Balochistan. An alternative explanation says the name means "Land of the Pure". By the end of the 1930s, Muhammad Ali Jinnah, leader of the Muslim League and considered the founding father of Pakistan, had also decided that the only way to preserve Indian Muslims from Hindu domination was to establish a separate Muslim state.

CREATION OF PAKISTAN

In 1940 the Muslim League formally endorsed the partitioning of British India and the creation of Pakistan as a separate Muslim state. During pre-independence talks in 1946, therefore, the British government found that the stand of the Muslim League on separation and that of the Congress on the territorial unity of India were irreconcilable. The British then decided on partition and on August 15, 1947, transferred power dividedly to India and Pakistan. The latter, however, came into existence in two parts: West Pakistan, as Pakistan stands today, and East Pakistan, now known as Bangladesh. The two were separated by 1,600 km (1,000 mi) of Indian territory.

PROBLEMS OF PARTITION

The division of the subcontinent caused tremendous dislocations of populations. Some 6 million Hindus and Sikhs moved from Pakistan into India, and about 8 million Muslims migrated from India to Pakistan. The demographic shift was accompanied by considerable inter-ethnic violence, including massacres, that reinforced bitterness between the two countries. This bitterness was further intensified by disputes over the accession of the former native states of India to either country. Nearly all of these 562 widely scattered polities had joined either India or Pakistan; the princes of Hyderabad, Junagadh, and Kashmir, however, had chosen to join neither country.

On August 15, 1947, these three states became technically independent, but when the Muslim ruler of Junagadh, with its predominantly Hindu population, joined Pakistan a month later, India annexed his territory. Hyderabad's Muslim prince, ruling over a mostly Hindu population, tried to postpone any decision indefinitely, but in September 1948 India also settled that issue by pre-emptive annexation. The Hindu ruler of Jammu and Kashmir, whose subjects were 85 per cent Muslim, decided to join India. Pakistan, however, questioned his right to do so, and a war broke out between India and Pakistan. Although the UN subsequently resolved that a plebiscite be held under UN auspices to determine the future of Kashmir, India continued to occupy about two thirds of the state and refused to hold a plebiscite. This deadlock, which still persists, has intensified suspicion and antagonism between the two countries.

PRE-REPUBLICAN ERA

The first independent government of Pakistan was headed by Prime Minister Liaquat Ali Khan. Muhammad Ali Jinnah was Governor-General until his death in 1948. From 1947 to 1951 the country functioned under unstable conditions. The government endeavoured to create a new national capital to replace Karachi, organize the bureaucracy and the armed forces, resettle refugees, and contend with provincial politicians who often defied its authority. Failing to offer any programme of economic and social reform, however, it did not capture the popular imagination. In his foreign policy Liaquat established friendly relations with the United States, when he visited President Harry S. Truman in 1950. Liaquat's United States visit injected bitterness into Pakistan's relations with the Union of Soviet Socialist Republics (USSR) because Liaquat had previously accepted an invitation from Moscow that never materialized in a visit. The United States gave no substantial aid to Pakistan until three years later, but the USSR, Pakistan's close neighbour, had been alienated.

After Liaquat was assassinated in 1951, Khwaja Nazimuddin, an East Pakistani who had been Governor-General since Jinnah's death, became Prime Minister. Unable to prevent the erosion of the Muslim League's popularity in East Pakistan, however, he was forced to yield to another East Pakistani, Muhammad Ali Bogra, in 1953. When the Muslim League was routed in East Pakistani elections in 1954, the Governor-General dissolved the constituent assembly as no longer representative. The new assembly that met in 1955 was no longer dominated by the Muslim League. Muhammad Ali Bogra was then replaced by Chaudhuri Muhammad Ali, a West Pakistani. At the same time, Iskander Mirza became the Governor-General of the country. The new constituent assembly enacted a bill, which became effective in October 1955, integrating the four West Pakistani provinces into one political and administrative unit. The assembly also produced a new constitution, which was adopted on March 2, 1956. It declared Pakistan an Islamic republic. Mirza was elected Provisional President.

CABINET SHIFTS

The new constitution notwithstanding, political instability continued because no stable majority party emerged in the National Assembly. Prime Minister Ali remained in office only until September 1956, when he was succeeded by Huseyn Shaheed Suhrawardy, leader of the Awami League of East Pakistan. His tenure lasted for slightly more than a year. When President Mirza discovered that Suhrawardy was planning an alliance between East and West Pakistani political forces by supporting the presidential aspirations of Firoz Khan Noon, leader of the Republican Party, he forced the prime minister to resign.

The succeeding coalition government, headed by Ismail Ibrahim Chundrigar, lasted only two months before it was replaced by a Republican Party Cabinet under Noon. President Mirza, however, found that his influence among the Republicans was diminishing and that the new prime minister had come to an understanding with Suhrawardy. Against such a coalition Mirza had no chance of being re-elected president. He proclaimed martial law on October 7, 1958, dismissed Noon's government, and dissolved the national assembly. The president was supported by General Muhammad Ayub Khan, Commander-in-Chief of the armed forces, who was named chief martial law administrator. Twenty days later Ayub forced the president to resign and assumed the presidency himself.

AYUB YEARS

Ayub ruled Pakistan almost absolutely for more than ten years, and his regime made some notable achievements, although it did not eliminate the basic problems of Pakistani society. A land reforms commission appointed by Ayub distributed some 900,000 hectares (2.2 million acres) of land among 150,000 tenants. The reforms, however, did not erase feudal relationships in the countryside; about 6,000 landlords still retained an area three times larger than that given to the 150,000 tenants. During Ayub's regime developmental funds to East Pakistan increased more than threefold. This had a noticeable effect on the economy of the eastern part, but the disparity between the two sectors of Pakistan was not eliminated.

Perhaps the most pervasive of Ayub's changes was his system of Basic Democracies. It created 80,000 basic democrats, or union councillors, who were leaders of rural or urban areas around the country. They constituted the electoral college for presidential elections and for elections to the national and provincial legislatures created under the constitution promulgated by Ayub in 1962. The Basic Democratic System had four tiers of government from the national to the local level. Each tier was assigned certain responsibilities in administering the rural and urban areas, such as maintenance of primary schools, public roads, and bridges. Ayub also promulgated an Islamic marriage and family laws ordinance in 1961, imposing restrictions on polygamy and divorce, and reinforcing the inheritance rights of women and minors. For a long time Ayub maintained cordial relations with the United States, stimulating substantial economic and military aid to Pakistan.

This relationship, however, deteriorated in 1965, when another war with India over Kashmir broke out. The United States then suspended military and economic aid to both countries, thus denying Pakistan badly needed weapons. The USSR then intervened to mediate the conflict, inviting Ayub and Prime Minister Lal Bahadur Shastri of India to Tashkent. By the terms of the so-called Tashkent Agreement of January 1966, the two countries withdrew their forces to pre-war positions and restored diplomatic, economic, and trade relations. Exchange programmes were initiated, and the flow of capital goods to Pakistan increased greatly. The Tashkent Agreement and the Kashmir war, however, generated frustration among the people of Pakistan and resentment against President Ayub. Foreign Minister Zulfikar Ali Bhutto resigned his position and agitated against Ayub's dictatorship and the "loss" of Kashmir. In March 1969 Ayub resigned. Instead of transferring power to the speaker of the National Assembly, as the constitution dictated, he handed it over to the commander-in-chief of the army, General Agha Muhammad Yahya Khan. Yahya became President and declared martial law.

FALL OF DHAKA

In an attempt to make his regime more acceptable, Yahya dismissed almost 300 senior civil servants and identified 30 families that were said to control about half of Pakistan's gross national product. To curb their power Yahya in 1970 issued an ordinance against monopolies and restrictive trade practices. He also made commitments to transfer power to civilian authorities, but in the process of making this shift, his intended reforms broke down. The greatest challenge to Pakistan's unity, however, was presented by East Pakistan, led by Sheikh Mujibur Rahman, leader of the Awami League, who insisted on a federation under which East Pakistan would be virtually independent. He envisaged a federal government that would deal with defence and foreign affairs only; even the currencies would be different, although freely convertible. His programme had great emotional appeal for East Pakistanis. In the election of December 1970 called by Yahya, Sheikh Mujib– as Mujibur Rahman was generally called– won by a landslide in East Pakistan, capturing a clear majority in the National Assembly. The Pakistan People's Party (PPP) formed by Bhutto in 1967 emerged as the largest party in West Pakistan.

Suspecting Sheikh Mujib of secessionist politics, Yahya in March 1971 postponed indefinitely the convening of the National Assembly. Mujib in return accused Yahya of collusion with Bhutto and established a virtually independent government in East Pakistan. Yahya opened negotiations with Mujib in Dhaka in mid-March, but the effort soon failed. Mujib was arrested and brought to West Pakistan to be tried for treason. Meanwhile Pakistan's army went into action against Mujib's civilian followers, who demanded freedom and independence for East Pakistan, or Bangladesh ("Bengali Nation") as it was to be called. There were a great many casualties during the ensuing military operations in East Pakistan, during which the Pakistani army attacked the poorly armed population. India claimed that nearly 10 million Bengali refugees crossed its borders and stories of West-Pakistani atrocities abounded. The Awami league took refuge in Calcutta and established a government-in-exile. India finally intervened on December 3, 1971, and the Pakistani army surrendered 13 days later.

On December 20 Yahya relinquished power to Bhutto, and in January 1972 the independent state of Bangladesh came into existence. When the Commonwealth of Nations admitted Bangladesh later that year, Pakistan withdrew from membership, not to return until 1989. However, the Bhutto government gave diplomatic recognition to Bangladesh in 1974.

BHUTTO GOVERNMENT

Under Bhutto's leadership a diminished Pakistan began to rearrange its national life. Bhutto nationalized basic industries, insurance companies, domestically owned banks, and schools and colleges. He also instituted modest land reforms that benefited tenants and middle-class farmers. He removed the armed forces from the process of decision-making, but to placate the generals he allocated about 6 per cent of the gross national product to defence. In 1973 the National Assembly adopted the country's fifth constitution. Bhutto became Prime Minister, and Fazal Elahi Chaudhry replaced him as President.

Although discontented, the military remained silent for some time. Bhutto's nationalization programme and land reforms further earned him the enmity of the entrepreneurial and capitalist class, while religious leaders saw in his socialism an enemy of Islam. His decisive flaw, however, was his inability to deal constructively with the opposition. His rule grew heavy-handed. In general elections in March 1977 nine opposition parties united in the Pakistan National Alliance (PNA) to run against Bhutto's PPP. Losing in three of the four provinces, the PNA alleged that Bhutto had rigged the vote. It boycotted the provincial elections a few days later and organized demonstrations throughout the country that lasted for six weeks.

ZIA REGIME

When the situation seemed to be deadlocked, the army Chief of Staff, General Muhammad Zia Ul-Haq, staged a coup on July 5, 1977, and imposed another military regime. Bhutto was tried for political murder and found guilty; he was hanged on April 4, 1979. Zia formally assumed the presidency in 1978 and established Shari'ah (Islamic law) as the law of the land. The constitution of 1973 was initially amended, then suspended in 1979, and benches were constituted at the courts to exercise Islamic judicial review. Interest-free banking was initiated, and maximum penalties were provided for adultery, defamation, theft, and the consumption of alcohol.

On March 24, 1981, Zia issued a provisional constitutional order, operative until the lifting of martial law. It envisaged the appointment of two vice-presidents and allowed political parties that had been approved by the election commission before September 30, 1979, to function. All other parties, including the PPP, now led by Bhutto's widow and by his daughter, Benazir, were dissolved, and by international relief agencies. In September 1981 Zia accepted a six-year economic and military aid package (worth US$3.2 billion) from the United States. After a referendum in December 1984 endorsed Zia's Islamic-law policies and the extension of his presidency until 1990, Zia permitted elections for parliament in February 1985. A civilian Cabinet took office in April, and martial law ended in December. Zia, however, was dissatisfied and, in May 1988, he dissolved the government and ordered new elections. Three months later he was killed in an aeroplane crash, and a caretaker military regime took power.

Benazir Bhutto A civil servant, Ghulam Ishaq Khan, was appointed President, and Benazir Bhutto became Prime Minister after the PPP won the general elections held in November 1988. She was the first female political leader of a modern Islamic state. In August 1990 President Ishaq Khan dismissed her government, charging misconduct, and declared a state of emergency. Bhutto and the PPP lost the October elections after she was arrested for corruption and abuse of power. The new prime minister, Nawaz Sharif, head of the Islamic Democratic Alliance, continued the programme of privatizing state enterprises and encouraging foreign investment begun in the 1980s. He also promised to bring the country back to Islamic law and to ease continuing tensions with India over Kashmir. The charges against Bhutto were resolved, and she returned to lead the PPP.

In April 1993 Ishaq Khan once again used his presidential power, this time to dismiss Sharif and to dissolve parliament. However, Sharif appealed to the Constitutional Court of Pakistan, which stated that Khan's actions were unconstitutional and reinstated Sharif as Prime Minister. Sharif and Khan subsequently became embroiled in a power struggle that paralysed the Pakistani government. In an agreement designed to end the stalemate, Sharif and Khan resigned together in July 1993, and elections were held in October of that year. The PPP won and Bhutto was again named Prime Minister. Farooq Ahmad Khan Leghari became the new president in November 1993.

NUCLEAR PROLIFERATION

With Bhutto in office, relations between India and Pakistan became more tense. Bhutto openly supported the Muslim rebels in Indian-held Jammu and Kashmir, who were involved in sporadic fighting against the Indian army. She also announced that Pakistan would continue with its nuclear weapons development programme, raising concerns that a nuclear arms race could start between Pakistan and India, which is believed to have had nuclear weapons since the 1970s. In February 1992, when the Pakistani government admitted to having nuclear capability, it claimed that its nuclear weapons programme had been stopped at the level achieved in 1989—that is, with an actual nuclear device far from completion. In 1996 the United States returned to a policy of delaying delivery of military equipment to Pakistan owing to China having supplied nuclear-weapons-related materials in 1995. Relations between Pakistan and India deteriorated in early 1996, when each country accused the other of conducting nuclear tests, though the first officially confirmed tests did not take place for another two years.

Pakistan has generally been considered a moderate Islamic state; Islamic fundamentalists won only nine National Assembly seats in the 1993 elections; however, during the 1990s Islamic activists seemed to be gaining in influence. There were persistent reports of discrimination against religious minorities. The incidents increased after 1991 when the National Assembly ruled that the criminal code should conform to Islamic law and the death sentence was made mandatory for a blasphemy conviction.

In February 1995 the position of religious minorities was highlighted by the conviction and sentencing to death of two Christians, one aged 14, for the alleged writing of blasphemous remarks on a mosque wall in a village in Punjab province. The imposition of the death sentence on a child and questions surrounding the evidence provoked an outcry within Pakistan, as well as abroad. The High Court at the end of the month overturned the conviction, saying there was no evidence to sustain it; earlier the original complainant, an Imam (Muslim prayer leader) in the village, had withdrawn his charges. The government, which had supported the changes in the law, appeared caught in a dilemma. Benazir Bhutto described herself as "shocked" by the sentences but declined to intervene. However, following the High Court ruling she said there would be a review of the law.

In June 1995 violence flared in Karachi over Bhutto's alleged condemnation of the ethnically based Mohajor Qaumi Movement, leaving over 290 people dead; all-party talks with the movement were convened immediately afterwards, but did not bring the hoped-for ceasefire in the city. In October a number of army officers were arrested over an attempted Islamic fundamentalist coup. Tension with India following a mysterious rocket strike on a mosque in Pok, bordering Indian-controlled Kashmir, escalated into heavy fighting along the Kashmir ceasefire line in January 1996. In April 1996 the former Pakistan cricket captain Imran Khan formed an anti-government political group, the Justice Movement, while bombings and political violence took place in Lahore and elsewhere.

NAWAZ GOVERNMENT AND RECENT DEVELOPMENTS

In November 1996 Bhutto's government was for the second time dismissed by the president under renewed charges of corruption and misrule. The National Assembly was dissolved for the third time since civilian rule replaced military rule. Following Bhutto's petitioning of the Supreme Court to reinstate her, the court voted by a 6-1 majority to reject her appeal. On February 3, 1997, elections were held in order to replace the Bhutto government. A low turnout (around 30 per cent), mainly because of widespread disgust over politics, nevertheless produced a vast majority for former prime minister Sharif. The PML faction led by Sharif won 130 out of 217 seats, with Bhutto's PPP winning only 20 seats. Despite his large majority and his election having been welcomed by the business community, Sharif has to contend with a president vying for greater influence, indicated in his setting-up of a special council that gives the military an official governmental role and which reflects the military's perennial influence in the country's political process. Sharif also faces widespread economic problems and rising crime and violence.

Passed a constitutional amendment removing the president's power to dissolve the assembly. This controversial ability had been used to dismiss three elected governments since 1985. The rupee was devalued in October by 8.5 per cent, an action followed (later that month) by the announcement a three-year financing package from the IMF amounting to US$1,558 million; a World Bank loan of US$250 million was announced in December. Following a constitutional crisis, during which Sharif had accused President Leghari and the chief justice of trying to undermine his government, Leghari unexpectedly resigned his position in December; the chief justice was dismissed from his post. Sharif's position was further enhanced when his nominee for the presidential office, Muhammad Rafiq Tarar, was successfully elected.

A year after enquiries into corruption allegations against the Bhutto family begun, 12 corruption cases were filed with Pakistan's accountability commission in January 1998. Although the family's Swiss bank accounts had been frozen in September, courts in the United Kingdom questioned the legality of the request for release of all documents held in the United Kingdom pertaining to the Bhutto's finances and dealings. Talks with India resumed in January regarding the possibility of a resolution to the Kashmir situation. A complementary working party has been established, which also covers the issue of the disputed Himalayan territory of Siachen. In April Pakistan openly tested a surface-to-surface missile with a range of 1,500 km (930 mi). Following five underground nuclear tests by India in May 1998, Pakistan responded within days with six nuclear tests. The events further heightened tensions between the two countries.

CHAPTER 5

MORE ABOUT PAKISTAN

Pakistan, the Indus land, is the child of the Indus in the same way as Egypt is the gift of Nile. The Indus has provided unity, fertility. Communication, direction and the entire landscape to the country. Its location marks it as a great divide as well as a link between Central Asia and South Asia. But the historical movements of the people from Central Asia and South Asia have given to it a character of its own and have established closer relation between the people of Pakistan and those of Central Asia in the field of Culture, Language, literature, food, dress, furniture and folklore. However, it is the Arabian Sea that has opened the doors for journey beyond to the Arabian world through the Gulf and Red Sea right into the ancient Civilization of Mesopotamia and Egypt. It is this Sea voyage that gave to the Indus Land its earliest name of Meluhha because the Indus people were characterized as Malahha (Sailor) in the Babylonian records. It is for this reason that the oldest Civilization of this land, called Indus Civilization, had unbreakable bonds of Cultural and trade link with the Gulf States of Dubai, Abu Dabi, Sharja, Qatter, Bahrain and right from Oman to Kuwait. While a Meluhhan village sprang up in ancient Mesopotamia (Modern Iraq), the Indus Seals, painted Pottery, Lapislazuli and many other items were exchanged for Copper, tin and several other objects from Oman and Gulf States. It is to facilitate this trade that the Indus writing was evolved in the same Proto-symbolic style as the contemporary cuneiform writing of Mesopotamia. Much later in history it is the pursuit of this seaward trade that introduced Islam from Arabia in to Pakistan. The twin foundations of cultural link have helped build the stable edifice of Islamic Civilization in this Country. All these cultural developments are write large in the personality of the people of Pakistan.

As in many other Countries of the world, man in Pakistan began with the technology of working on old stone by using quartzite and flint found in Rohri hills and stone pebbles found in the Soan Valley. The oldest stone tool in the world, going back to 2.2 million years old, has been found at Rabat, about fifteen miles away from Rawalpindi, thus breaking the African record. The largest hand Axe has also been found in the Soan Valley. Although man is still hiding in some corner, the Soan pebble stone age Culture show a link with the Hissar Culture in Central Asia. Later about fifty thousand B.C. at Sangho Cave in Mardan District man improved his technology for working on Quartz in order to chase the animal in closed Valleys. Still later he worked on micro quartz and chert or flint and produced arrows, knives. Scrapers and blades and hunted the feeling deer and ibexes with bow and arrow. Such an hunting scene is well illustrated on several rock carvings, particularly near Chilas in the Northern Areas of Pakistan along the Karakorum Highway - a style of rock art so well known in the trans-Pamir region of Tajikistan and Kirghizstan. However, the first settled life began in the eight millennium B.C. when the first village was found at Mehergarh in the Sibi Districts of Baluchistan comparable with the earliest villages of Jericho in Palestine and Jarmo in Iraq. Here their mud houses have been excavated and agricultural land known for the Cultivation of Maize and Wheat. Man began to live together in settled social life and used polished stone tools, made pots and pans, beads and other ornaments. His taste for decoration developed and he began to paint his vessels, jars, bowls, drinking glasses, dishes and plates. It was now that he discovered the advantage of using metals for his tools and other objects of daily use. For the first time in seventh millennium B.C. he learnt to use bronze. From the first revolution in his Social, Cultural and Economic life. He established trade relation with the people of Turkamenistan, Uzbekistan, Iran and other Arab world.

He not only specialized in painting different designs on pottery, made varieties of pots and used Cotton and Wool but also made terra-cotta figurines and imported precious stones from

Afghanistan and Central Asia. This early bronze age Culture spread out in the country side of Sindh, Baluchistan, Punjab and North West Frontier Province.

And this early beginning led to the concentration of population into small towns. Such as Kot Digi in Sindh and Rehman Dheri in Dera Ismail Khan District. It is this social and Cultural change that led to the rise of the famous cities of Mohenjodaro and Harappa, the largest concentration of population including artisans, craftsman, businessmen and rulers. This culminated in the peak of the Indus Civilization, which was primarily based on intensive irrigated land agriculture and overseas trade and contact with Iran, Gulf States, Mesopotamia and Egypt. Dams were built for storing river water, land was Cultivated by means of bullock-harnessed plough - a system that still prevails in Pakistan, granaries for food storage were built, furnace were used for controlling temperature for making red pottery and various kinds of ornaments, beads of carnelian, agate and terra-cotta were pierced through, and above all they traded their finished goods with Central Asia and Arab world. It is these trade divided that enriched the urban populace who developed a new sense of moral honesty, discipline and cleanliness, and above all a social stratification in which the priests and the mercantile class dominated the society. The picture of high civilization can be gathered only by looking at the city of Mohenjodaro, the first planned city in the world, in which streets are aligned straight, parallels to each other, with a cross streets cutting at right angles. It is through these wide streets that wheeled carriages, drawn by bulls or asses, moved about, carrying well-adorned persons seated on them, appreciating the closely aligned houses, made of pucca bricks, all running straight along the streets. And then through the middle of the streets ran stone dressed drains covered with stone slabs - a practice of keeping the streets clean from polluted water, for the first time seen in the world.

The Indus Civilization is the first literate Civilization of the subcontinent. The cities were centers of art and craft. Where the artisan produced several kinds of goods that were exported to other countries. Sailing boats sailed out from Mohenjodaro and anchored in the port of the Gulf, which region was perhaps known as Dilmin. However, it was the city administration that managed the urban life in strict discipline and controlled the trade in their hands. The discipline is derived from the strict practice of meditation (yoga) that was practiced by the elite of the city, who appear to have trimmed their beard and hair combed and tied with golden fillets. The body was covered with a shawl bearing trefoil designs on them. Such a noble man with a sharp nose and long wish eyes shows a contrast with a bronze figurine of a dancing and singing girl, plying music with her fully bang led hand, as we find today with the Cholistan ladies having bangled hands. Obviously there were distinctive ethnic groups of people in Mohenjodaro but the dominant class of rulers and merchants appear to be distinctive from the rest of the population. It is these literate people who interacted with the Arabian people and continued to maintain strict discipline in the society. It is they who developed astronomy, mathematics, and science in the country along with numerical symbols, weights and measures but they thoroughly intermixed in the society and also believed in the local cult of tree and tree deities and animal totems. The most prominent animals as attested in the seals are bull, buffalo, elephant, tiger, rhinoceros, alligator and deer and ibexs. However, Mesopotamian influences are seen in the figures of Gilgamash, Enkidu, joint statue of the bull and man and other animals with several heads and bodies. However, the unique local concept is that of highly meditative man, seated in his heels, with three or four heads, and combining in himself the power to control the animals probably with a crown of horns or some times a tree overhead. It is this supreme deity, depicted on Seals, that draws the serpent worshippers and overpowers the animals. A part from these there was no concept of nature worship as we find in the Vedas of the Aryans. The ritual consisted of offerings through the intermediary of mythological composite animals to the tree deity. These dose not appear to have been any concept of animals sacrifice nor worship of any idol or idols. The Indus civilization lasted for nearly five hundred years and flourished up to 1750 B.C. when we notice the movements of nomadic tribes in Central Asia. As a result the Asian trade system was greatly disturbed. Consequently the trade and industry of the Indus people greatly suffered with the result that led to the end of the Civilization. The cities vanished, the noble lost their position. The writing finished. The common people met with the influx of new horse-riding pastoralists who hardly understood the system of irrigated agriculture and hence the value of dams. Such nomadic tribes are known from the large number of graves and their village settlements all over Swat, Dir and Bajaur right up to Taxila. In the Northern Areas of Pakistan different group of such tribes, known as Dardic people are known from their graves. The tribes of the plains are recognized as different groups of the Aryans from the hilly tribes of the North the ancestors of the Kalash people and those who now speak Shina, Burushaski and other Kohistani languages. They had nothing to do with the cities as we find them building small villages nor did they know irrigation. In fact they believed in nature gods, one of them Indra destroyed the dams and spelled disaster on the local Dasyus who differed from them in color, creed and language. These Aryans conquerors developed there own religion of the Vedas, practiced animal sacrifice and gradually built up tribal kingdoms all over the Indus Valley. The most prominent being that of Gandhara with capitals at Pushkalavati (modern Charsadda) and Taxila, the last having been the older capital of Takshaka, the king of serpent worshippers. Taksha-sila (a Sanskrit word, literally translated in to Persian Mari-Qila) survive in modern Margala. It become the strong hold of the Aryans, whose great epic book Mahabarata was for the first time recited here. Since that time Takshka-sila or Taxila lying on the western side of Margala remained the capital of the Indus land, which was called Sapta-Sindhu (the land of seven rivers) by the Aryans. It because of this central location, en routs from Central to South Asia that the new capital of Pakistan has been established at Islamabad on the eastern side of Margala hill, thus giving a historical link from the most ancient to modern time and new significance to Pakistan as a link between Central and South Asia.

The city of Taxila began to grow from 6th century B.C. onward when Achaemenian kings by name Cyrus and Darius joined this city by road and postal services with their own capital at Persepolis in Iran. Here one can see the Aryan village at Hatial mound lying above the pre-Aryan bronze age capital of Takshakas (Serpent worshippers). One can also visit the Achaemenian city at Bhir mound, where old bazars and royal palace, with long covered drain, have been discovered. Land route trade with Iran and the west once again started with the issue of coin currency for the first time in the Indus land. But the most important was the great use of iron technology, which produced several kind of iron tools, weapons and other objects of daily use as known as from the excavations at Taxila. Above all a new writing known as Kharoshti was developed here. At the same time the oldest University of the world was founded at Taxila, where taught the great grammarian Panini, born at the modem village of Lahur in Sawabi district of the Frontier Province. It is the basis of this grammar that modem linguistics has been developed. It is in this University that Chandragupta Maurya got his education, who later founded the first subcontinental empire in South Asia. He developed the Mauryan city at Bhir mound in Taxila, where ruled his grandson, Ashoka, twice as governor. He introduced Buddhism in Gandhara and built the first Buddhist monastery, called Dharmajika Vihara, at Taxila. Ashoka has left behind his Rock Edicts at two palaces, one at Mansehra and another at Shahbazgari, written in Kharoshti.

Long before the rise of Chandragupta Maurya the Achaemenian empire, that had extended from Pakistan to Greece and Egypt, had collapsed under the onslaught of Alexander of Macedonia. He first finished with the Greek city states, united the Greeks, and dashed forward to annex the Achaemenian empire and hence proceeded to all those places where the Achaemenian had ruled. In this march they come to Taxila in 326 B.C. where he was welcomed by the local king Ambhi in his palace at Bhir mound. It is here as well as at Bhira in Jhelam district that Alexander's remains can be seen. However, he fought the greatest battle on the bank of the Jhelam river opposite the present village of Jalalpur Sharif against Porus, the head of the heroic Puru tribe, whose descendents still supply military personal to the Pakistan army. Alexander's battle place was at Mong, where he founded a new city, called Nikea, the city of victory. The other city which he founded was called Bucaphela after the name of his horse that died here. However, the most captivating site is at Jalalpur Shaif, laying on the bank of river let Gandaria, perhaps Sikanaria, where Alexander's monument has now been built on the spot where he stopped for about two months before launching his attack on Porus.

The Achaemenian and Alexander's contacts with Pakistan are very important from the point of view of educational and

Cultural history. The Achaemenian brought the learning and science of Mesopotamia Civilization that enriched the University of Taxila. They also introduced their administrative system here, on the basis of which the famous book on political science, called Arthasastra was written in Sanskrit language in Taxila by Kautilya, known as Chanakya, the teacher of Chandragupta Maurya. It is this book that was adapted for the administrative of the Mauryan empire. On the basis of Achaemenian currency the Mauryan punch marked coins. So well known in Taxila, were produced. It is their Aramic writing, used by Achaemenian clerks, that led to the development of Kharoshti in Pakistan and trade with the sematic world that created the Brahmi writing in India. On the other hand Alexander brought Greek knowledge and science to Taxila and introduced Greek type of coin currency. 'It is Taxila that philosophers and men of learning of the two countries met and developed science, mathematics and astronomy. Above all Alexander left behind large number of Greeks in Central Asia, who founded the Bactrian Greek kingdom in mid-third century B.C. it is the descendants of these Bactrian Greeks who later advanced in to Pakistan and built up the Greek kingdom here and built up their own city at Sirkap in Taxila. This is the second well planned city in Pakistan. The Greeks introduced their language, art and religion in the country of Gandhara, where ruled thirteen Greek kings and queens. Their language lasted more than five hundred years and their art and religion and considerable influence on the flourish of Gandhara Civilization.

This civilization was the result of interaction of several peoples who followed the Greeks, the Scythians, the Parthians and Kushans who came one the other from Central Asia along the Silk Road and integrated them selves into the local society. It is under their patronage that Buddhism evolved here into its new Mahayana form and this become the religion of the contemporary people in Pakistan. Under their encouragement the Buddhist monks moved along the Silk Road freely and carried this religion to central Asia, China, Korea and Japan. It is again the trade along the silk road that was particularly controlled by the Kushana emperors, who built a mighty empire with Peshawar as their Capital, the boundaries of which extended from the Aral Sea to the Arabian Sea and from Afghanistan to the Bay of Bengal. It is the dividends of trade that enriched Pakistan and led to the development of Gandhara Art, which mirrors the social, religious and common man's life of the time. It is an art that was blend of the Greek classical and local arts, which created the finest statues of Buddha and Buddhisattvas that today decorate the museums all over the world. At the same time the sculpture depict the whole life of the Buddha in a manner that is unsurpassed. Many Greek themes, their gods, typical toilet trays, Greek life scenes showing musicians, drinking bouts and love making are presented in there natural fashion. The Kushanas period was the golden age of Pakistan as the Silk Road trade brought unparalleled prosperity to the people of the country.

The luxury items produced in the country enrich the museum at Taxila at that show the Cultural and trends of life of the time. Gandhara art is the high water achievement of the people of Pakistan. Mahayana Buddhism was the inspiring ideal of the time and the Buddhist Stupas and monasteries survive in every nook and corner of the hills. It was this time that the country was known as Kushana-shahar, the land of the Kushanas, to which came the Romanships to carry the luxury goods in exchange for Roman Siler and Gold, that were used by the Kushana emperors and as a result their gold currency flooded the country and all along the Silk road. It is these Kushana kings who have gifted the national dress of shalwar and kamiz and sherwani to Pakistan. Their dress and decorations are deeply imprinted on the Indus land, that is now Pakistan.

Then came from Central Asia the Huns and the Turks who gave to Pakistan the present ethnic, their Culture, Food and Adab. The Jats, Gakkhars, Janjuas (Jouanjouan of the Chinese) and Gujars all trekked into Pakistan and made their home here. The Rajput rose and founded the feudal system in Punjab and Sindh in the same way the Pashtuns, who borrowed the surname of Gul and later the title of Khan from the Mongols, their Sardari system in Baluchistan, and slowly developed the *wadera* practice in the Indus delta region of Sindh. This feudal arrangements, which was the result of confederated tribes of the Huns, led to new administrative system in the country and created a new form of land management that has lasted until today. The tribes have fused into the agricultural society but their brotherhoods have survived and they have given a permanent character to Pakistan.

In the early eight Century A.D. the Arabs brought Islam in Sindh and Multan built up the kingdom of Al-Mansura in Sindh. At the same time their east ward Sea trade introduced porcelain and called on were from China and popularized glass were from Iran Syrianew materials that can be seen in the excavations at Bambhor in Sindh. With the Muslims Turks came the Sufis and Darveshas from Central Asia. Iran and Afghanistan and they spread Islam all over the country. It is Sultan Muhamud of Ghazni who made Lahore the city of Data Saheb as his second capital. However, the city of Multan become famous as the city of Saints although it lay en route the camel caravan that carried on trade between Pakistan and Central Asia right up to Baku in Azerbaijan. It is these cities that the famous Muslims monuments of old are to be seen. As a result of the Saintly activity Pakistan become a land of Islamic Civilization. In several villages and cities we now find the Dargah of these Muslims Saints. While Shaahbaz Kalandar is a well known in Sindh, Baba Farid Shakarganj presides over Pak Pattan in Punjab, Buner Baba rules over the Frontier region, and Syed Ali Hamdani is the real Sufi Saint in Kashmir. The capital city of Islamabad enshrines the well known Golra Sharif and Barri Imam. It is in these Saints who influenced the development of Sufi literature in all the languages of Pakistan and their monumental tombs that attract the people from all the country. In the old city of Thatta at Makli hill several tombs and Mausolea are spread over the place that surpass in the beauty of stone carving but much more than this they evidence the historical evolution of architecture from 12th century A.D. to the Mughal time.

This was a period of great change in the historical integration of the people in Pakistan when the country was brought closer to Central Asia and the Arab world. The mixing of several tribes from both these regions transformed the ethnic complex of the country. Just as in the period of Kushanas of Mahayana type rose here and the Buddhist monks out from this land along the Silk road to carry the massage of the Buddha, now it was the Arabs and the Muslims Saints from Central Asia who came in the reverse direction and flocked in the prosperous land of Pakistan. New trade route were opened in the reverse direction from those countries into the Indus land. From the Huns to the Turks the age of cavalry dominated the life scene. Many Rock carvings in Central Punjab show men riding, even standing on horse back and brandishing their swords and shooting arrows. Hence forward Polo game become common and sword dance was common, as seen in the Rock carving near Chilas. The foundation of Muslims state was firmly laid, in which the dominate position first occupied by the Arabs in Sindh and Multan and later by the Gaznavid and Ghorid Sultans who made the Indus country as their spring board from the onward conquest of India. A beautiful monument in memory of sultan Ghori can be seen at Suhawa on the National Highway. It was therefore in the fitness of things that the first missile made in Pakistan was named after Ghori. Several Muslims kingdoms grew up in this country. Beginning from north we find the Trakhan ruling dynasty, who came from trans-pamir region here and become supreme in the Gilgit area. The descendent of Shah Mir founded the Muslims Sultanate in Kashmir maintained its independents until the time of the Mughal emperor Akbar. The Pushtun tribes made their movements and asserted their independence in the land watered by the western branch of the Indus River. The Langhas and later the Arghuns become the Master of Multan. The Sama ruling dynasty started a new era of Cultural development and prosperity in Sindh. The Baluchis in concert with Brahuis leapt forward not only to build their kingdom in Baluchistan but also migrated eastward and northward. Apart from these political shape of the country, there was an unparalleled development in art and architecture, literature and music, and particularly new social integration took place on the basis of the patronage of local languages, such as Baluchi, Sindhi, Panjabi, Pashto, Kashmiri, Shina and Burushaski. All these languages received literary form with the support of the Muslims rulers and the first time their literatures began to take shape. They received influence from Arabic and Persian and added many themes from the Folklores as well as from those of Central Asia. Such an unusual developments transformed the society with the stories from Shahnama and Hazar Dastan and with the Folk-tales from Lila-Majnun, Sasi-Punnu and Hir-Ranjha. The stringed instruments, the dholak and the dhap and aslo flute and trinklets gave a new tone to the life of the people of Multan, Thatta, Maarha Shrif in D.I. Khan, Swat and Kashmir, and finally Gilgit, Hunza and

Balistan created the finest architecture of the time. That was the period of new religious activity in the country side when Islam become the dominant religion of the people who were directly linked in religious ties with the people of Central Asia, Iran, Afghanistan, Turkey and Arab world.

The migrant people had brought the new technology of straining the horse from Central Asia and Iran. Wherever the horse galloped right up the comer of Bengal and Orissa, the Turks and Afghans advanced from Pakistan and established new empires. Here the artisans and craftsman gathered in new center, cities began to grow with new craft mohallas, and they began to specialise in the products of Shawl and carpets in Kashmir, chapkan, chadar and dopatta in Panjab and Chitral and Northern Areas, tile work in Multan, Hala and Hyderabad, block printing in Sindh and fine carpentry in Chiniot, Bhira and Dera Ismail Khan. As a result several families occupied themselves in traditional crafts and passed them on to their own children.

Then came the Mughal emperors, descendent of Amir Timur, who, following the Mongol ruler Changiz Khan, had embarked on building a new world empire on the basis of organizing a new type of cavalry and making a new disciplined army in the unites of hundred and thousand. The later still survive in the name of Hazara both in Pakistan and Afghanistan. The first Mughal emperor, Zahiruddin Muhammad Babar, who had to come out from Farghan, brought a new taste of poetry, baghicha and architectural forms from the natural environment and landscape from Farghana and Samarkand, latter city reflecting the delicious water of Zarafshana (golden) river. Babar built his first terraced garden in Kabul and then choose the beautiful spot at Kalda or Kakkar Kahar in Chakwal district and built here Bagh-i-Safa on the very spot marked by this throne seat. It was again terraced garden watered by a near by spring. At the old Bhira on the bank of Jehlum he built a fort and then proceeded to Shah Dara (the Royal pass Gate) that opened his route the city of Lahore. At Shah Dara several garden were laid by the Mughal noblemen but only one is preserved inside Jehangir tomb that was built by his queen Nur Jehan who lies buried in another mausoleums. The tomb along with the garden is now desolate. There is also Kamran's baradari, without the garden, that still defies the flood of the Ravi river.

When the Mughal emperors followed Babar one after the other, they choose the old Lahore on the bank of Ravi to their main Urban centers in Punjab. It was developed as a city of gardens with numerous gardens around but the main Mughal fortress was built in an Island, surrounded by the Ravi on the three sides and only on the east it was joined to the city proper. Here third Mughal emperor Akbar transferred his capital from Agra to meet the challenge of cousin Mirza Hakim. Here he laid the foundation of a typical Mughal citadel with royal residences, called Akbari Mahal and Jehangiri Mahal, with a prominent Diwan-i-Am built in the traditional Iranian style, all constructed in red sand stone imported from Rajasthan. Later Akbar's grandson Shah Jehan, the King of architecture, transformed many buildings and renewed to his taste with white marble. He added Diwan-i-Khas that overlooked Ravi, his palace and Turkish Bath and still more important the Moti Masjid, the gem of monuments, with beautiful decorative designs in precious stones set in marble.

However, his choicest building is the Shish Mahal, the Mirror Palace that was the constructed by the side of a Charbagh style garden with running water channel and fountains, but later destroyed by the British, and quadrangles remodeled. Such garden, called Mehtab, can be seen in other quadrangles in the Fort. The Shish Mahal is the luxurious place of resort particularly during summer months with rest rooms of a long hall at its either end, opening on to the brilliantly dazzling Veranda that looks at the marble paved quadrangle with a fountain in the middle side. The mirror reflects the stars and the bedrooms presents, in its ceiling, the panorama of a star lit Sky. On the western side there is a unique building of Bengali style, called Naulakha, whose brilliance of precious stone outshone the natural setting of flowers and tree leaves that decorate the walls. Alas ! British soldiers have robbed many of the precious stones. Even then the Shish Mahal, even in its changed character by the Sikhs, presents a dazzling brilliance in its perfect creation by the Mughal emperor Shah Jehan. It is the climax of Mughal luxury surpassed nowhere in the world.

The exterior wall of the Shish Mahal one can see the beautiful mosaic paintings that depict everyday sport of the Mughal princes for the enjoyment of the people who used to gather below the fort not only to have a view of the emperor sitting in the Jharokha but also to admire the brilliance of color on the wall. Here one can observe galloping horses, humped camels, elephant ride, hunting scene, animal fights, horse man plying polo or chaughan, camel fights, figures of angels, demon head sand moving clouds, horse and elephant riders crossing Swords and verities of floral and geometrical designs. There are three gates to enter the fort, all three of them showing different tastes. The Masti (or correctly Masjid) Gate on the east shows Akbar's taste of red sand stone. The Shahburj gate on the west presents the fine mosaic decorations of the time of Jehangir. The last is the Alamgiri gate built by Emperor Aurangzeb, showing tasteful simple entrance with multiple facetted Tower at either end, crowned by Kiosks.

From Shish Mahal one can have a magnificent view of the Badashahi Masjid built by Aurangzeb on a spot regained after the river Ravi shifted further away. Its magnificent Stair way leading to the elegant red sand stone gate way on the east is highly impressive. It is on the left side that later the tomb of Allama Iqbal was built. The gate way, which is preserved the relic of the Prophet and also in one of the copy of the Holy Qur'an with brilliant calligraphy, leads into a wide open courtyard, having a washing pond in its middle, and rows of cells on its sides. On its west is the main prayer chamber of oblong shape marked by four tall corner towers. On its roof are three marble dooms of bulbous shape that attract the eye from a long distance. The interior of the mosque has chaste decoration in the mehrab chamber that opened in to equally well decorated side aisles. It has a Verandah on the front that is again tastefully decorated. But the most elegant are the tall towers at four corners of the quadrangle, from the top of which one can have an unforgettable view of the city of Lahore.

There are two other beauties in the city of which the greatest monumental gems of Lahore. The first is the most chaste fully painted mosque of Wazir Khan, which was once the center of religious and educational activities during the Mughals period. In its original design the mosque was fronted by an open maidan that presented from a distance a marvellous view of the mosque. It was built by Ilmuddin Ansari, hailing from the old trading city of Chiniot, but later he gave rise to the city of Wazirabad. He was raised to the high post of governor by Shah Jehan for his devoted service and great skill of Hikmat. But of greater importance in his taste of decorative architecture which he has translated into this mosque. The mosque plan, which is typical Mughals style but for its squat domes has tall minarets crowned by tasteful Chhatris. The most attractive is the mosaic ornamentation of the facade, the minars, and particularly the mihrab, which remains unsurpassed in its setting and choice of decorations and calligraphic work. In its charging decoration the mosque symbolises high sense of taste and marks a magnificent attraction in Lahore, to which both Shah Jehan as well as his officials gave a new face of color and charm.

And yet the greatest jewel of the city of Lahore is the Shahlimar Bagh, the unique pleasure resort that has been gifted to the world by the Mughal emperors. With paying a visit to this garden one can hardly understand the Mughal love for pleasances. In its creation what a real pleasure they have bestowed to the people of Lahore. The garden symbolises the elixir of life that the Mughals alone could imagine. They had long left Farghana but the beauteous charm of its terraced fields lingered behind that has been recaptured in the Cahrbagh style of the garden in Shahlimar, as Taj Mahal in Agra is the symbol of unforgettable love of emperor Shah Jehan, in the form of unique architectural creation, for the beloved queen Mumtaz Mahal, so is the Shahlimar, the epitome, of Shala (fire of love), the embodiment of the highest playful joy in life that the emperor and empress could have in this world. The garden is a combination of Charbaghs, water channels, fountains, Cascades, water falls and bathing hall in three different terraces, each terrace headed by beautiful pavilions for a pause of pleasurable enjoyment and then to pass on the other ponds of joy, inset with showering fountains, each terrace presenting varieties in scenic complex. Starting from a elaborate gate way in the south, with a water fountain in its middle chamber, we enter the open space, surrounded on right and left, by residential quarters, having long walkways, in the middle of either side of a channel marked by fountain, that join together on the four sides on a watery platform. And then we pass to the first pavilion that looks at a square pond remarkable sitting a cascade of a water falling down below the pavilion, series of fountains around a central seat for musicians and dancers and smaller pavilions at the four corners. From the top pavilion the elite royalties draw their pleasure from the scenic panorama in front and from the corner pavilions guests could roll in pleasance and enjoy the music of the running fountains coupled with the music of the singers and dancers. The next lower terrace begin with a rare bathing hall in the middle with water fountains lower down and lighted lamps in the arched niches of the walls. Here one could cool the legs during summer months—a novel way of cooling the atmosphere in the days when there were no electricity and air conditioners. And thus we find here a thrilling atmosphere where natural art has been channelised in the service of man. What a creation of charming loveliness that is combined with cooling water in various forms to soothe the evening of warm Lahore.

That is not all of Mughal architecture. If one likes to see the Mughal fondness for hunting, one can go to Sheikhopura, not from Lahore, and admire the construction of Hiran Minar by emperor Jehangir on the spot his dearly loved deer died. That Minar stand by the side of a tank which has in its middle a three storied pavilion for a general view around. If one can interested to see the defence arrangements of the Mughals, one can go to Attock on the bank of the Indus river, where Akbar's built a magnificent fort, made arrangements for crossing the river by boat-bridge and laid a new road south of the Kabul river leading to Peshawar through the Khyber pass to Kabul. And then come to Attock the empress Nur Jehan, who constructed here a caravan Serai, known as Begum Ki Serai, with a platform at the four corners and living rooms cooled by the Indus breeze. It is from one of the top platform that one could look at the magnificent expanse of the Indus river, full of flowing life and natural beauty, that perhaps will remain as the lasting memory of the Indus land, that is Pakistan.

CULTURAL HERITAGE OF PAKISTAN

The land where the Islamic Republic of Pakistan is situated today had been a seat of world's leading Civilizations from the time immemorial. There is plenty of evidence from the pre-historic and historic period to support this argument, e.g. fossil jaws of apes, circa 14 millions years old found from Pothohar. They belong to a species named "Sivapithecus Pakininsis", said to be the ancestor of Man. A 2 million years old earliest stone hand axe. Now on display in Islamabad Museum, Islamabad. The legacy of our predecessors at the time of our independence, on August 14, 1947, came to us as a treasure which may be called as Pakistan's national heritage. So rich and diversified is this heritage that Pakistani nation can be proud of its glorious past, be Islamic, Post Islamic or pre-Islamic period as far back as pre-historic times. No other country of the world can produce the treasure of by gone days as can be found in Pakistan. It is now incumbent upon us to treasure our national heritage and save it from further deterioration and theft.

The establishment of NFCH is much appreciated and a great interest is shown by the general public hence since its establishment in 1994 hundreds of proposals were received from different agencies and individuals for the conservation, preservation and publication of the Pakistan's national heritage. It is hoped that with the continued patronage of the government, the Philanthropists and the Business Community to the NFCH we shall be able to achieve the aforesaid goal. The Cultural Heritage of Pakistan is spread over the centuries, starting from pre-historic times to the present day and which may be summarized in the following periods:

- Indus Civilization;
- Gandhara Civilization;
- Islamic Period;
- Sikh Period;
- British Period;
- Post independence Period.

INDUS CIVILIZATION

This land also witnessed the glorious era of Indus civilization about 8000 years B.C when the first village was found at Mehargarh in the Sibi District of Balochistan comparable with the earliest villages of Jericho in Palestine and Jarmo in Iraq. Here, during the last decade i.e., 1980's, the French and Pakistani archaeologists have excavated mud built houses of the Mehergarh people and their agricultural land known for the cultivation of maize and wheat, together with polished stone tools, beads and other ornaments, painted jars and bowls, drinking glasses, dishes and plates.

The archaeologists believe that by 7000 B.C., the Mehergarh people learnt to use the metal for the first time. From the first revolution of agricultural life the man moved to another great revolution in his social, cultural and economic life. He established trade relations with the people of Turkmenistan, Uzbekistan, Iran and the Arab world. He not only specialized in painting different designs of pottery, made varieties of pots and used cotton and wool but also made terra-cotta figurines and imported precious stones from Afghanistan and Central Asia. This early bronze age Culture spread out in the countryside of Sind, Balochistan, Punjab and North West Frontier Province of Pakistan.

This early beginning led to the concentration of population into the small towns, such as Kot Diji in Sind and Rahman Dheri in Dera Ismail Khan district. It is this social and cultural exchange that led to the rise of the famous cities of Mohenjodaro and Harappa, with largest concentration of population including artisans, craftsmen, businessmen and rulers. This culminated in the peak of the Indus Civilization which was primarily based on intensively irrigated agricultural land and overseas trade and contact with Iran, Gulf States, Mesopotamia and Egypt. Dames were built for storing river water, land was cultivated by means of bullock-harnessed plough - a system which still prevails in Pakistan, granaries for food storage were built, furnace was used for controlling temperature for making red pottery and various kinds of ornaments, beads of carnelian, agate, and terra-cotta were pierced through and above all they traded their finished goods with Central Asia and Arab world. It is these trade dividends that enriched the urban populace who developed a new sense of moral honesty, discipline and cleanliness combined with a social stratification in which the priests and the mercantile class dominated the society. The picture of high civilization can be gathered only by looking at the city of Mohenjodaro, the First Planned City in the World, in which the streets are aligned straight, parallel to each other with cross streets cutting at right angles. It is through these wide streets that wheeled carriages, drawn by bulls or asses, moved about, carrying well-adorned persons seated on them appreciating the closely aligned houses made of pucca-bricks, all running straight along the streets. And then through the middle of the streets ran stone dressed drains covered with stone slabs - a practice of keeping the streets clean from polluted water, seen for the first time in the world.

FASTING BUDDHA

The Zenith of Gandhara Art, flanked by Gandhara Jewellery Found from Sirkap, Taxila

This is the land which attracted Alexander the great from Macedonia in 326 B.C., with whom the influence of Greek culture came to this part of the world. During the 2nd century B.C., it was here that Buddhism was adopted as the state religion which flourished and prevailed here for over 1000 years, starting from 2nd century B.C., until 10th century A.D. During this time Taxila, Swat and Charsaddah (old Pushkalavati) became three important centres for culture, trade and learning. Hundreds of monasteries and stupas were built together with Greek and Kushan towns such as Sirkap and Sirsukh both in Taxila. It was from these centres that a unique art of sculpture originated which is known as Gandhara Art all over the world. Today the Gandhara Sculptures occupy a prominent place in the museums of England, France, Germany, USA, Japan, Korea, China, India and Afghanistan together with many private collections world over, as well as in the museums of Pakistan. Nevertheless, the zenith of this Gandhara Art is one and only "Fasting Buddha" now on display in Lahore Museum, Lahore.

Finally, the light of Islam penetrated in this part of the world as early as 7th century AD. from the west with the Arabs and during the 10th century AD from the north with the Turks. Islam replaced the early way of life of worshipping idols and introduced new philosophy of faith in one God. With Islam it came a new culture in this land from Arabia and Central Asia. Hence, a new type of architecture, hitherto unknown in this area, was introduced. Tens of thousands of Mosques, Madrasahs, tombs and gardens were created by the Muslim rulers all over the Sub-Continent. The new style of Islamic architecture prevailed and matured in this land for over a thousand years. The most important contribution of the Muslim rulers to this land, however, is a new language 'Urdu' which became the national language of Pakistan since its independence in 1947.

ISLAMIC PERIOD

The light of Islam penetrated in this part of the world as early as 712 A.D from the west with the Arab General Muhammad bin Qasim and during the 10th century A.D from the north with the Turk Sultan Mahmud of Ghaznah (better known as Mahmud Ghaznavi). Islam replaced the early way of life of worshipping idols and introduced new philosophy of faith in one God. With Islam it came a new culture in this land from Arabia and Central Asia. Hence, a new type of architecture, hitherto unknown in this area, was introduced. Tens of thousands of Mosques, Madrasahs, tombs and gardens were created by the Muslim rulers all over the Sub-Continent. The new style of Islamic architecture prevailed and matured in this land for over a thousand years. The direct influence of the Muslim Rulers was not only confined to the architecture; their food added a variety of new dishes in the Sub-Continental cuisine. The national dress of Pakistan, " Shalwar Qamiz" is also a direct gift of the Muslim Turks.

Since the mother tongue of the Muslim Rulers was Arabic, Turkish and Farsi, it was only natural that the local languages of the Sub-Continent were greatly influenced and new language was introduced. Thus the most important contribution of the Muslim rulers to this land is a new language 'Urdu' which became the national language of Pakistan since its independence in 1947.

CHAPTER 6

LAND

PROVINCES

BALOCHISTAN

Balochistan is the largest province of Pakistan with an area about 343,000 sq. km. Although it is bigger than the British Isles, its population is only about one million. This is perhaps due to its tough terrain and scarcity of water. To its south is Arabian sea, to its west-Iran, and to its north is Afghanistan. It also shares boundaries with the provinces of Punjab, Sind and NWFP. Makran-an important coastal town of Balochistan is almost entirely desert with low, dry hills rising from 300 meters to 2500 meters in the north. To its west, in the proximity of Iran, more expansive desert plains reign supreme. This is where the Chagai and Toba Kakar Mountain Ranges form the borders of Iran, Afghanistan and Pakistan. In winter the temperature falls to as low as–30° Celsius while in summer it ranges from 18 to 30° C. One of the oldest Neolithic sites (6000 BC) is to be found at Mehr Ghar just south of Bolan Pass. This culture faded away in 3000 BC about the same time that the Indus Valley Civilization emerged.

Balochistan never became part of the Mughal Empire, and effectively remained an autonomous frontier tributary. Makran, once a thriving region with its capital in Panjgur and Commercial point in Tiz with 'great warehouses, palm groves and a beautiful mosque, with people of all nations', simply dried up. From Balochistan passes the route of the Euro-Asian Highway– from Zahedan in Iran to Taftan in Balochistan and on to Quetta. Another alternative road turns south from Kandahar in Afghanistan into Chaman in Balochistan - this was the route for Freight bound for Afghanistan arriving through Karachi harbour. Apart from its importance as a transit area, there are mineral resources which are just beginning to be tapped. The Sui district has one of the largest gas deposits in the world. Balochistan is a province of contrasts. It has some of the bleakest landscape in the country with grim, jagged mountains, barren and arid land where the sparse greenery shrivels and wilts, but hidden away are some stunningly beautiful places.

Not many people know that Quetta, the capital of Balochistan, is considered as Mecca for gliding enthusiasts. The climatic conditions are such that from June till September, warm air currents, also known as thermals, rise up from the Quetta valley to great heights. This phenomenon offers excellent conditions for gliding and soaring. It may surprise many that Quetta Flying Club is in existence since early 1960s. Flying for upto 9 hours, non-stop, and distances flown in excess of 200 kms. are common. About 80 kms. north-east of Quetta is the famous town of Ziarat, a place where the father of the nation spent his last days. Ziarat boasts of Juniper forest, only one of its kind in the world. Some trees have ages in excess of thousand years. In winters, the rolling hills with the carpet of Juniper forests and snow claded tops present beautiful scenic view

NWFP

The North-West Frontier Province is the smallest of all the provinces. It is also abbreviated as NWFP. It shares a common border for over 1,100 km (680 miles) with Afghanistan. It also shares border with Baloohistan on the west and Punjab on the east. The city of Peshawar is its capital. The northern half of the province consists of five river valleys. Running roughly parallel, north to south, are the Chitral, Dir, Swat, Indus and Kunhar (Kaghan) valleys. These valleys are green and wooded on their southern sections owing to Monsoon rains. Northern Chitral and the upper regions of the Indus Valley are mountainous deserts, where cultivation depends entirely on irrigation. The regions south of Pesawar are below the monsoon belt and consist of low, rocky mountains.

About half of the province, along its border with Afghanistan, is tribal. There are autonomous regions governed by tribal law under supervision of the Pakistan Government. The Khyber Pass, the route from Peshawar to Kabul into Afghanistan, is the feature of the province most widely known in the world beyond. To visit the pass one needs a special permit from the Political Agent. The Mughals, Afghans, Sikhs, British and Russians have suffered defeat at the hands of Pathans. They are divided into numerous sub-tribes and clans, each defending its territory and honour. The Pathans serve as Pakistan's first line of defense along the Durand Line, the border drawn in 1893 by Sir Mortimer Durand, the then foreign secretary of British India.

PUNJAB

The Punjab meaning "Land of Five Rivers", is the second largest province of Pakistan. It is the richest, most fertile and most heavily populated province of Pakistan. Important cities include, Lahore—the Provincial Capital, Multan, Rawalpindi, Gujranwala, Wazirabad, Rahimyarkhan, Khanewal, Sargodah, Faisalabad and Bahawalpur. The province of Punjab shares its boundaries with NWFP in the north-west, Balochistan in the west, Sind in the South and India on the East. There are five rivers in Punjab, thus the name Punjab. "Punj" means five and "ab" means water in the Punjabi language. When "Punj" and "ab" are put together they make the phrase "five waters" in English. The five rivers are: Indus, Jhelum, Chenab, Ravi and Sutlej.

Punjab is home to over 70 million people, which is more than half the population of the entire country. This province is a land of contrasts, from the alluvial plain of the Indus River and its tributaries to the sand-dunes of the Cholistan Desert, from the verdant beauty of the pine-covered foothills of the Himalayas to the convoluted lunar landscape of the Potwar Plateau and the Salt Range.

Lahore became one of the greatest Mughal cities in subcontinent in the 17th century. There was a town near Lahore which was the birthplace of Guru Nanak, the 15th century founder of the Sikh religion. Lahore was the capital from which Maharaja Ranjit Singh ruled his 19th century Sikh Empire. The British coveted this fertile region, and overthrew the Sikhs in 1849, annexing Punjab to their Indian dominions, with Lahore as its provincial capital. It was in Lahore where the All India Muslim

League passed, on 23 March 1940, its Resolution for the Creation
of Pakistan. Lahore continues to be the capital of Punjab even
today. The best time to visit northern Punjab is in the spring, from
February to April, and in the autumn, from September to
November. Southern Punjab is extremely hot in summer, so
Multan is at its best in winter, from November to February.
Punjab, like Sind is full of historical and archaeological sites.
Lahore and Multan themselves offer rich historical and cultural
attractions along with treasures of archaeological sites.

SINDH

Sindh is the third largest province of Pakistan. To its west
and north-west is the Province of Batochistan, to the north-east is
Punjab, to its south and south-east is India and to its south-west
is the Arabian Sea. Major cities of Sindh indude the port city of
Karachi which also happens to be the largest port of Pakistan. It
is also the largest city of the country in terms of population.
Sukkur, Hyderabad, Larkana and Jacobabad are other major
cities. Karachi, the largest and the most papulous city is a colourful
combination of the old and new. There are narrow twisting lanes
and alleys of the old city throbing with life along-side the wide
metalled roads and elegant modern buildings.

Karachi offers a variety of pleasant attractions: wide sunny
beaches, deep-sea fishing, yachting, golf and horse racing throughout
the year. The restaurants in the city provide a wide variety of
Pakistani and Western cuisine, its markets and bazaars offer a
variety of shopping including indigenous handicrafts, rugs and
carpets. Karachi was a small port town about 150 years ago. With
the development of its harbour it gradually grew into a large city
and an important centre of trade and industry. Karachi was the
first capital of Pakistan. About 64 kms (40 miles) east of Karachi
is the famous archaeological site Bhambore. Some scholars identify
it with Debal, the port city where the Arab General Mohammad
Bin Qasim landed in 712 AD.

Pakistan's old and most popular folk-story of Sassi-Pannu, like
Romeo-Juliet in the west, is known to have originated here.
Hyderabad, 164 km north of Karachi is the second largest city
in Sindh and one of the largest in Pakistan. Hyderabad is situated
on the banks of the Indus River. The buildings are topped by

badgirs that look like chimneys on roof tops. They catch the cool breezes which blow steadily in a south-west direction from late April till late June. Hyderabad is hot for most of the year.

The streets give this city a mediaeval look. On the northern side there are tombs from the Talpur and Kalhora periods. The tomb of Ghulam Shah Kalhora is one of the finest. A desert oasis, similar to Jaisalmer in Rajasthan, is the city of Sukkur. Just across the Indus, on the other side, is the town of Rohri, which is fairly prosperous and an important rail and road junction. About eight km away are remains of the ancient city of Aror where Alexander the Great is said to have camped.

Kot Diji, a small but archaeologically very important town is 51 kms south of Khairpur town in the Khairpur District of Sindh. According to Archaeologists, the discovery of this pre-historic site has furnished information of high significance since it pushed back the pre-history of Pakistan by atleast another 300 years from about 2,500 BC to 2,800 BC. Evidence of new cultural element of pre-Harappan and pre-Mohenjodaro dates has been found at Kot Diji. The excavations there have proved that the Indus Valley Civilisations borrowed or developed some of the basic cultural elements of the Kot Dijians. In Mohenjodaro (Mound of dead) on the west-bank of the Indus in Sindh are the remains of one of the earliest and a most developed urban civilisations of the ancient world. It was discovered in 1922.

The Indus Valley Civilisation flourished from 3,000 to 15,00 BC. It was contemporary to the ancient civilisations of Egypt and Mesopotamia. At its prime, it comprised of atleast 400 cities and towns along the Indus and its tributaries, covering most of the present day Pakistan and stretching north-west as far as modern Kabul and east as far as modern Delhi. The most imposing remain is the great bath which consisted of an open quandrangle with verandahs on four sides, galleries and rooms at the back, a group of halls on the north and a large bathing pool. The ruins of the Indus Valley Civilisation face imminent danger from the rising water tables and salinity. Government of Pakistan in cooperation with UNESCO is making all possible efforts to avert this danger and save Mohenjodaro.

Officially Islamic Republic of Pakistan, republic in south Asia, bordered on the north and north-west by Afghanistan, on the north-east by Jammu and Kashmir, on the east and south-east by India, on the south by the Arabian Sea, and on the west by Iran. The status of Jammu and Kashmir is a matter of dispute between India and Pakistan. Pakistan became an independent state in 1947. Until December 1971 it included the province of East Pakistan (previously East Bengal), which, after its secession from Pakistan, assumed the name Bangladesh. The area of Pakistan is 796,095 sq km (307,293 sq mi), excluding the section of Jammu and Kashmir under its control. The capital of Pakistan is Islamabad, Karachi is the largest city.

LAND AND RESOURCES

Pakistan is mostly a dry country characterized by extremes of altitude and temperature. It is divided by the River Indus, which enters the country in the north-east and flows south into the Arabian Sea. The Indus forms the demarcation line between two of Pakistan's main topographic areas–the Indus Plain, which extends principally along the eastern side of the river, and the Balochistan Plateau, which lies to the south-west. Four other topographic areas are the coastal plain, a narrow strip of land bordering the Arabian Sea; the Kharan Basin, to the west of the Balochistan Plateau; and the Thar Desert (or Great Indian Desert), which straddles the border with India in the south-east; and the mountains of the north and north-west, including the Hindu Kush.

The Indus Plain in Pakistan varies in width from about 80 to 320 km (50 to 200 mi) and covers an area of about 518,000 sq km (200,000 sq mi). From north to south it includes portions of two main regions, namely, the Punjab Plain and the Sind Plain. The Punjab region is drained by the Sutlej, Ravi, Chenab, and Jhelum rivers, which are tributaries of the Indus; and supply the irrigation system that waters the Indus Plain. The upland Balochistan Plateau is bordered by a series of mountain ranges; among these are the Tobakakar Range, the Siahan Range, the Sulaiman Range, and the Kirthar Range. The highest peak in the northern mountains is Tirich Mir (7,690 m/25,230 ft) in the Hindu Kush. The Sefid Koh Range is pierced by the Khyber Pass on the Pakistan-Afghanistan border.

The highest peak in Pakistan is K2 (also known as Mount Godwin-Austen). Rising 8,611 m (28,250 ft) above sea level in the Karakorum Range, the peak is located in the region of Jammu and Kashmir controlled by Pakistan. K2 is the second-highest mountain in the world, after Mount Everest. A range of natural hazards disrupt or claim life: these include frequent earthquakes, which may be severe especially in the north and west, and flooding along the Indus after heavy rains in July and August. The country overall has limited natural fresh water resources and many people do not have access to clean drinking water. As in many developing countries, deforestation, soil erosion, and desertification are also major problems.

CLIMATE

The climate of Pakistan varies widely with topography, but is generally continental in type. In the mountain regions of the north and west, temperatures fall below freezing during the winter. In the Indus Plain area, temperatures range between about 32° and 49° C (90° and 120° F) in summer; the winter average is about 13° C (55° F). Throughout most of Pakistan rainfall is scarce. The Punjab region receives the most precipitation more than 508 mm (20 in) per year. The arid regions of the south-east and south-west receive less than 127 mm (5 in) annually. Most rain falls between July and September.

NATURAL RESOURCES

Pakistan's resources are primarily agricultural. Mineral resources include salt, chromite, coal, gypsum, limestone, iron ore, sulphur, clay, graphite, manganese, copper, oil, and natural gas, but many known mineral deposits, particularly iron ore and coal, are low grade. Oil was first discovered in small quantities in 1915; intensive exploration during the 1980s revealed several new fields, notably in Sindh Province. Large natural gas fields were discovered in the 1950s on the border between Balochistan and Punjab provinces.

PLANTS AND ANIMALS

The vegetation of Pakistan varies according to elevation and rainfall. In much of the country the natural vegetation is limited to drought-resistant grasses and stunted trees. Alpine flora grows on the higher mountain slopes. The wetter slopes are wooded; species include spruce, evergreen oak, chir or cheer pine, and a cedar known as the deodar. Pakistan has a varied animal life. Species include deer, boar, bear, crocodile, and waterfowl. In the freshwater and salt-water areas, fish of many varieties are found. Marine species indude herring, mackerel and sharks, as well as shellfish.

POPULATION

The ethnic background of Pakistan's population is extremely varied, largely because the country lies in an area that has been repeatedly invaded since earliest times. The people come from such ethnic stocks as Dravidian, Indo-Aryan, Greek, Scythian, Hun, Arab, Mongol, Persian, Turkish, and Afghan.

POPULATION CHARACTERISTICS

Pakistan, a highly populated country, has a population (1995 estimate) of about 129,808,000 (not including the disputed territories of Jammu and Kashmir), yielding an average population density of about 163.1 people per sq km (422 per sq mi). The birth rate in Pakistan in 1995 was 38.4 births for every 1,000 people. Average life expectancy is 62 years for men and 64 years for women. About 32 per cent of the people live in urban areas. There were an estimated 1.5 million refugees from Afghanistan in the country in 1994.

PRINCIPAL CITIES

Pakistan's largest city and commercial and industrial centre is Karachi, with a population (1981 census) of about 5.1 million. Other significant urban centres are Lahore (2.92 million), an industrial centre; Faisalabad (1.1 million), a centre of the cotton industry; Rawalpindi (928,000), an industrial and military centre; Hyderabad (795,000), an agricultural and manufacturing centre; Multan (730,000), and Peshawar (555,000), the hub of trade with Afghanistan. Islamabad (201,000) is the federal capital of Pakistan. Pakistan has four provinces-North-West Frontier, Balochistan, Punjab and Sindh plus the Federal Capital Territory of Islamabad and federally administered tribal areas.

RELIGION

Islam is the faith of about 97 per cent of the people. Some 77 per cent of Muslims are Sunni; 20 per cent are Shiite. Hinduism and Christianity form the leading minority religions; other religious groups include Sikhs, Parsees, and a small number of Buddhists. The constitution defines Pakistan as an Islamic nation and, as amended in 1986 and 1991, makes Islamic Shari'ah law the supreme law of Pakistan. Freedom of religion is guaranteed, however, by the constitution.

LANGUAGE

The national language of Pakistan is Urdu, but comparatively few people use it as their mother tongue. Punjabi is probably the most widely spoken language, followed by Sindhi, Pashto, Saraiki, and Baloch respectively. English is extensively used by educated people and is the official language of Pakistan.

EDUCATION

About 34 per cent of adult Pakistanis are literate. Although the constitution prescribes free and compulsory primary education, this remains a goal to be achieved; only about 40 per cent of five-to nine-year-olds are enrolled in school. Five years has been established as the period of primary school attendance. Adult literacy programmes play an important role in boosting literacy levels. Pakistan spends an estimated 2.7 per cent of its gross national product (GNP) on education. In the mid 1990s about 16.7 million pupils were enrolled in primary and pre-primary schools, and about 5.7 million students attended the various forms of secondary school including vocational schools. In addition, about 794,000 students attended institutions of higher education. Pakistan has 24 universities, mostly established in the late 19th century. Among the leading universities are the University of Karachi (founded 1951), the University of the Punjab (1882), in Lahore; the University of Peshawar (1950); the University of Sind (1947), in Dadu; and the University of Agriculture (1909), in Faisalabad.

CULTURE

As a Muslim nation, Pakistan is strongly influenced by the culture and traditions of Islam. Hindu and British influences, however, are widespread in the country. Karachi is the seat of some of the most important libraries in Pakistan; these include the Liaquat Memorial Library, the Central Secretariat Library, and the University of Karachi library. Also of note are the National Archives of Pakistan, in Islamabad, and the Punjab Public Library, in Lahore. The National Museum of Pakistan, in Karachi, contains important materials from the Indus Valley Civilizations, as well as Buddhist and Islamic artefacts. Cultural materials are also displayed in the Lahore Museum and in the Peshawar Museum. There is an Industrial and Commercial Museum in Lahore.

ECONOMY

The economy of Pakistan grew by an average 5.1 per cent annually during the period from 1965 to 1980, despite setbacks in the early 1970s caused fay the secession of East Pakistan in 1971. During the 1980s and early 1990, following the introduction of economic liberalization policies, the rate increased, and gross domestic product (GDP) growth remains strong, running at roughly 5 per cent per annum. The current growth target for GDP is 7 per cent. The budget deficit was reduced to 5.6 per cent of GDP at the end of 1994-1995, having been 8 per cent two years earlier. Pakistan attracted US$2,600 million in foreign investment in 1996 from bilateral and multilateral sources. Despite these improvements, the economy remains vulnerable to crisis and the majority of the nation's citizens remain poor and heavily dependent on the agricultural sector for their livelihoods. This is largely a result of the country's high rate of population increase; but political factors, in particular heavy military spending and continuing sectarian and political violence, have also slowed economic growth and modernization.

In 1994 Pakistan's GNP was about US$60,000 million, giving an average per capita income of US$460. The trade deficit rose to US$22,200 million in 1995, over three times that of 1994. As a result, a number of stabilization reforms were introduced in 1995, which included a 7 per cent devaluation of the Pakistani rupee. The government of Pakistan has been deeply involved in directing the country's economy; most major industries were nationalized during the 1970s. Pakistan receives considerable economic assistance from foreign countries and from international organizations. The government has been under pressure from the International Monetary Fund (IMF) and other donors to continue the economic reforms and austerity measures begun in 1993. In mid-December 1995 the IMF approved a US$600 million standby loan and urged Pakistan to move forward with economic liberalization.

Since the 1980s, as part of efforts to increase growth and employment private companies have been allowed into previously state-controlled sectors, such as banking, water, and other utilities. Public-debt servicing accounts for 35 per cent of budget expenditure, military spending accounts for about 26 per cent, and development, 23 per cent. The 1988-1993 seventh five-year plan allowed private investors to set up businesses without having to seek government permission—as previously—in all economic sectors except arms and alcohol production. Many people go abroad to work. The Eighth Five-Year Plan is running from 1993-1998; there is also a perspective plan for 1993-2008. The annual budget in the mid-1990s included an estimated US$12,500 million in revenue and US$14,000 million in expenditure.

AGRICULTURE, FORESTRY, AND FISHING

About 27 per cent of Pakistan's total land area, predominantly in the Indus Valley, is considered arable; most cultivated land is irrigated. Agriculture and related activities involve almost half the work force and provide over one quarter of GDP. By the late 1970s an intensive land-reform effort had resulted in the expropriation of some 1.2 million hectares (3 million acres) from landlords, the distribution of almost half of this to tenants, and the limitation of individual holdings to 40 hectares (100 acres) of irrigated, or 81 hectares (200 acres) of non-irrigated land.

Formerly an importer of wheat, Pakistan achieved self-sufficiency in grain by the mid-1970s, and is now also a major exporter of rice. Principal crops in 1995 (with output in tonnes) included sugar cane, 47.2 million; wheat, 17.0 million; rice, 5.7 million; cotton, 1.8 million; and maize, 1.3 million. Most people living in rural areas keep some animals; those living in the arid upland areas, such as the Balochistan Plateau, are generally pastoralists, living nomadic or semi-nomadic lives. The livestock population in the mid-1990s included an estimated 19 million cattle, 29 million sheep, 44 million goats, 20 million buffalo, 4 million donkeys, 1.1 million camels, and 135 million chickens. About 5 per cent of Pakistan is forested. Most of the 29 million cum (1,024 million cu ft) of roundwood harvested in 1994 was used as fuel. Fishing resources are extensive. In 1994 the total catch was about 552,000 tonnes, most of it obtained from the Indian Ocean. The fish caught include sardines, sharks, and anchovies; the shrimp catch is also important, up Mining in 1995 the most important minerals (with annual production in tonnes) included gypsum (620,000), rock salt (890,000), limestone (9.7 million), bauxite (4,400), chromite (13,000), and coal and lignite (3 million). Crude oil production was about 19.9 million barrels, and production of natural gas was about 17.7 million cu m (625 million cu ft).

MANUFACTURING

Pakistan's manufacturing capacity is increasing and production has been steadily expanding. In the mid-1990s manufacturing accounted for about 18 per cent of GDP, as compared with 14 per cent in 1965; the service sector, including the state bureaucracy, accounted for 31 per cent. Important products include processed foods; leather; clothing and footwear: cotton and jute textiles; cotton, silk, and rayon doth; refined petroleum; cement; fertilizers; sugar; cigarettes; soda ash; bicycles: steel billets and sheets; and chemicals. Handicraft products, such as pottery and carpets, are also important. Government policy since the late 1970s has been to encourage private-sector investment in industry. However, the largest plants are still mainly state owned, including those producing cement, fertilizer, steel, and ghee (clarified butter) for cooking.

ENERGY

About 60 per cent of Pakistan's electricity is produced in thermal installations, and most of the rest is generated in hydroelectric facilities, including the large Tarbela project on the River Indus. Pakistan also has a small nuclear sector, a nuclear power plant situated near Karachi contributes under 1 per cent of total output. Pakistan's output of electricity in 1995 was 53.3 billion kWh, based on an installed generating capacity of 8,430 MW.

CURRENCY AND BANKING

The monetary unit of Pakistan is the Pakistani rupee of 100 paisa (44 rupees equal US$1; 1998). The State Bank of Pakistan, established in 1948, is the central bank. It issues banknotes; manages currency, credit, the public debt, and exchange controls; and supervises the commercial banks. Pakistani banks were nationalized in 1974. A number of major foreign banks (21) maintain offices in the country. The practices of banks and other financial institutions are regulated, in part, by Islamic law. They are not permitted, under 1985 legislation, to pay interest on domestic transactions, or under a 1991 Federal Shari'ah (Islamic) Court ruling to charge interest. Instead banks operate a system of investment partnerships with customers.

COMMERCE AND TRADE

Pakistan's foreign trade consists largely of exports of raw materials and basic products such as cotton yam, and imports of manufactured products. In 1996 exports earned about US$8,300 million and imports cost US$12,000 million. The chief exports were textiles and fabrics: clothing; rice; carpets and rugs; leather; fish; and cotton. The main imports were machinery; electrical equipment; petroleum products; transport equipment; oils and fats; metal and metal products; and organic chemicals. Pakistan's leading trade partners included Japan, the United States, the United Kingdom, Germany, Saudi Arabia, and France. Tourism is of increasing importance in Pakistan's foreign currency earnings. In 1994 there were around 454,353 tourist arrivals; the foreign exchange receipts from tourism in 1994 were US$126.2 million.

TRANSPORT

Lack of a modern transport network has been a major hindrance to Pakistan's development. Its terrain, laced with rivers and mountains, presents formidable obstacles to internal land transport. The country has about 216,564 km (134,572 mi) of roads, of which 53 per cent are all-weather roads. In 1996 there were 732,100 motor vehicles in Pakistan, with a ratio of 135 people per car. The railway network operated by Pakistan Railways totals about 8,160 km (5,070 mi) of track. Karachi is the principal port; a second major port, Muhammad bin Qasim, was opened in the early 1980s. Pakistan International Airlines (PIA), 56 per cent government owned, provides domestic as welt as overseas service to about 30 countries. The main international airports serve Karachi, Lahore, Islamabad, Peshawar, and Quetta.

COMMUNICATIONS

In the mid-1990s Pakistan had more than 2.5 million telephones, 12 million radios, and 2.5 million television sets. The Pakistan Television Corporation transmits eight channels. Transmissions first began in Lahore in 1964, followed by Karachi in 1966. Newspapers are mainly printed in Urdu and English. In 1994 Pakistan had 130 dailies and 269 weeklies, most with small circulations. The major dailies are concentrated in Lahore and Karachi. The average circulation of all dailies in the mid-1990s was just over 1 million.

GOVERNMENT

Pakistan is an Islamic republic with a federal system of government. Following the secession of East Pakistan in 1971, Pakistan adopted a new constitution in 1973 to replace the one in operation since 1956. Following the military coup d'etat of 1977, however, a system of martial law was put into effect, and most aspects of the 1973 constitution were suspended. In 1985 parliamentary government was re-established, martial law was ended, and the constitution restored, after amendments extending the powers of the president, including those of appointing and dismissing ministers and vetoing new legislation. Legislation enacted in 1991 made Shari'ah, or Islamic law, the supreme law of the land. A constitutional court rules on matters relating to the constitution, and can overrule presidential decisions. On April 1, 1997, the federal legislature revoked sections of the constitution's eighth amendment, in effect reducing the powers of the president in order to restore power to the elected government. The legislation, known as the 13th amendment, has brought the presidency back under the control of the prime minister; the president may not dismiss parliament without the prime minister's permission.

EXECUTIVE AND LEGISLATURE

According to the 1973 constitution, as amended in 1985, the head of state of Pakistan is a president, elected to a five-year term by a college of deputies from the federal and provincial assemblies.

The chief executive is the prime minister, who is responsible to the legislature. Legislative power is vested in the bicameral federal legislature (Majilis-e-Shoora). The National Assembly has 217 seats, including 10 reserved for religious minority representatives. Members are directly elected by universal suffrage for terms of up to five years. The Senate has 87 seats (two for women). Members are indirectly elected by the provincial legislatures; senators serve six-year terms.

POLITICAL PARTIES

During the period of martial law (1977-1985) political parties were first severely limited in their activities and then, in October 1979, banned outright. They were allowed to resume their activities in December 1985. The first proper elections after the ending of military rule were won by the Pakistan People's Party (PPP), founded in the 1960s by Zulfikar Ali Bhutto, and the dominant party in the country in the period before martial law. Bhutto's daughter, Benazir, became Prime Minister, but was dismissed by the president in August 1990. After a short period of emergency rule, new elections in October 1990 were won by the Islamic Democratic Alliance. The PPP became the main opposition party until 1993 when a new crisis led to the dismissal of the prime minister and a general election, which returned the PPP and Benazir Bhutto to power. The Pakistan Muslim League (PML) emerged as the main opposition party, and won the 1997 elections with a huge majority.

JUDICIARY

The highest court in Pakistan is the Supreme Court. The judicial system in each province is headed by a High Court. A Federal Shari'ah Court has been established to determine whether any law is wholly or partially un-Islamic. In 1991 parliament passed a law obliging the criminal code to conform to Islamic law. In 1992 the death penalty, in abeyance since 1986, was reintroduced.

LOCAL GOVERNMENT

Pakistan is divided into four provinces—Balochistan, North-West Frontier Province, Punjab, and Sindh—the Federal Capital Territory of Islamabad, and the federally administered tribal areas along the north-west border with Afghanistan. Provincial governors, appointed by the president of Pakistan, are assisted by elected provincial legislative assemblies. For local government purposes, the provinces are subdivided into divisions, districts, and agencies. The tribal areas—Khyber, Kurram, Malakand, Mohmand, North Waziristan, and South Waziristan—are officially administered by political agents responsible to the federal government. The laws of Pakistan do not operate in these areas, and they are administered according to the traditional customs of their people. PoK, the western part of the area of Jammu and Kashmir controlled by Pakistan, has its own government, president, prime minister, and courts. The northern portion—Gilgit, Diamir, and Baltistan—is directly administered by the federal government.

HEALTH AND WELFARE

Health services in Pakistan are limited by a lack of finance and facilities. In 1994 the country had about 66,200 doctors (1 per 2,064 people) and some 80,900 beds in hospitals and clinics. In 1976 an old-age pension system was inaugurated, but it covers relatively few Pakistanis. In 1996 the infant mortality rate was 79 deaths for every 1,000 live births. Pakistan spends an estimated 3.5 per cent of GDP on health care.

DEFENCE

Military service in Pakistan is voluntary. In 1995 the country's armed forces had about 587,000 members, with 520,000 in the army, 45,000 in the air force, and 22,000 in the navy. Pakistan is not a signatory to the Nuclear Non-Proliferation Treaty (NPT), and officially became a nuclear power when it conducted underground tests in May 1998. As a proportion of GDP, Pakistan's spending on defence is around three times that of its main rival nation, India; arms imports in 1993 amounted to US$430 million.

INTERNATIONAL ORGANIZATIONS

Pakistan is a member of the UN, the Commonwealth of Nations, and the Colombo Plan.

CHAPTER 7

GEOGRAPHY

GEOGRAPHICAL FACTS

Location: Southern Asia, bordering the Arabian Sea, between India on the east and Iran and Afghanistan on the west and China in the north.

Geographic coordinates: 30 00 N, 70 00 E.

Map references: Asia

Area:

total: 803,940 sq km
land: 778,720 sq km
water: 25,220 sq km

Area - comparative: slightly less than twice the size of California.

Land boundaries:

total: 6,774 km
border countries: Afghanistan 2,430 km, China 523 km, India 2,912 km, Iran 909 km

Coastline: 1,046 km

Maritime claims: *contiguous zone:* 24 nm

continental shelf: 200 nm or to the edge of the continental margin
exclusive economic zone: 200 nm
territorial sea: 12nm

Climate: mostly hot; dry desert; temperate in northwest; arctic in north

Terrain: flat Indus plain in east; mountains in north and northwest; Balochistan plateau in west

Elevation extremes

Lowest point: Indian Ocean 0 m.
Highest point: K2 (Mt. Godwin-Austen) 8,611m

Natural resources: land, extensive natural gas reserves, limited petroleum, poor quality coal, iron ore, copper, salt, limestone

Land use

arable land: 27%
permanent crops: 1%
permanent pastures: 6%
forests and woodland: 5%
other: 61% (1993 est.)

Irrigated land: 171,100 sq km (1993 est.)

Natural hazards : frequent earthquakes, occasionally severe especially in north and west; flooding along the Indus after heavy rains (July and August).

Environment - current issues : water pollution from raw sewage, industrial wastes, and agricultural runoff; limited natural fresh water resources; a majority of the population does not have access to potable water; deforestation; soil erosion; desertification.

Environment - international agreements

Party to: Biodiversity, Climate Change, Desertification, Endangered Species, Environmental Modification, Hazardous Wastes, Law of the Sea, Marine Dumping, Nuclear Test Ban, Ozone Layer Protection, Ship Pollution, Wetlands *signed, but not ratified:* Marine Life Conservation.

Geography - note: controls Khyber Pass and Bolan Pass, traditional invasion routes between Central Asia and the Indian Subcontinent.

Pakistan, officially Islamic Republic of Pakistan, is bounded on the north and northwest by Afghanistan, on the northeast by Jammu and Kashmir, on the east and southeast by India, on the south by the Arabian Sea, and on the west by Iran.

The status of Jammu and Kashmir is a matter of dispute between India and Pakistan. Until December 1971 Pakistan included the province of East Pakistan; at that time, however, East Pakistan seceded from Pakistan and assumed the name Bangladesh. The capital of Pakistan is Islamabad, the largest city of the country is Karachi.

CLIMATE

Pakistan has three seasons: winter (November-March) is warm and cooled by sea breezes on the coast; summer (April-July) has extreme temperatures and the monsoon season (July-September) has the highest rainfall on the hills. Karachi has little rain. The best time to visit southern Pakistan is between November and March, when the days are cool and clear. The best time to visit northern Pakistan is from April to October.

Pakistan is a Muslim nation in southern Asia. The country's official name is the Islamic Republic of Pakistan. About 97 per cent of its people practise Islam, the Muslim religion.

Religion was the chief reason for the establishment of Pakistan as an independent nation. The separation in 1947 of British India into the Muslim state of Pakistan (with two sections West and East) and largely Hindu India was never satisfactorily resolved.

A third war between these countries in 1971 resulted in East Pakistan seceding and becoming the separate nation of Bangladesh. A dispute over the state of Kashmir is ongoing. In response to Indian nuclear weapons testing, Pakistan conducted its own tests in 1998.

Size: Total land area estimated to be 796,095 square kilometers.

Topography: Three major geographic areas: northern highlands, Indus River plain, and Balochistan Plateau.

Climate: Generally arid; hot summers, cool or cold winters; wide variations of temperature in given locale and between coastal area on Arabian Sea and glacial regions of northern areas; little rainfall.

PHYSICAL ENVIRONMENT

Located in the northwestern part of the South Asian subcontinent, Pakistan became a state as a result of the partition of British India on August 14, 1947. Pakistan annexed PoK after the Indo-Pakistani War of 1947-48. Initially, Pakistan also included the northeastern sector of the subcontinent, where Muslims are also in the majority. The East Wing and West Wing of Pakistan were, however, separated by 1,600 kilometers of hostile Indian territory. The country's East Wing, or East Pakistan, became the independent state of Bangladesh in December 1971.

BOUNDARIES

Pakistan occupies a position of great geostrategic importance, bordered by Iran on the west, Afghanistan on the northwest, China on the northeast, India on the east, and the Arabian Sea on the south . The total land area is estimated at 803,940 square kilometers. The boundary with Iran, some 800 kilometers in length, was first delimited by a British commission in 1893, separating Iran from what was then British Indian Balochistan. In 1957 Pakistan signed a frontier agreement with Iran, and since then the border between the two countries has not been a subject of serious dispute.

Pakistan's boundary with Afghanistan is about 2,250 kilometers long. In the north, it runs along the ridges of the Hindu Kush (meaning Hindu Killer) mountains and the Pamirs, where a narrow strip of Afghan territory called the Wakhan Corridor extends between Pakistan and Tajikistan. The Hindu Kush was traditionally regarded as the last northwestern outpost where Hindus could venture in safety. The boundary line with Afghanistan was drawn in 1893 by Sir Mortimer Durand, then Foreign Secretary in British India, and was acceded to by the Amir of Afghanistan that same year. This boundary, called the Durand Line, was not in doubt when Pakistan became independent in 1947, although its legitimacy was in later years disputed periodically by the Afghan government as well as by Pakhtun tribes straddling the Pakistan-Afghanistan border. On the one hand, Afghanistan claimed that the Durand Line had been imposed by a stronger power upon a weaker one, and it favored the establishment of still another state to be called Pashtunistan or Pakhtunistan. On the other hand, Pakistan, as the legatee of the British in the region, insisted on the legality and permanence of the boundary. The Durand Line remained in effect in 1994.

In the northeastern tip of the country, Pakistan controls about 84,159 square kilometers of the former princely state of Jammu and Kashmir. This area, consisting of PoK (11,639 square kilometers) and most of the Northern Areas (72,520 square kilometers), which includes Gilgit and Baltistan, is the most visually stunning of Pakistan. The Northern Areas has five of the world's seventeen highest mountains. It also has such extensive glaciers that it has sometimes been called the "third pole." The boundary line has been a matter of pivotal dispute between Pakistan and India since 1947, and the Siachen Glacier in northern Kashmir has been an important arena for fighting between the two sides since 1984, although far more soldiers have died of exposure to the cold than from any skirmishes in the conflict.

From the eastern end of the Afghanistan-Pakistan border, a boundary of about 520 kilometers runs generally southeast between China and Pakistan, ending near the Karakoram Pass. This line was determined from 1961 to 1965 in a series of agreements between China and Pakistan. By mutual agreement, a new boundary treaty is to be negotiated between China and Pakistan when the dispute over Kashmir is finally resolved between India and Pakistan.

The Pakistan-India cease-fire line runs from the Karakoram Pass west-southwest to a point about 130 kilometers northeast of Lahore. This line, about 770 kilometers long, was arranged with United Nations (UN) assistance at the end of the Indo-Pakistani War of 1947-48. The cease-fire line came into effect on January 1, 1949, after eighteen months of fighting and was last adjusted and agreed upon by the two countries in the Simla Agreement of July 1972. Since then, it has been generally known as the Line of Control.

The Pakistan-India boundary continues irregularly southward for about 1,280 kilometers, following the line of the 1947 Radcliffe Award, named for Sir Cyril Radcliffe, the head of the British boundary commission on the partition of Punjab and Bengal in 1947. Although this boundary with India is not formally disputed, passions still run high on both sides of the border. Many Indians had expected the original boundary line to run farther to the west, thereby ceding Lahore to India; Pakistanis had expected the line to run much farther east, possibly granting them control of Delhi, the imperial capital of the Mughal Empire.

The southern borders are far less contentious than those in the north. The Thar Desert in the province of Sindh is separated in the south from the salt flats of the Rann of Kutch by a boundary that was first delineated in 1923-24. After partition, Pakistan contested the southern boundary of Sindh, and a succession of border incidents resulted. They were less dangerous and less widespread, however, than the conflict that erupted in Kashmir in the Indo-Pakistani War of August 1965. These southern hostilities were ended by British mediation, and both sides accepted the award of the Indo-Pakistan Western Boundary Case Tribunal designated by the UN Secretary General. The tribunal made its award on February 19, 1968, delimiting a line of 403 kilometers that was later demarcated by joint survey teams. Of its original claim of some 9,100 square kilometers, Pakistan was awarded only about 780 square kilometers. Beyond the western terminus of the tribunal's award, the final stretch of Pakistan's border with India is about 80 kilometers long, running west and southwest to an inlet of the Arabian Sea.

TOPOGRAPHY AND DRAINAGE

Pakistan is divided into three major geographic areas: the northern highlands; the Indus River plain, with two major subdivisions corresponding roughly to the provinces of Punjab and Sindh; and the Balochistan Plateau. Some geographers designate additional major regions. For example, the mountain ranges along the western border with Afghanistan are sometimes described separately from the Balochistan Plateau, and on the eastern border with India, south of the Sutlej River, the Thar Desert may be considered separately from the Indus Plain. Nevertheless, the country may conveniently be visualized in general terms as divided in three by an imaginary line drawn eastward from the Khyber Pass and another drawn southwest from Islamabad down the middle of the country. Roughly, then, the northern highlands are north of the imaginary east-west line; the Balochistan Plateau is to the west of the imaginary southwest line; and the Indus Plain lies to the east of that line.

The northern highlands include parts of the Hindu Kush, the Karakoram Range, and the Himalayas. This area includes such famous peaks as K2 (Mount Godwin Austen, at 8,611 meters the second highest peak in the world), and Nanga Parbat (8,126 meters), the twelfth highest. More than one-half of the summits are over 4,500 meters, and more than fifty peaks reach above 6,500 meters. Travel through the area is difficult and dangerous, although the government is attempting to develop certain areas into tourist and trekking sites. Because of their rugged topography and the rigors of the climate, the northern highlands and the Himalayas to the east have been formidable barriers to movement into Pakistan throughout history.

South of the northern highlands and west of the Indus River plain are the Safed Koh Range along the Afghanistan border and the Sulaiman Range and Kirthar Range, which define the western extent of the province of Sindh and reach almost to the southern coast. The lower reaches are far more arid than those in the north, and they branch into ranges that run generally to the southwest across the province Balochistan. North-south valleys in Balochistan and Sindh have restricted the migration of peoples along the Makran Coast on the Arabian Sea east toward the plains.

Several large passes cut the ranges along the border with Afghanistan. Among them are the Khojak Pass, about eighty kilometers northwest of Quetta in Balochistan; the Khyber Pass, forty kilometers west of Peshawar and leading to Kabul; and the Baroghil Pass in the far north, providing access to the Wakhan Corridor.

Less than a one-fifth of Pakistan's land area has the potential for intensive agricultural use. Nearly all of the arable land is actively cultivated, but outputs are low by world standards. Cultivation is sparse in the northern mountains, the southern deserts, and the western plateaus, but the Indus River basin in Punjab and northern Sindh has fertile soil that enables Pakistan to feed its population under usual climatic conditions.

The name *Indus* comes from the Sanskrit word *Sindhu,* meaning ocean, from which also come the words *Sindh, Hindu,* and *India.* The Indus, one of the great rivers of the world, rises in southwestern Tibet only about 160 kilometers west of the source of the Sutlej River, which joins the Indus in Punjab, and the Brahmaputra, which runs eastward before turning southwest and flowing through Bangladesh. The catchment area of the Indus is estimated at almost 1 million square kilometers, and all of Pakistan's major rivers—the Kabul, Jhelum, Chenab, Ravi, and Sutlej—flow into it. The Indus River basin is a large, fertile alluvial plain formed by silt from the Indus. This area has been inhabited by agricultural civilizations for at least 5,000 years.

The upper Indus Basin includes Punjab; the lower Indus Basin begins at the Panjnad River (the confluence of the eastern tributaries of the Indus) and extends south to the coast. In Punjab (meaning the "land of five waters") are the Indus, Jhelum, Chenab, Ravi, and Sutlej rivers. The Sutlej, however, is mostly on the Indian side of the border. In the southern part of the province of Punjab, the British attempted to harness the irrigation power of the water over 100 years ago when they established what came to be known as the Canal Colonies. The irrigation project, which facilitated the emergence of intensive cultivation despite arid conditions, resulted in important social and political transformations.

Pakistan has two great river dams: the Tarbela Dam on the Indus, near the early Buddhist site at Taxila, and the Mangla Dam on the Jhelum, where Punjab borders PoK. The Warsak Dam on the Kabul River near Peshawar is smaller. These dams, along with a series of head works and barrages built by the British and expanded since independence, are of vital importance to the national economy and played an important role in calming the raging floodwaters of 1992, which devastated large areas in the northern highlands and the Punjab plains.

Pakistan is subject to frequent seismic disturbances because the tectonic plate under the subcontinent hits the plate under Asia as it continues to move northward and to push the Himalayas ever higher. The region surrounding Quetta is highly prone to earthquakes. A severe quake in 1931 was followed by one of more destructive force in 1935. The small city of Quetta was almost completely destroyed, and the adjacent military cantonment was heavily damaged. At least 20,000 people were killed. Tremors continue in the vicinity of Quetta; the most recent major quake occurred in January 1991. Far fewer people were killed in the 1991 quake than died in 1935, although entire villages in the North-West Frontier Province were destroyed. A major earthquake centered in the North-West Frontier Province's Kohistan District in 1965 also caused heavy damage.

CHAPTER 8

SOCIETY AND CULTURE

SOCIETY

Pakistani society is ethnically diverse yet overwhelmingly Muslim. It is largely rural yet beset by the problems of hyper urbanization. Since its independence in 1947, Pakistan has enjoyed a robust and expanding economy—the average per capita income in the mid-1990s approached the transition line separating low-income from middle-income countries—but wealth is poorly distributed. A middle-class is emerging, but a narrow stratum of elite families maintains extremely disproportionate control over the nation's wealth, and almost one-third of all Pakistanis live in poverty. It is a male-dominated society in which social development has lagged considerably behind economic change, as revealed by such critical indicators as sanitation, access to health care, and literacy, especially among females. Increasing population pressure on limited resources, together with this pattern of social and economic inequity, was causing increased disquietude within the society in the early 1990s.

Pakistan was created in 1947, as a homeland for Muslims in South Asia, and about 97 per cent of Pakistanis are Muslim. The founders of Pakistan hoped that religion would provide a coherent focus for national identity, a focus that would supersede the country's considerable ethnic and linguistic variations. Although this aspiration has not been completely fulfilled, Islam has been a pervasive presence in Pakistani society, and debate continues about its appropriate role in national civic life. During the 1990s,

Islamic discourse has been less prominent in political controversy, but the role that Islamic law should play in the country's affairs and governance remains an important issue.

There is immense regional diversity in Pakistan. Pakhtuns, Baloch, Punjabis, and Sindhis are all Muslim, yet they have diverse cultural traditions and speak different languages. Ethnic, regional, and—above all—family loyalties figure far more prominently for the average individual than do national loyalties. Punjabis, the most numerous ethnic group, predominate in the central government and the military. Baloch, Pakhtuns, and Sindhis find the Punjabi preponderance at odds with their own aspirations for provincial autonomy. Ethnic mixing within each province further complicates social and political relations.

Expectations had been raised by the return of democracy to Pakistan in 1988 after the death of Mohammad Zia-ul-Haq, by the continued economic expansion in the 1990s, and by some observable improvement in the volatile relations among ethnic groups that had so divided the country in years past. Also in the early 1990s, previously peripheralized social movements, particularly those concerning women and the environment, assumed a more central role in public life. As bilateral and multilateral development assistance has dwindled, non governmental organizations (NGOs) committed to economic and social development have emerged and begun to take on important responsibilities. Nonetheless, the problems that confront Pakistan pose a significant threat to its cohesion and future.

Sociologists speak of a loss of a sense of social contract among Pakistanis that has adversely affected the country's infrastructure: the economy, the education system, the government bureaucracy, and even the arts. As population pressure increases, the failure of the populace to develop a sense of publicly committed citizenship becomes more and more significant. The self-centeredness about which educator Ishtiaq Husain Qureshi complained soon after independence is increasingly noticeable in many areas of social life. Although many people once imagined that economic development would by itself improve the quality of life, few any longer believe this to be true.

Family or personal interest and status take precedence over public good in Pakistan. Thus traffic laws are often enforced solely according to a person's political clout rather than due process, and admission to school depends more upon connections or wealth than on ability.

Failure to develop civic-minded citizenship is also evident in public administration and imbalanced government spending. For example, military expenditures vastly exceed combined expenditures on health and education. The bureaucracy, a legacy of the British colonial period, has not modernized sufficiently to incorporate new technologies and innovations despite efforts by the government staff colleges. Although in the mid-1980s the World Bank forecast the advancement of Pakistan to the ranks of middle-income countries, the nation had not quite achieved this transition in the mid-1990s. Many blame this fact on Pakistan's failure to make significant progress in human development despite consistently high rates of economic growth. The annual population growth rate, which hovered between 3.1 and 3.3 per cent in the mid-1990s, threatens to precipitate increased social unrest as greater numbers of people scurry after diminishing resources.

An anonymous Pakistani writer has said that three things symbolized Pakistan's material culture in the 1990s: videocassette recorders (for playing Hindi films), locally manufactured Japanese Suzuki cars, and Kalashnikov rifles. Although the majority of the people still reside in villages, they increasingly take social cues from cities. Videocassette tapes can be rented in many small villages, where residents also watch Cable News Network (CNN)—censored through Islamabad—on televisions that are as numerous as radios were in the 1970s. The cities are more crowded than ever; parts of Karachi and Lahore are more densely populated even than Dhaka, the capital of Bangladesh. In many areas, tiny Suzuki automobiles have replaced the bicycles and motorcycles that were in great demand merely a decade earlier. Whereas urban violence was traditionally related to blood feuds, it has become more random and has escalated dramatically.

CULTURE

The pleasures of Pakistan are ancient: Buddhist monuments, Hindu temples, Islamic palaces, tombs, pleasure grounds and Anglo-Mogul mansions—some in a state of dereliction which makes their former grandeur more emphatic. Sculpture is dominated by Graeco-Buddhist friezes, and crafts by ceramics, jewellery, silk goods and engraved woodwork and metalwork. Pakistan's flotillas of mirror-buffed and chrome-sequinned vintage Bedford buses and trucks are dazzling works of art. Traditional dances are lusty and vigorous: music is either classical, folk or devotional; and the most patronized literature is a mix of the scholastic and poetic. Cricket is Pakistan's greatest sports obsession and national players are afforded hero status - unless, of course, they proselytise young and wealthy English women, then marry them.

Nearly all Pakistanis are Muslim, and Islam is the state religion. Christians are the largest minority, followed by Hindus and Parsees, descendants of Persian Zoroastrians. Note that dress codes are strictly enforced: to avoid offence invest in a *shalwar qamiz* - a long, loose, non-revealing garment worn by both men and women.

Pakistani food is similar to that of northern India, with a dollop of Middle Eastern influence thrown in for good measure. This means menus peppered with baked and deep-fried breads *(roti, chapattis, puri, halwa* and *nan)*, meat curries, lentil mush *{dhal)*, spicy spinach, cabbage, peas and rice, and of course that staple of hippies, the sturdy Hunza pie. Street snacks - *samosas* and *tikkas* (spiced and barbecued beef, mutton or chicken) - are delicious, while a range of desserts will satisfy any sweet tooth. The most common sweet is *barfi* (it pays to overtook the name), which is made of dried milk solids and comes in a variety of flavours. Though Pakistan is officially 'dry', it does brew its own beer and spirits which can be bought (as well as imported alcohol) from specially designated bars and top-end hotels.

CHAPTER 9

ENVIRONMENT AND POLLUTION

ENVIRONMENT

Pakistan is divided into three major geographic areas: the northern highlands; the Indus River plain, with two major subdivisions corresponding roughly to the provinces of Punjab and Sindh; and the Balochistan Plateau. Some geographers designate additional major regions. For example, the mountain ranges along the western border with Afghanistan are sometimes described separately from the Balochistan Plateau, and on the eastern border with India, south of the Sutlej River, the Thar Desert may be considered separately from the Indus Plain. Nevertheless, the country may conveniently be visualized in general terms as divided in three by an imaginary line drawn eastward from the Khyber Pass and another drawn southwest from Islamabad down the middle of the country. Roughly, then, the northern highlands are north of the imaginary east-west line; the Balochistan Plateau is to the west of the imaginary southwest line; and the Indus Plain lies to the east of that line.

The northern highlands include parts of the Hindu Kush, the Karakoram Range, and the Himalayas. This area includes such famous peaks as K2 (Mount Godwin Austen, at 8,611 meters the second highest peak in the world), and Nanga Parbat (8,126 meters), the twelfth highest. More than one-half of the summits are over 4,500 meters, and more than fifty peaks reach above 6,500 meters. Travel through the area is difficult and dangerous, although the government is attempting to develop certain areas into tourist and trekking sites. Because of their rugged topography and the rigors of the climate, the northern highlands and the Himalayas to the east have been formidable barriers to movement into Pakistan throughout history.

South of the northern highlands and west of the Indus River plain are the Safed Koh Range along the Afghanistan border and the Sulaiman Range and Kirthar Range, which define the western extent of the province of Sindh and reach almost to the southern coast. The lower reaches are far more arid than those in the north, and they branch into ranges that run generally to the southwest across the province Balochistan. North-south valleys in Balochistan and Sindh have restricted the migration of peoples along the Makran Coast on the Arabian Sea east toward the plains. Several large passes cut the ranges along the border with Afghanistan. Among them are the Khojak Pass, about eighty kilometers northwest of Quetta in Balochistan; the Khyber Pass, forty kilometers west of Peshawar and leading to Kabul; and the Baroghil Pass in the far north, providing access to the Wakhan Corridor.

Less than a one-fifth of Pakistan's land area has the potential for intensive agricultural use. Nearly all of the arable land is actively cultivated, but outputs are low by world standards. Cultivation is sparse in the northern mountains, the southern deserts, and the western plateaus, but the Indus River basin in Punjab and northern Sindh has fertile soil that enables Pakistan to feed its population under usual climatic conditions. The name Indus comes from the Sanskrit word Sindhu, meaning ocean, from which also come the words Sindh, Hindu, and India. The Indus, one of the great rivers of the world, rises in southwestern Tibet only about 160 kilometers west of the source of the Sutlej River, which joins the Indus in Punjab, and the Brahmaputra, which runs eastward before turning southwest and flowing through Bangladesh. The catchment area of the Indus is estimated at almost 1 million square kilometers, and all of Pakistan's major rivers—the Kabul, Jhelum, Chenab, Ravi, and Sutlej—flow into it. The Indus River basin is a large, fertile alluvial plain formed by silt from the Indus. This area has been inhabited by agricultural civilizations for at least 5,000 years.

The upper Indus Basin includes Punjab; the lower Indus Basin begins at the Panjnad River (the confluence of the eastern tributaries of the Indus) and extends south to the coast. In Punjab (meaning the "land of five waters") are the Indus, Jhelum, Chenab, Ravi, and Sutlej rivers. The Sutlej, however, is mostly on the Indian side of the border. In the southern part of the province of Punjab, the British attempted to harness the irrigation power of the water over 100 years ago when they established what came to be known as the Canal Colonies. The irrigation project, which facilitated the emergence of intensive cultivation despite arid conditions, resulted in important social and political transformations. Pakistan has two great river dams: the Tarbela Dam on the Indus, near the early Buddhist site at Taxila, and the Mangla Dam on the Jhelum, where Punjab borders PoK. The Warsak Dam on the Kabul River near Peshawar is smaller. These dams, along with a series of headworks and barrages built by the British and expanded since independence, are of vital importance to the national economy and played an important role in calming the raging floodwaters of 1992, which devastated large areas in the northern highlands and the Punjab plains.

Pakistan is subject to frequent seismic disturbances because the tectonic plate under the subcontinent hits the plate under Asia as it continues to move northward and to push the Himalayas ever higher. The region surrounding Quetta is highly prone to earthquakes. A severe quake in 1931 was followed by one of more destructive force in 1935. The small city of Quetta was almost completely destroyed, and the adjacent military cantonment was heavily damaged. At least 20,000 people were killed. Tremors continue in the vicinity of Quetta, the most recent major quake occurred in January 1991. Far fewer people were killed in the 1991 quake than died in 1935, although entire villages in the North-West Frontier Province were destroyed. A major earthquake centered in the North-West Frontier Province's Kohistan District in 1965 also caused heavy damage.

CLIMATE

Pakistan lies in the temperate zone. The climate is generally arid, characterized by hot summers and cool or cold winters, and wide variations between extremes of temperature at given locations. There is little rainfall. These generalizations should not, however, obscure the distinct differences existing among particular locations.

For example, the coastal area along the Arabian Sea is usually warm, whereas the frozen snow-covered ridges of the Karakoram Range and of other mountains of the far north are so cold year round that they are only accessible by world-class climbers for a few weeks in May and June of each year.

Pakistan has are four seasons: a cool, dry winter from December through February; a hot, dry spring from March through May; the summer rainy season, or southwest monsoon period, from June through September; and the retreating monsoon period of October and November. The onset and duration of these seasons vary somewhat according to location. The climate in the capital city of Islamabad varies from an average daily low of 2°C in January to an average daily high of 40°C in June. Half of the annual rainfall occurs in July and August, averaging about 255 millimeters in each of those two months. The remainder of the year has significantly less rain, amounting to about Fifty millimeters per month. Hailstorms are common in the spring.

Pakistan's largest city, Karachi, which is also the country's industrial center, is more humid than Islamabad but gets less rain. Only July and August average more than twenty-five millimeters of rain in the Karachi area; the remaining months are exceedingly dry. The temperature is also more uniform in Karachi than in Islamabad, ranging from an average daily low of 13°C during winter evenings to an average daily high of 34°C on summer days. Although the summer temperatures do not get as high as those in Punjab, the high humidity causes the residents a great deal of discomfort. Most areas in Punjab experience fairly cool winters, often accompanied by rain. Woollen shawls are worn by women and men for warmth because few homes are heated. By mid-February the temperature begins to rise; springtime weather continues until mid-April, when the summer heat sets in. The onset of the southwest monsoon is anticipated to reach Punjab by May, but since the early 1970s the weather pattern has been irregular. The spring monsoon has either skipped over the area or has caused it to rain so hard that floods have resulted. June and July are oppressively hot. Although official estimates rarely place the temperature above 46°C, newspaper sources claim that it reaches 51°C and regularly carry reports about people who have succumbed to the heat. Heat records were broken in Multan in June 1993, when the mercury was reported to have risen to 54°C. in August the oppressive heat is punctuated by the rainy season, referred to as barsat, which brings relief in its wake. The hardest part of the summer is then over, but cooler weather does not come until late October.

POLLUTION

Little attention was paid to pollution and environmental issues in Pakistan until the early 1990s. Related concerns, such as sanitation and potable water, received earlier scrutiny. In 1987 only about 6 per cent of rural residents and 51 per cent of urban residents had access to sanitary facilities; in 1990 a total of 97.6 million Pakistanis, or approximately 80 per cent of the population, had no access to flush toilets. Greater success has been achieved in bringing potable water within reach of the people; nearly half the population enjoyed such access by 1990. However, researchers at the Pakistan Medical Research Council, recognizing that a large proportion of diseases in Pakistan are caused by the consumption of polluted water, have been questioning the "safe" classification in use in the 1990s. Even the 38 per cent of the population that receives its water through pipelines runs the risk of consuming seriously contaminated water, although the problem varies by area. In Punjab, for example, as much as 90 per cent of drinking water comes from groundwater, as compared with only 9 per cent in Sindh.

The central government's Perspective Plan (1988-2003) and previous five-year plans do not mention sustainable development strategies. Further, there have been no overarching policies focused on sustainable development and conservation. The state has focused on achieving self-sufficiency in food production, meeting energy demands, and containing the high rate of population growth, not on curtailing pollution or other environmental hazards. In 1992 Pakistan's *National Conservation Strategy Report* attempted to redress the previous inattention to the nation's mounting environmental problem. Drawing on the expertise of more than 3,000 people from a wide array of political affiliations, the government produced a document outlining the current state of environmental health, its sustainable goals, and viable program options for the future. Of special concern to environmentalists is the diminishing forest cover in watershed regions of the northern highlands, which has only recently come under close scrutiny. Forest areas have been thoughtlessly denuded. Deforestation, which occurred at an annual rate of 0.4 per cent in 1989-90, has contributed directly to the severity of the flooding problem faced by the nation in the early 1990s. As industry has expanded, factories have emitted more and more toxic effluents into the air and water. The number of textile and food processing mills in rural Punjab has grown greatly since the mid-1970s, resulting in pollution of its rivers and irrigation canals. Groundwater quality throughout the country has also suffered from rapidly increasing use of pesticides and fertilizers aimed at promoting more intensive cropping and facilitating self-sufficiency in food production.

The *National Conservation Strategy Report* has documented how solid and liquid excreta are the major source of water pollution in the country and the cause of widespread waterborne diseases. Because only just over half of urban residents have access to sanitation, the remaining urban excreta are deposited on roadsides, into waterways, or incorporated into solid waste. Additionally, only three major sewage treatment plants exist in the country; two of them operate intermittently. Much of the untreated sewage goes into irrigation systems, where the wastewater is reused, and into streams and rivers, which become sewage carriers at low-flow periods. Consequently, the vegetables grown from such wastewater have serious bacteriological contamination. Gastroenteritis, widely considered in medical circles to be the leading cause of death in Pakistan, is transmitted through waterborne pollutants. Low-lying land is generally used for solid waste disposal, without the benefit of sanitary landfill methods. The National Conservation Strategy has raised concerns about industrial toxic wastes also being dumped in municipal disposal areas without any record of their location, quantity, or toxic composition. Another important issue is the contamination of shallow groundwater near urban industries that discharge wastes directly into the ground.

Water in Karachi is so contaminated that almost all residents boil it before consuming it. Because sewerage and water lines have been laid side by side in most parts of the city, leakage is the main cause of contamination. High levels of lead also have been found in water in Islamabad and Rawalpindi. Air pollution has also become a major problem in most cities. There are no controls on vehicular emissions, which account for 90 per cent of pollutants. The *National Conservation Strategy Report* claims that the average Pakistani vehicle emits twenty-five times as much carbon monoxide, twenty times as many hydrocarbons, and more than three and one-half times as much nitrous oxide in grams per kilometer as the average vehicle in the United States. Another major source of pollution, not mentioned in the *National Conservation Strategy Report,* is noise. The hyperurbanization experienced by Pakistan since the 1960s has resulted in loose controls for heavy equipment operation in densely populated areas, as well as in crowded streets filled with buses, trucks, automobiles, and motorcycles, which often honk at each other and at the horse-drawn tongas (used for transporting people) and the horse-drawn *rehras* (used for transporting goods).

CHAPTER 10

CLIMATE

Pakistan has three seasons: winter (November-March) is warm and cooled by sea breezes on the coast; summer (April-July) has extreme temperatures and the monsoon season (July-September) has the highest rainfall on the hills. Karachi has little rain. The best time to visit southern Pakistan is between November and March, when the days are cool and clear. The best time to visit northern Pakistan is from April to October.

Pakistan lies in the temperate zone. The climate is generally arid, characterized by hot summers and cool or cold winters, and wide variations between extremes of temperature at given locations. There is little rainfall. These generalizations should not, however, obscure the distinct differences existing among particular locations. For example, the coastal area along the Arabian Sea is usually warm, whereas the frozen snow-covered ridges of the Karakoram Range and of other mountains of the far north are so cold year round that they are only accessible by world-class climbers for a few weeks in May and June of each year.

Pakistan has are four seasons: a cool, dry winter from December through February; a hot, dry spring from March through May; the summer rainy season, or southwest monsoon period, from June through September; and the retreating monsoon period of October and November. The onset and duration of these seasons vary somewhat according to location. The climate in the capital city of Islamabad varies from an average daily low of 2°C in January to an average daily high of 40°C in June. Half of the annual rainfall occurs in July and August, averaging about 255 millimeters in each of those two months. The remainder of the year has significantly less rain, amounting to about fifty millimeters per month. Hailstorms are common in the spring. Pakistan's largest city, Karachi, which is also the country's industrial center, is more humid than Islamabad but gets less rain. Only July and August average more than twenty-five millimeters of rain in the Karachi area; the remaining months are exceedingly dry. The temperature is also more uniform in Karachi than in Islamabad, ranging from an average daily low of 13°C during winter evenings to an average daily high of 34°C on summer days. Although the summer temperatures do not get as high as those in Punjab, the high humidity causes the residents a great deal of discomfort.

Most areas in Punjab experience fairly cool winters, often accompanied by rain. Woollen shawls are worn by women and men for warmth because few homes are heated. By mid-February the temperature begins to rise; springtime weather continues until mid-April, when the summer heat sets in. The onset of the southwest monsoon is anticipated to reach Punjab by May, but since the early 1970s the weather pattern has been irregular. The spring monsoon has either skipped over the area or has caused it to rain so hard that floods have resulted. June and July are oppressively hot. Although official estimates rarely place the temperature above 46°C, newspaper sources claim that it reaches 51°C and regularly carry reports about people who have succumbed to the heat. Heat records were broken in Multan in June 1993, when the mercury was reported to have risen to 54°C. In August the oppressive heat is punctuated by the rainy season, referred to as *barsat,* which brings relief in its wake. The hardest part of the summer is then over, but cooler weather does not come until late October.

CHAPTER 11

INDIA-PAKISTAN WARS

Name given to the series of conflicts between India and Pakistan since 1947, when the Indian subcontinent was partitioned and the two countries became independent of Great Britain. The most violent outbreaks came in 1947-48, 1965, and 1971. The roots of the conflicts lie in the hostility between Hindus and Muslims and, initially, in the disposition of self-governing princely states.

THE 1947-48 WAR

The first war arose over Kashmir, in NW India, in 1947 when Muslim subjects revolted and were supported by Pakistani troops. The Hindu ruler appealed to India for aid, agreeing to cede the state to India in return. India moved quickly to consolidate its position in Kashmir, pushing Pakistan's "volunteers" back. Conflicts also arose in the Punjab and in Bengal. The undeclared war in Kashmir continued until Jan. 1, 1949, when a truce was arranged through UN mediation; negotiations between India and Pakistan began and lasted until 1954 without resolving the Kashmir problem.

THE 1965 WAR

The second war began in Apr., 1965, when fighting broke out in the Rann of Kutch, a sparsely inhabited region along the West Pakistan-India border. In August fighting spread to Kashmir and to the Punjab, and in September Pakistani and Indian troops crossed the partition line between the two countries and launched air assaults on each other's cities. After threats of intervention by China had been successfully opposed by the United States and Britain, Pakistan and India agreed to a UN-sponsored cease-fire and withdrew to the pre-August lines. Prime Minister Shri Lal Bahadur Shastri of India and President Ayub Khan of Pakistan met in Tashkent, USSR (now Tashkent, Uzbekistan), in Jan., 1966, and signed an agreement pledging continued negotiations and respect for the cease-fire conditions. After the Tashkent Declaration another period of relative peace ensued.

THE 1971 WAR

Indo-Pakistani relations deteriorated when civil war erupted in Pakistan, pitting the West Pakistan army against East Pakistanis demanding greater autonomy. The fighting forced 10 million East Pakistani Bengalis to flee to India. When Pakistan attacked Indian airfields in Kashmir, India attacked both East and West Pakistan. It occupied the eastern half, which declared its independence as Bangladesh, on Dec. 6, 1971. Under great-power pressure, a UN cease-fire was arranged in mid-December, after Pakistan's defeat. Pakistan lost its eastern half, an army of 100,000 soldiers, and was thrown into political turmoil. Zulfikar Ali Bhutto emerged as leader of Pakistan, and Mujibur Rahman as prime minister of Bangladesh. Tensions were alleviated by the Shimla accord of 1972, and by Pakistan's recognition of Bangladesh in 1974, but tensions have periodically recurred.

THE KARGIL CONFLICT

The Kargil conflict was the result of the Pakistan's plan of "Operation Topac" which was formulated by General Zia in 1988. The "Operation Topac" was to be completed in two phases. The first phase of this plan was implemented by Pakistan against India in 1989 and as a result of the implementation of the phase II of this Pakistan plan happened the present Kargil war. To counter Kargil war India had to conduct "Operation Vijay".

We contain valuable information and facts to enhance the knowledge of the people. It is the first hand information concerning Kargil Conflict between India and Pakistan. It highlights India's politio-military supremacy over Pakistan. It contains facts concerning the aggression, the situation which encouraged Pakistan to attempt an open aggression in Kargil region on Indian side of the line of control (LoC).

INDO-PAKISTANI CONFLICT OF 1947-48

The first war between India and Pakistan began in October 1947 and ended in December 1948. The origins of the first war between India and Pakistan can be traced to the final status of

Kashmir following the establishment of an independent India and Pakistan August 15, 1947. British policy held that the various princely states would have to accede to either Pakistan or India based on geographic location and on demographics. While the final status of many of the states was easily concluded, Kashmir and two other states presented special problems. Kashmir was strategically located between India and Pakistan and though it was led by a Hindu Maharaja, Muslims made up the majority of the population. Sikhs and Hindus made up the other major ethnicities though they were a minority compared to the Muslim population. Though required to choose between the India and Pakistan the Maharaja was unable to decide which state to join.

Both states applied a significant degree of pressure to sway Kashmir's government. Pakistan felt that as it was the established state for Muslims in South Asia that Kashmir should accede to it rather than India. Tensions between Pakistan and the government of Kashmir grew as the Maharaja's indecision frustrated Pakistan and pro-Pakistani factions within Kashmir. Hostilities began in early October 1947 when a tribal rebellion broke out in Poonch in southwest Kashmir. By October 20th the Pakistani Army entered the conflict in support of the tribal forces in a multi-pronged effort designed to capture Uri, Jhangar, Rajuara, and Naushera in the opening days of the campaign. Pakistan's timetable was to capture the capital of Kashmir, Srinagar, within a week.

Tribal and Pakistani forces experienced significant successes in the opening days of the conflict as they were able to take Dommel on the first day and overpowered a Kashmiri government battalion at Muzaffarabad by October 23. Tribal and Pakistani forces met fierce resistance at Uri, where Kashmiri government forces, despite the desertion of many of its Muslim troops, were able to delay the Pakistani forces for two days until it was destroyed. Retreating Kashmiri forces were able to destroy a key bridge thus delaying Pakistani forces for an additional day. Pakistani efforts to the south in the Jammu region were less successful as Pakistani forces faced significant resistance and were prevented from gaining most of the towns and locations that Pakistan attempted to capture.

Following the fall of Uri, Pakistani and tribal forces took Baramula and began to march on Srinagar. The Pakistani-backed forces were able to damage an important power station, located in Mahura, that supplied electricity to Srinagar. In the following days the invading forces were able to get within a few miles of the airfield near Srinagar. Up to this point the Pakistani-backed forces had faced opposition only from the Kashmiri government forces. The Maharaja, facing overwhelming odds and near certain defeat, asked India for military support. India agreed to help provided that Kashmir acceded to India and that the Prime Minister of Kashmir agreed to the accession. Both the Maharaja and the Prime Minister agreed to these terms and on October 26 the Maharaja signed the instrument of Accession.

India's 161st infantry Brigade was deployed and thwarted the advance of the tribal forces. In early November 1947, the 161st using armored cars, counterattacked, surprising the Pakistani forces and successfully broke through the their defenses. The 161st was flown into the airfield at Srinagar and from there was able to repulse the Pakistani-backed forces. Initial successes allowed the Indians to secure the airfield and to return power to Srinagar. The momentum of the Indian counterattack forced the Pakistani forces into a full retreat allowing elements of the 161st to retake Baramula and Uri. Despite early successes, the Indian army suffered a setback in December because of logistical problems. Furthermore, many of the Indian soldiers were ill prepared for fighting in the mountainous region of Kashmir and Jammu, few were experienced at high altitude combat nor were they prepared for the cold. These setbacks were significant as the Pakistani-backed forces were able to capitalize on these problems and to push back Indian forces from the border area.

In the spring of 1948, the Indian side mounted another offensive to retake some of the ground that it had lost. Pakistani regulars were introduced into the conflict later in the year, targeting the city of Jammu. The fighting from the spring through December 1948 was widespread as Pakistani forces conducted operations in both the north and the south. The intensity of the conflict and the inability to foresee a quick end to the conflict without Involving considerable resources on the part of India to expel the Pakistani forces led Indian leaders to approach the United Nations who ultimately introduced Observers in June 1948. A UN brokered cease-fire went into effect on Jan. 1, 1949.

THE 1947-48 WAR SCENARIO

It was Jinnah's idea of sending 'Razakars' into the valley and draw the Kashmiris' will towards their side. However, things did not go as he had envisaged. What turned out was a bloody orgy of plunder and rape against any human, Hindu or Muslim, who stood in the way of the tribesmen. This was the first fatal mistake that Pakistan had made regarding Kashmir, a mistake that only alienated it from the population. Maharaja Hari Singh entered in to a standstill agreement with India and Pakistan. However, Pakistan felt that Jammu and Kashmir being a Muslim-dominated state, it should accede to Pakistan in accordance with the general principles of Partition. Suspecting the intentions of the Maharaja and anxious to secure the state without loss of time. It launched an invasion on Jammu and Kashmir on October 20, 1947. Pakistan initially utilised tribesmen from the North West Frontier Province, ex- soldiers, deserters from the state forces and personnel of the regular army supposedly on leave.

On October 24, 1947, the Maharaja requested the Government of India for military aid and on October 26 signed the 'Instrument of Accession to India' with the concurrence of Sheikh Abdullah. On October 27, India despatched troops to the state. While efforts to clean up the valley were going on, the Government of India also appealed to the UN to intervene in the case and get Pakistan to stop its aggression. A memorandum was presented to the Security Council on December 30, 1947. Broadly, the Indian Army's operations in Jammu and Kashmir fall into two parts: the initial response to clear the raiders from the Valley, and to recapture maximum territory lost and link up isolated garrisons.

One should remember that the political and social set-up of the two new nations were totally different from what it is now. India and Pakistan were non-players on the world stage. Both States were insufficient in military capabilities and had a non-existent economy. Kashmir had not yet woken up to the realities of political independence. At this juncture, Pakistan made its first great blunder, of unleashing terror that it could not control. This alienated the people from Pakistan instead of endearing them to it. In the words of General Mohd Musa, later commander-in-chief of the Pakistan Army, "It seems that the tribesmen who had gone to Kashmir to help the Muslim population of the state against their ruthless oppressors and in resisting their tyranny, were not guided by the so-called leaders who were actuated by personal motives of self-glorification."

This conflict did bring out salient features in the political and military spheres that would not have come up had the situation not arisen. In the political sphere, it must be remembered that the 1947-48 war was really forced on India in its infancy. There was not much time to react, or any preparation possible. It should also be remembered that no military assistance could be rendered unless the state acceded to India. Such a situation needed sagacity of a high order to understand the vital national interests at that point of time. Pakistan always supported the 'Two Nation Theory' and thus Muslim-dominated lands came under its domain. India, on the other hand, always went by people's will. Thus, while accepting the Instrument of Accession, it ensured that the request had the support of the people, as represented by the major political party, the Muslim National Conference, led by Sheikh Abdullah.

Had the Indian forces been allowed to continue the operation for a few months more, perhaps the enemy could have been evicted even from the remainder of the territory under its occupation. However, being conscious of the need to restore peace and having complete faith in the UN to ensure justice, the Indian government agreed to the cease-fire. A unique feature of these operations was the excellent rapport that developed between the local civilian population and the military that went to their aid. Senior political personalities like Bakshi, Dhar and Nazir maintained constant liaison with the Army and even accompanied them during operations. Even the locals aided the military by providing valuable intelligence and logistics. As the areas were liberated, the Army extended medical help, built roads and helped in the reconstruction of a ravaged state.

The period during 1947-48 is unthinkable by today's standards. Every document of this episode in Kashmir's history clearly points out towards the unnecessary evil act of Pakistan.

INDO-PAKISTAN WAR OF 1965

The second indo-Pakistani conflict (1965) was also fought over Kashmir and started without a formal declaration of war. The war began in August 5, 1965 and was ended Sept. 22,1965. The war was initiated by Pakistan who since the defeat of India by China in 1962 had come to believe that Indian military would be unable or unwilling to defend against a quick military campaign in Kashmir, and because the Pakistani government was becoming increasingly alarmed by Indian efforts to integrate Kashmir within India. There was also a perception that there was widespread popular support within for Pakistani rule and that the Kashmiri people were dissatisfied with Indian rule.

After Pakistan was successful in the Rann of Kutch earlier in 1965, Ayub Khan (by nature a cautious person) was pressured by the hawks in his cabinet (led by Z.A. Bhutto) and the army to infiltrate the cease-fire line in Kashmir. The action was based on the incorrect premise that indigenous resistance could be ignited by a few saboteurs. Ayub resisted the idea as he foresaw India crossing the international frontier in retaliation at a point of its choosing. The Bhutto faction, which included some prominent generals, put out the canard that Ayub's cowardice stemmed from his desire to protect his newly acquired wealth. It was boasted at the time that one Pakistani soldier was equal to four Indian soldiers and so on. On August 5, 1965 between 26,000 and 33,000 Pakistani soldiers crossed the Line of Control dressed as Kashmiri locals headed for various areas within Kashmir. Indian forces, tipped off by the local populace, crossed the cease fire line on August 15.

The initial battles between India and Pakistan were contained within Kashmir involving both infantry and armor units with each country's air force playing major roles. It was not until early September when Pakistani forces attacked Ackhnur that the Indians escalated the conflict by attacking targets within Pakistan itself, forcing the Pakistani forces to disengage from Ackhnur to counter Indian attacks. The largest engagement of the war occurred in the Sialkot region where some 400 to 600 tanks squared off. Unfortunately the battle was indecisive. By Sept. 22 both sides had agreed to a UN mandated cease-fire ending the war that had by that point reached a stalemate.

Overall, the war was militarily inconclusive; each side held prisoners and some territory belonging to the other. Losses were relatively heavy—on the Pakistani side, twenty aircraft, 200 tanks, and 3,800 troops. Pakistan's army had been able to withstand Indian pressure, but a continuation of the fighting would only have led to further losses and ultimate defeat for Pakistan. Most Pakistanis, schooled in the belief of their own martial prowess, refused to accept the possibility of their country's military defeat by "Hindu India" and were, instead, quick to blame their failure to attain their military aims on what they considered to be the ineptitude of Ayub Khan and his government.

Pakistan was rudely shocked by the reaction of the United States to the war. Judging the matter to be largely Pakistan s fault, the United States not only refused to come to Pakistan's aid under the terms of the Agreement of Cooperation, but issued a statement declaring its neutrality while also cutting off military supplies. The Pakistanis were embittered at what they considered a friend's betrayal, and the experience taught them to avoid relying on any single source of support. For its part, the United States was disillusioned by a war in which both sides used United States—supplied equipment. The war brought other repercussions for the security relationship as well. The United States withdrew its military assistance advisory group in July 1967. In response to these events, Pakistan declined to renew the lease on the Peshawar military facility, which ended in 1969. Eventually, United States–Pakistan relations grew measurably weaker as the United States became more deeply involved in Vietnam and as its broader interest in the security of South Asia waned.

Iran, Indonesia, and especially China gave political support to Pakistan during the war, thus suggesting new directions in Pakistan that might translate into support for its security concerns. Most striking was the attitude of the Soviet Union. Its post-Khrushchev leadership, rather than rallying reflexively to India's side, adopted a neutral position and ultimately provided the good offices at Tashkent, which led to the January 1966 Tashkent Declaration that restored the status quo ante. The aftermath of the 1965 war saw a dramatic shift in Pakistan's security environment, instead of a single alignment with the United States against China and the Soviet Union, Pakistan found itself cut off from United States military support, on increasingly warm terms with China, and treated equitably by the Soviet Union. Unchanged was the enmity with which India and Pakistan regarded each other over Kashmir. The result was the elaboration of a new security approach, called by Ayub Khan the "triangular tightrope"—a tricky endeavor to maintain good ties with the United States while cultivating China and the Soviet Union. Support from other developing nations was also welcome. None of the new relationships carried the weight of previous ties with the United States, but, taken together, they at least provided Pakistan with a political counterbalance to India.

THE CHALLENGE : PAKISTAN ATTACKS INDIAN AIR FIELDS

The 1965 War

In September, 1965, the long standing border disputes, communal tensions and conflict over the question of Kashmir flared up in a full-scale war between India and Pakistan.

The War of Rann of Kutch

Skirmishes at the Rann of Kutch flared up almost accidentally in the spring of 1965, and India and Pakistan found themselves drawn into the first of their two undeclared wars. The dispute goes back to the days of the British rule in India. The Rann was the bone of contention between the princely state Kutch and British Indian province of Sind. When British India was partitioned, the issue was inherited by India, to whom Kutch acceded, and Pakistan, whom Sind joined, involving some 3,500 miles of territory leading to frequent border incidents, from January 1965 onwards.

By all accounts the Indian forces were badly mashed in the Kutch area by the Pakistan army. It was at the Common Wealth conference at Britain, that the British Prime Minister Harold Wilson successfully persuaded both India and Pakistan to sign an agreement on June 30 to resolve the dispute. Failing to do so bilaterally, a tribunal was set up which announced its verdict on February 19, 1965 by giving 350 sq. miles in Northern part to Pakistan and the rest of Rann area to India.

The War in Kashmir

Events in Kashmir were also moving towards a climax. The application of articles 356 and 357 of the Indian constitution to the Kashmir state, which enabled the President of India to establish President rule in Kashmir and legislate there, were efforts to amalgamate Kashmir completely into the Indian union. Sheikh Abdullah, the Kashmiri leader took extensive foreign tours to enlist international support for the Kashmiri cause. But he was arrested and the Kashmir legislative assembly adopted the constitutional amendments bill on March 30, providing:

(A) the Sadar-i-Riyasat would henceforth be known as Governor
     and would be appointed by President of India instead of
     being elected by the local assembly.
(B) the Prime Minister would be styled as Chief Minister, as in
     the states of the Indian union.

The Lahore Offensive

At 3:00 a.m. on September 6, without a formal declaration
of war, Indians crossed the international border of West Pakistan
and launched a three-pronged offensive against Lahore, Sialkot
and Rajasthan. There was a fierce tank battle on the plains of
Punjab. The domestic Indo-Pak conflict transformed into an
international conflict and raised super power concerns.

The U.S. suspended military supplies to both sides during
the Indo-Pak war. Both the Soviet Union and the United States
took a united stand to curtail the conflict within the boundaries
of Indo-Pakistan from escalating into a global conflict. China had
threatened to intervene and offered military support on behalf of
Pakistan Because India was the offender and Pakistan, the Defender.
It was the fear of India being crashed by Pakistan and also the
chance of China also getting in the War that both the Soviet Union
and the United States pressured the UN to arrange for an immediate
cease-fire, to keep China away from this conflict. In there opinion
if China also attacked, India would be History.

The main diplomatic effort to stop the fighting was conducted
under the United Nations auspices and a cease-fire came into
effect on September 23, 1965. The Soviet Union which remained
neutral when India and Pakistan went to war in September 1965,
played the broker afterward at Tashkent.

A Soviet Government communique, formally announced
on December 8 that the Indian Prime Minister Shastri and the
Pakistani President Ayub would meet at Tashkent on January 4,
1966. The Tashkent conference lasted from January 4 to January
10. The Soviet Premier Kosygin earned the praise as a peace
maker. The main achievement of the conference was to withdraw,
not later than February 25, 1966, all armed personal to the position
held before August 5, 1964.

BANGLADESHI WAR OF INDEPENDENCE INDO-PAKISTANI WAR OF 1971

The third war between India and Pakistan took place between November 22 (when the Indian's began providing active artillery support to the separatists) and Dec. 17, 1971. The origins of the third Indo-Pakistani conflict (1971) were different from the previous conflicts. The Pakistani failure to accommodate demands for autonomy in East Pakistan in 1970 led to secessionist demands in 1971. In March 1971, Pakistan's armed forces launched a fierce campaign to suppress the resistance movement that had emerged but encountered unexpected mass defections among East Pakistani soldiers and police. The Pakistani forces regrouped and reasserted their authority over most of East Pakistan by May.

As a result of these military actions, thousands of East Pakistanis died at the hands of the Pakistani army. Resistance fighters and nearly 10 million refugees fled to sanctuary in West Bengal, the adjacent Indian state. By midsummer, the Indian leadership, in the absence of a political solution to the East Pakistan crisis, had fashioned a strategy designed to assist the establishment of the independent nation of Bangladesh. As part of this strategy, in August 1971, India signed a twenty-year Treaty of Peace, Friendship, and Cooperation with the Soviet Union. One of the treaty's clauses implied that each nation was expected to come to the assistance of the other in the event of a threat to national security such as that occurring in the 1965 war with Pakistan. Simultaneously, India organized, trained, and provided sanctuary to the Mukti Bahini (meaning Liberation Force in Bengali), the East Pakistani armed resistance Fighters.

Unable to deter India's activities in the eastern sector, on December 3, 1971, Pakistan launched an air attack in the western sector on a number of Indian airfields, including Ambala in Haryana, Amritsar in Punjab, and Udhampur in Jammu and Kashmir. The attacks did not succeed in Inflicting substantial damage. The Indian air force retaliated the next day and quickly achieved air superiority. On the ground, the strategy in the eastern sector marked a significant departure from previous Indian battle plans and tactics, which had emphasized set-piece battles and slow advances. The strategy adopted was a swift, three-pronged assault of nine infantry divisions with attached armored units and close air support that rapidly converged on Dhaka, the capital of East Pakistan. Lieutenant General Sagat Singh, who commanded the eighth, twenty-third, and Fifty-seventh divisions, led the Indian thrust into East Pakistan. As these forces attacked Pakistani formations, the Indian air force rapidly destroyed the small air contingent in East Pakistan and put the Dhaka airfield out of commission. In the meantime, the Indian navy effectively blockaded East Pakistan. Dhaka fell to combined Indian and Mukti Bahini forces on December 16, bringing a quick end to the war.

Action in the western sector was divided into four segments, from the cease-fire line in Jammu and Kashmir to the marshes of the Rann of Kutch in northwestern Gujarat. On the evening of December 3, the Pakistani army launched ground operations in Kashmir and Punjab. It also started an armored operation in Rajasthan. In Kashmir, the operations were concentrated on two key points, Punch and Chhamb. The Chhamb area witnessed a particularly intense battle where the Pakistanis forced the Indians to withdraw from their positions. In other parts of Kashmir, the Indians made some small gains along the cease-fire line. The major Indian counteroffensive came in the Sialkot–Shakargarh area south and west of Chhamb. There, two Pakistani tank regiments, equipped with United States-made Patton tanks, confronted the Indian First Armored Corps, which had British Centurion tanks. In what proved to be the largest tank battle of the war, both sides suffered considerable casualties.

Within hours of outbreak of hostilities, the Indian Missile Boat Group was ordered to execute operation Trident, the code name for the first attack on Karachi. The task group consisting of three OSA class missile boats, escorted by two Kamorta class anti-submarine patrol vessels, regrouped off Okha and charged towards Karachi. At 2150 hrs on December 4, the task group was 70 nautical miles south-west of Karachi. Soon thereafter, the task group detected patrolling Pakistani naval ships on their sensors. The deadly missiles were heading towards their targets which were soon hit. PNS Khyber, a destroyer and PNS Muhafiz, a minesweeper were sunk. Another Pakistani destroyer Shajehan was badly damaged. The fuel storage tanks at Karachi harbour were set ablaze, causing heavy loss. Operation Trident was a thundering success with no damage to any of the ships of the Indian Naval Task Group, which returned safely. Operation Trident had introduced to the war, the first ever ship launched missiles in the region.

Enthused by the success of this attack, the Indian Navy planned another offensive operation, code named Python. The continued presence of the Indian Navy's larger ships is the area gave enough indication to the Pakistani naval authorities that more offensive operations were in the offing. The Pak aerial surveillance was stepped up and their ships attempted to outsmart the Indian Navy by mingling with merchant shipping. Notwithstanding these measures by the Pakistanis, operation Python was launched on the night on December 8 and 9, 1971. Despite bad weather and rough seas, the task group consisting of missile boat Vinash and two multipurpose frigates, executed the attack with razor sharp precision. INS Vinash approached close to the Karachi coast and fired four missiles. The first missile struck the fuel tanks at the Keamari Oil Farm. The other three missiles hit the merchant tankers Harmattan, Gulf Star and the Pakistani naval tanker Dacca. More than 50 per cent of the total fuel requirement of the Karachi zone was reported to have been blown up. Operation Python was another great success. Though the Indian conduct of the land war on the western front was somewhat timid, the role of the Indian air force was both extensive and daring. During the fourteen-day war, the air force's Western Command conducted some 4,000 sorties. There was little retaliation by Pakistan's air force, partly because of the paucity of non-Bengali technical personnel. Additionally, this lack of retaliation reflected the deliberate decision of the Pakistan Air Force headquarters to conserve its forces because of heavy losses incurred in the early days of the war.

WAR BREAKS ON DECEMBER 3RD 1971
Part One : Origin of the Crisis

The Setting

The partition of the Indian Subcontinent in 1947 created two independent countries: India and Pakistan. India, which became independent on 15 August 1947, stood for a secular, equitable polity based on the universally accepted idea that all men are created equal and should be treated as such. Pakistan, which officially came into existence a day earlier, was based on the premise that Hindus and Muslims of the Subcontinent constitute two different nationalities and cannot coexist. The Partition created two different countries with most Muslim majority areas of undivided India going to the newly created nation, Pakistan. Pakistan was originally made up of two distinct and geographically unconnected parts termed West and East Pakistan. West Pakistan was made up of a number of races including the Punjabis (the most numerous), Sindhis, Pathans, Balochis, Mohajirs (Muslim refugees from India) and others. East Pakistan, on the other hand, was much more homogeneous and had an overwhelming Bengali-speaking population.

The Roots of Discord

Although the Eastern wing of Pakistan was more populous than that the Western one, political power since independence rested with the Western elite. This caused considerable resentment in East Pakistan and a charismatic Bengali leader called, Sheikh Mujibur Rehman, most forcefully articulated that resentment by forming an opposition political party called the Awami League and demanding more autonomy for East Pakistan within the Pakistani Federation. In the Pakistani general elections held in 1970, the Sheikh's party won the majority of seats, securing a complete majority in East Pakistan. In all fairness, the Sheikh should have been Prime Minister of Pakistan, or at least the ruler of his province. But West Pakistan's ruling elite were so dismayed by the turn of events and by the Sheikh's demands for autonomy that instead of allowing him to rule East Pakistan, they put him in jail.

Origins of the Crisis

The dawn of 1971 saw a great human tragedy unfolding in erstwhile East Pakistan. Entire East Pakistan was in revolt. In the West, General Yahya Khan, who had appointed himself President in 1969, had given the job of pacifying East Pakistan to his junior, General Tikka Khan. The crackdown of 25 March 1971 ordered by Tikka Khan, left thousands of Bengalis dead and Sheikh

Mujibur Rehman was arrested the next day. The same day, the Pakistani Army began airlifting two of its divisions plus a brigade strength formation to its Eastern Wing. Attempts to dis-arm Bengali troops were not entirely successful and within weeks of the 25 March massacres, many former Bengali officers and troops of the Pakistani Army had joined Bengali resistance fighters in different parts of East Pakistan.

The Pakistani Army conducted several crackdowns in different parts of Bangladesh, leading to massive loss of civilian life. The details of those horrific massacres, in which defenceless people were trapped and machine-gunned, is part of Bangladeshi history. Survivors compare it to the Nazi extermination of Jews. At the same time, the Pakistani Administration in Dhaka thought it could pacify the Bengali peasantry by appropriating the land of the Hindu population and gifting it to Muslims. While this did not impress the peasantry, it led to the exodus of more than 8 million refugees (more than half of them Hindus) to neighbouring India. West Bengal was the worst affected by the refugee problem and the Indian government was left holding the enormous burden. Repeated appeals by the Indian government failed to elicit any response from the international community and by April 1971, the then Indian Prime Minister, Mrs. Indira Gandhi, decided that the only solution lay in helping Bengali freedom fighters, especially the Mukti Bahini, to liberate East Pakistan, which had already been re-christened Bangladesh by its people.

Pakistan felt it could dissuade India from helping the Mukti Bahini by being provocative. The Pakistan Air Force (PAF) in East Pakistan took to attacking suspected Mukti Bahini camps located inside Indian territory in the state of West Bengal. In the Western and Northern sectors too occasional clashes, some of them quite bloody, took place. Pakistan was suggesting that should India continue with its plans it should expect total war as in 1965. Only this time, the Pakistanis would concentrate their forces in the West and thereby aim at capturing as much as Indian territory as possible. The Indians, on the other hand, would be fighting a war on two fronts (while at the same time keeping a fearful eye on the Chinese borders). Given this scenario, the Pakistanis felt that India at best would be able to capture some territory in East Pakistan and lose quite a bit in the West. In the end, the Pakistanis

knew that the Western powers would intervene to stop the war
and what would matter is who had the most of the other's territory
Confident that another war would be as much of a stalemate as
the 1965 Conflict, the Pakistanis got increasingly bold and finally
on 3 December 1971 reacted with a massive co-ordinated air strike
on several Indian Air Force stations in the West. At midnight, the
Indian Prime Minister Mrs. Indira Gandhi in a broadcast to the
nation declared that India was at war with Pakistan. As her words
came on in million of Indian homes across the Subcontinent, the
men at the front were already engaged in bitter combat...

Part Two : War is Declared

PAF Strikes

For all practical purposes, the war started at about 5:40 pm
on 3 December when Pakistan Air Force (PAF) combat aircraft
struck nine Indian airfields along the Western borders. The air
strikes were followed by a massive attack on the strategic Chhamb
sector in the north. In the East, it was the Indian Army which went
on the offensive. By late that night, artillery shells were raining
down all along the Western and Eastern borders. India and
Pakistan were locked in a two-front war. In the West, the Indian
Army had very limited offensive aims and was relegated more to
a holding role. The initiative lay with Pakistan. In this theatre,
Pakistan had near parity with India in armour and artillery while
India had more infantry divisions. Pakistan's most successful thrust
was in Chhamb where the 23rd Pakistani Division (along with two
additional infantry brigades, one extra armoured brigade and
Corps artillery units) under the able leadership of Major General
Iftikhar Khan completely overwhelmed the forward defensive
positions of the Indian 10 Division commanded by Major General
Jaswant Singh. Chhamb village was taken and the Pakistanis
threatened to advance towards Jammu, the summer capital of the
state of Jammu & Kashmir. Heavy fighting continued in this sector
for a week until the indecisiveness of the Indian Divisional
commander forced the Indian Corps Commander to intervene
personally and launch heavy attacks to push the Pakistanis back
to a non-threatening position. The Pakistanis surprisingly failed to
take advantage of their initial successes in this sector and actually
depleted the forces available to their commander, who was killed
on 10 December in a helicopter crash.

Acting in accordance with its strategy to grab as much territory in the West as possible, Pakistan also launched a major attack on Punch in the state of Jammu & Kashmir. This attack, unlike the one on Chhamb, was completely repulsed, although here the Indian Army was at a locational disadvantage since the Pakistanis controlled the heights around the town. Smaller attacks were launched by Pakistan in Punjab at Fazilka and Hussainiwala. Here the forward Indian defences were breached but the Pakistani Army could not sustain its attacks. A more ambitious armoured thrust in the deserts of Rajasthan was similarly stopped in the famous Battle of Longewal. In all, it appeared that the Pakistani military high command could not make up its mind as to where it should deliver its main punch and kept pulling back until it was too late. The Indian Army chief, General Sam Maneckshaw, had a completely different set of problems. His strategy had to take into account the Chinese, with whom the Indian Army had fought a full blown war only nine years earlier. The Chinese were now firm Pakistani allies and had been making threatening noises ever since India resolved to intervene in the East Pakistan issue. General Maneckshaw, despite the disappointment of his Corps and divisional commanders, had to hold back his Army in the West, keep a watchful eye on the long and difficult Chinese borders and, at the same time, ensure that his Eastern Army secured its objective of grabbing a good chunk of East Pakistani territory within 2 to 3 weeks. The Indian aim was to install a Bangladeshi interim government in East Pakistani territory before the cessation of hostilities. It was not all clear in the beginning whether things would work out quite the way as planned.

Part Three : Entering the East

Modest Aims, Ambitious Action

One of the less remarked upon aspects of the 1971 war was the varied character of the key men who planned and executed the operations. Best known was of course the flamboyant Indian Army Chief, General Sam Maneckshaw, a Parsee who had won the Military Cross in WW II. To the Indian public, it was General Maneckshaw with his twirled moustache, Gorkha cap and baton, who was the symbolic hero. Yet, there were below him, an equally varied and extra ordinary set of men, who planned and executed

their own battles. The Western Army was commanded by an
Anglo-Indian Lt. Gen. K.P. Candeth and the Eastern Army,
headquarters at Calcutta, by a Sikh, Lt. Gen. J.S. Aurora. General
Aurora's a brilliant Chief of Staff was Major. Gen. J.F.R. Jacob,
the scion of an old Jewish family of Calcutta. Together these men
planned and executed the lightning operations of December 1971.

The 4th morning saw Indian forces and Mukti Bahini guerrillas
ready for battle with the Pakistanis, who were by now well dug
in and waiting for the Indian assault. The Indian forces easily
outnumbered the Pakistanis by a ratio of about 2:1. However,
according to conventional infantry wisdom, an attacking Army
requires a three-is-to-one superiority in numbers to attack. India
did not have that. Besides, the Pakistani Army commander in the
East, General A.A.K. Niazi, was determined merely to delay the
Indian advance. For, in this war, the real battle was against time.
The longer it took the Indian to secure their limited objectives,
the greater the probability of the United Nations intervening to
stop the war and effect a stalemate. Pakistan was confident that
a stalemate was all that the Indians could get. Towards this
strategy, General Niazi, had fortified the towns and approaches
to the East Pakistani heartland and had boasted before the war
began that should hostilities begin, he would take the battle inside
India. The brief given by the Indian Army chief, General
Maneckshaw, to the Eastern Command was very limited. The aim
was to occupy only two areas of East Pakistan - Chittagong and
Khulna - so that an interim Bangladeshi government could be
established. The capture of the whole of East Pakistan was not
even conceived. A major problem was the geography and terrain
of East Pakistan. Three major rivers - the Brahmaputra, the Ganga
and the Meghna - divided East Pakistan into four natural regions.
Each of the rivers were major ones - all of them wider than any
European river. Each sub-region was further divided into several
pockets cut by smaller rivers and their tributaries. The idea that
an attacking army could bridge these, fight the enemy and then
take territory, all within a couple of weeks, was ludicrous.

Lt. General Aurora's Chief of Staff, Major General Jacob,
however, did not entirely agree with the Indian Army top brass.
"I think the aim of the government was to take as much territory
as possible in East Pakistan so as to establish and Bangladeshi

government in their own territory. "Army Headquarters issued an operations instruction according to which our main objectives were to take Chittagong and Khulna ports, which were termed the entry ports. But we at Eastern Command felt differently. We felt that Dhaka was the geo-political centre of Bangladesh and therefore any campaign to be successful had to capture Dhaka." The Eastern Command went ahead with its own plans, although Army Headquarters felt it was too ambitious and could not be achieved. Jacob's commander, Lt. Gen. Aurora, provided full support for his Army's own plans and allowed Jacob to pull down troops kept in reserve for a possible attack by the Chinese. Some of these troops had to be brought into battle so hurriedly that the only way was to paradrop them. This was accomplished with the help of the IAF and soon soldiers geared to fight the Chinese in the high mountains found themselves in the tropical riverine areas of Tangail in East Pakistan.

'We realised that any campaign to be successful had to be swift. The United Nations was putting great pressure on us and also the Russians had indicated that they did not want to exercise their veto any more," Jacob explained. "Therefore any campaign had to be quick. We realised that Niazi (the Pakistani Army commander in East Pakistan) was going to fortify the towns and defend them in strength. We therefore decided not attack any towns but bypass them using subsidiary tracks to get to our objective: Dhaka."

The immense practical problem of moving thousands of troops and tonnes of equipment across rivers and marshes was accomplished largely due to the efforts of the Army Corps of Engineers, and with a lot of local help. The IAF chipped in by using helicopters to lift entire battalions across larger rivers that could not be quickly bridged by the Engineers. In most places, the swiftly moving contingents quickly overcame enemy resistance and moved forward. The Pakistanis for the most part, were completely taken by surprise. Within 6 days of the war, Indian troops were deep inside East Pakistani territory and moving fast. The Mukti Bahini section of the advancing forces played a crucial role in guiding the Indian Army through the treacherous riverine areas and providing critical intelligence. It is doubtful whether the Indian Army could have moved so fast and decisively without the help of the Bangladeshis. At any rate, by the seventh day of the war, the Pakistani Army High Command, headquarters in Rawalpindi, was in a complete panic.

Part Four : Blockade from the Seas

The 1971 war was the first, and only, occasion when the Indian political leadership exhibited a proper understanding of the use of military power for achieving a clear national aim. In past conflicts, Indian leaders either had no clear aim in mind and were merely reacting to events or they were confused about how best to use the military power available to them. During the 1962 India-China war, for instance, the Indian government ordered the Indian Air Force to withdraw its fighter bomber squadrons from the north east and not to hit the invading Chinese. IAF bombers could have changed the course of the 1962 war had it been allowed to hit the thin and tenuous Chinese logistics lines. Similarly, in the 1965 India-Pakistan conflict, the Navy was ordered to keep its ships in port and not engage in any offensive action against Pakistan. The Pakistani Navy was given a free hand and it managed to lob a few shells at one point in the Western Coast. The Indian Navy's chance to see some action came only in 1971 December.

Since East and West Pakistan were two separate geographical entities more than 1,600 miles apart, the only way Pakistani forces in East Pakistan could be sustained was through the sea. The Indian Prime Minister, Mrs. Indira Gandhi, decided that the Navy would be given the strategic task of denying both East and West Pakistan access to war supplies. The aim in short was a complete naval blockade of both parts of Pakistan. The bigger aim was of course to ensure that the conflict was not perpetuated beyond the time required to capture a chunk of East Pakistani territory. The Indian Navy's best and biggest warship at that time was its sole aircraft carrier, *INS Vikrant,* a carefully preserved World War II vintage carrier built in Britain. Ideally, a task force centred around the *Vikrant* should have been used to block Karachi, which at that time was West Pakistan's sole deep water port. However, one of *Vikrant's* main boilers was out of operation and the ship could not maintain the kind of speed required for maneuvering in a situation where the air threat would be considerable. It was decided that the *Vikrant* would be used to blockade the ports in East Pakistan, and destroy the riverine craft used by the Pakistanis there.

Vikrant in Action

The day war was declared, the *Vikrant,* which had been anchored off the northern-most tip of the Andaman & Nicobar chain of islands, moved towards the principal East Pakistani port, Chittagong. The Pakistanis, having learnt that *Vikrant* was positioned in the Bay of Bengal, despatched one of their submarines, *PNS Ghazi,* to the east. The Pakistani submarine thought it could sneak into Vizag harbour, the principal naval port in the Indian east coast. It was, however, detected and sunk before it could cause any damage. The *Vikrant* continued unhindered. Rear Admiral (retired) P.D. Sharma, who was then an aviator aboard the *Vikrant,* recalls what it was like:

"Fighter pilots practice for years and when they finally get an opportunity to see real action, it is thrilling - it is the moment one has been waiting for all one's life. And it was so for us aboard the *Vikrant* on 4th December 1971... The first sortie was mounted against Cox's Bazaar. Eight Sea Hawks went in led by the squadron commander. I was in the second sortie which attacked Chittagong. This was in the afternoon of the 4th because it took some time for the *Vikrant* to dose in the range to Chittagong.

"We went in low level, pulled up and carried out repeated attacks on the airfield. In the first attack itself we inflicted considerable damage. We withdrew for the night and sailed towards the Mangla- Khulna area. Our next attacks were on those harbours. Then we came back to Chittagong. And by the time we were through with that area, especially Chittagong harbour, Chittagong airfield and the approaches to Chittagong, the scene was something to be seen. The place had been devastated. There were ships that had turned turtle, there were half-sunk ships by the quay side, the airfield was pockmarked with craters and no ship could even think of approaching the place."

The Attack on Karachi

The most dramatic naval plan was drawn up by the Western Naval Command. It was decided that the main attack on Karachi harbour would be launched by tiny PT-15 missile boats instead of regular warships. There were several reasons for this decision. Regular ships without air cover would be vulnerable whereas the tiny missile boats would present difficult, fast-moving targets. Moreover, the Navy wanted to try out the missiles to see how effective they could be in real action, although this kind of use of missile boats, which were designed for coastal defence and not for long range offensive action of any kind, was highly unorthodox. At any rate, three missile boats were chosen for the mission and despatched in the dead of night from Bombay harbour. Leading the missile boat squadron was Commodore (Retired) Babru Bahan Yadav: "The task given to us was not easy. Our ships were little more than boats and did not have the range to go all the way to Karachi on their own steam. So an oiler was placed about half-way to the target and we were able to refuel and carry on.

As we neared their coast, we found some of their ships patrolling the area. The boat on my left was detailed to engage the contact. That boat was the first Indian warship to fire a missile in anger. Two missiles were fired and both were direct hits. It is interesting to recall that the radar contact which was on our screen slowly diminished and then suddenly disappeared. We were very jubilant at that time. Later, we found that this has been a Pakistani destroyer. Very soon another ship was located right in front of my boat. We fired a couple of missiles as well but did not sink it. The boat on our right was ordered to attack the ship. It did so and managed to cripple it completely. We thought we had sunk it but later the Pakistanis claimed that the ship had been badly crippled and put out of action but not sunk. Anyway, as we continued, both the other boats could not keep up and had to turn back. Only *Nipat,* the boat I was on, could proceed towards Karachi harbour. We pressed on and fired missiles on Karachi which hit the oil installations there. The attack took place just 1 minute before midnight and we could see the flames from the oil installations lighting up the sea. It looked like *Diwali* (Indian festival of lights and firecrackers)."

It took a few more days for Commodore Yadav's boat to return to harbour as they had to take evasive action and ran out of fuel. In the meanwhile, the Pakistanis who were hunting for the boat put out a message that an Indian vessel had been sunk. *Nipat,* the only boat not accounted for at that time, was presumed sunk. But *Nipat* returned, thanks to the ingenuity of its engineers who managed to take out pump oil and use it to run the engines. The Indian Navy accomplished the task assigned to it within the first few days of the war. No enemy shipping could move in or out of its harbours. Merchant ships did not dare approach Karachi. Control of the seas around both wings of Pakistan was with the Indian Navy.

Part Five : Battle of Longewal

An Audacious Plan

The Battle of Longewal, fought in the deserts of the Indian state of Rajasthan, merits inclusion in any account of the 1971 India-Pakistan war because of the sheer audacity of the Pakistani generals who had planned it. Had it succeeded, India would have lost thousands of kilometres of a vast expanse of desert. But there is a fine line between the daring and the foolhardy. Did Pakistani generals cross that dividing line? The Rajasthan sector was rather thinly held by both the Indians and by the Pakistanis for the simple reason that the Thar desert is not conducive to vehicular movement. Unlike in North Africa where the desert surface is relatively hard and the coastal areas allow for easy movement of traffic, the loose shifting sands of the Thar cannot be crossed by wheeled vehicles and even tracked vehicles are liable to get bogged down. The region also has very few dirt tracks and even fewer paved roads. On the Pakistani side, the principal town is Rahimiyar Khan which is also an important railway junction connecting prosperous Pakistani Punjab in the north with the barren province of Sindh and its capital, Karachi, in the south. On the Indian side, the four principal towns are Jaisalmer, Barmer, Bikaner and Jodhpur. The major portion of Indian forces in 1971 were concentrated near the border towns of Barmer and Jaisalmer, both of which are supported by a forward air force base. The original Indian plan was to attack Rahimiyar Khan from Jaisalmer with a view to cutting off the main railway artery in West Pakistan.

The Pakistani plan was no less ambitious and a surprise attack was launched along the Gabbar-Longewal axis. The main axis lay to the north, connecting the Indian town of Jaisalmer with the Pakistani town of Islamgarh and Rahimiyar Khan beyond it.

The intruding Pakistani armoured column and accompanying towed artillery was spotted by an Indian patrol on 4th December after it had come 16 km into Indian territory. The first reports were dismissed, until the enemy took up position just 300 metres away from the isolated Indian Army company located at Longewal. The unit had no anti-tank weapons or mines. The Pakistanis could have overrun the post within hours. But the Indian company commander, Major Kuldip Singh Chandpuri, showed presence of mind by bringing in the company's recoilless guns and heavy machine guns and directing concentrated and sustained fire at the enemy positions. The Pakistanis were taken aback by the extent of the fire and felt that the Indians must have a much larger force at Longewal than reported by their Intelligence. Instead of storming the post and carrying on to Jaisalmer as was the plan, the Pakistanis encircled the post and decided to set up their artillery to soften it up before attacking.

By this time, the GOC of 12 Indian Infantry Division based at Tanot north of Jaisalmer was fully in the picture and realised that the Pakistanis had launched a full-scale armoured thrust to take Jaisalmer by outflanking 12 Division's main forces concentrated in the Tanot-Kishengarh area. Later it was discovered that the commanding officer of 18 Pakistani Army Division had planned to breakfast at Ramgarh and have dinner at Jaisalmer before proceeding on to Jodhpur. In complete contrast to the Pakistani divisional commander's audacity was over-cautiousness of the Indian generals. Confronted by the surprise attack, both the Indian divisional commander and his senior in charge of Southern Command dithered. They neither continued with their planned attack on Rahimiyar Khan nor did they send a large enough force to engage the Pakistani intruders. The job of relieving pressure on the beleaguered Indian company was left to the Indian Air Force.

The IAF at that time had only two oldish Hawker Hunter aircraft positioned at Jaisalmer and that too mainly for reconnaissance purposes. Among the two pilots posted there was Squadron Leader R.N. Bali:" It was on the 4/5th night that we learnt of a change in plans and that we had to take on the enemy tank thrust at Longewal. It was sometime after midnight when we received our orders and it took 2 to 3 hours to change the role of our aircraft from air defence to ground attack. But we had to wait till first light to launch our mission... "We saw enemy tanks strewn around in an area in a radius of more than 30 kilometres since the enemy tanks had started taking evasive action. We had to split our basic two-level missions into one level so that each aircraft could go in turn by turn. We were lucky in the sense that there was no enemy air opposition in the first phase and we could afford to put in more time over the target and see what we were destroying."

Part Six : Air War in the East

IAP Continues Flying in Support of Army

The air war began on 22 November, 1971, several days before the formal start of hostilities. The first encounter was so dramatic and happened in full view of so many ordinary people on the ground that it would endure in public memory as one of the most vivid moments of the war. The concept of air battle, so remote till then to ordinary Indians, would become an integral part of the concept of warfare. *Rupak Chattopadhyay* describes what happened...

The scene of action was in the eastern sector, a few minutes flying time away from Calcutta, the largest Indian metropolis in the east. The provocation was the repeated intrusion by groups of PAF F-86 Sabres into a salient inside Indian territory. This salient called Boyra was being used by Bangladeshi Mukti Bahini guerrillas to launch attacks inside East Pakistan. The Pakistani Army in the east had reacted angrily by launching a full scale attack in that sector but had had to beat a retreat after losing 13 tanks and many men. The job of messing up the Mukti Bahini was given to the PAF Sabres which began crossing into Indian territory, strafing the area and slipping back into Pakistani air space. The IAF had to get them while they were in Indian air space. The window was small: barely a couple of minutes wide, and the PAF fighters had to be intercepted over a 3 km wide corridor surrounded on three sides by Pakistani territory.

Four IAF Gnats were ordered to scramble at about 2:49 on 22 November afternoon to take on four Sabres strafing the Indian salient. The Gnats got three Sabres. The IAF formation leader,

Flight Lieutenant R. Massey: Flight Lieutenant M. A. Ganapathy
and Flying Officer D. Lazarus each got one Sabre. One Sabre
crashed into a pond in Chaugacha on the East Pakistani side of
the border, while the other two went down over Indian territory.
Flt. Lt. Parvez Mehdi Qureshi and Fg Offr Khalil Ahmed, the two
PAF pilots who ejected over India were captured and produced
before a crowded press conference the next day. The action was
splashed in newspaper front pages all over the country and the
three pilots who scored hits became national heroes overnight.
This encounter set the tone of the air battles that were to follow.
News of the incident and the famous gun camera shots were
splashed across newspaper headlines the world over and the tiny
Gnat acquired a reputation of being the Sabre killer. Conversations
picked up in the air suggested that PAF fighters were instructed
not to engage with Gnats, although this small aircraft could easily
be out flown by Sabres and Starfighters. The PAF also subsequently
withdrew some its aircraft from East Pakistan leaving a sole
squadron of Sabres to grapple with the eleven IAF squadrons
positioned in the east.

Protecting the Skies

A major reason for India's rapid successes in the 1971
conflict was the excellent co-ordination effected between the
Indian Air Force (IAF) and the Army. Air Chief Marshal P.C. Lal,
the IAF's low profile chief, appreciated that the IAF's primary role
would be to fly in support of the Army. Achieving complete air
superiority was not the primary aim, especially on the western
front where the Pakistani Air Force (PAF) had massed its squadrons,
leaving only one squadron of F-86 Sabres for the defence of the
east. The Indians had more aircraft but most of them were
generally much older than the aircraft in the PAF's inventory. The
IAF's pride and the most advanced aircraft of the time was the
MiG-21. But the MiG-21 required long runways not always available
in many of the frontline air bases and required expert handling.
The IAF's primary interceptor continued to be the Folland Gnat,
a tiny but highly maneuverable aircraft that had been passed over
by its British manufacturers. The Gnats flew the highest number
of sorties during the war. The lAF's primary ground attack aircraft
were the old British built Hunters, the positively ancient Canberras
and the spanking new Sukhoi- 7s (acquired in 1968). The IAF also

operated the indigenous Marut HF-24 fighters, which were somewhat under powered and difficult to maneuver, and a number of other obsolete types including the Harvard IIR's, the Vampires and Mysteres.

The PAF's mainstay was the F-86F Sabre, which was in service with many NATO countries although it belonged to a line that had been in production since the time of the Korean War. The Sabre was an excellent aircraft and had been substantially modified over the years to keep up with evolving Soviet combat aircraft. In 1971, the PAF Sabres included the ones upgraded to '40s' standards and newer Mk.6s from Canada. Pakistan also had the F-104 Starfighter, touted as the most sophisticated aircraft of the day. The rest of PAF's inventory was made up of Mirage-IIIs, newer Chinese variants of the MiG-19 (F-6s) and American B-57 bombers. A few IAF pilots had flown Sabres in the United States and knew the fine handling properties of their enemy's main combat fighter. The Indians rated the Mirage-III as the best PAF fighter but that aircraft was not seen as much as it was hoped. The IAF, despite its superiority in numbers, knew it would be a tough fight but was fully prepared for a no-holds barred contest.

Air Superiority in the East

The IAF's strength in the east was made up of 4 squadrons of Hunters, one of Su-7s, 3 of Gnats and 3 of the newer MiG-21s. The IAP also was prepared to hit any Chinese incursions into Indian territory in the eastern Himalayas. As it turned out, the Chinese did not stir and the IAF managed to knock out the PAF squadron within 2 days of the outbreak of war. The IAF had gone into action within hours of Pakistan's pre-emptive strikes of 3/4 December 1971. Counter air sorties in the east were so successful that the PAF was neutralized within hours of the outbreak of war. In their first raid on the 4th of December a four ship formation of MiG-21 FLs from the No.28 Squadron took out the runways at Tezgaon air base near Dhaka. Three Sabres attempting to intercept the MiGs were taken out by a combination of cannon fire and K-13 missiles. For the remainder of the war, round the clock attacks on the Kurmitola and Tezgaon air bases kept them, and the PAF non-operational.

Meanwhile, later that day Hunters from No. 14 Squadron struck Chittagong Harbour as a prelude to strikes from the carrier INS Vikrant. The Hunters were to continue flying interdiction missions for the remainder of the war in, shooting up ammunition dumps and other fixed installations. Gnats and Sukhoi Su-7s flew many missions in support of army units as they moved swiftly towards Dhaka, delivering ordnance such as iron bombs to take out enemy bunkers which occasionally posed an obstacle to advancing infantry. Canberras repeatedly struck Jessore forcing the enemy to abandon this strategic city. On the 11th of December three converted An-12s from the No.44 Squadron struck the Jaydebpur Ordnance factory in East Pakistan. Once Kurmitola and Tezgaon were put out of action the IAF had gained complete air superiority over East Pakistan.

The story of the old Caribou transporters speaks a lot about the mood of the times. Two of these old Canadian transporters were posted at Hashimara during the war and were used during the Tangail air drop and for minor missions. The Caribou air crew were getting restless. They wanted a piece of the action. Finally, Eastern Air Command agreed by allowing them to bomb Dhaka by night. The PAF had been knocked out by then but the Pakistanis still had plenty of Chinese made multi-barrel anti-aircraft guns, which could be pretty devastating. The Caribous were fitted with old World War II bombs and told to circle Dhaka for as long as they could during the night. While the pilots droned over Dhaka along with the occasional AN-12 keeping the Pakistanis awake, an airman aboard the Caribou once in a while pushed out a bomb from the open back. None of the bombs caused significant damage but they kept the Pakistani generals getting much sleep. After the surrender, one Pakistani general was to angrily remark about the damned aircraft which did not allow any of them to sleep for a week or more.

Part Seven : Air War in the West

The Western Air Situation

Pakistani military analysts writing after the War tried to make out that the Pakistani Air Force (PAF) was heavily outnumbered even in the West. One writer claims that Pakistan had just 10 squadrons against 44 fielded by India. Such absurd assertions notwithstanding, fact is in 1971 the Indian Air Force (IAF) had a total of about 34 effective combat squadrons plus three under strength Canberra bomber squadrons and one AN-12 transporter squadron, which as it turned out played a remarkable role as modified bombers during the War. Of these Indian squadrons, ten were in the East (plus one Canberra squadron) and four were kept as reserves for protecting the inner cities. This meant the IAF had about 20 front-line combat squadrons in the West. Some of the front-line Indian squadrons were broken up and posted at different stations. This could be one reason for confusion on the Pakistani air intelligence side - and considerable exaggeration.

The Pakistanis, according to the IISS (International Institute of Strategic Studies) Military Balance 1971, had 19 squadrons including two B-57B light bomber and one recce squadron. According to our studies, the Pakistanis had about 14 effective combat squadrons in the West excluding the B-57B bombers and recce aircraft. However, PAF squadrons tended to have more aircraft per squadron than the IAF. This was further bolstered by the acquisition of an unspecified number of F-86 Sabres, Mirage IIIs, Starfighters (from Jordan) and about 15 Chinese F-6s in the months prior to the war. These aircrafts were not accounted for the IISS in its 1971 Military balance or in any other report. Also, the serviceability of PAF Sabres was much higher - meaning more aircraft could be fielded. The Indians had 16 aircraft per combat squadron but the effective availability during the war was 12 per squadron. Bomber and transporter squadron had 10 aircraft each of which about 6 to 8 were serviceable at any given time. Many PAF squadrons, in contrast, had as many as 25 aircraft. Thus, while the PAf was outnumbered in the West, at no point was it ever fighting against overwhelming odds.

More important, the PAF on the whole was far better equipped to fight a modem air war than the IAF. The Pakistanis, for instance, had very effective air-to-air missiles which the Indians lacked. American made Sidewinder missiles were fitted on Chinese-made F-6 aircraft, on Sabres and on Starfighters. These were accurate missiles and accounted for at least three kills by PAF fighters in air-to-air combat. The Indians had only their guns and cannons to rely on. The Soviet-made MiG-21 was the only aircraft in the IAF's inventory fitted with missiles. But the missiles - the infamous K-13 - were a poor copy of the American Sidewinders and were so useless that they were scrapped after the war. The other major advantage, and a critical one, the Pakistanis had was their radar and communication system built by the Americans. In most parts, particularly Punjab, the PAF had a real time radar surveillance system, the ability to track low flying aircraft coming over Pakistan and the means to guide their aircraft right to intruding enemy aircraft. India had nothing in comparison. Instead of low level radar, the IAP had to rely on men posted near the borders. Every time a suspected enemy aircraft flew over, the observation post had to call in on their high frequency radio sets to warn the sector controllers. Even the medium and high level radar cover available to the IAF was poor with the result that each forward base had to earmark between one to two combat squadrons just for air defence. It was a primitive and wasteful system - and the Pakistanis knew it. The technologically inferior but numerically superior Indian Air Force could be tackled quite easily by a smaller but more modem force. This is what prompted the PAF to launch pre-emptive strikes against forward Indian air bases on 3 December 1971.

IAF Counter Strike

Within 30 minutes of the Pakistani President General Yahya Khan's declaration of war against India at 1630 hours on 3rd December 1971, Pakistani fighter bombers struck five Indian airfields - Srinagar, Avantipur, Pathankot, Amritsar and the advanced landing ground at Faridkot. More strikes by PAF B-57 bombers followed at night against Ambala, Agra, Halwara, Amritsar, Pathankot, Srinagar, Sirsa, Adampur, Nal, Jodhpur and Jamnagar. Not a single aircraft was destroyed in these raids and runways damaged were repaired within a matter of hours.

The IAF's counter strike in the west was mounted on much greater scale than in the east. Within hours of the first PAF strike, converted An-12s from No.44 Squadron (led by Wg Cmdr Vashist) struck ammunition dumps in the Changa Manga forests. In one of the first counter air sorties of the war, Sukhois from No-222 Squadron struck Risalwala air field, while aircraft from the No. 101 attacked Pasrur. The No. 101 was to later become involved in providing support to the 10 Infantry Division in the

Sialkot Sector, eventually destroying over 60 enemy tanks. Keamri oil installations near Karachi harbour were struck twice on the 4th by a three ship Hunter formations. And No.27 Squadron's Hunters continuously strafed enemy positions around Poonch and Chhamb. The four antiquated Harvard/Texans of the IAF also joined in ground support missions, their slow speed being particularly useful in hitting enemy gun emplacements in the valleys and gorges of Kashmir. Three counter air strikes were mounted on the 4th by Hunters of No.20 Squadron against PAF airfields at Peshawar, Chaklala and Kohat. The raids left 8 aircraft destroyed on the ground, including at least 1 Mirage III. Maruts from No. 10 Squadron were heavily involved in counter air operations, hitting targets upto 200 miles inside Pakistani territory.

The second day of the war began with a Canberra strike against Masroor air base and other strategic installations around Karachi. A force of eight Canberras flying lo-lo over the Arabian sea set strategic and military installations around Karachi alight. A similar raid was mounted on the 6th. The success of these missions being confirmed by Photo Recon. Canberras reporting "the biggest blaze ever seen over South Asia" On the 5th , one four-ship formation from No. 20 struck Chaklala for a second time in as many days destroying a C-130 and an Twin Otter on the ground. A second four-ship formation went for radar installation around Lahore and Walton. And a third raid by No.20 was mounted against the radar site at Sakesar, unfortunately two Hunters were lost during this mission. Later that day Maruts from the Nos. 10 and 220 Squadrons, and their MiG escorts moved against rail heads at Sundra, Rohri and Mirpur Khas. Between the 5th and the 12th , two Sukhoi squadrons flying form Halwara and Adampur repeatedly struck railway marshalling yards around Lahore.

One of the most celebrated actions of the 5th and 6th December is contribution of four Hunters from the ATW in the defeat of a Pakistani armoured force at Longewala. A previous section covers this in great detail. The AN-12s were also quite busy on the 6th. A bombing raid by the AN-12s early in the day destroyed a Pakistani brigade in the Haji Pir salient. Later that day HQ 18 (Pakistan) Division at Fort Abbas was bombed, as were

areas around Bhawalpur. The 7th of December got off to a rather
bizarre start; a Marut from the No. 220 Squadron, on its way back
from a bombing raid against Rohri, actually engaged and brought
down with cannon fire an F-86 sent up to intercept it. Surprisingly
no Maruts were ever lost to enemy aircraft, although four were
downed by ground fire. Two days later an enemy Shenyang F-
6 was to be brought down by a ground attack aircraft - this time
a Su-7 from No.32 Squadron. Between the 7th and the 12th,
Sukhoi and Mystere Squadrons were engaged in support of I and
XI Corps in the Fazilka-Ferozepur sector. The Indian Army's
efforts in the Fazilka area were also assisted by bombing raids by
No.44 Squadron's AN-12s. A four-ship formation flying at 180 ft
above sea level struck Pakistani installations across from Fazilka
on the 9th.

As fighting in the west intensified, the Pakistanis launched an
offensive against Poonch on the 10th. To break up this offensive
Canberras dropped 28,000 lbs. of ordnance on the enemy. On
the 11th, in even larger interdiction sorties the Canberras delivered
36,000 lbs. of ordnance against enemy emplacements and tank
farms. Despite the damage, the Canberras inflicted on the enemy,
four of the force were lost to ground fire. The war in 1971 revealed
the true air-air combat capabilities of the MiG-21, altering
perceptions held about it as an outcome of its disappointing
performance in the Arab-Israeli war of 1967. The MiGs on both
fronts had ample opportunity to engage the enemy in aerial
combat. The five squadrons that served on the western front
conducted frequent armed reconnaissance missions deep into
enemy territory to lure out PAF fighters. All Su-7 and Marut raids
were given MiG-21 cover. Unfortunately for the Indian pilots who
flew in the northern sector (Western Air Command) there was
little by way of aerial engagements. On the 11th a Gnat of the
No.23 Squadron engaged and severely damaged a Mirage over
Pathankot. Those who flew with the South Western Air Command
were luckier. On the 12th a Jordanian F-104A Starfighter, on loan
to the PAF was shot down by cannon fire by a MiG-21 FL of No.47
Squadron flying from Jamnagar.

A Marut strike against Naya Chor on the 16th was intercepted
by three PAF Shenyang F-6s. In the ensuing dogfight one of the
F-6's was brought down by cannon fire from one of the two MiG

escorts from the No.29 Squadron. No Indian aircraft were lost in
the engagement and the Maruts were able to hit their targets. The
following morning a low flying Starfighter was destroyed by a
MiG-21 scrambled from Utterlai. A few hours later MiG-21 escorts
of a Marut mission near Umarkot destroyed a pair of Starfighters.
While the performance MiGs were shooting down enemy fighters,
the lumbering Antonovs were contributing more than their share
to victory in the West. The Rohri railway yards which had
remained under attack from day one of the war were hit by a pair
of An-12s at dusk on the 13th. The following day the Antonovs
delivered their coup-de-main against the enemy's fighting
capabilities. On the evening of the 14th a three-ship formation of
the Antonovs flying from Jodhpur struck the Sui Gas Plant. The
damage caused by these aircraft was so extensive that it took six
months to restore gas production at Sui to even 50% of capacity.
Happily all three aircraft taking part in the mission were recovered
safely, landing at Utterlai. Sadly however, that very night, Fg Offr
N.S. Sekhon of the No. 18 Squadron lost his life as he gallantly
engaged 6 enemy Sabres over Srinagar by himself. Before being
shot down Sekhon's Gnat managed to score hits on two of the
enemy for which he was awarded the Param Vir Chakra
posthumously.

The An-12s flew in the bombing role for the last time on the
17th. A mixed formation of Canberras and Antonovs commanded
by Vashist sortied against Skardu air field in Pakistani occupied
Kashmir. Of the thirty six bombs dropped on the runway by the
Antonovs, twenty eight hit the target while two fell within yards
of it (this was confirmed by a PR sortie later the same day). On
the way back, Vashist's aircraft was chased by two Mirages. In
order to evade them he climbed down into a valley and kept
circling for twenty minutes until the Mirages gave up and left. The
most astonishing thing about the An-12 bombing raids is that none
of the eleven (ten bombers and one flying command post) converted
aircraft were lost, although many were peppered by ack ack. The
ease with which these rather slow aircraft could strike deep into
enemy territory is testimony to the ineffectiveness of the Pakistani
Air Force during the winter of 1971. Only the absence of modern
weapons delivery systems for its air-to-surface weapons prevented
the India Air Force from causing more damage than it did.

Who Won the Air Wars

One of the last enduring debates on the 1971 War is the outcome of the air war. Both sides continue to claim that it won the air war. This debate continues because victory in the air is more difficult to quantify than victory on land or sea. In the land and sea wars, India emerged as the clear victor both in terms of objectives attained and losses/gains versus the enemy. In the air war, even estimates of losses on both sides are widely divergent. Immediately after the war, the official Indian Government figures given out were 86 Pakistan Air Force (PAF) aircraft destroyed as against 42 Indian Air Force (IAF) lost. The Pakistanis later claimed that they had actually won the air war by destroying over a 100 Indian aircraft while losing only 36 of their own. The truth, as usual, is somewhere in between.

Unlike in 1965, the Indian Air Force in 1971 handled claims of aerial victories by its pilots with great maturity. No "kills" were awarded until all claims could be verified, preferably by photo reconnaissance missions. Almost immediately after the War was over, the Air Chief asked the Halwara station commander, Air Marshal C.V. Gole, to visit every IAF station in the West to ascertain the performance of various squadrons. "Later, we had access to other information as well and we worked out a pretty accurate picture of losses on both sides", he explains. But discrepancies could well remain. For instance, Gole recalls that one SAM battery had fired missiles at a couple of attacking Pakistani B-57 bombers. One was hit and streaming smoke. A few hours later, some villagers called to say that they had found the debris of the Pakistani aircraft. On investigation it was found that what remained was not the debris of an aircraft but that of a missile. The hit was not taken into account. It was only much after the war that some Pakistani report spoke about a B-57 pilot who had become "Shaheed" after he tried to bail out his burning aircraft but could not make it.

Pakistani claims of their own losses are less than reliable. The main cause of this confusion has to do with various "Official" histories of the PAF quoting different figures. It has been estimated by some observers, based on signal intercepts from the PAF, that the PAF lost at least seventy-two aircraft (including at least fifty-five combat types). Pakistan itself admits to the loss of twenty-nine combat aircraft on the ground. Only 16 were claimed to have been shot down over India. Add to this the 13 Sabres destroyed by the PAF itself at Dhaka. Even then the figure comes to 58. However, a lot of this is inaccurate. After almost a year's of research, we at SAPRA INDIA believe that the losses of combat aircraft on both sides were as follows :

Combat Aircraft Losses

Description	Pakistan	India
Air to Air	19	19
Ground Fire	15	35
On Ground	29	2
Total	63	56

*   Combat aircraft and bomber losses only. Transporters and Recce PAF aircraft shot down or destroyed on the ground not included.

**   PAF losses include 13 aircraft destroyed by PAF on the ground at Dhaka.

The PAF lost many more aircraft on the ground not only because the Indians launched many more counter air operations than the Pakistanis but also because the PAF itself destroyed 13 of its Sabres in Dhaka within a few days of the war. PAF's No. 14 squadron with about 18 aircraft felt it had been abandoned by its higher command and left to face the onslaught of ten full Indian squadrons. After a couple of gallant actions by Pakistani pilots, the PAF commanders in East Pakistan appear to have decided that the game was not worth the effort. The last aerial engagement in East Pakistan took place on 4 December. Even if the Pakistani claim that the Indians lost more aircraft is accepted, does it suggest that the Pakistanis won the air war? The answer is a clear no. Because war, in the ultimate analysis, is not a numbers game. Winning a war has to do with achieving clear objectives. For the IAF, the aim was twofold: first, to prevent the PAF from messing with the Indian Army's advances, logistics and launching points; and second, to seriously impair Pakistan's capacity to wage war. The PAF's job was to do the opposite. The pre-emptive air strikes on 3rd December were aimed at knocking out a good part of the IAF while it was on the ground. This failed for the simple reason that the Indians had learnt their lessons of the 1965 war and had constructed fortified pens and bunkers to store their aircraft. More important, young IAF fliers proved they had the grit to go out and fight, even if it meant losing one's life.

By the end of the first week of the war, PAF fighters in the West appeared to have lost their will to fight. By this time, the IAF was repeatedly hitting secondary targets including railway yards, cantonments, bridges and other installations as well as providing close air support to the Army wherever it was required. The most dangerous were the close air support missions which involved flying low and exposing aircraft to intense ground fire. The IAF lost the most aircraft on these missions as is proved by the high losses suffered by IAF Sukhoi-7 and Hunter squadrons But their pilots flew sortie after sortie keeping up with the Army and disrupting enemy troop and tank concentrations. Once it was known that the Indian Army was knocking at the gates of Dhaka, the PAF in the West virtually gave up flying. During the last few days of the war, the IAF brass ordered attacks on PAF airfields with the sole purpose of drawing out their aircraft. But that rarely succeeded as the PAF aircraft for the most part remained secured inside their pens, refusing to come out and fight. The strongest indictment of the Pakistani Air Force was made not by an Indian but by the Pakistani leader, Zulfiqar Ali Bhutto, who took over from General Yahya Khan after the 1971 defeat. On taking over, he made a speech in which he castigated the PAF chief Air Marshal Rahim Khan and several other officers by name.

A better analysis of effectiveness of the two air forces is provided by the losses per sortie figure. The IAF flew at least double the number of combat sorties per day than the PAF, thereby exposing itself to ground fire and enemy interdiction. Despite this, the lAF's attrition rate of 0.86 per 100 sorties during the 1971 War compares favourably with the Israeli rate of 1.1 in the Yom Kippur War. The PAF's overall attrition rate works out to 2.47 (including transporters and recce aircraft lost on the ground). If aircraft destroyed on the ground are not taken into account, the rate works out to 1.12, which is still very high given that PAF aircraft never really stood back to fight. The question of loss is important but, in the ultimate analysis, secondary. Achieving air superiority cost the IAF dearly in 1971 but in the end it managed to achieve complete dominance over the skies in both East and West Pakistan.

Part Eight : Defending the West

Limited Plans

The Indian Army HQ's plans on the western front clearly demonstrate that India's aim was not the destruction of Pakistan. Operations instructions issued to commanders on the western front were quite limited and the larger aim was to ensure that the Indian Army took as much as territory from the Pakistanis and conceded as little of Indian territory as possible. India felt that whoever held the most territory would end up as the winner because the final word on the war would only be spelt out during the post-war negotiations that were expected to follow. Pakistani commanders were aware of this basic dynamic and had concentrated virtually all their forces in the West. Their Air Force was equipped with Star-fighters, new Chinese F-6s and newer versions of the F-86 Sabre. Their Army had a lot of fire power in the form of heavy artillery, new Chinese built T-59 tanks, and US-built Patton tanks. India had been preparing for war for some months but the Pakistanis were not perturbed. They felt that any Indian advance in the East could be held up for a while during which their concentrated forces in the West would seize strategically important Indian territory. In the end, India would be forced to negotiate and, the Pakistanis hoped, India's strategic designs would be frustrated. Bangladesh would never come into being.

The First Blow

Pakistan struck the first blow by attacking nine Indian air bases on 3 December 1971 and followed up by a massive attack on Chhamb. The Chhamb attack was stopped—but at a cost. Many of the major battle plans drawn up before the outbreak of war had to be hastily changed - even abandoned in some cases. One very disappointed soldier was Major. General. Z.C. Bakshi, commanding the 26 Indian Infantry Division. "I toured the front-lines in my jeep, flying my flag, and there was no problem," recalls the General. "At one or two places, Pakistani soldiers even saluted my jeep. And I knew we could break through these lines and threaten Sialkot town, which was the objective given to my Division." Major. General, Bakshi had a reputation of being a fighter and had done brilliantly in the previous war. When he took over 26 Division, in the southern part of the state of Jammu & Kashmir, a major worry was a dagger-shaped strip of territory measuring 170 square kilometres under Pakistani control that protruded into the Indian side. This "dagger" threatened an important link town called Akhnur. After studying the map a few times, Bakshi told his subordinates that this was no "dagger" but a chicken's neck: "We shall squeeze this part like a chicken's neck as soon as the war begins." And he did just that. Within two days of the outbreak of the war, the "chicken's neck" had been wrung by one brigade under 26 Division. But the more ambitious plan to move towards Sialkot was never effected. "After the Pakistani thrust at Chhamb, headquarters was in a in flap and they took away one of my brigades and told me to not to attack," says Bakshi. "All those brilliant plans prepared before the war went to waste all because people could not keep their cool in the heat of battle and let one temporary reverse cloud their judgement.

The Indians had prepared just two other offensive plans for the entire western sector, which stretches from Ladakh (Jammu & Kashmir) in the north to the salt water marshes of the Runn of Kutch (Gujarat) in the south. The terrain in this sector is highly varied and begins with tall snow covered mountains in the north, then turns into riverine flats before moving to scrub covered stretches and rich farmland further south in the plains of Indian Punjab. Below Punjab, is the state of Rajasthan, made up mostly of desert. The desert stops short of the state of Gujarat and gives way to vast dry flat lands ending with the marshes of Kutch, which eventually merge into the Arabian Sea. The western border is long - more than the distance between Paris and Moscow - and many an army has perished in the past in these areas. Taking territory here is a costly enterprise and the Indians knew it. This is why the overwhelming majority of its Army divisions were (and continue to be) termed as 'holding" formations as opposed to "strike" formations. The emphasis traditionally has been on defence rather than offense. The responsibility of defending the entire western sector was the responsibility of two Indian Army commands - the

Western Command and the Southern Command. In 1971, India had just one strike formation, the 1 Corps. The other divisions under the Western and Southern commands were all designated holding formations. Though the holding corps also engaged in offensive action, these were all limited and not geared to carry the battle deep into enemy territory.

The three offensive missions drawn up by Indian Army Headquarters included the aborted 26 Division plan to move towards Sialkot, a major thrust by 1 Corps to capture the 30 km thick Shakargarh bulge which juts into the region between north Punjab and south Jammu & Kashmir, and a plan to move across the deserts to cut off the rail link between Pakistan's Punjab and Sindh provinces. The first two of these actions were to be carried out by Western Command, the largest of the two commands. The other command - Southern Command - was responsible for the borders south of Anupgarh at the northernmost edge of Rajasthan right down to the Arabian Sea. Due to the difficult terrain in the south, only two Indian Army divisions from Southern Command took part in the fighting and their battles is part of the story of Longewala. All the battles that took place in the Western sector are two numerous to be recounted here but the fight for Shakargarh deserves mention. For, here the fighting was particularly bitter with the most lives lost on both sides. As for the Pakistanis, despite grandiose pre-war plans, their only notable success was in Chhamb. In other areas, Pakistani units fought tenaciously but got nowhere because of the failure of their higher command.

Attack by 1 Corps

The Shakargarh Bulge points to the north Punjab town of Pathankot, which is squeezed between the mountains rising in the east and the Pakistani border on the west. Pathankot is strategically important for the defence of Jammu & Kashmir and the northern parts of Himachal Pradesh. This was also the Headquarters of India's only strike corps, commanded at that time by Lt. General. K.K. Singh. His forces included three infantry divisions, two independent armoured brigades, two independent artillery brigades and the equivalent of about two engineers brigades. The corps was, however, tied down due to defensive commitments that took up more than a division's worth of troops. The Pakistanis too had a formation designated 1 Corps opposite its Indian counterpart. This too was a heavy formation possessing considerable strike force. It was made up of two infantry divisions and four independent armoured brigades, apart from artillery and other support units. The Pakistanis also had committed considerable reserves for this sector, which they were able to bring in with surprising agility.

The Indian corps commander decided to attack the bulge from three sides: one division (54 Div) was to attack from Samba, a town in the north of the bulge where he had shifted his HQ: another (39 Div) was deployed more towards the western tip of the bulge: and the other (36 Div) was to commence from the southern part of the bulge. All these divisions had far less than their full complement of units and in practice had to operate at the brigade level. The fighting showed that in the end it is not only plans but hard fighting that decides the course of battles.

The advances of 39 Division under Major General B.R. Prabhu was a series of disasters right from the beginning. Although his units crossed the enemy lines easily enough, they got bogged down in minefields and could not secure their objectives. To be fair, the Div commander had none of his brigades and had to make do with one brigade and two independent armoured brigades less a regiment. This made him a little cautious and somewhat disinclined to rally his forces forward. This caused major problems for the other two depleted divisions which were pressing ahead only to find their flanks exposed because of 39 Div's lack of progress.

54 Div attacking from the north was the most active although during the initial days of the war two of its three brigades had been taken away for the protection of Chhamb. Nevertheless Major General W.A.G. Pinto, commanding the Div, and his able armoured brigade commander, Brigadier A.S. Vaidya (later General Vaidya, who became Chief of Army Staff), made tremendous progress. By 15 December 1971, the Div had control of all the points overlooking the Shakargarh-Zafarwal road. The big test was the crossing of the Basantar river, which had been mined by the Pakistanis and the minefield continued for 1,400 metres. The Pakistanis also had more than four independent armoured brigades worth of armour to throw at the Indians, which was far more than

what the attackers had. The most formidable task was the river crossing.

By this time, the Pakistanis had got wind of the plan and had thrown in two infantry brigades and one armoured brigade to prevent the formation of a successful bridgehead. The Pakistani Air Force too was called in to fly relentless sorties against the Indian build-up. The Indian battalions and the brave engineers literally had to run through a wall of fire to establish crossing points and move across. The bridgehead was secured but the enemy was not dispersed. One Indian battalion had its commanding officer shot by Pakistanis infiltrating the bridgehead. Other units suffered horrendous losses in the concentrated artillery fire and aerial bombing. The Indian units pressed on regardless and by 15 December had established a bridgehead.

The Pakistanis tried to destroy the bridgehead by launching a series of counter-attacks headed by tanks of Pakistan's 8 Independent Armoured Brigade. Indian tanks were rushed in to stop the Pakistanis from breaking through. Two Indian tank regiments tried and were virtually decimated. Finally, the third Indian armoured regiment (17 Horse) held the Pakistanis with the help of three Indian infantry battalions. The fighting here was easily the most desperate in the war with the Pakistanis losing as many as 46 tanks in less than a days of fighting. The Pakistanis counter-attack was eventually stopped by nothing less than sheer grit. If anybody could tell the story best, it was Major Nisar, squadron commander of Pakistan's 13 Cavalry.

The Pakistani armoured counter-attacks were stopped by 17 Horse and in the end it was just 3 tanks of a troop commanded by Captain V. Malhotra that ultimately took on one of the final Pakistani assaults from an entire squadron of tanks Leading the Pakistani squadron was Major Nisar. He was amazed to find his advance stopped by just three tanks. But before he could get over his surprise, he found most of his tanks hit. One of the Indian tanks, commanded by young Second Lieutenant Arun Khetarpal was responsible for most of the damage. Even after both the other tanks or their commanders were put out of action, Khetarpal continued to fight until his tank was hit by Major Nisar's tank and caught fire. He was ordered to abandon his tank but he refused.

He kept engaging the Pakistani tanks and stopped Major Nisar's tank with a hit. Although Nisar's tank ground to a halt it managed to fire one last shot at Khetarpal's stricken tank, killing the Second Lieutenant instantly. Major Nisar escaped by leaping out of his burning tank. The attack was stopped but out of the three squadron commanders only one lived to tell the tale - Captain Malhotra. After the cease fire, Major Nisar paid a courtesy calls across the lines to pay his complements. He only found Captain Malhotra. Khetarpal was one of the few Indians in the country's 50 year history to have received the highest award for gallantry, the *Param Vir Chakra*. His posthumous citation read: "His calculated and deliberate decision to fight from a burning tank was an act of valour and self-sacrifice beyond the call of duty."

But that is just what thousands of other soldiers did in the fighting in the Shakargarh bulge. The Pakistanis too fought to the man and in many areas, the fighting often ended up in hand-to-hand combat. From all accounts, this is the area where the Pakistanis fought for every inch of soil and the Indian shed blood for every yard they captured. The Indians clung on to every inch of territory they had conquered and the Indian Army's third *Param Vir Chakra* was won on these very killing fields. Major Hoshiar Singh led the forward company of the 3 Grenadiers into battle into the bridgehead and took a village called Jarpal. The Pakistanis counter-attacked later the same day. Hoshiar Singh undaunted went from trench to trench to rally his men disregarding the bullets flying all around him. His behaviour so encouraged the men that they took on a battalion sized attack the next morning even after being pounded by artillery in which Hoshiar Singh was seriously wounded. He continued to move amongst his men and kept up the fire against the enemy. When one of his machine gun crews was knocked out by a shell, he personally took over and shot a number of Pakistanis. At the end of the days fighting, over 85 Pakistani soldiers were found dead in front of their trenches.

That was the end of the Pakistani counter-attacks but the Indians could get no further as the cease-fire came into effect on the same evening. The Indians had halted their advance just 7 kilometres short of Zafarwal. Some Indian military historians have been critical of 1 Corps' actions, arguing that much more could have been achieved had the corps commander not dispersed his resources and had not been forced to tie down a major chunk of his assets for defensive purposes. But this is not quite fair considering that the actual offensive was late in starting and the Indians had actually less than a week to gain their objectives. Besides, this area was traversed by numerous rivers, ditches and defended embankments. The enemy had re-inforced the area in depth and laid extensive minefields all over the place. They also had significant artillery fire and were supported by the PAF. Making headway under such conditions in so limited a time was difficult.

Soldiers on both sides fought hard and if, in the end, the whole affair was a stalemate, it was justly so. Had the war dragged for even a week more, things would certainly have been very different. That is why the Pakistani high command despite having lost all its strategic objectives readily agreed to a cease-fire. The Indian Army in the west proved that the regimental colours its men carried were still a matter of honour. The stories of the 1971 War ensured that those traditions would be carried on by many generations of fighting men in the years to come. Most of all, Indian troops had learnt that after all was said and done, honour in battle meant standing one's ground and fighting - even to the last man or tank if necessary.

THE KARGIL CONFLICT

The Kargil conflict was the result of the Pakistan's plan of "Operation Topac" which was formulated by General Zia in 1988. The "Operation Topac" was to be completed in two phases. The first phase of this plan was implemented by Pakistan against India in 1989 and as a result of the implementation of the phase II of this Pakistan plan happened the present Kargil war. To counter Kargil war India had to conduct "Operation Vijay".

We contain valuable information and facts to enhance the knowledge of the people. It is the first hand information concerning Kargil Conflict between India and Pakistan. It highlights India's politio-military supremacy over Pakistan. It contains facts concerning the aggression, the situation which encouraged Pakistan to attempt an open aggression in Kargil region on Indian side of the line of control (LoC).

Introduction

The valleys of Suru, Drass, Wakha and Bodkarbu lie midway between the alpine valleys of Kashmir and the fertile reaches of the Indus Valley and Ladakh. The region falls within India's political boundaries, the ones that were threatened by Pakistan as recently as a year ago and ended in the Kargil War. It is also integral to Baltistan in its ethnicity, while geographically it fits into Ladakh.

HISTORY

Until 1947, Kargil once served as an important trading and transit centre linking Ladakh with Gilgit (Pakistan), and the lower Indus Valley. There were also important trading links between the villages of the Suru Valley and the Zanskar Valley, and even 20 years ago it was not uncommon to see yak trains making their way from Padum all the way into the Kargil Bazaar. It was also an important commercial point in the Pan-Asian trade network.

Numerous caravans carrying exotic merchandise comprising silk, brocade, carpets, felts, tea, poppy, ivory et al, transited the town on their way to and from China, Tibet, Yarkand and Kashmir. The old Bazaar displayed a variety of Central Asian and Tibetan commodities even after the cessation of Central Asian trade in 1949, until these were exhausted about two decades back. Similarly, the ancient trade route passing through the township was lined with several caravanserai.

Now, since 1975, travellers of numerous nationalities have replaced traders of the past and Kargil has regained its importance as a centre for travel-related activities. Located in the midst of a Himalayan region with tremendous potential for adventure activities, Kargil serves as an important base for adventure tours in the heart of the Himalayas. It is also the take-off station for visitors to the exotic Zanskar Valley.

Kargil, next to the roaring Suru River, is the second-largest town in Ladakh, but is not really little more than one long main road called Main Bazaar Road, with innumerable little lanes branching off (watch out for wide trucks). If you have time, walk up Hospital Road for some interesting views of the area. There are also picturesque fields and villages across the Qatilgah Bridge, at the end of Balti Bazaar Road. The Tourist Reception Centre is next to the taxi stand, just off the main road. Open 10 AM to 4 PM on normal working days, it rents out trekking gear.

GEOGRAPHY

Kargil, situated at 2704 metres above sea level, lies 204 km east of Srinagar, 234 km west of Leh, and is the second largest urban centre of Ladakh and the headquarters of the district that shares its name. Kargil is an overnight halt on the way to Leh for tourists travelling between Srinagar, and is also the point where you turn south in the direction of the Zanskar Valley.

The town nestles along the rising hillsides of the lower Suru basin. Two tributaries of the Suru River that meet here are the Drass and the Wakha. The lands that lie along the narrow valley, as also the rising hillsides, are intensively cultivated in neat terraces, to grow barley, wheat, peas, a variety of vegetables and other cereals. Thick plantations of poplars and willows, besides apricot, apple and mulberry, adorn the valley bottom and the hills. The town, along with the adjoining villages, forms a rich oasis against the backdrop of the undulating lunar mountain-scape. Kargil is famous for the fine apricots that are grown here. In May, the entire countryside abounds with fragrant white apricot blossoms, while in August, the ripening fruit washes the land in hues of orange.

THE KARGIL CONFLICT AND "OPERATION VIJAY"

Planning of invasion

Invasion planned 14 years ago

The Pakistani Army had planned the invasion of the Kargil Drass region 14 years ago to cut off India's road connection to Siachen, according to the weekly *"Tokbeer"*, brought out by pro-army Jammait-e-Islami. The brain behind this strategy was Brigadier Azizuddin, who was given charge of the Pakistani brigade in PoK in 1985, the year India and Pakistan held talks on a no war pact proposed by Pakistan and a treaty of peace and friendship proposed by India. In its latest issue, the weekly says that the brigadier conceived the invasion plan after an intensive tour and study of the topography of PoK but was called back to Rawalpindi before he could implement it.

Dawat Al Irshad is behind intrusion

About 40 km from Lahore on way to Rawalpindi is a town called Muridke. In November every year, thousands of Islamic fundamentalists gather there to participate in the annual international convention of the Dawat Al Irshad. The Dawat is the Parent body of the Lashkar-i-Toiba, the militant organisation that has sent in most of the intruders who had occupied Indian territory, besides regular Pakistani soldiers, in this sector as well as Drass and Batalik sub-sector. Intelligence sources said, though other organisations such as the Hizbul Mujahideen and Harkat-Jehad-e-lstami are still active in the state, it is the Lashkar which is the mainstay of the insurgents now. In their convention last year, Hafiz Saeed, chief of the Dawat, and other leaders of the organisation such as Maulana Amir Harriza, had made public their plans to "capture" Jammu and Kashmir. Yet, it seems, the Indian authorities took no precautionary measures.

After having been taught about Islamic tenets in hundreds of madarsas that are being run by the Dawat (these are besides those madarsas which are being run be other organisations such as the Jamiat-ul-Ulema-i-lslam and Jamaat-e-lslami), these teenagers are trained in warfare at dozens of training camp being run by the Lashkar in the mountainous terrain near Muzaffarabad in PoK and at Kunar in Afghanistan. Army sources say the intruders are carrying light machine guns, an assortment of assault rifles and shoulder-fired Stinger missiles which the US had supplied to the Afghan groups. By one estimate, 80 per cent of these missiles were not used in Afghanistan and are now being made use of by the intruders.

Bin Laden 'Worked in Tandem with Pak'

Osama bin Laden is working closely with the Pakistani Government in pushing the intruders into Kargil, according to western intelligence reports quoted here. Bin Laden is working with the Pakistani Government through two groups, Al Badr and Harkat-ul-Ansar, say the reports. The intruding force is said to include several hundred of Bin Laden's Islamic fighters along with regulars from the Pakistani Army. These reports indicate a larger percentage of trained terrorists in the intruding force than the Indian Government has indicated.

A report in "The Daily Telegraph" indicated that while the Indian Army had claimed that the intruders were mostly Pakistani troops in disguise. Western intelligence believes that many are Afghan, Pakistani and even international Muslim militants backed by Pakistan's ISI (Interservices Intelligence). The report said the "ISI is known to train, arm and fund Islamic terrorist groups". The report said many of the ISI-trained intruders belong to Al Badr, which it described as "a terrorist group linked to Osama Bin Laden". An earlier report had mentioned Bin Laden's links with the Harkat-ul-Ansar, the group that was behind the abduction of five Western hostages in Kashmir in 1995. The Harkat-ul-Ansar is assisted by the ISI, according to the report, which said "several former members of Pakistan's intelligence agencies, who now live in exile in Britain, have been giving information to Scotland Yard on this matter." The report also said that Harkat-ul-Ansar and the ISI were working towards "Pakistani's complete control of Kashmir". The links between Osama and the Pakistani Government through the ISI, Al Badr and the Harkat-ul-Ansar indicate that leaders of a Private army" that Pakistan has helped to build up will have considerable say in deciding the position of the intruders in Kargil. A report in Jane's Intelligence Review said in 1997 Bin Laden had declared that his aim was to target "US soldiers". In an interview last year he changed that position to say that "we do not differentiate between those dressed in military uniform and civilians. They are all targets in this fatwa (edict)". According to the report published in the June edition of Jane's Intelligence Review, Bin Laden has been targeting the US interests and failing of late.

Pakistan army organisation

The Pakistan army is commanded by the Chief of the Army Staff who sits in the General Headquarters, Rawalpindi. He is assisted by Principal Staff Officers who are two or three star generals.

Force structure	Enemy power
Corps HQ	Total 9 corps HQ

Pakistan army's new doctrine of offensive-defence was tested during Exercise 'Zarb-e-Momin', its biggest ever manoeuvre in 1989. After this, exercise, the army is viewed as a force capable of undertaking a strategic offensive on land, including the possibility of taking the war into enemy territory, rather than waiting to be hit as in 1965 and 1971 wars. The Pakistan army has 45 days of reserve ammunition and fuel in stock. Pakistan boasts premier defence institutes like the Command and Staff College, Quetta, and the National Defence College. Every year around 2,000 army officers are sent to foreign countries for training with over 75% going to the US. The army has more than 50 officers with Ph D.

Armed Div	Total 2 in number
Groups Arty Bde	19 groups of artillary
Area Comand	1 area command
Indep Armed Bde	7 independent armoured brigades
Indep Inf Bde	9 independent infanty brigades
Engr Bde	7 engineering brigades
SF Group	1 special force
Armed Recce Regt	3 armoured regiments
Armed Comd (1)	1 armoured command
Aviation	17 aviation wings

Main battle tanks 2,000 main battle tanks Artillery pieces

Eight Indians who work behind the scene

When the (COAS) Chief of Army Staff, Gen. V.P. Malik, held a press conference in the midst of the Kargil conflict, diplomatic circles were surprised. They may not have known that the unprecedented move of a war-time Army chief holding a press briefing was part of New Delhi's proactive strategy in dealing with international option. Behind this Strategy is the core group of the Advisory Board of the National Security Council which has been meeting daily to advise the government on handling of the Kargil issue. It comprises National Security Adviser to the Prime Minister. Brajesh Mishra, noted analyst on strategic affairs K. Subrahmanyam, former foreign secretary J.N. Dixit, former defence and home secretary N.N. Vohra, former Air Chief, Air Chief Marshal S K Mehra, Major General (Retd.) Afsir Karim and economist Sanjaya Baru, Satish Chandra, convener of the NSC Secretariat, is also the convener of this group.

Mr. Mishra decided to constitute the group after criticism that the 27-member National Security Advisory Board (NSAB) was too disparate and unwieldy to advise the government during a crisis.

However, despite this core group's four-week existence and the key task that it is performing, information on it is hard to come by.

However, another member was more accommodating and confirmed that the group has been active for the past four weeks. But he refused to comment on the manner in which the group interacted with the political leadership, particularly Prime Minister Vajpayee. Unlike the NSAB which does not receive any classified information, this core group is being provided with sensitive information ranging from the day's reports from the frontline, telegrams from various embassies, assessments from the concerned ministries and a constant review of the economic situation. Asked whether the events have followed the expectation of the group, this member said, 'Things have happened more or less as we had envisaged.

Sources say this group has been responsible for guiding the overall approach of low-profile diplomacy and stem action on the ground. It endorsed the broad approach that pushed Pakistan on the defensive on the battlefield and isolated it in the international community. More important, it persuaded the government and the armed forces to allow open access to the media despite occasional negative reporting.

A Tough Challenge for IAF Pilots

The use, of air power to dislodge the Pakistan supported infiltrators Kashmir's Drass sector posed a challenge to pilots flying strike aircraft. To begin with, air strikes by jet fighters in high-altitude terrain is rare in the history of military aviation. Although the Indian Air Force is known to have earmarked a squadron each of MiG-21B and MiG 27M for altitude strike missions, the IAFs doctrine published in 1996 categorically rules out employment of air power for internal security duties. Further, the nature of the terrain, unpredictable weather conditions and flying parameters impose serious constraints on the performance of highspeed aircraft. IAF pilots are mostly trained for radar-evading, low-level strikes in the plains and semi-hilly terrain. The IAF has never seriously oriented its fighter pilots to carry out air strikes in high altitude terrain. Since the infiltrators are holding ridges at heights of 15,000 to 18,000 feet, IAF aircraft have been launching bombs and rockets from heights of about 18,000 to 20,000 feet while flying at speeds over 700 km an hour. At such speeds, all mountain peaks look the same frioin the air. To compound matters, the infiltrators enjoy the advantage of spreading out over vast areas in small groups, and hiding in mountain folds and behind ridges. This requires many more strike sorties and sustained bombing of positions over large mountain tracts. The atmosphere is rarified at altitudes of 20,000 feet. Therefore, aircraft fly at a much faster 'true' speed. This has two implications. First, the radius of the turning aircraft increases substantially which reduces tile flexibility for maneouvre. Should the pilot need to turn in an emergency, the aircraft could well cross the Line of Control (LoC). Second, the aircraft will take longer to pull up after striking targets.

Chronology of Events

"A Kannada proverb sums up the Kargil crisis: In broad day light he fell into a well that he had recognized even in dark night."

Some time in March, heavily armed Pakistan backed intruders dug themselves in at heights of 16000-18000 ft. on Indian side of the LoC along an 80 km. stretch north of Kargil.

Then followed the following sequence of events as reported by leading national Indian daily news papers.

April 1, 1999 : Intruders establish themselves 6-7 km. inside LoG, set up strong points near Jubar ridge.

May 6 : Infiltrators first sighted.   .

May 9-11 : Indian Patrol led by Major Rohit Gour moved down on Jubar ridge.

May 15 : Eight Killed in Kargil Shelling. At least eight Indians including seven army men and around 15 Pakistani militants have been killed in heavy exchange of fire continuing for the past two days in Kargil sector of Jammu and Kashmir. Meanwhile, talking to newsmen in Leh, Defence Minister George Fenandes denied reports that Pakistan has captured a border post in Kargil sector.

—Express, May 16, 1999

May 16 : Infiltrators hushed in one of the biggest counter-insurgency operations, Army on Saturday started flushing out Pakistan backed infiltrators from the Line of Control (LoC) in Kargil sector of Jammu and Kashmir where at least 23 people, including 15 Pakistanis, have been killed in exchange of fire since May 9.

–Indian Express, May 17, 1999

May 17 : Kargil Shelling. An army counter offensive has cut off 100 Pakistani infiltrators holed up in Drass sector in Jammu and Kashmir. The infiltrators who suffered heavy casualties have fled from one of the ridgelines after a bold manoeuvre by Indian solders.

–Indian Express, May 18, 1999

May 18 : Kargil still in the line of fire. The Kargil sector of Kashmir is witnessing over a week-long gun battle between the Indian troops and the Pakistan Army in which nearly 70 persons have lost lives, a majority of them infiltrators, though the army here is maintaining an enigmatic silence. However, there is no official word on the subject in the valley, and all the details are pouring in from the Army headquarters in Delhi . It has now taken more than a week for the Army to dislodge the armed intruders from the ridge lines with gunshots and heavy artillery gunfire. This brings out the enormity and the intensity of fight posed by infiltrators, reportedly backed by regular Pakistan Army personnel. The reports of 300-odd militants intrusion, provoking the Army to marshall unprecedented resources to push back the infiltrators, has recast the whole security scenario in the state that has been in the grip of secessionist militancy for the past decade. Other reports indicate that there are more than 150 militants waiting to cross over from other sectors along the Line of Control (LoC) and that would obviously stretch the Army's resources to the limit.

What was part of the speculation has been officially confirmed that the Indian troops had abandoned some of their posts in the Kargil sector during winter. Pakistan Army or infiltrators having taken advantage of that, occupied the posts resulting in the crisis on the border which has now spilled over to Kargil town. Apart from Kargil, there are reports from other sectors along the LoC

like Uri, Kupwara, Budhi, Rajouri and Poonch that a large number
of militants were waiting to cross over. These intensified infiltration
bids have complicated matters for the security forces.

—Hindustan Times, May 19, 1999

May 19: 52 Militants Killed in Kargil Sector in a major
offensive, the Army has gunned down 52 heavily armed Pakistan-
backed militants and injured many others since Sunday in Kargil
sector of Jammu and Kashmir where they had infiltrated under
heavy artillery fire by Pakistan Army since May 9, official sources
said here today. The Army has lost nine men in the operation
which began yesterday to flush out militants entrenched in four
of the seven ridges in the Kargil mountains, the sources said,
however, the names and ranks of the Army men killed had not
been disclosed. So far, 52 bodies of militants have been recovered
which included 28 in Batalik, 10 in Kaksar and 11 each in Drass
and Mushkoh regions, the sources said, adding that while the
number of injured militants was high, their figure was being
ascertained. An estimated 350 Militants, dressed like local
shepherds, had been pushed in by Pakistan Army under the cover
of artillery gunfire to which Indian Army had given a befitting
response. The sources said the operation is on to clear the rest
of the ridges being occupied by the trained militants. Meanwhile,
an Army spokesman said that fresh attempts were being made
by Islamabad to push in more infiltrators from Pak-occupied
Kashmir. J and K Chief Minister Farooq Abdullah visited Kargil
and Drass today and flew over the area of operations. He was
accompanied by top Army officials. Heavy Pakistani artillery fire
was reported near Turtuk post in Kargil sector, besides Batalik
and Drass areas. However, India troops kept the infiltrators across
the ridge line despite the latter having the advantages of height,
the sources added.

—Indian Express, May 20, 1999

May 20: *Army Recaptures Strategic Positions in Kargil* : The
Indian Army achieved a major success this morning when it recaptured certain strategic positions along the Kargil sector and
hoped that it would be able to fully clear the area in the next two
to three days. Speaking for the first time about the over 10-days
long gun battles in Kargil, provoked by the infiltration of 300 to

400 Pushtoo speaking militants, Corps Commander Lt. Gen. Krishan Pal told media persons here this morning that the Indian Army has reached a position which would enable "us to resolve the situation to our advantage in the next two to three days". He said the infiltration bid was "fully backed by the Pakistan Army and ISI", to "revive the proxy war". He said the Army has "encircled these infiltrators and would soon neutralise them". He said there was nothing of much concern. The infiltrators are trapped in high ridges and results would soon be there for all to see. They have been blocked and their routes cut by the Army. The Corps Commander said the response of the Indian Army to this situation was "swift, well-focussed and hard-hitting". Gen. Krishan Pal, providing a detailed account of the situation said, infiltrators had occupied the posts in the unheld areas and "there was no question of the Pakistan Army capturing any of the posts. No post has been captured". He said all reports in this regard were mischievous and baseless. He admitted that 12 soldiers have lost their lives in these gun battles. He added: 'We have seen through the designs of the Pakistan Army and would deal with this local situation locally and not allow it to be spilled over to other sectors". The Corps Commander said "radio intercepts have revealed that cadres and 78 others have been wounded". "The toll could be higher", he said. He said the infiltrators are being fought in piecemeal fashion because of the terrain.

—Hindustan Times, May 21, 1999

May 20: Pakistani Army had Crossed LoG The on going cross-border artillery barrage in Kargil sector reveals a well-rehearsed and calculated Pakistan Army plan to intrude into Indian territory with an aim to disrupt road links to Leh and escalate tension in the region, claim Defence Ministry sources. Sources say that the so called infiltrators had actually intruded six to seven kilometers across the Line of Control (LoC) and established reinforced concrete cement bunkers on the ridge-lines in Drass-Kargil Batalik axis. The Indian Army after considerable effort has not been able to push back these intruders and are in the process of evicting them. The "infiltrators" are holding position and directing artillery five on to the Indian Army installations in Kargil sector, gives credence to the fact that the intruders are actually regular Pakistan Army troops.

The Pakistan Army plan to hold ground is evident from the fact that the established bunkers have coordinated defence with arcs of artillery fire overlapping each other in accordance with an established military strategy. Although Defence Minister George Fernandes sought to play down the Kargil situation by saying that the Army was more than equipped to tackle the scenario, it is apparent that it would take quite some time for the Army to evict the intruders. Sources say that the Pakistani game plan in the Kargil sector was hatched in January this year, with "infiltrators" occupying areas that were vacated by Indian Army as they become inaccessible during the winter. However, the Indian Army came to know about their presence forward area ammunition dump in Kargil was blown and the first convoy to Leh on the national highway 1 Alpha came under artillery fire in the first week of this month. The pattern of artillery firing revealed that shells were being directed to the military targets by these infiltrators positioned on the ridge-tops. Till last year, it is understood that artillery firing was being directed through STD booths in the area. Sources say that this intrusion has led to a lot of rethinking in the top echelons of the Indian Army as it is felt that such moves by the adversary should have been anticipated and a contingency plan to put in place. It is understood that intelligence reports since February this year have indicated presence of infiltrators in this area.

—Hindustan Times, May 21, 1999

May 21 : *Army to Counter Pak Plan to Alter LoG :* When the Pakistan army chief was making an unscheduled visit to his frontline 62 Brigade in Skardu today, a determined Army Headquarters here was weighing the option of expanding its positions along the rest of the Line of Control (LoC) instead of letting it remain localised in the Kargil area". On the second day of the eviction operations launched against Pakistani soldiers and their militants, a senior South Block official said: If the Pakistanis are aiding and abetting the alteration of the LoC, there is no reason for us to let it be a localised issue. We too may make gains on the LoC and we may well exercise that option." He was alluding to the infiltration attempt by around 300 Pakistani-militants and soldiers as well as yesterday's statement by the Director General of the Inter Services Public Relations in Rawalpindi, Brig

Rashid Qureshi, to the Pakistani media. Qureshi had declared that the LoC was not a "demarcated line". The South Block official pointed out that the LoC was the outcome of the 1949 Karachi Ceasefire Agreement and the 1972 Simla Agreement. "On both occasions, the contours of the LoC were determined by military officials from India and Pakistan, who then signed and accepted the respective positions. That is how the ceasefire line came to become the LoC," he said. The ability of the infiltrators to hold on to the ridge lines along the LoC has convinced observers here that Pakistani soldiers are part of the operation. The entire operation, said the sources, was planned at the highest levels in Islamabad and Rawalpindi and involved both the Pakistan Army as well as the Directorate of Inter Services Intelligence (ISI). They also pointed out that Pakistan Prime Minister Nawaz Sharif was given a briefing at the ISI Headquarters, as unusual but significant event. The entire operation being coordinated by the Pakistan Army's 62 Brigade, which has its headquarters at Skardu, and the Minimarg based 80 Brigade; both in the Baltistan portions of Pakistan Occupied Kashmir. They come under the command of the Force Commander Northern Areas, a formation of more than a division strength.

—Indian Express, May 22, 1999.

May 22 : Pak Fire Disrupts Supply Line, dislocates villagers. The heaviest ever border skirmish between Indian troops and the Pakistan-backed infiltrators in Ladakh's Kargil region has led to exodus of about 25,000 people, disrupted tourism and the arterial supply line to Leh and Siachen. Sources in the Government say that townsfolks from Kargil, Drass and smaller habitations along the firing range of the infiltrators had moved to interiors without adequate arrangements. The Infiltrators, who continue to hold positions along a vital ridge between Kargil and Drass, have reportedly been shelling the sole road link to Ladakh—the 434 kms. Srinagar-Leh Highway on one hand and the trekkers paradise— the Kargil Zanaskar road on the other. The sources said the shells have landed 60 km inside the Indian territory disrupting life in the hitherto safer zones of the barren Himalayan peaks.

The Pak offensive in Kargil is aimed at diverting troops from counter-insurgency operations in Kashmir to enable infiltrators and mercenaries to sneak in well in time to scuttle the ensuing Lok Sabha and panchayat elections.

"Kargil-Drass is not a suitable terrain for movement of infiltrators," sources in the Home Ministry said. The area is a barren wasteland with glacial peaks of 16,000 to 17,000 feet altitude and a small population of Shia Muslims, who have not shown any propensity towards insurgency. The sources said there were indications of a large group of infiltrators having managed to wriggle across to Kashmir via Baltal, an alternate alpine route to Amarnath cave. From there the mercenaries can get an easy access to Wadwun valley in Doda Valley. The incident has shocked all the agencies engaged in counter insurgency operations in Kashmir. It is a serious lapse on the part of Indian planner that we could not visualise the infiltrators taking such an inhospitable route as this one," a senior officer told the leading newspaper.

Pakistan, it seems has achieved two main motives through the skirmish - one they have opened a new front for Indian troops in Kashmir and secondly, it has managed to divert Army troops from Kashmir, where the infiltrators were finding it difficult to sneak in from. Significantly, the ridge line since captured by the infiltrators had been in control of Pakistan army till 1981. It gives strategic advantage of dominating the vital Srinagar-Leh Highway. This road is the only supply line for the entire region, which remains cut off for nearly seven months due to snowfall. Last year Pak shelling had adversely hit tourism in Ladakh and the economy of the apricot- growing region had come to a halt. This year too infiltrators fire has hit Kargil, the biggest town of the region, and Drass, the second coldest inhabited place in Asia.

–Indian Express, May 23, 1999

May 25 : 660 infiltrators, but no intelligence failure: The Army for the first time today acknowledged the presence of about 600 infiltrators inside Indian territory and another 400 across the Line of Control, and said a four-pronged attack was under way to recover the higher ridgelines in the Batalik, Kaksar, Drass and Mushkoh areas. Some supply lines have been cut off and most positions have been isolated. While declining to admit to an intelligence failure, additional director-General (military operations) Maj. Gen Joginder Jaswant Singh conceded at a press conference in South Block today that the Army did not have any prior information on Pakistan's sinister and evil design. In the operations thus far, he added, 17 soldiers have died and 90 have sustained injuries. Three officers are among the 14 missing, presumed dead or taken prisoner. The casualty list on the infiltrators' side is said to number over 100. Asked about the use of air power to flush the infiltrators, Singh refused to answer, simply saying, a response would be given "as we deem militarily fit". The crisis, Maj. Gen Singh said, began on May 6 when an army patrol spotted 9-10 persons in black dress and long coats moving on the ridge east of Batalik. A reconnaisance patrol the next day drew heavy artillery fire from Pakistani gun positions. When troops clashed with the infiltrators on May 8, it had become apparent that the higher ridgelines had already been occupied. And when the clashes intensified. Pakistani artillery targeted Kargil, Drass and Batalik, destroying an ammunition point. Major Gen Singh also said that Pakistan army chief General Parvez Musharraf had on at least two occasions visited Skardu, headquarters of 62 Brigade, one of two brigades now suspected to be spearheading the infiltration operations. Musharraf s most recent visit is said to have been on May 21.

–Indian Express, May 26, 1999

SAGA OF PATRIOTISM

Home they brought her warriors dead
'She nor swoon'd, 'nor utter'd cry .
All her maidens, watching, said,
'She must weep or she will die.'

–Tennyson

Describing the Kargil Martyr's saga of patriotism

"Sobbing wives, broken mothers, stoic fathers, bewildered children, Flag-draped coffins of officers and jawans coming home, With unrelenting regularity, these tragic images of the Kargil conflict filled the nation's consciousness. As the last bugle sounds, TV cameras pick up the ineffable sorrow of the moment, its microphones record a brave sound bite, newspaper reporters are at hand. A father says, "My son died for the motherland, that's enough for me." A young widow looks at her four-year-old and whispers, "when he grows up, he too will defend the nation like his father." Glowing tributes about the supreme sacrifice that the dead man made fill the air. For that moment at least, there is a public recognition of a very personal loss."

SAGA OF PATRIOTISM

As the operation Vijay started views of bravery, courage, patriotism and of course martyrdom poured from the battle front in Kargil. Following are some important news Hero wise telling the saga of patriotism.

Grinadier Yogendra Singh Yadav   Lt. Manoj Kumar Pandey
Cantain Vikram Batra   Major Padmapani Acharya
Majar Rajesh Singh Adhikari   Major Sonam Wangchuk
Lt. Keishing Clifford Nongrum   Major Vivek Gupta
Cantain Anuj Nayyar   Rifleman Sanjay Kumar

CHAPTER 12

LEADERS OF PAKISTAN

HEADS OF STATE

Governors-General

Mohammad Ali Jinnah	15 Aug. 1947 - 11 Sep. 1948	
Khawaja Nazimuddin	14 Sep. 1948 - 17 Oct. 1951	
Ghulam Mohammad	17 Oct. 1951 - 6 Oct. 1955	(+1956)
Iskander Ali Mirza	6 Oct 1955 - 23 Mar 1956	(+1969) military

Presidents of the Republic

Iskander Ali Mirza	23 Mar 1956 - 27 Oct 1958	(+1969)
Mohammad Ayub Khan	27 Oct 1958 - 25 Mar 1969 military	(+1974)
Agha Mohammad Yahya Khan	25 Mar. 1969 - 20 Dec. 1971	(1980) military[1]
Zulfiqar Ali Bhutto	20 Dec. 1971 - 13 Aug. 1973	(+1979)
Fazal Elahi Chaudhry	14 Aug. 1973 - 16 Sep. 1978	(+1982)
Mohammad Zia ul-Haq	16 Sep. 1978 - 17 Aug. 1988	(+) k military
Ghulam Isaq Khan	17 Aug 1988 - 18 Jul 1993 (acting to 13 Dec 1988)	n/p
Wasim Sajjad	18 Jul 1993 - 14 Nov. 1993	
Farooq Ahmed Khan Leghari	14 Nov. 1993 - 2 Dec. 1997	
Wasim Sajjad	2 Dec. 1997 - 1 Jan. 1998	
Mohammad Rafiq Tarar	1 Jan. 1998 - 20 Jan. 2001	
Pervez Musharraf	20 Jun 2001 -	military

---

1. Chief Martial Law Administrator to 31 Mar 1969 and then president of the Republic.

PRIME MINISTERS

Nawabzada Liaquat Ali Khan	19 Jul. 1947 - 16 Oct. 1951	(+) a
Khawaja Nazimuddin	17 Oct. 1951 - 17 Apr 1953	(+1964)
Mohammad Ali Bogra	17 Apr. 1953 - 12 Aug. 1955	(+1963)
Chaudhry Mohammad Ali	12 Aug. 1955 - 12 Sep. 1956	(+1980)
Husain Shaheed Suhrawardy	12 Sep. 1956 - 17 Oct. 1957	(+1963)
Ismail Ibrahim Chundrigar	17 Oct. 1957 - 16 Dec. 1957	(+1960)
Malik Firooz Khan Noon	16 Dec. 1957 - 24 Oct. 1958	(+1970)
Mohammad Ayub Khan military	24 Oct. 1958 - 27 Mar. 1969	(+1974)
Agha Mohammad Yahya Khan[1]	27 Mar 1969 - 7 Dec. 1971	(+1980) military
Nurul Amin	7 Dec. 1971 - 24 Dec. 1971	(+1974)
Zulfiqar Ali Bhutto	24 Dec. 1971 - 5 Jul. 1977	(+1979)
Mohammad Zia ul-Haq	5 Jul 1977 - 24 Mar 1985	(+1988) military
Mohammad Khan Junejo	24 Mar. 1985 - 29 May 1988	(+1993)
Mohammad Zia ul-Haq military	9 Jun 1988 - 17 Aug 1988	(+) k
Benazir Bhutto	2 Dec. 1988 - 6 Aug. 1990	
Ghulam Mustapha Jatoi	6 Aug 1990 - 6 Nov. 1990	
Mian Mohammad Nawaz Sharif	6 Nov. 1990 - 18 Apr 1993	PML-N
Balakh Sher Mazari	18 Aprl 1993 - 26 May 1993	PML-N
Mian Mohammad Nawaz Sharif	26 May 1993 - 18 Jul. 1993	PML-N
Moeen Qureshi	18 Jul 1993 - 19 Oct. 1993	n/p
Benazir Bhutto	19 Oct. 1993 - 15 Nov. 1996	PPP
Malik Miraj Khalid (interim)	5 Nov 1996 - 17 Feb. 1997	n/p
Mian Mohammad Nawaz Sharif	17 Feb 1997 - 12 Oct. 1999	
Pervez Musharraf[2]	12 Oct. 1999 -	military

1. As Chief Martial Law Administrator.
2. The factor ruler to 15 Oct. 1999, then Chief Executive and (since 25 Oct. 1999) chairman of a military/civilian National Security Council.

MOHAMMAD ALI JINNAH

Father of the Nation Quaid-i-Azam Mohammad Ali Jinnah's achievement as the founder of Pakistan, dominates everything else he did in his long and crowded public life spanning some 42 years. Yet, by any standard, his was an eventful life, his personality multidimensional and his achievements in other fields were many, if not equally great. Indeed, several were the roles he had played with distinction: at one time or another, he was one of the greatest legal luminaries India had produced during the first half of the century, an 'ambassador of Hindu-Muslim unity, a great constitutionalist, a distinguished parliamentarian, a topnotch politician, an indefatigable freedom-fighter, a dynamic Muslim leader, a political strategist and, above all one of the great nation-builders of modern times.' What, however, makes him so remarkable is the fact that while similar other leaders assumed the leadership of traditionally well-defined nations and espoused their cause, or led them to freedom, he created a nation out of an inchoate and down-trodden minority and established a cultural and national home for it. And all that within a decades. For over three decades before the successful culmination in 1947, of the Muslim struggle for freedom in the South-Asian sub-continent, Jinnah had provided political leadership to the Indian Muslims: initially as one of the leaders, but later, since 1947, as the only prominent leader- the Quaid-i-Azam. For over thirty years, he had guided their affairs; he had given expression, coherence and direction to their legitimate aspirations and cherished dreams; he had formulated these into concrete demands; and, above all, he had striven all the while to get them conceded by both the ruling British and the numerous Hindus the dominant segment of India's population. And for over thirty years he had fought, relentlessly and inexorably, for the inherent rights of the Muslims for an honourable existence in the subcontinent. Indeed, his life story constitutes, as it were, the story of the rebirth of the Muslims of the sub-continent and their spectacular rise to nationhood, phoenix-like.

Early Life

Born on December 25, 1876, in a prominent mercantile family in Karachi and educated at the Sindh Madrassat-ul-Islam and the Christian Mission School at his birth place, Jinnah joined the Lincoln's Inn in 1893 to become the youngest Indian to be called to the Bar, three years later.

Starting out in the legal profession with nothing to fall back upon except his native ability and determination, young Jinnah rose to prominence and became Bombay's most successful lawyer, as few did, within a few years. Once he was firmly established in the legal profession, Jinnah formally entered politics in 1905 from the platform of the Indian National Congress. He went to England in that year along with Gopal Krishna Gokhale (1866–1915), as a member of a Congress delegation to plead the cause of Indian self-government during the British elections. A year later, he served as Secretary to Dadabhai Noaroji (1825–1917), the then Indian National Congress President, which was considered a great honour for a budding politician. Here, at the Calcutta Congress session (December 1906), he also made his first political speech in support of the resolution on self-government.

Political Career

Three years later, in January 1910, Jinnah was elected to the newly-constituted Imperial Legislative Council. All through his parliamentary career, which spanned some four decades, he was probably the most powerful voice in the cause of Indian freedom and Indian rights. Jinnah, who was also the first Indian to pilot a private member's Bill through the Council, soon became a leader of a group inside the legislature. Mr. Montagu (1879–1924), Secretary of State for India, at the close of the First World War, considered Jinnah "perfect mannered, impressive-looking, armed to the teeth with dialectics..." Jinnah, he felt, "is a very clever man, and it is, of course, an outrage that such a man should have no chance of running the affairs of his own country."

For about three decades since his entry into politics in 1906, Jinnah passionately believed in and assiduously worked for Hindu-Muslim unity. Gokhale, the foremost Hindu leader before Gandhi, had once said of him, "He has the true stuff in him and that freedom from all sectarian prejudice which will make him the best ambassador of Hindu-Muslim Unity: And, to be sure, he did become the architect of Hindu-Muslim Unity: he was responsible for the Congress-League Pact of 1916, known popularly as Lucknow Pact—the only pact ever signed between the two political organisations, the Congress and the All-India Muslim League, representing, as they did, the two major communities in the sub-continent.

The Congress-League scheme embodied in this pact was to become the basis for the Montagu-Chemlsford Reforms, also known as the Act of 1919. In retrospect, the Lucknow Pact represented a milestone in the evolution of Indian politics. For one thing, it conceded Muslims the right to separate electorate, reservation of seats in the legislatures and weightage in representation both at the Centre and the minority provinces. Thus, their retention was ensured in the next phase of reforms. For another, it represented a tacit recognition of the All-India Muslim League as the representative organisation of the Muslims, thus strengthening the trend towards Muslim individuality in Indian politics. And to Jinnah goes the credit for all this. Thus, by 1917, Jinnah came to be recognised among both Hindus and Muslims as one of India's most outstanding political leaders. Not only was he prominent in the Congress and the Imperial Legislative Council, he was also the President of the All-India Muslim and that of the Bombay Branch of the Home Rule League. More important, because of his key-role in the Congress-League entente at Lucknow, he was hailed as the ambassador, as well as the embodiment, of Hindu-Muslim unity.

Constitutional Struggle

In subsequent years, however, he felt dismayed at the injection of violence into politics. Since Jinnah stood for "ordered progress", moderation, gradualism and constitutionalism, he felt that political terrorism was not the pathway to national liberation but, the dark alley to disaster and destruction. Hence, the constitutionalist Jinnah could not possibly, countenance Mohandas Karamchand Gandhi's novel methods of Satyagrah (civil disobedience) and the triple boycott of government-aided schools and colleges, courts and councils and British textiles. Earlier, in October 1920, when Gandhi, having been elected President of the Home Rule League, sought to change its constitution as well as its nomenclature, Jinnah had resigned from the Home Rule League, saying: "Your extreme programme has for the moment struck the imagination mostly of the inexperienced youth and the ignorant and the illiterate. All this means disorganisation and choas". Jinnah did not believe that ends justified the means.

In the ever-growing frustration among the masses caused by colonial rule, there was ample cause for extremism. But, Gandhi's doctrine of non-cooperation, Jinnah felt, even as Rabindranath Tagore (1861–1941) did also feel, was at best one of negation and despair: it might lead to the building up of resentment, but nothing constructive. Hence, he opposed tooth and nail the tactics adopted by Gandhi to exploit the Khilafat and wrongful tactics in the Punjab in the early twenties. On the eve of its adoption of the Gandhian programme, Jinnah warned the Nagpur Congress Session (1920): "You are making a declaration (of Swaraj within a year) and committing the Indian National Congress to a programme, which you will not be able to carry out". He felt that there was no short-cut to independence and that Gandhi's extra-constitutional methods could only lead to political terrorism, lawlessness and chaos, without bringing India nearer to the threshold of freedom.

The future course of events was not only to confirm Jinnah's worst fears, but also to prove him right. Although Jinnah left the Congress soon thereafter, he continued his efforts towards bringing about a Hindu-Muslim entente, which he rightly considered "the most vital condition of Swaraj". However, because of the deep distrust between the two communities as evidenced by the country-wide communal riots, and because the Hindus failed to meet the genuine demands of the Muslims, his efforts came to naught. One such effort was the formulation of the Delhi Muslim Proposals in March, 1927. In order to bridge Hindu-Muslim differences on the constitutional plan, these proposals even waived the Muslim right to separate electorate, the most basic Muslim demand since 1906, which though recognised by the Congress in the Lucknow Pact, had again become a source of friction between the two communities, surprisingly though, the Nehru Report (1928), which represented the Congress-sponsored proposals for the future constitution of India, negated the minimum Muslim demands embodied in the Delhi Muslim Proposals.

In vain did Jinnah argue at the National convention (1928): 'What we want is that Hindus and Mussalmans should march together until our object is achieved... These two communities have got to be reconciled and united and made to feel that their interests are common". The Convention's blank refusal to accept Muslim demands represented the most devastating setback to Jinnah's life-long efforts to bring about Hindu-Muslim unity, it meant "the last straw" for the Muslims, and "the parting of the ways" for him, as he confessed to a Parsee friend at that time. Jinnah's disillusionment at the course of politics in the sub-continent prompted him to migrate and settle down in London in the early thirties. He was, however, to return to India in 1934, at the pleadings of his co-religionists, and assume their leadership. But, the Muslims presented a sad spectacle at that time. They were a mass of disgruntled and demoralised men and women, politically disorganised and destitute of a clear-cut political programme.

Muslim League Reorganised

Thus, the task that awaited Jinnah was anything but easy. The Muslim League was dormant: primary branches it had none; even its provincial organisations were, for the most part, ineffective and only nominally under the control of the central organisation. Nor did the central body have any coherent policy of its own till the Bombay session (1936), which Jinnah organised. To make matters worse, the provincial scene presented a sort of a jigsaw puzzle: in the Punjab, Bengal, Sindh, the North West Frontier, Assam, Bihar and the United Provinces, various Muslim leaders had set up their own provincial parties to serve their personal ends. Extremely frustrating as the situation was, the only consultation Jinnah had at this juncture was in Allama Iqbal (1877–1938), the poet-philosopher, who stood steadfast by him and helped to charter the course of Indian politics from behind the scene.

Undismayed by this bleak situation, Jinnah devoted himself with singleness of purpose to organising the Muslims on one platform. He embarked upon country-wide tours. He pleaded with provincial Muslim leaders to sink their differences and make common cause with the League. He exhorted the Muslim masses to organise themselves and join the League. He gave coherence and direction to Muslim sentiments on the Government of India

Act, 1935. He advocated that the Federal Scheme should be scrapped as it was subversive of India's cherished goal of complete responsible Government, while the provincial scheme, which conceded provincial autonomy for the first time, should be worked for what it was worth, despite its certain objectionable features. He also formulated a viable League manifesto for the election scheduled for early 1937. He was, it seemed, struggling against time to make Muslim India a power to be reckoned with.

Despite all the manifold odds stacked against it, the Muslim League won some 108 (about 23 per cent) seats out of a total of 485 Muslim seats in the various legislature. Though not very impressive in itself, the League's partial success assumed added significance in view of the fact that the League won the largest number of Muslim seats and that it was the only all-India party of the Muslims in the country. Thus, the elections represented the first milestone on the long road to putting Muslim India on the map of the sub-continent. Congress in Power With the year 1937 opened the most momentous decade in modern Indian history. In that year came into force the provincial part of the Government of India Act, 1935, granting autonomy to Indians for the first time, in the provinces.

The Congress, having become the dominant party in Indian politics, came to power in seven provinces exclusively, spurning the League's offer of cooperation, turning its back finally on the coalition idea and excluding Muslims as a political entity from the portals of power. In that year, also, the Muslim League, under Jinnah's dynamic leadership, was reorganised de novo, transformed into a mass organisation, and made the spokesman of Indian Muslims as never before. Above all, in that momentous year were initiated certain trends in Indian politics, the crystallisation of which in subsequent years made the partition of the sub-continent inevitable. The practical manifestation of the policy of the Congress which took office in July, 1937, in seven out of eleven provinces, convinced Muslims that, in the Congress scheme of things, they could live only on sufferance of Hindus and as "second class" citizens. The Congress provincial governments, it may be remembered, had embarked upon a policy and launched a programme in which Muslims felt that their religion, language and culture were not safe. This blatantly aggressive Congress policy was seized upon by Jinnah to awaken the Muslims to a new consciousness, organize them on all-India platform, and make them a power to be reckoned with. He also gave coherence, direction and articulation to their innermost, yet vague, urges and aspirations. Above all, he filled them with his indomitable will, his own unflinching faith in their destiny.

The New Awakening

As a result of Jinnah's ceaseless efforts, the Muslims awakened from what Professor Baker calls (their) "unreflective silence" (in which they had so complacently basked for long decades), and to "the spiritual essence of nationality" that had existed among them for a pretty long time. Roused by the impact of successive Congress hammerings, the Muslims, as Ambedkar (principal author of independent India's Constitution) says, "searched their social consciousness in a desperate attempt to find coherent and meaningful articulation to their cherished yearnings. To their great relief, they discovered that their sentiments of nationality had flamed into nationalism". In addition, not only had they developed" the will to live as a "nation", had also endowed them with a territory which they could occupy and make a State as well as a cultural home for the newly discovered nation. These two pre-requisites, as laid down by Renan, provided the Muslims with the intellectual justification for claiming a distinct nationalism (apart from Indian or Hindu nationalism) for themselves. So that when, after their long pause, the Muslims gave expression to their innermost yearnings, these turned out to be in favour of a separate Muslim nationhood and of a separate Muslim state.

"We are a nation", they claimed in the ever eloquent words of the Quaid-i-Azam—"We are a nation with our own distinctive culture and civilization, language and literature, art and architecture names and nomenclature, sense of values and proportion, legal laws and moral code, custom; and calendar, history and tradition, aptitudes and ambitions; in short, we have our own distinctive outlook on life and of life. By all canons of international law, we are a nation". The formulation of the Muslim demand for Pakistan in 1940 had a tremendous impact on the nature and course of Indian politics. On the one hand, it shattered for ever the Hindu dreams of a pseudo-Indian, in fact, Hindu empire on British exit from India: on the other, it heralded an era of Islamic renaissance and creativity in which the Indian Muslims were to be active participants. The Hindu reaction was quick, bitter, malicious.

Equally hostile were the British to the Muslim demand, their hostility having stemmed from their belief that the unity of India was their main achievement and their foremost contribution. The irony was that both the Hindus and the British had not anticipated the astonishingly tremendous response that the Pakistan demand had elicited from the Muslim masses. Above all, they failed to realize how a hundred million people had suddenly become supremely conscious of their distinct nationhood and their high destiny. In channelling the course of Muslim politics towards Pakistan, no less than in directing it towards its consummation in the establishment of Pakistan in 1947, none played a more decisive role than did Quaid-i-Azam Mohammad Ali Jinnah. It was his powerful advocacy of the case of Pakistan and his remarkable strategy in the delicate negotiations, that followed the formulation of the Pakistan demand, particularly in the post-war period, that made Pakistan inevitable.

Cripps Scheme

While the British reaction to the Pakistan demand came in the form of the Cripps offer of April, 1942, which conceded the principle of self-determination to provinces on a territorial basis, the Rajaji Formula (called after the eminent Congress leader C. Rajagopalachari, which became the basis of prolonged Jinnah-Gandhi talks in September, 1944), represented the Congress alternative to Pakistan. The Cripps offer was rejected because it did not concede the Muslim demand the whole way, while the Rajaji Formula was found unacceptable since it offered a "moth-eaten, mutilated" Pakistan and that too appended with a plethora of pre-conditions which made its emergence in any shape remote, if not altogether impossible. Cabinet Mission, the most delicate as well as the most tortuous negotiations, however, took place during 1946-47, after the elections which showed that the country was sharply and somewhat evenly divided between two parties—the Congress and the League—and that the central issue in Indian politics was Pakistan.

These negotiations began with the arrival, in March 1946, of a three-member British Cabinet Mission. The crucial task with which the Cabinet Mission was entrusted was that of devising in consultation with the various political parties, a constitution-making machinery, and of setting up a popular interim government. But, because the Congress-League gulf could not be bridged, despite the Mission's (and the Viceroy's) prolonged efforts, the Mission had to make its own proposals in May, 1946. Known as the Cabinet Mission Plan, these proposals stipulated a limited centre, supreme only in foreign affairs, defence and communications and three autonomous groups of provinces. Two of these groups were to have Muslim majorities in the north-west and the north-east of the subcontinent, while the third one, comprising the Indian mainland, was to have a Hindu majority. A consummate statesman that he was, Jinnah saw his chance. He interpreted the clauses relating to a limited centre and the grouping as "the foundation of Pakistan", and induced the Muslim League Council to accept the Plan in June 1946; and this he did much against the calculations of the Congress and to its utter dismay.

Tragically though, the League's acceptance was put down to its supposed weakness and the Congress put up a posture of defiance, designed to swamp the League into submitting to its dictates and its interpretations of the plan. Faced thus, what alternative had Jinnah and the League but to rescind their earlier acceptance, reiterate and reaffirm their original stance, and decide to launch direct action (if need be) to wrest Pakistan. The way Jinnah manoeuvred to turn the tide of events at a time when all seemed lost indicated, above all, his masterly grasp of the situation and his adeptness at making strategic and tactical moves. Partition Plan By the close of 1946, the communal riots had flared up to murderous heights, engulfing almost the entire subcontinent. The two peoples, it seemed, were engaged in a fight to the finish. The time for a peaceful transfer of power was fast running out. Realising the gravity of the situation, His Majesty's Government sent down to India a new Viceroy—Lord Mountbatten. His protracted negotiations with the various political leaders resulted in 3 June (1947) Plan by which the British decided to partition the subcontinent, and hand over power to two successor States on 15 August, 1947. The plan was duly accepted by the three Indian parties to the dispute—the Congress the League and the Akali Dal (representing the Sikhs).

Leader of a Free Nation

In recognition of his singular contribution, Quaid-i-Azam Mohammad Ali Jinnah was nominated by the Muslim League as the Governor-General of Pakistan, while the Congress appointed Mountbatten as India's first Governor-General. Pakistan, it has been truly said, was born in virtual chaos. Indeed, few nations in the world have started on their career with less resources and in more treacherous circumstances. The new nation did not inherit a central government, a capital, an administrative core, or an organized defence force. Its social and administrative resources were poor; there was little equipment and still less statistics. The Punjab holocaust had left vast areas in a shambles with communications disrupted. This, along with the en masse migration of the Hindu and Sikh business and managerial classes, left the economy almost shattered.

The treasury was empty, India having denied Pakistan the major share of its cash balances. On top of all this, the still unorganized nation was called upon to feed some eight million refugees who had fled the insecurities and barbarities of the north Indian plains that long, hot summer. If all this was symptomatic of Pakistan's administrative and economic weakness, the Indian annexation, through military action in November 1947, of Junagadh (which had originally acceded to Pakistan) and the Kashmir war over the State's accession (October 1947–December 1948) exposed her military weakness. In the circumstances, therefore, it was nothing short of a miracle that Pakistan survived at all. That it survived and forged ahead was mainly due to one man—Mohammad Ali Jinnah. The nation desperately needed in the person of a charismatic leader at that critical juncture in the nation's history, and he fulfilled that need profoundly. After all, he was more than a mere Governor-General: he was the Quaid-i-Azam who had brought the State into being.

In the ultimate analysis, his very presence at the helm of affairs was responsible for enabling the newly born nation to overcome the terrible crisis on the morrow of its cataclysmic birth. He mustered up the immense prestige and the unquestioning loyalty he commanded among the people to energize them, to raise their morale, land directed the profound feelings of patriotism that the freedom had generated, along constructive channels. Though tired and in poor health, Jinnah yet carried the heaviest part of the burden in that first crucial year. He laid down the policies of the new state, called attention to the immediate problems confronting the nation and told the members of the Constituent Assembly, the civil servants and the Armed Forces what to do and what the nation expected of them. He saw to it that law and order was maintained at all costs, despite the provocation that the large-scale riots in north India had provided. He moved from Karachi to Lahore for a while and supervised the immediate refugee problem in the Punjab. In a time of fierce excitement, he remained sober, cool and steady. He advised his excited audience in Lahore to concentrate on helping the refugees to avoid retaliation, exercise restraint and protect the minorities. He assured the minorities of a fair deal, assuaged their inured sentiments, and gave them hope and comfort. He toured the various provinces, attended to their particular problems and instilled in the people a sense of belonging. He reversed the British policy in the North-West Frontier and ordered the withdrawal of the troops from the tribal territory of Waziristan, thereby making the Pathans feel themselves an integral part of Pakistan's body-politics. He created a new Ministry of States and Frontier Regions, and assumed responsibility for ushering in a new era in Balochistan. He settled the controversial question of the states of Karachi, secured the accession of States, especially of Kalat which seemed problematical and carried on negotiations with Lord Mountbatten for the settlement of the Kashmir Issue.

The Quaid's last Message

It was, therefore, with a sense of supreme satisfaction at the fulfilment of his mission that Jinnah told the nation in his last message on 14 August, 1948: "The foundations of your State have been laid and it is now for you to build and build as quickly and as well as you can". In accomplishing the task he had taken upon himself on the morrow of Pakistan's birth, Jinnah had worked himself to death, but he had, to quote Richard Symons, "contributed more than any other man to Pakistan's survival". He died on 11 September, 1948. How true was Lord Pethick Lawrence, the former Secretary of State for India, when he said, "Gandhi died by the hands of an assassin; Jinnah died by his devotion to

Pakistan".

A man such as Jinnah, who had fought for the inherent rights of his people all through his life and who had taken up the somewhat unconventional and the largely misinterpreted cause of Pakistan, was bound to generate violent opposition and excite implacable hostility and was likely to be largely misunderstood. But what is most remarkable about Jinnah is that he was the recipient of some of the greatest tributes paid to any one in modern times, some of them even from those who held a diametrically opposed viewpoint.

The Aga Khan considered him "the greatest man he ever met", Beverley Nichols, the author of 'Verdict on India', called him "the most important man in Asia", and Dr. Kailashnath Katju, the West Bengal Governor in 1948, thought of him as "an outstanding figure of this century not only in India, but in the whole world". While Abdul Rahman Azzam Pasha, Secretary General of the Arab League, called him "one of the greatest leaders in the Muslim world", the Grand Mufti of Palestine considered his death as a "great loss" to the entire world of Islam. It was, however, given to Surat Chandra Bose, leader of the Forward Bloc wing of the Indian National Congress, to sum up succinctly his personal and political achievements. "Mr. Jinnah", he said on his death in 1948, "was great as a lawyer, once great as a Congressman, great as a leader of Muslims, great as a world politician and diplomat, and greatest of all as a man of action, By Mr. Jinnah's passing away, the world has lost one of the greatest statesmen and Pakistan its life-giver, philosopher and guide". Such was Quaid-i-Azam Mohammad Ali Jinnah, the man and his mission, such the range of his accomplishments and achievements.

NAWABZADA LIAQUAT ALI KHAN

Nawabzada Liaquat Ali Khan, the second son of Nawab Rustam Ali Khan, was born on October 1896 in a Madal Pathan (Nausherwan) family. After his graduation in 1918 from M.A.O. College, Aligarh, Liaquat Ali Khan was offered by the British Government to join the Indian Civil Services but he rejected the offer on the plea that he wanted to serve his nation. He was married to his cousin, Jehangir Begum in 1918. After his marriage, he went to London for higher education. In 1921, he obtained a degree in Law from Oxford and was called to Bar at Inner Temple in 1922. On his return from England in 1923 Liaquat decided to enter politics with the aim to liberate his homeland from foreign yoke. From the very beginning, he was determined to get rid of injustices and ill treatment meted out to the Indians by the British. In his early life, Liaquat Ali, like most of the Muslim leaders of his time, believed in Indian Nationalism but gradually his views changed. He was approached by the Congress leaders to join their party, but he refused and joined Muslim League in 1923. When Quaid-i-Azam, with the help of some other Muslim leaders, decided to put a new life in the Muslim League and held its annual session in May, 1924 at Lahore, Liaquat, like many other young Muslims, attended the session. Liaquat Ali started his parliamentary career from the U.P. Legislative Assembly in 1926 as an independent candidate. Later he formed his own party, the Democratic Party, in the Legislative Assembly and was elected its leader. He remained the member of the U.P. Legislative Council till 1940 when he was elected to the Central Legislative Assembly. In his parliamentary career, Liaquat Ali Khan established his reputation as an eloquent, un-purchasable, principled and honest spokesman who never compromised his principles even in front of severe odds. He always used his influence and good offices for the liquidation of communal tension and bitterness. He took active part in the legislative business. He was one of the members of the Muslim League delegation, which attended the National Convention held at Calcutta to discuss the Nehru Report, in December 1928. Liaquat Ali's second marriage with Begum Raana took place in 1933. Begum Raana was a distinguished economist and an educationalist who stood through the thick and thin of Liaquat Ali's political life career. She proved to be a valuable asset to his political career as well as his private life. Quaid-i-Azam in those days was in England in self-exile. The Newly wed couple had a number of meetings with the Quaid and convinced him to come back to India to take the leadership of the Muslims of the region. When Quaid-i-Azam, on his return to India, started reorganizing Muslim League, Liaquat was elected as the Honorary Secretary of the party on April 26, 1936. He held the office till the establishment of Pakistan in 1947. In 1940, he was made the deputy leader of the Muslim League Parliamentary party. Quaid-i-Azam was not able to take active part in the proceedings of the Assembly on account of his heavy political work thus the whole burden of protecting Muslim interests in the Assembly fell on Liaquat's shoulders. Liaquat was also the member of Muslim Masses Civil Defense Committee, which was formed to keep the Muslims away from the Congress activities and to strengthen the League's mission.

Liaquat won the Central Legislature election in 1945-46 from the Meerut Constituency in U.P. He was also elected Chairman of League's Central Parliamentary Board. He assisted Quaid-i-Azam in his negotiations with the members of the Cabinet Mission and the leaders of the Congress during the final phase of freedom movement. When the Government asked Muslim League to send their nominees for representation in the Interim Government, Liaquat was asked to lead the League group in the cabinet. He was given the portfolio of Finance, which he handled brilliantly. He influenced the working of all the departments of the Government and presented a poor man's budget. His policies as Finance Minister helped in convincing the Congress to accept the Muslim demand of a separate homeland.

After independence, Quaid-i-Azam and Muslim League had no better option than Liaquat to be appointed as the head of Pakistani government. Being the first Prime Minister of the country, Liaquat had to deal with a number of difficulties facing Pakistan in its early days. Liaquat All Khan helped Quaid-i-Azam in solving the riots and refugee problem and setting up an effective administrative system for the country. After the death of Quaid-i-Azam, Liaquat tried to fill in the vacuum created by the departure of the Father of the Nation. Under his Premiership Pakistan took its first steps in the field of constitution making as well as foreign policy. Objective Resolution, presented by him in the Legislative Assembly, was passed by the house on March 12, 1947. Under his leadership a team also drafted the first report of the Basic Principle Committee. His efforts in signing Liaquat-Nehru pact on minorities in 1950 reduced tension between India and Pakistan. In May 1951, he visited USA and set the course of Pakistan's foreign policy towards closer ties with the West.

On October 16, 1951, when Liaquat was expected to make some important announcement in a public meeting at Municipal Park, Rawalpindi, he was assassinated by Saad Akbar. The murderer was immediately shot dead by the security people and thus the clue to the real culprit was removed forever. Liaquat Ali Khan was officially given the title of Shaheed-i-Millat but the question of who was behind his murder, is yet to be answered.

KHAWAJA NAZIMUDDIN [1894—964]

Khawaja Nazimuddin was born in July 1894. He was educated at Muhammadan Anglo Oriental College, Aligarh and Cambridge University. He was elected Chairman Dacca Municipality 1922—29 and in 1937 he was appointed as Home Minister. He remained the leader of Muslim League parliamentary party in Bengal legislative assembly from 1942 to 1943. He headed Muslim League Ministry from 1943 to 1945. He also remained member of All India Muslim League working committee from 1937—1947.

Khawaja Nazimuddin was Chief Minister of Bengal in 1947. He then succeeded Jinnah as Governor General in September 1948. After Liaquat All Khan's assassination, he was appointed Prime Minister of Pakistan—a post he held from 1951 to 1953.

Khawaja Nazimuddin died in 1964.

MUHAMMAD ALI BOGRA

Muhammad Ali was born in Bogra in an aristocratic Nawab family. Officially he was carrying the family name Bogra. He studied at the Calcutta University and in 1937 he was elected to the Bengal legislative assembly.

In 1943, Muhammad Ali became parliamentary secretary to Khawaja Nazimuddin, the then Chief Minister of Bengal. Later in 1946, he became Finance and Health Minister of the province.

After the formation of Pakistan, he was appointed Ambassador to Burma in 1948, High Commissioner to Canada in 1949 and finally Ambassador to USA in 1952.

Khawaja Nazimuddin, the then Prime Minister of Pakistan was dismissed by the Governor General, Malik Ghulam Muhammad in April 1953, and Muhammad Ali Bogra was appointed Prime Minister on April 17, 1953 by the Governor General.

Muhammad Ali Bogra was very renowned diplomat but almost unknown as a politician. His appointment as Prime Minister came as a surprise to political observers and public alike, and it was widely suspected that his transfer from Washington to Karachi, elevation to the office was a prelude to closer relations between the US and Pakistan.

Only three days after the new premier's nomination, the US President Eisenhower asked Congress for authority to ship hundreds and thousands of tons of wheat to Pakistan. The US was at that time conducting a vigorous anti-Communist policy and looking for friends in Asia. Pakistan entered into defense pacts with it.

After the dissolution of the Constituent Assembly in 1954 by the Governor-general, Muhammad Ali was again invited to form a new cabinet call "ministry of all talents."

Muhammad Ali Bogra was replaced by Chaudhary Muhammad Ali in August 1955 after the second Constituent Assembly was elected. Muhammad Ali again resumed his assignment as ambassador to the USA. He died in the year 1969 and has been buried in the family grave of Bogra Nawab Palace.

CHAUDHARY MUHAMMAD ALI

Chaudhary Muhammad Ali was born on July 15, 1905 at Jullundur. He took his M.Sc. degree in 1927 from the University of Punjab. Ch. Muhammad Ali joined Indian Audit and Accounts Service in 1928 and was deputed as Accountant General to Bahawalpur state in 1932. In 1936, he joined Government of India as private secretary to Finance Minister, Sir Grigg. In 1945 he was appointed financial advisor for war and supply, a post never before held by an Indian.

During the drafting of the partition plan, Ch. Muhammad Ali was one of the two secretaries to the partition council, presided over by Lord Mountbatten.

On the establishment of Pakistan he became secretary general of the new government and played a key role in it's organization. In 1951, he became Finance Minister and in 1955 Prime Minister of the country. Under his leadership the Constituent Assembly adopted the constitution of the Islamic Republic of Pakistan.

HUSAIN SHAHEED SUHRAWARDY [1892—1963]

Husain Shaheed Suhrawardy was born on September 8, 1892 into an illustrious Muslim family from Midnapore in West Bengal, India. Suhrawardy's mother was the first Muslim woman to pass the senior Cambridge examination. He graduated with honors in Science from St. Xaviares College. In 1913, he obtained masters degree in Arabic from Calcutta University. Suhrawardy received BCL degree from Oxford University and was called to the Bar from Grey's Inn in 1918.

In 1920, Suhrawardy married Begum Niaz Fatima.

In 1921, he was elected to the Bengal Legislative Assembly. For a brief period, he served as secretary, Calcutta Khilafat Committee. In 1923 he was appointed deputy leader of Swaraj Party. Next year he was elected deputy mayor of Calcutta. In 1936 he became the General Secretary of the Bengal provincial Muslim League. After the 1937 elections, Suhrawardy was appointed Minister for Labour and Commerce. After serving briefly in the Fazlul Haq's ministry, he joined Khawaja Nazimuddin's ministry in 1943 as Civil Supplies Minister.

After the 1946 elections, Suhrawardy formed government in Bengal, the only Muslim League government in the sub-continent. In 1949, he formed East Pakistan Awami Muslim League, and in 1953 he renamed it as 'Awami League'.

Suhrawardy along with A. K. Fazlul Haq and Maulana Bhashani established United Front in 1953 in Dhaka, which won the 1954 general elections. The same year he joined Muhammad All Bogra's ministry as Law Minister. However, with the change of government in 1955, Suhrawardy took charge of the leadership of opposition.

H. S. Suhrawardy became the fifth Prime Minister of Pakistan on September 12, 1956. During his tenure, he tried to remove economic disparity between the two wings. Suhrawardy resigned from premiership in October 1957, due to President's refusal to convene a meeting of parliament to seek a vote of confidence.

Ailing from heart disease for a long time, Suhrawardy succumbed to death on December 5, 1963.

IBRAHIM ISMAIL CHUNDRIGAR

Ibrahim Ismail Chundrigar was horn in 1897 at Ahmedabad He passed his B.A. and L.L.B examinations from Bombay University and then started practising law in 1920. In 1937 elections, he was elected as a member of the Bombay Legislative Council on All India Muslim League's ticket. A year later, he was elected as the deputy leader of the party in the legislative assembly. He remained the president of Bombay Muslim League from 1940 to 1945. When Quaid-i-Azam was asked to nominate the members of Muslim League for the interim government in 1946, the Quaid selected I.I. Chundrigar as one of his nominees.

After the independence of Pakistan, Chundrigar was appointed as the Minister for Trade and Commerce in the first cabinet of the newly established county. Next he served as the Ambassador of Pakistan at Kabul. After that, he was appointed as the Governor of North-West Frontier Province and also served as Governor of the Punjab from November 1951 to May 1953. In August 1955 he assumed the charge as the Law Minister in the Federal Cabinet and served in the same capacity till August 1957. After the resignation of Suhrawardy, Iskander Mizra asked I.I. Chundrigar to establish his ministry in the center. Himself, a leader of Muslim League, Chundrigar formed his government on October 18, 1957 with the help of the Republican Party, Krishak Sramik Party and Nizam-i-Islam Party. His tenure as Prime Minister of Pakistan proved to be the shortest one, as he failed to maintain the support of his coalition partners at a time when the President of the country was involved in palace intrigues. He was forced to resign on December 11, 1957 and thus could only remained Prime Minister of Pakistan for less than two months. During his short tenure, he raised his voice in favour of Separate Electorates.

I.I. Chundrigar was more of a lawyer than a politician. He gained a lot of popularity as a constitutional lawyer, when he pleaded the case of Maulvi Tameezuddin for the restoration of the first Constituent Assembly of Pakistan. He died on September 26, 1960.

FEROZ KHAN NOON

Malik Feroz Khan Noon belonged to one of the most influential landlord families of the Punjab. He was born in 1893. After receiving his early education from Athison College, Lahore he went to London from where he did his Masters in 1916. During his stay at London he also passed the exam of Bar at Law. On his return, Noon practised law at Lahore High Court from 1917–1926. Then he joined politics and was appointed as Minister of Health and Education in the Punjab cabinet. He served as High Commissioner for India in London from 1936–1941. He was appointed as the member of the Viceroy's Executive Council in 1941 and retained the position till 1945. Simultaneously, he held the position of the Defence Minister of India from 1942–1945. He was the first Indian to be raised to that prestigious position during the British rule.

In October 1947, Quaid-i-Azam Muhammad Ali Jinnah, with the desire to bring unity among the Muslim Ummah, sent Feroz Khan Noon as his special envoy to some countries of the Muslim World. This one-man delegation was the first official mission sent abroad by the Government of Pakistan. The aim of the mission was to introduce Pakistan, to explain the reasons of its creation, to familiarize the Muslim countries with its internal problems and to get the moral and material support from the brethren countries. Noon performed the role assigned to him in a successful manner. Keeping his political and administrative experience in consideration, Feroz Khan Noon was appointed as the Governor of East Pakistan. However, he himself was more interested in the politics of the Punjab. Along with Nawab of Mamdot and Mumtaz Daultana, he remained one of the main contenders for the Chief Ministership of the Punjab during late 1940s and early 1950s. He finally succeeded in achieving his aim in 1953 and remained Chief Minister of the province till 1955. In 1956, he assumed charge as Foreign Minister of Pakistan in Suhrawardy's Cabinet.

Being a close friend of Iskander Mirza, Feroz Khan Noon was the key pin in organizing the Republican Party in Punjab. He remained the President of the party and it was also on the platform of this party that Noon was elected as the Prime Minister of Pakistan, on December 16, 1957. Though President Iskander

Mirza's support played an important role in the establishment of Noon's Ministry, but later on Mirza considered Noon as an obstacle in his way of obtaining absolute power. When Martial Law was enforced in the country on October 7, 1958, Noon's tenure as Prime Minister automatically came to an end.

Apart from politics, Feroz Khan Noon also proved his capabilities in the field of academics. He wrote a total of five books, including his autobiography, 'From Memory'. His wife, Vigar-un-Nisa Noon, though not originally from Pakistan, spent her entire life working for the betterment of people of Pakistan, proving herself to be a great social worker.

AGHA MOHAMMAD YAHYA KHAN

Born , Feb. 4, 1917, near Peshawar, India, died Aug. 10. 1980, Rawalpindi, Pakistan.

President of Pakistan (1969–71), a professional soldier who became commander in chief of the Pakistani armed forces in 1966.

Yahya was born to a family that was descended from the elite soldier class of Nadir Shah, the Persian ruler who conquered Delhi in the 18th century. He was educated at Punjab University and later graduated first in his class.

GHULAM MUHAMMAD

The third Governor General of Pakistan, Ghulam Muhammad was born at Lahore in 1887. He graduated from Aligarh University and joined the Imperial Service. Initially he served in the railway board, during the war he served in the capacity of controller of general supplies and purchase.

During the First Round Table Conference, Ghulam Muhammad represented the Nawab of Bhopal. He also served as advisor finance in the state of Hyderabad Deccan. After independence he joined Central Cabinet as Finance Minister.

After the assassination of Liaquat All Khan, Ghulam Muhammad became Governor-General by replacing Khawaja Nazimuddin.

In April 1953, he dismissed Khawaja Nazimuddin's cabinet and latter dismissed the Constituent Assembly in October, 1954 by declaring emergency.

ZULFIKAR ALI BHUTTO

Zulfikar Ali Bhutto was born on January 5, 1928. He was the only son of Sir Shah Nawaz Bhutto.

Zulfikar Ali Bhutto completed his early education from Bombay's Cathedral High School. In 1947, he joined University of Southern California (USC), and later joined University of California at Berkeley in June 1949. After completing his degree with honors in political science at Berkeley in June 1950, he was admitted to Oxford.

Zulfikar Ali Bhutto married Nusrat Isphahani on September 8, 1951. He was called to bar at Lincoln's Inn in 1953 and in the same year his first child, Benazir Bhutto was born on June 21. On his return to Pakistan, Bhutto started practising law at Dingomal's.

In 1954, when one unit scheme envisaging combining of the four provinces of Punjab, Sind, NWFP and Baluchistan into one unit to be called 'West Pakistan' was enforced, Bhutto opposed the scheme vehemently. In 1958, Zulfikar Ali Bhutto joined President Mirza's cabinet as Commerce Minister. After Ayub Khan took over, Bhutto joined the cabinet as the youngest member. In 1963, he took over as Foreign Minister from Muhammad Ali Bogra.

His first major achievement was to conclude Sino-Pakistan boundary agreement on March 2, 1963. In mid-1964, Bhutto helped convince Ayub of the wisdom of establishing closer economic and diplomatic links with Turkey and Iran. The trio formed RCD later on. In June 1966, Bhutto left Ayub's cabinet over differences concerning Tashkent agreement.

Zulfikar Ali Bhutto launched Pakistan People's Party (PPP) after leaving the cabinet of Ayub Khan. In the general elections held in December 1970, PPP won a large majority in West Pakistan but, failed to reach an agreement with Sheikh Mujib-ur-Rehman, the majority winner from East Pakistan. Following the 1971 war and the separation of East Pakistan, Yahya Khan resigned and Bhutto took over as President and Chief Martial Law Administrator on December 20, 1971.

In early 1972, Bhutto nationalized ten categories of major industries, and withdrew Pakistan from Commonwealth of Nations and SEATO when Britain and other western countries recognized the new state of Bangladesh. On March 1, he introduced land reforms, and on July 2, 1972, signed Simla Agreement with India which paved way for the return of occupied lands and Pakistani POWs captured in East Pakistan in the 1971 war.

After the National Assembly passed the 1973 constitution, Bhutto was sworn-in as the Prime Minister of the country.

On December 30, 1973, Bhutto laid the foundation of Pakistan's first steel mill at Pipri, near Karachi. On January 1, 1974, Bhutto nationalized all banks. On February 22, 1974, the Second Islamic Summit was inaugurated in Lahore. Heads of States of most of the thirty eight Islamic countries attended.

Following a political crisis in the country, Bhutto was imprisoned by General Zia-ul-Haq who imposed Martial Law on July 5, 1977.

On April 4, 1979, the former Prime Minister was hanged, after the Supreme Court upheld the death sentence passed by the Lahore High Court. The High Court had given him death sentence in the case of murder of the father of a dissident PPP politician.

Zulfikar Ali Bhutto was buried in his ancestral village, at Garhi Khuda Baksh next to his father's grave.

GENERAL MUHAMMAD ZIA-UL-HAQ [1924—88]

Muhammad Zia-ul-Haq was the General who enforced Marshal Law for the third time in the brief history of Pakistan. Second child and the eldest son of Muhammad Akram, a teacher in the Army, Zia-ul-Haq was born on August 12, 1924 at Jalandhar. After receiving his early education from Government High School Simla, he did his B.A Honors from St. Stephen College, Delhi. He was commissioned in the British Army in 1943 and served in Burma, Malaya and Indonesia during the Second World War. When the war was over, he decided to join armoured core. At the time of Independence, like most of the Muslim officers in the British Army, Zia-ul-Haq opted to join Pakistan Army. As a Major he got an opportunity to do a training course in the Commander and Staff College of United States of America in 1963-64. During the war of 1965, he acted as the Assistant Quarter Master of 101

Infantry Division, which was posted at Kiran sector. He remained posted at Jordon from 1967-70, where he trained military men of the country. He was appointed as Core Commander of Multan in 1975.

On April, 1 1976, in a surprise move, the then Prime Minister of Pakistan, Zulfikar Ali Bhutto, appointed Zia-ul-Haq as the Chief of the Army Staff. It is interesting to note that five senior Generals were superseded. Bhutto probably wanted somebody as the head of the armed forces, who would not prove to be a threat for him and the best available option was the simple General, who apparently was interested only in offering prayers and playing golf. However, history proved Bhutto wrong, and Zia-ul-Haq proved to be much smarter than he looked. When the political unsuitability reached its climax due to the deadlock between Bhutto and the leadership of Pakistan National Alliance (PNA) on the issue of general elections, Zia-ul-Haq took advantage of the situation. On July 5, 1977, he carried out a bloodless coup overthrowing Bhutto's government and enforced Martial Law in the country.

After assuming power as Chief Martial Law Administrator, Zia-ul-Haq promised to hold National and Provincial Assembly elections in the next 90 days and to hand over power to the representatives of the nation. However, in October 1977 he announced the postponement of the electoral plan and decided to start an accountability process of the politicians. In a statement he said that he changed his decision due to the strong public demand for the scrutiny of political leaders who had indulged in malpractice in the past. The Disqualification Tribunal was formulated and many former Members of Parliament were disqualified from participating in politics at any level for the next seven years. A white paper was also issued which criticized the activities of PPP's government under Zulfiqar Ali Bhutto.

With the retirement of Fazl Ellahi, Zia-ul-Haq also assumed the office of President of Pakistan on September 16, 1978. In the absence of a parliament, Zia-ul-Haq decided to set up an alternative system. He introduced Majlis-i-Shura in 1980. Most of the members of the Shura were intellectuals; scholars, ulema, journalists, economists and professionals belonging to different fields of life. The Shura was to act as a board of advisors for the President. The idea of establishing this institution was not bad but the main problem was that all 284 members of the Shura were to be nominated by the President and thus there was no room available for the difference of opinion.

In the mid-1980s, Zia-ul-Haq decided to fulfil his promise of holding elections in the country. But before handing over the power to the public representatives, he decided to secure his position. Referendum was held in the county in December 1985 and the masses were given the option to elect or reject the General as the future president of Pakistan. According to the official result, more than 95% of the vote cast, were in favour of Zia-ul-Haq and he was elected as President for the next five years. Here one should not ignore the fact that the question asked in the referendum was phrased in a way that Zia-ul-Haq's win was related to the process of Islamization in the country.

After being elected as President, Zia-ul-Haq decided to hold elections in the country in March 1985 on non-party basis. Most of the political parties decided to boycott the elections but election results showed that many victors belonged to one party or the other. To make things easier for him, the General nominated the Prime Minister from amongst the members of the Assembly. To many, his nomination of Muhammad Khan Junejo as the Prime Minister was because he wanted a simple person at the post, who could act as a puppet in his hands. Before handing over the power to the new government he made certain amendments in the constitution and got them endorsed from the parliament before lifting the sate of emergency in the county. Due to this eighth amendment in the constitution, the powers of President were increased and the President possessed complete power to take any step, which he deems fit, on the plea of safeguarding national integrity.

As the time passed, the parliamentarians wanted to have more freedom and power. By the beginning of 1988, rumours about the differences between the Prime Minister and Zia-ul- Haq were in the air. The general feeling was that the President, who had enjoyed absolute power for eight long years, was not ready to share it with anybody else. On May 29, 1988, Zia-ul-Haq finally dissolved the National Assembly and removed the Prime Minister under article 58 (2) B of the amended constitution. Apart from many other reasons, Junejo's decision to sign the Geneva Accord against the wishes of Zia-ul-Haq proved to be one of the major factors responsible for him going back home. After 11 years, Zia-ul-Haq once again made the same promise with the nation to hold fresh elections within next 90 days. With Benazir Bhutto back in the country and Muslim League leadership annoyed with the President over the decision of May 29, Zia-ul-Haq was trapped in the most difficult situation of his political life. The only option left for him was to repeat history and to postpone the elections once again.

However, before taking any decision, Zia-ul-Haq died in an air crash near Bahawalpur on August 17, 1988. The accident proved to be very costly for the country as almost the entire military elite of Pakistan was on the board. Though United States' Ambassador to Pakistan was also killed in the misfortune, yet many do not rule-out US involvement in the sabotage. They believe that United States could not afford Pakistan to oppose Geneva Accord and thus they removed the biggest hurdle in their way. The remains of Zia-ul-Haq were buried in the premises of Faisal Mosque, Islamabad. The tragic death brought a large number of mourners to attend his funeral, which proved to be one of the biggest in the history of the country.

During his rule, Zia-ul-Haq tried his utmost to maintain close ties with the Muslim World. He made vigorous efforts along with other Muslim States to bring an end to the war between Iran and Iraq. Pakistan joined the Non-Aligned Movement in 1979 during Zia-ul-Haq's term. It was also he who fought a war by proxy in Afghanistan and saved Pakistan from a direct war with Soviet Union.

MUHAMMAD KHAN JUNEJO [1932—92]

Muhammad Khan Junejo was born on August 18, 1932 at Sindhri, Sind. After completing his senior Cambridge, he went to U.K. for a diploma in Agriculture.

Junejo started his political career at the age of twenty one. In 1962, he was elected Member Provincial Assembly, West Pakistan from Sanghar. He was appointed Minister in the West

Pakistan cabinet in July 1963 and held the portfolios of Health, Basic Democracies and Local Government, Works, Communications and Railways.

After partyless polls were held for the national and provincial assemblies in 1985, Muhammad Khan Junejo was appointed Prime Minister by General Zia. He was however, dismissed on May 29, 1988 by the President using discretionary power given under the eighth amendment.

Muhammad Khan Junejo was elected member of the National Assembly in 1990, and died of illness in 1992.

GHULAM MUSTAFA JATOI [1931]

Ghulam Mustafa Jatoi was born on August 14, 1931, at New Jatoi, Sind. Eldest of the four brothers, Ghulam Mustafa's father. Khan Bahadur Ghulam Rasul Khan Jatoi was member of the Sind legislative assembly.

Ghulam Mustafa was educated at Karachi Grammar School and passed his senior Cambridge. In 1952, he went to England for his bar at law, but had to return home within one year due to his father's serious illness.

He was elected to the first Provincial Assembly of West Pakistan in 1958, and was re-elected in 1965.

Jatoi joined Pakistan People's Party in March 1969. In 1970, he was elected to the National Assembly on PPP ticket. In 1973, he was elected Chief Minister of the Sind, and held this office till 1977. He was re-elected in March 1977. After the imposition of Martial Law, Jatoi remained associated with the Movement for Restoration of Democracy (MRD). Twice he was arrested in 1983 and 1985. Later, he founded the National People's Party.

In 1989, he was elected to the National Assembly in the by-elections from Kot Addu. After joining Islami Jamhoori Ittehad (IJI), Jatoi was elected leader of the combined opposition parties in the National Assembly in 1989.

Ghulam Mustafa Jatoi was appointed caretaker Prime Minister in 1990, by President Ghulam Ishaq Khan. He relinquished his office after Nawaz Shareef was elected as Prime Minister in the October 1990 elections.

He was again elected a Member of the National Assembly as a result of October 1993 elections, but lost his seat in the elections held in February 1997.

His two sons, Tariq Jatoi and Ghulam Murtaza Jatoi are also in politics.

MIAN MUHAMMAD NAWAZ SHARIF
[BORN 1949]

Muhammad Nawaz Sharif was born in Lahore, on December 25, 1949. He is the eldest son of Muhammad Sharif, a joint owner of Ittefaq Group of Industries.

Nawaz Sharif did his schooling from St. Anthony's High School. After graduating from Government College Lahore, he obtained his law degree from the Punjab University.

Nawaz Sharif remained member of the Punjab Provincial Council for some time. He joined the Punjab cabinet as Finance Minister in 1981. He was able to raise the allocation of funds in the development of rural areas to seventy per cent, out of the annual development program in the province. He also held the portfolio of Sports and was able to reorganize the sports activities in the province.

In the general elections of 1985, Nawaz Sharif won with overwhelming majorities, both in the National, and Provincial Assemblies. On April 9, 1985, he was sworn in as Chief Minister of Punjab. On May 31, 1988, he was appointed caretaker Chief Minister, after the dismissal of assemblies by General Zia. Nawaz Sharif was again elected as Chief Minister after the 1988 general elections. A massive uplift of Murree and Kahuta was done during his term as Chief Minister, Punjab.

On November 6, 1990, Nawaz Sharif was sworn in as the Prime Minister of the country, after his alliance, IJI won the October 24, 1990 elections. However, Nawaz Sharif could not complete his term of five years, and was dismissed by the President in April 1993. He was reinstated by the superior judiciary, but had to resign along with the President in July 1993.

During his tenure as the Prime Minister, efforts were made to strengthen the industrial sector with the help of private sector.

Projects like Ghazi Brodha, Gawadar Mini port, were initiated. Land was distributed among landless peasants in Sindh. Relations with the Central Asian Muslim republics were strengthened and ECO was given a boast. To end the Afghan crisis, "Islamabad Accord" was reached between various Afghan factions. His most important contribution was economic progress despite American sanctions on Pakistan through Pressler Amendment.

Pakistan Muslim League again won the elections held in February 1997, and Mian Nawaz Sharif was re-elected as Prime Minister with an overwhelming majority.

Taking advantage of his absolute majority in the National Assembly, he added a landmark in the constitutional history of Pakistan by repealing the controversial 8th Amendment. This 13th Constitutional Amendment stripped the President of his powers, under Article 52(b) of the 8th Amendment, to dismiss the Prime Minister and dissolve the National Assembly. He added another milestone to the constitution when his Parliament adopted the anti-defection 14th Amendment Bill. His development venture of the Lahore-Islamabad motorway has also been appreciated by a segment of society

MALIK MERAJ KHALID [BORN 1916]

Malik Meraj Khalid was born in 1916, in a small village near Lahore. He studied law and began practice in 1948. He was elected to the Provincial Assembly in 1965. He joined the Pakistan People's Party soon after its inception in 1968 and was appointed President of Lahore PPP. He was re-elected to the National Assembly in 1970.

Zulfikar Ali Bhutto included Meraj Khalid in his cabinet as Minister for Food and Agriculture and Under developed Areas in December 1971. In November 1972 he was appointed Chief of the Party's Parliamentary Affairs and in 1975 he was given the portfolios of Social Welfare, Local Government and Rural Development. Later he was elected speaker of the National Assembly.

After the execution of Zulfikar Ali Bhutto in April 1979, he was nominated member of the PPP central committee. But he resigned from the party's central committee in January 1988. He was again appointed the Speaker of National Assembly in 1988. He lost elections in 1993 and remained aloof from politics for sometime and served as the rector of International Islamic University.

He was nominated as head of the interim government in November 1996 and remained in power till February 1997.

BENAZIR BHUTTO (BORN 1953)

Benazir Bhutto, the eldest child of Zulfikar Ali Bhutto was born on June 21, 1953 in Karachi. She attended Lady Jennings Nursery School and then Convent of Jesus and Mary in Karachi. After two years of schooling at the Pindi Presentation Convent she was sent to the Jesus and Mary Convent at Murree. She passed her O level examination from here at the age of fifteen. In April 1969 she got admission in the US at Harvard University's Radcliffe College. In June 1973 Benazir graduated from Harvard University with a degree in Political Science. After graduating from Harvard in 1973, Benazir joined Oxford University in the fall of 1973. Just before graduation, Benazir was elected to the Standing Committee of the most prestigious Oxford Union Debating Society.

In 1976, she graduated in PPE (politics, philosophy and economics). In the autumn of 1976 Benazir returned once again to Oxford to do a one-year Postgraduate course. In January 1977, she was elected the President of the Oxford Union. Benazir Bhutto returned to Pakistan in June 1977. She wanted to join the Foreign Service but her father wanted her to contest the assembly election. As she was not yet of age, Benazir Bhutto assisted her father as an advisor.

In July 1977, General Zia-ul-Haq imposed Martial Law. During the Martial Law, Benazir spent almost five years in detention at various jails and ten months in solitary confinement. She was allowed to proceed abroad on medical grounds in January 1984, after spending nearly six and half years in jail. She went into exile in England for two years.

In July 1984 her younger brother Shah Nawaz died under mysterious circumstances in Paris. She came back to Pakistan to bury her youngest brother. A year later she came back to Pakistan to fight the elections for National and Provincial Assemblies held by General Zia-ul-Haq. On her return on April 10, 1986, one million people at Lahore airport welcomed her. She attended mammoth rallies all over Pakistan and kept in close touch with the Movement for Restoration of Democracy (MRD). On December 18, 1987, Benazir married Asif Ali Zardari in Karachi. She contested the elections, which were held on non-party basis by Ghulam Ishaq Khan. Ghulam Ishaq Khan had taken over as acting President after the death of General Zia, who died on 17th August 1988 in an air crash at Bahawalpur.

Benazir Bhutto approached the Supreme Court of Pakistan seeking enforcement of the fundamental rights guaranteed to the political parties under Article 17(2) of the 1973 constitution to hold the elections on Party basis. The Supreme Court gave its verdict in favour of the political parties. The PPP—without forming an alliance with any party—was able to win 94 out of the 207 seats in the National Assembly. With the cooperation of 8 MQM members and 13 members of the federally Administered Tribal areas, the PPP was able to get a clear majority in the National Assemblies. Benazir Bhutto was nominated as the Prime Minister on 1st December, 1988 and Ghulam Ishaq Khan was nominated the President of Pakistan.

Benazir Bhutto became the youngest Prime Minister at the age of thirty-five and the first Muslim woman to lead a Muslim nation in modern times. During her first term, she started People's Program for economic uplift of the masses. Benazir Bhutto also lifted a ban on the student unions and trade unions. The PPP government hosted the fourth SAARC Summit held in Islamabad in Dec., 1988.

Domestic issues and foreign Policy issues along with differences between her Government and the establishment led to the dismissal of her Government by President Ishaq Khan on 6th August, 1990.

Benazir returned to power again, by winning the October, 1993 Elections. The PPP had won the largest share with 86 seats and formed a new Government with the help of alliances, but her government was dismissed by President Farooq Ahmad Khan Leghari on corruption charges in November, 1996.

Her publications include "Daughter of the East" and "Foreign Policy Perspective."

ISKANDER MIRZA

Iskander Mirza was born in 1899, in a feudal family of Bengal. Educated at Elphinstone College, he was sent by the British to Sandhurst Academy in England for army training in 1918. On his return he was inducted in the British Indian Army in 1919. In 1926 he left the army, joined the Indian political Service and was posted as Assistant Commissioner in North-West Frontier Province. He was promoted to District Officer in 1931. Much of his career as a District Officer was spent in the Tribal Areas. Before the creation of Pakistan, he served the Ministry of Defense, Government of India as a Joint Secretary. At the time of partition, he was appointed as a member of the team which was to divide the personnel and assets between the Indian and Pakistan Army.

Being the senior most Muslim Civil Servant in the Indian Ministry of Defence, Iskander Mirza was appointed as the first defense secretary of Pakistan at the time of Independence. He served in the same position for about seven years. With the dismissal of the United Front's ministry in East Pakistan, Governor General Ghulam Muhammad decided to enforce Governor's rule in the province and appointed Iskander Mirza as Governor in May 1954. Assuming charge of the province, he openly declared that he would not hesitate to use force in order to establish peace in the province. The first step he took as Governor was to order the arrest of 319 persons, including the two most outspoken leaders, Mujib al Rahman and Yusuf Ali Choudhury. By mid June, the number of persons arrested had reached 1051, including 33 assembly members and two Dhaka University Professors. By doing so he might have been able to bring immediate peace but had sown a permanent seed of hatred for the Central government in the hearts of people of East Pakistan.

From October 1954 to August 1955, Iskander Mirza served as the Interior Minister, and then as the Minister of States and Frontier Regions in the cabinet of Prime Minister, Muhammad Ali Bogra. Ghulam Muhammad, due to his illness, went on two months leave and thus Iskander Mirza assumed the duties of acting Governor General on August 7, 1955. However, this acting charge was made permanent in the times to come. He appointed Chaudhry Muhammad Ali, another bureaucrat, as the Prime

Minister of the country. When the Constitution of 1956 was adopted, the title of the head of the state of Pakistan was changed from Governor General to President but the duties and powers of the office did not change to a great extent. The Constituent assembly unanimously elected Iskander Mirza as the first President of Pakistan.

Primarily, Iskander Mirza was a Civil Servant and it is widely believed that he lacked parliamentary spirit. He was of the view that because of the lack of training in the field of democracy and low literacy rate among the masses, democratic institutions can not flourish in Pakistan. He never had a very high opinion about Pakistani politicians and once referred to them as 'mostly crooks and scalawags'. He wanted controlled democracy for Pakistan with more powers for the civil bureaucracy. He believed that the Magistrate should be given the same powers, which he used to enjoy during the British Raj. He thought that politicians should be given the power to make policy but they should not interfere in administration, Iskander Mirza was also a great advocate of the One Unit scheme. In his opinion religion was to be kept at a distance from politics.

History documents that like his predecessor, Ghulam Muhammad, Iskander Mirza was also a power hungry person and wanted to dominate the political scene of the country by hook or by crook. Being the head of the state, he always remained active in power politics and played the role of a king-maker. He proved to be an expert in palace intrigues. He took full advantage of the weakness of the politicians and played them against each other. To offset the influence of the Muslim League, he played an active role in the creation of Republican Party. During his short span of four years as the head of the state, four Prime Ministers were changed. Most historians believe that Iskander Mirza was the one mainly responsible for this political unstability.

Iskander Mirza felt threatened from the reorganization of Muslim League and the alliance of Awami League with the Punjabi groups in mid 1958. On October 7, he issued a proclamation abrogating the 1956 constitution. According to the proclamation, the central and the provincial assemblies were dissolved and the first Martial law was enforced in the country. Iskander Mirza himself remained President and appointed Ayub Khan as the Martial Law Administrator and supreme commander of the armed forces. Ayub Khan proved to be smarter than the politicians and refused to act as puppet in the hands of the President. On October 27, Ayub Khan compelled Iskander Mirza to leave the country, assumed the title of President himself and announced that martial law would continue in order to give legal cover to certain reforms he wanted to put through.

Iskander Mirza spent rest of his life in a hotel room in London.

GHULAM ISHAQ KHAN [1915]

Ghulam Ishaq Khan was born on January 20, 1915 in Ismail Khel, Bannu district of NWFP. He did his graduation in Chemistry and Botany and joined NWFP Civil Service in 1940.

After the unification of West Pakistan into one unit in 1955, Ishaq Khan was appointed Provincial Secretary of West Pakistan for Irrigation Development. In this capacity he represented the provincial government in federal planning commission.

In 1958, he became Member WAPDA. In 1966, he was appointed Federal Finance Secretary and promoted to Secretary General Defense during Bhutto's term.

General Zia appointed him Advisor on Finance and later on as Federal Finance Minister. Ishaq Khan represented his country in various international conferences, which included UN conferences on finance, IMF, OIC and Asian Development Bank.

In February 1985, Ishaq Khan was elected Chairman Senate. After the death of General Zia, Ishaq Khan took over as President of the country on August 17, 1988. He was elected President on December 13, 1988 as he was the consensus candidate of PPP and IJI.

In 1993, Ghulam Ishaq Khan was forced to resign from his office due to differences with the Prime Minister.

During his tenure, Ishaq Khan dismissed the governments of Benazir Bhutto and Nawaz Sharif, using discretionary powers given to the President of the state under eighth constitutional amendment.

CHIEF EXECUTIVE OF ISLAMIC REPUBLIC OF PAKISTAN: GENERAL PERVEZ MUSHARRAF

Date of Birth:

August 11, 1943.

Zodiac Sign:

LEO.

Place of Birth:

Born in a Haveli, situated at Mohallah Kacha Saad Ullah, Old Delhi.

Parents:

Father Syed Musharraf Uddin a graduate of Aligarh University, worked in Civil Supplies Delhi. After the division, he joined Foreign Department and took the retirement as a secretary foreign affairs.

Mother had taken her Master degree from Lucknow University, recently she had taken the retirement from UNO agency in ISB.

Siblings:

Two children Ayla and Bilal, both happily married. They have a granddaughter, Mariam from Ayla.

Favourite Pastime:

General has always loved the outdoors and spends most of his leisure time playing Squash, Badminton or Golf. The General also takes keen interest in water sports, is an enthusiastic canoeist and loves to sail. An avid reader he is well versed in Military History, being his favourite subject.

Favourite Personality:

Kamal Atta Turk.

Foreign Languages:

Turkish.

Military Career:

He joined the Pakistan Military Academy in 1961 and was commissioned in an elite Artillery Regiment in 1964. He saw action in 1965 war as a young officer in the Khem Karan, Lahore and Sialkot Sectors with a self-propelled Artillery Regiment. He was awarded Imtiazi Sanad for gallantry. He later volunteered and served for seven years in the Special Service Group "Commandos". He also participated in the 1971 war as Company Commander in a Commando Battalion.

General Musharraf has the privilege of commanding two self-propelled Artillery Regiments. As a Brigadier, he had the distinction of commanding an Infantry Brigade as well as Armoured Division Artillery. On promotion to the rank of Major General on 15th January, 1991, he was given the command of an Infantry Division and later of a prestigious strike Corps as Lieutenant General on 21st October, 1995.

General Musharraf has served on various important staff and instructional appointments during his career. These include Deputy Military Secretary at the Military Secretary's Branch, member of Directing Staff both at the Command and Staff College, Quetta and the National Defense College. He has also remained the Director General Military Operations at the General Headquarters.

A graduate of Command and Staff College, Quetta and the National Defense College, General Pervez Musharraf also distinguished himself at the Royal College of Defense Studies, United Kingdom. Commenting on his performance in his report remarked, "A capable, articulate and extremely personable officer, who made a most valuable impact here. His country is fortunate to have the services of a man of his undeniable quality".

General Pervez Musharraf was promoted to the rank of General on 7th October, 1998 and appointed Chief of Army Staff. He was given the additional charge of Chairman Joint Chiefs of Staff Committee on 9th April, 1999 and is performing duties as the Chief Executive of Pakistan since 12th October, 1999. He also continues to hold the office of Chief of Army Staff and Chairman Joint Chiefs of Staff Committee.

MUHAMMAD RAFIQ TARAR [BORN 1929]

On January 1, 1998, Mr. Muhammad Rafiq Tarar, took the oath of office as the ninth President of Islamic Republic of Pakistan. He secured an all time high number of votes from an electoral college consisting of total membership of the two houses of the Parliament and the four provincial legislatures. No one before him received such overwhelming support from the elected representatives of the people of Pakistan.

Muhammad Rafiq Tarar was born on November 2, 1929, in a middle-class family of village Pirkot in District Gujranwala near Lahore. After graduating from Islamia College, Gujranwala in 1949, Mr. Tarar secured his Law Degree (L.L.B.) from Law College, Lahore, in the year 1951. The same year he was enrolled as a pleader. In October 1955, he was enrolled as an advocate in the Lahore High Court. He established a practice in Gujranwala before rising to the position of Chairman, Punjab Labour Court in 1970. Four years later he entered the High Court and was appointed as Chief Justice of Lahore High Court. Earlier, during his days as Judge of the LHC, he also served as member Pakistan Election Commission. Mr. Justice Muhammad Rafiq Tarar was elevated as the Judge of the Supreme Court of Pakistan in 1991 from which he retired in November 1994 on attaining the age of 65 years.

Following his retirement from Judiciary in March 1997, Mr. Tarar moved from a legal to a political career. He was elected as Member, Senate on PML (N) ticket. On December 31,1997, he was elected as the President of Pakistan. His appointment as the President is widely attributed to his close ties with the family of the then Prime Minister of Pakistan, Mian M. Nawaz Sharif.

On June 20, 2001, by virtue of a Provisional Constitutional Order, he was replaced by Gen. Pervez Musharraf, who himself became the President.

Mr. Tarar fondly recounts his light moments, mostly relating to his role as a volunteer in relief camps set up by Muslim Students Federation for refugees from the riot-torn India to Pakistan in 1947. Mr. Tarar has a passion for poetry and literature. He has a deep insight into classic Persian Literature. He is married and has four children, three sons and one daughter.

CHAPTER 13

BASIC ROOTS OF ISLAM

TAUHEED (ONENESS OF GOD)

QUALITIES THAT EXISTS IN GOD

- *Eternal:* That He is from ever and will be for ever. Death is not for him.
- *Capable:* That He is capable of doing everything, with His own consent.
- *Knowledgeable:* That He knows everything at its root, without any aid. He don't have any need of eyes, ears, hands, nose, etc. or any other means for His knowledge. He knows everything from ever and is never forgetful of anything.
- *Truthful:* That He is Truth Worthy.
- *One:* God is Absolutely One and only One, having no parts of any kind. He is Unique, nothing is similar to Him.
- *Absolute:* He is Absolute in the Absolute sense.
- *Greater:* He is Absolute and Perfect Creator. He created everything from nothing. The Almighty Creator brings to existence everything with utmost Perfection and nothing in His Universe is imperfect.
- *Originator:* He is the Originator of all causes and effects with no effect on Him.
- *Ever-Present:* His presence is Absolutely ubiquitous.
- *Independent:* He is Absolutely independent of anything and everything that exists.

QUALITIES THAT DOES NOT EXIST IN GOD

- *Partnership:* He has no partner or colleague of any kind and at any stage.

- *Composition:* God is not a compound of any kind. Every thing may be made up of atoms or sub-atomic particles. These atoms and sub-atomic particles are its creations, then how He can be made-up of these?
- *Location:* We cannot locate God in space, yet He is present everywhere. His position can never be specified. It is His creations that can be located in space at some particular position.
- *Assimilation:* That He cannot be mixed, merged or fused with any other thing.
- *Alteration:* He is free from alteration. He is same every time and every place. Change of any kind cannot the with God. He is never child, old, asleep, awaked, napping, etc.
- *Perceptible:* That He is invisible and not detectable directly. However, He can be seen through His creations only. No one can see Him, any time and anywhere. No entity in His Universe can ever comprehend His true state. No one in the world can ever physically define Him. Ascribing a shape to the One who is beyond our limited perceptions would be tantamount to lying and giving a false appearance and a false representation. In addition, to believe that one can see God in the physical sense of sitting on a throne like some mythical being is certainly an untrue statement and should never be accepted.
- *Needy:* He is never in need of anyone. Everyone has need of Him, always.
- His qualities are not part of Himself. He and His qualities are not different thing. It is also specific to God only. Every other thing has itself and qualities different things.
- *Analogous:* He is not similar to anything. If anything comes to mind to be the God, then it is not God.
- *Birth:* He begets not, nor is He begotten.
- *Death:* He will never be dead.
- *Travel:* He don't change from one place to another. See Location above.
- *Time:* He has no effect of time. See alternation above.
- *Sex:* Sex cannot be defined for God.

How the God is One

- If there was partner of God, it would have created disturbance in Universe.

- Partnership is a defect of God, that cannot be in God.
- All Messengers of God (Prophets) are from one God. They all said that He is one. If there were other god, then he must have sent his messengers.
- If we suppose two gods, then one of them will be able to remove other or not. If first is able to remove other, then the second is not god. If first is not able to remove other, then he cannot be god.
- God told his Prophets that He is one. If He tell them a lie, then lie is a defect, defect cannot be in God.

AADAL (JUSTICE)

- Essentially part of Tauheed (Oneness of Allah)
- Aadal is the belief that God is just.
- He will reward or punish any person according to his deeds and thus the notion of predestination (where all decisions are God's and not any one else's) in one's deeds does not exist.
- It is absolutely forbidden in Islam to believe that the Almighty, Merciful Allah planned our destiny and that the good and the bad are just His Will and there is no choice for us between them (God forbid!).
- Those who ascribe to such lies do so because they want to blame their own evils on Allah and claim the good for themselves!
- Although the attribute of Allah's Justice is not a separate entity of Allah for certainly the Almighty God can never be compartmentalized nor defined in any relative terms, it is nonetheless absolutely compulsory to believe and fully understand the importance of this attribute in Islam so as not to allow the evil suggestions of Iblees (curse of Allah be upon him and his progeny) and his companions from leading us astray.

How the God is Just

- Unjust is defect, that cannot be in God.
- Unjust is due to some need, God is not needy.
- God has discarded unjust, then how He can be unjust?
- God has announced that He is Just through all His Book revealed on the humans.
- Just is present in everything He has created.

- If we suppose that he is unjust then we cannot guarantee his truthfulness.

Nabuwwat—The Prophet Hood
(Messenger—Courier System of Allah)

- Nabuwwat is the belief in the Prophets (PBUT) of God who excel all other persons for whom they are sent for.
- All prophets of Allah are perfect and sinless (ma'soom).
- Prophet Muhammad Mustafa (PBUH&HF) is the last of the prophets sent by God and the sealer of prophets for NO more are to come, EVER!
- The total number of prophets (PBUT) that were sent by God to mankind is 124,000 and every nation on earth was given guidance through them. In fact, all major religions today on earth can be traced to have these divinely guided teachers as their original propagators of the Truth of Allah.
- The best of His messengers all came from the same tree i.e. family lineage and many of them are mentioned in the Holy Qur'an which describes who they were and what their mission on earth was.
- It is important to note that no prophet on earth ever negated or rejected any of the other divinely ordained prophets and thus their message was always the same and one in purpose. Each established the law of the One and Only God and showed the way of life for humans to observe.
- From the very first creation of mankind, there was always a prophet on earth which was Prophet Adam (PBUH). This guidance from the Merciful Allah to establish His complete laws continued to the last Prophet Muhammad (PBUH&HF) who exemplified the letters of the law in his most perfect behaviour.
- He completed and perfected the one and only True religion, Islam.
- With the revelation of the last Holy Book, the Qur'an, which is the most protected and perfect book of God with us, he established as part of his mission, every conceivable and practical law for mankind to follow in order to attain spiritual perfection.
- Great prophets such as Nuh (Noah), Ibrahim (Abraham), Ismail (Ishmael), Ishaaq (Isaac), Yaqoob (Jacob), Yusuf

(Joseph), Dawood (David), Sulaiman (Solomon), Musa (Moses), Yahya (John), and Isa (Jesus),–(Peace be upon them all)–all came from the one blessed lineage of Prophet Adam (PBUH) and ended with the last Messenger, Muhammad (PBUH&HF).

It is also important to note that anyone who ascribes imperfections or mistakes to these divinely guided personalities is ascribing it directly to Allah who is certainly free from such. Acceptance of such ideas is also rejection of the message of Allah entirely. Thus with prophethood, a believer has to accept in their complete message

Imamat (Guidance)

- Imamat is the belief in the divinely appointed leadership after the death of the Holy Prophet (PBUH&HF) to protect and guide mankind with the revealed Truth, the Holy Qur'an and the true practices of the Holy Prophet himself.
- The roles of these leaders is an integral part in the protection of all the Messengers and their divine Messages.
- The Almighty Allah appointed through the Holy Prophet himself, twelve Guides (Imams) to protect mankind from misrepresenting and misinterpreting the Truth.
- Belief in this is most important in Islam and no doubts about their positions should be allowed.
- They are indeed sinless (ma'soom) and perfect in the highest sense of the word.
- The Imams have direct knowledge from God, and their verdict is the verdict of God.
- After the Holy Prophet, only they can interpret and guide mankind in every aspect of life and death and all believers must acquire guidance from them or else they will certainly be lost.
- They do NOT bring any new laws nor do they ever innovate their own laws. They always exemplify and elucidate the practical (Sunnah) and the written (the Holy Qur'an).
- It is also important to note that they NEVER disagree with each other in their manners and duties nor in their representations of the Divine Laws.

- They are from the best and the most blessed and purified lineage of the last Holy Prophet Muhammad (PBUT) and their names are as follows:

    1. Imam Ali ibn Abu Talib, the cousin and son-in-law of the Holy Prophet who called him his only brother in this world and in the next,
    2. Imam Hasan son of Ali,
    3. Imam Husain son of Ali,
    4. Imam Ali son of Husain,
    5. Imam Muhammad son of Ali,
    6. Imam Ja'far son of Muhammad,
    7. Imam Musa son of Ja'far,
    8. Imam Ali son of Musa,
    9. Imam Muhammad son of Ali,
    10. Imam Ali son of Muhammad,
    11. Imam Hasan son of Ali,
    12. and the last and living Imam Muhammad son of Hasan, the establisher of the Truth till the end of this world (PBUT).

- There is no successor to the Twelfth Holy Imam Muhammad ibnul Hassan (PBUH) and he is LIVING today but is in occultation and appears only to those who are most in need and to those who are most virtuous and pious. By the Command of Allah, he will reappear to all when he will establish true justice on earth and will rule mankind compassionately with utmost perfection as is the Will of the Almighty Allah. He will abolish the evil establishments on earth and mankind will live under true guidance as should have been many centuries ago!

Sifate Thubutiyyah

The positive attributes which are benefiting Allah are Sifate Thubutiyyah. They are many in number, but only eight of them are usually mentioned. They are:

1. *QADEEM :* It means that Allah is Eternal, i.e.. He has neither beginning nor end. Nothing except Allah is eternal.
2. *QAADIR :* It means that Allah is Omnipotent, i.e.. He has power over every thing and every affair.

3. *AALIM* : It means that Allah is Omniscient, i.e.. He knows every thing. Even our unspoken intentions and desires are not hidden from Him.

4. *HAI* : It means that Allah was always alive and will remain alive for ever.

5. *MUREED* : It means that Allah has His own will and discretion in all affairs. He does not do anything under compulsion.

6. *MUDRIK* : It means that He is All-Perceiving, as 'Samii' (All-Hearing), 'Basser' (All-Seeing). Allah sees and hears every thing without any need of eyes or ears.

7. *MUTAKALLIM* : It means that Allah is the master of the word, i.e.. He can create speech in anything, as He did in a tree for Hadhrat Musa (A.S) and in the "Curtain of Light" for our Holy Prophet (S.A.W.)

8. *SADIQ* : It means that Allah is true in his words and promises. It is impossible to fix any limit to His attributes. This list is not exhaustive but is essential to understand the Glory of Allah. These attributes are not acquired but are inherent in the conception of Divinity.

Sifate Salbiyyah

The negative attributes which cannot be found in Allah because they are below His dignity are called "Sifate Salbiyyah." They are many, but like "Sifate Thubutiya" only eight are listed here. They are:

1. *SHAREEK* : The word "Shareek" means a colleague or partner. Allah has neither a colleague nor a partner in His Divinity.

2. *MURAKKAB* : This word means "Compound" or "Mixed". Allah is neither made, nor composed, of any material. He cannot be divided even in imagination.

3. *MAKKAN* : It means "Place". Allah is not in a place because He has no body, and He is everywhere because His power and knowledge is magnificently apparent everywhere.

4. *HULOOL* : It Means "Entering". Nothing enters into Allah nor does He enter into anything or anybody. Therefore, the belief of Incarnation in any form is abhorrent to the conception of Divinity.

5. *MAHALLE HAWADIS :* This means "Subject to changes". Allah cannot change.
6. *MAR-I :* It means "Visible". Allah is not visible. He has not been seen, is not seen and will never be seen.
7. *IHTIYAJ :* It means "Dependence" or "Need". Allah is not deficient in any virtue, so he does not need anything. He is All-Perfect.
8. *SIFATE ZAID :* This means "Added Qualifications." The attributes of Allah are not separate from His Being, when we say that God is Omnipotent and Merciful, we do not mean that His Power and Mercy are something different from His Person. We see that a child is born without any power; and then he acquires strength day by day. It is so because power is not his person. God is not like this. He is Power Himself; Mercy Himself; Knowledge Himself; Justice Himself; Virtue Himself; Truth Himself; and so on.

It will thus be seen that according to Islam ALLAH is the name of God as perceived in the light of the above Positive and Negative Attributes. In other words, ALLAH is the Creator of the Universe, Self-Existent, the source of all perfection and free from all defects.

Names of Allah

The proper name which Islam uses for God is "ALLAH". "ALLAH" means "One 'Who deserves to be loved" and "Into Whom everyone seeks refuge." This word, grammatically speaking, is unique. It has no plural and no feminine. So this name itself reflects light upon the fact that Allah is one and only one; He has neither any partner nor any equal. The name cannot properly be translated by the word "God" because God can be transformed in 'gods' and goddesses".

Two more frequently used names are Rahman and Rahim. Rahman signifies that Allah is Merciful and that His Mercy encompasses each and everything in the universe without any distinction on account of faith or belief He makes, creates and sustains everything and every man whether he be a Muslim or Kafir.

Rahim signifies that the Mercy of Allah on the Day of Judgement will surround the true believers only, and that unbelievers and hypocrites will be left out.

It is apparent that both of these names signify a distinct aspect of God's Mercy. His Mercy in this world, as signified by 'Rahman' is general; and the one in the life-hereafter, as signified by 'Rahim' is special. It will be of interest to note that the word 'Rahman' cannot be used except for Allah, while 'Rahim' can be used for others also.

That is why it has been told by Imam that 'Rahman is a reserved name which denotes unreserved Mercy, and Rahim is an unreserved name which denotes Reserved Mercy."

ATTRIBUTES OF PERSON AND ACTION

Question: One of the names of Allah is 'Khaliq' i.e. Creator As Allah was Creator from ever, does it not follow that the 'created things, i.e., the universe is from ever?

Answer: Allah was not creating from ever. If you study carefully you will find that the attributes of God, as mentioned in the above chapter, may easily be divided into two groups:

First, there are those attributes which can never be separated from the conception of divinity. For example we say that God is Qaadir (Omnipotent), Aalim (Omniscient) and Hai (Ever-living). These are such attributes which can never be separated from the conception of God, because there never was a time when God was not Omnipotent, Omniscient or Living. He was Qaadir, Aalim and Hai for ever, and will remain Qaadir, Aalim and Hai for ever. Such attributes refer to the person of Allah, and are, therefore, called 'Sifaat-e-Dhat' (Attributes of person of Allah).

Second, there are the attributes which describe the actions of Allah. For example, we say that Allah is 'Khaaliq' (Creator), 'Raaziq' (Sustainer) etc. These are the Attributes which describe the actions of Allah, and are, therefore, called 'Sifaat-el Afaal' (Attributes of Actions of Allah).

These actions were not from ever, and therefore these attributes were not used for Allah, from ever. You know that Allah is 'Mureed'. He acts according to His own plan and His own Will. He is not like fire which burns without any intention or will of its own. Nor is He like the sun which goes on giving light and warmth without intention and will of its own. Allah works according to His own plan. He created when He wished, and not before that.

It does not mean that God had no power to create. The power to create was there for ever; because the 'Power' is not separate from His person. But the appearance of that power, and bringing it into effect, was not from ever. In short, Allah had power to create from ever, but He did not create from ever. And when He created. He was called Khaaliq; but not before that.

Likewise, when he sustained, He was called 'Raaziq'; when He forgave He was called 'Ghaffaar'; when He avenged, He was called 'Qahhaar'; when He gave life, He was called 'Muhyi', when He gave death, He was called 'Mumeet'.

Death

Death is not something which is debatable nor that which is talked about enough in western society. However it is a fact which every soul will taste. As Muslims we know that death is near and this world is not one to long for. If you love this world and wish to cling to it, it will be temporary and certainly will not last.

God Almighty commands in verse 11 of chapter 59 in the holy Qur'an:

'The Hour will certainly come: Therein is no doubt: yet most men believe not'.

Also in verse 15 of chapter number 99:

'And serve thy lord until there come unto thee the hour that is certain'.

We believe that one of Allah's positive attributes is that he is just beyond all injustice.

He does not treat his creatures without justice, nor does he rule them unfairly or cruelly, he rewards his obedient servants and punishes those who fall into sin. He does not compel his servants to do things which are not within their capabilities, nor does he punish them for more than the sins they have committed as was discussed in the previous issue of Read.

That which does not die and will never die is Allah. Us humans, will one day eventually leave this world. The setting of the sun each day is a poetical metaphor for our passing away. How good it is, if we meet with another day, just like the sun, beaming and bright on the horizon of the resurrection. This is important for the sunset is inevitable; death is a reality which, like it or not, must happen.

Verse 99 of chapter 23 in the holy Qur'an says of the unbelievers and those who, till the moment of death, continue in unacceptable ways :—

'Until when death overtakes one of them, he says: Send me back, my Lord, send me back'.

But their wish is unfulfilled, and verse 100 of chapter 23 confirms this:

'Haply I may do good in that which I have left. By no means? It is a (mere) word that he speaks; and before them is a barrier until the day they are raised'.

Some people run away from the remembrance of death, and do not give way to thoughts about it. It is as if they have drunk the water of eternity, and think to remain in this world forever. These people are drunk from the wine of neglectfulness. For they know but do not accept that the only thing that it is eternal and will not die is Allah. From the results of their neglectfulness of death, they will pass their lives aimlessly. They do not think to reform themselves; their time is spent like the hands of a turning clock, turning round and round, and how often will they be polluted with dreadful sins. There is not so much difference between their lives and the lives of animals.

THE MIGHTY WORDS OF ALLAH

'And when the blast shall sound, upon the day when a man shall flee from his brother, his mother, his father, his consort, his sons, every man that day shall have business to suffice him'. Verse 33-37 from Surat ABASA.

'Every soul shall taste of death, and you shall only be paid fully your reward on the resurrection day; then whoever is removed far away from the fire and is made to enter the garden, he indeed has attained the object; and the life of this world is nothing but a provision of vanities.' Verse 185 from Surat AL-e-IMRAN.

'Then how will it be when We shall gather them together on a day about which there is no doubt, and every soul shall be fully paid what it has earned, and they shall not be dealt with unjustly?' Verse 25 from Surat Al-e-IMRAN.

'Every soul must taste of death and We try you by evil and good by way of probation; Iman, faith, is an Arabic term which has come to be used in the regular vocabularies of Islamic countries, in such a way that today every Persian, Turkish or Urdu (speaking person) is familiar with its meaning. Even though we have stated that the term iman itself is generally widely-known; in order to have a clear and uniform idea, it is better to clearly define it with the help of some examples to limit its range of meaning and connotations.

When we believe in the honesty of someone to the extent that we completely trust that person without any worry, anxiety, hesitation or fear, say that we have faith or iman in this person.

When the truth of a topic is apparent to the point of conviction, we say that we have 'faith' in this subject. 'When we strongly believe in an intellectual system—or an ideological system in its European sense, or Islamic doctrine in our interpretation, when we feel such a strong attraction that it consequently becomes the foundation of our lives, and becomes such with conviction, more than that, with enthusiasm, ardour and inclination; when we re-align our lives and activities upon this basis, then we can say that we have 'faith' in this doctrine.

In light of the examples, it can be said that 'faith' means heart-felt confidence and trust in a person or creed.

Doubt and Hesitation

The opposite of faith is doubt, hesitation or faltering, whether towards a person, a subject, or towards a creed. Doubt and hesitation can take the form of complete indifference. It is possible that it might be mixed with optimism or pessimism, but its natural outcome is distrust. Even if a kind of optimism is interwined with it, one could not become devoted to or follow a person or a creed with doubt and hesitation, especially in cases where steadfastness and resoluteness will be required.

Let us objectively review the life of the human being and see what role faith plays in it. But let us not review past ages. Rather let us look at this very era of ours, an era which allegedly lacks faith. Are we really living in such an era? Is there no place left: for faith to have a role in the life of the human being? Can this era of scientific and industrial advances, development of public education, and an increased awareness of the human being of himself and the world surrounding be coupled with faith? Is it true that with the progress of science the age of faith has come to an end?

From Where do We Begin?

From where should we begin this objective review? From the scenes of the heroic struggles of the people of Lebanon, Iran, Algeria, Palestine, Vietnam and many others? Or from more tranquil scenes for example from the warm nucleus of the family or the school? As this discussion is arranged for students, if we were to directly go to the scenes of social struggle, we would have spoken according to the demand of the circumstances. If you have the patience it is better for us to examine the role of faith in the life of the human being in general in order to become better acquainted with the essence of the subject.

Childhood

The primary factor in a child's life, even in this age of science and technology the age of space exploration—is faith; life revolves around faith. The actions one performs so as to emulate others are due to one's faith in those who surround the child, that, is parents, siblings, nurse and so on; and the actions which one carries out according to one's discernment, spring from one's faith in one's own sense of direction.

The Faith of the Mother, Father and Teacher

A child's prosperity and proper and correct growth for life to a large extent depends upon the faith of the mother, father, teacher and all those who are responsible for the child. Only those who have faith in their works and duties are able to undertake these sensitive responsibilities. A mother who nurtures and physically and spiritually trains her children with love, care, faith, and a sense of responsibility towards them; a father who endeavours with love and faith to provide for the welfare and physical and mental health of the members of the family; a teacher who accepts the responsibility for the grave and delicate talks of teaching and education with love and faith undoubtedly play an influential role in a child's prosperity.

In family environments that are deprived of love, the lack of faith, a sound belief of the parents and children and their heart-felt respect for each-others rights are considered to be among the most important factors of the children's adverseness. This is true even from the point of view of today's very progressive science. The child does not feel peace or security in such a lifeless family surrounding. Gradually the child becomes pessimistic towards everything, even the self, and becomes deprived of the most valuable factors of progress and evolution, that is faith in the self and faith in one's environment.

Essentially a child's faith is largely a reflection of the faith of parents which has shone upon the pure and susceptible heart of the child, and from their attitude, which is mixed with love and faith toward the child and towards each other. Such is the case of the teacher at school, particularly during the first years of education.

Undoubtedly the best of our memories belongs to those days when we enjoyed the education and teaching of a diligent and faith-filled teacher in primary school or professor in the University.

Ravaging of Doubt and Suspicion

With the approach of adulthood, the type of faith of the period of childhood comes under doubt. Also during that very period of childhood, from time to time, the child is faced with incidents which would take away his faith from some one or something, but during this period, usually another type of faith replaces the withdrawn faith: faith which is opposite of the first, but not doubt. Sometimes the child changes his or her mind rapidly and successively. A child might not be on speaking terms with a play-mate for an hour but would reconcile with him or her in the next, and a sincere reconciliation it is at that.

Gradually this period passes and the period of adulthood and growth begins. During this period various physical and mental changes take place in the human being. Among them is the fact that the person might become doubtful and skeptical about many of the principles and beliefs held during childhood. The extent of this doubt and skepticism differs in individuals. In some persons it spreads to such an extent that it virtually encompasses everything.

Constructive Doubt

Doubt occurring during adulthood is one of the most effective factors in the evolution of the human being, on the condition that it be accompanied by love and faith, love and faith for research and investigation. Only this kind of doubt can be named constructive doubt although the work of doubt always ends in destruction; that is, the destruction of whatever we believed in. Construction relates to the research and investigation which we begin following this destruction.

CHAPTER 14

ISLAMIC RELIGION

"ALLAH DOES NOT PLACE BURDEN UPON A SOUL BEYOND WHAT IT CAN BEAR".

(Al Baqarah 2:286)

THE TRUE RELIGION

The Religion of Islam

The first thing that one should know and clearly understand about Islam is what the word "Islam" itself means. The religion of Islam is not named after a person as in the case of Christianity which was named after Jesus Christ, Buddhism after Gautama Buddha, Confucianism after Confucius, and Marxism after Karl Marx. Nor was it named after a tribe like Judaism after the tribe of Judah and Hinduism after the Hindus. Islam is the true religion of "Allah" and as such, its name represents the central principle of Allah's "God's" religion; the total submission to the will of Allah "God". The Arabic word "Islam" means the submission or surrender of one's will to the only true god worthy of worship "Allah" and anyone who does so is termed a "Muslim". The word also implies "peace" which is the natural consequence of total submission to the will of Allah. Hence, it was not a new religion brought by Prophet Muhammad (PBUH) I in Arabia in the seventh century, but only the true religion of Allah re-expressed in its final form.

Islam is the religion which was given to Adam, the first man and the first prophet of Allah, and it was the religion of all the prophets sent by Allah to mankind. The name of God's religion Islam was not decided upon by later generations of man. It was chosen by Allah Himself and clearly mentioned in His final revelation to man. In the final book of divine revelation, the Qur'an, Allah states the following:

"This day have I perfected your religion for you, completed My favour upon you, and have chosen for you Islam as your religion". *(Soorah Al-Maa'idah 5:3)*

"If anyone desires a religion other than Islam (submission to Allah (God) never will It be accepted of Him" *(Soorah Aal'imraan 3:85)*

"Abrahm was not a Jew nor Christian; but an upright Muslim." *(Soorah Aal'imraan 3:67)*

Nowhere in the Bible will you find Allah saying to Prophet Moses' people or their descendants that their religion is Judaism, nor to the followers of Christ that their religion is Christianity. In fact, Christ was not even his name, nor was it Jesus! The name "Christ" comes from the Greek word Christos which means the anointed. That is, Christ is a Greek translation of the Hebrew title "Messiah". The name "Jesus" on the other hand, is a latinized version of the Hebrew name Esau.

For simplicity's sake, I will however continue to refer to Prophet Esau (PBUH) as Jesus. As for his religion, it was what he called his followers to. Like the prophets before him, he called the people to surrender their will to the will of Allah; (which is Islam) and he warned them to stay away from the false gods of human imagination.

According to the New Testament, he taught his followers to pray as follows: "Yours will be done on earth as it is in Heaven".

THE MESSAGE OF ISLAM

Since the total submission of one's will to Allah represents the essence of worship, the basic message of Allah's divine religion, Islam is the worship of Allah alone and the avoidance of worship directed to any person, place or thing other than Allah. Since everything other than Allah, the Creator of all things, is Allah's creation; it may be said that Islam, in essence calls man away from the worship of creation and invites him to worship only its Creator. He is the only one deserving man's worship as it is only by His will that prayers are answered. If man prays to a tree and his prayers are answered, it was not the tree which answered his prayers but Allah who allowed the circumstances prayed for to take place. One might say, "That is obvious," however, to tree-worshippers it might not be. Similarly, prayers to Jesus, Buddha, or Krishna, to Saint Christopher, or Saint Jude or even to Muhammad, are not answered by them but are answered by Allah. Jesus did not tell his followers to worship him but to worship Allah. As the Qur'an states:

"And behold Allah will say: 'O Jesus the son of Mary Did you say to men, Worship me and my mother as gods besides Allah He will say—Glory to you I could never say what I had no right (to say')" *(Soorah Al-Maa'idah- 5:116)*

Nor did he worship himself when he worshipped but rather he worshipped Allah. This basic principle is enshrined in the opening chapter of the Qur'an, known as *Soorah Al-Faatihah, verse 4:*

"You alone do we worship and from you alone do we seek help".

Elsewhere, in the final book of revelation, the Qur'an, Allah also said:

"And your Lord says: 'Call on Me and I will answer your (prayer)'." (Soorsh *Mu'min 40:60)*

It is worth noting that the basic message of Islam is that Allah and His creation are distinctly different entities. Neither is Allah His creation or a part of it, nor is His creation Him or a part of Him.

This might seem obvious, but, man's worship of creation instead of the Creator is to a large degree based on ignorance of this concept. It is the belief that the essence of Allah is everywhere in His creation or that His divine being is or was present in some aspects of His creation, which has provided justification for the worship of creation though such worship may be called the worship of Allah through his creation. How ever, the message of Islam as brought by the prophets of Allah is to worship only Allah and to avoid the worship of his creation either directly or indirectly. In the Qur'an Allah clearly states:

"For We assuredly sent amongst every people a prophet, (with the command) worship means avoid false gods "*(Soorah Al-Nahl 16:36)*

When the idol worshipper is questioned as to why he or she bows down to idols created by men, the invariable reply is that they are not actually worshipping the stone image, but Allah who is present within it. They claim that the stone idol is only a focal point for Allah's essence and is not in itself Allah! One who has accepted the concept of the presence of God's being within His creation in any way will be obliged to accept this argument of idolatry. Whereas, one who understands the basic message of Islam and its implications would never concede to idolatry no matter how it is rationalized. Those who have claimed divinity for themselves down through the ages have often based their claims on the mistaken belief that Allah is present in man. They merely had to assert that although Allah according to their false beliefs, is in all of us. He is more present in them than in the rest of us. Hence, they claim, we should submit our will to them and worship them as they are either God in person or God concentrated within the person.

Similarly, those who have asserted the godhood of others after their passing have found fertile ground among those who accept the false belief of God's presence in man. One who has grasped the basic message of Islam and its implications could never agree to worship another human being under any circumstances. God's religion in essence is a clear call to the worship of the Creator and the rejection of creation-worship in any form. This is the meaning of the motto of Islam:

"Laa Elaaha Illallaah" (There is no god but Allah)

Its repetition automatically brings one within the fold of Islam and sincere belief in it guarantees one Paradise.

Thus, the final Prophet of Islam is reported to have said, "Any one who says: There is no god but Allah and dies holding that (belief) will enter paradise".

It consists in the submission to Allah as one God, yielding to Him by obeying His commandments, and the denial of polytheism and polytheists.

THE MESSAGE OF FALSE RELIGION

There are so many sects, cults, religions, philosophies, and movements in the world, all of which claim to be the right way or the only true path to Allah. How can one determine which one is correct or if, in fact, all are correct? The method by which the answer can be found is to clear away the superficial differences in the teachings of the various claimants to the ultimate truth, and identify the central object of worship to which they call, directly or indirectly. False religions all have in common one basic concept with regards to Allah. They either claim that all men are gods or that specific men were Allah or that nature is Allah or that Allah is a figment of man's imagination.

Thus, it may be stated that the basic message of false religion is that Allah may be worshipped in the form of His creation. False religion invites man to the worship of creation by calling the creation or some aspect of it God. For example, prophet Jesus invited his followers to worship Allah but those who claim to be his followers today call people to worship Jesus, claiming that he was Allah!

Buddha was a reformer who introduced a number of humanistic principles to the religion of India. He did not claim to be God nor did he suggest to his followers that he be an object of worship. Yet, today most Buddhists who are to be found outside of India have taken him to be God and prostrate to idols made in their perception of his likeness.

By using the principle of identifying the object of worship, false religion becomes very obvious and the contrived nature of their origin clear. As God said in the Qur'an:

That which you worship besides Him are only names you and your forefathers have invented for which Allah has sent down no authority: The command belongs only to Allah:

"He has commanded that you only worship Him; that is the right religion, but most men do not understand". *(Soorah Yoosuf 12:40).*

It may be argued that all religions teach good things so why should it matter which one we follow. The reply is that all false religions teach the greatest evil, the worship of creation. Creation-worship is the greatest sin that man can commit because it contradicts the very purpose of his creation. Man was created to worship Allah alone as Allah has explicitly stated in the Qur'an:

"I have only created Jinns and men, that they may worship me". *(Soorah Zaareeyaat 51:56)*

Consequently, the worship of creation, which is the essence of idolatry, is the only unforgivable sin. One who dies in this state of idolatry has sealed his fate in the next life. This is not an opinion, but a revealed fact stated by Allah in his final revelation to man: "Verily Allah will not forgive the joining of partners with Him, but He may forgive (sins) less than that for whom so ever He wishes". *(Soorah An-Nisaa 4:48 and 116).*

THE UNIVERSALITY OF ISLAM

Since the consequences of false religion are so grave, the true religion of Allah must be universally understandable and attainable, not confined to any people, place or time. There can not be conditions like baptism, belief in a man, as a saviour etc., for a believer to enter paradise. Within the central principle of Islam and in its definition, (the surrender of one's will to God) lies the roots of Islam's universality. Whenever man comes to the realization that Allah is one and distinct from His creation, and submits himself to Allah, he becomes a Muslim in body and spirit and is eligible for paradise. Thus, anyone at any time in the most remote region of the world can become a Muslim, a follower of God's religion, Islam, by merely rejecting the worship of creation and by turning to Allah (God) alone—it should be noted however, that the recognition of and submission to Allah requires that one chooses between right and wrong and such a choice implies accountability. Man will be held responsible for his choices, and, as such, he should try his utmost to do good and avoid evil. The ultimate good being the worship of Allah alone and the ultimate evil being the worship of His creation along with or instead of Allah. This fact is expressed in the final revelation as follows:

"Verily those who believe, those who follow the Jewish (Scriptures), the Christians and the Sabians and who believe In Allah and the last day, and work righteousness shall have their reward with their Lord; They will not be overcome by fear nor grief." *(Soorah Al-Baqarah 2:62).*

"If only they had stood by the law, the Gospel, and all the revelation that was sent to them from their Lord, they would have enjoyed happiness from every side. There Is from among them a party on the right course; but many of them follow a course that Is evil.". *(Soorah Al-.Maa'idah 5:66)*

RECOGNITION OF ALLAH

The question which arises here is, "How can all people be expected to believe in Allah given their varying backgrounds, societies and cultures? For people to be responsible for worshipping Allah they all have to have access to knowledge of Allah. The final revelation teaches that all mankind have the recognition of Allah imprinted on their souls, a part of their very nature with which they are created.

In *Soorah Al-A'raaf. Verses 172-173,* Allah explained that when He created Adam, He caused all of Adam's descendants to come into existence and took a pledge from them saying. Am I not your Lord? To which they all replied, " Yes, we testify to It.'

Allah then explained why He had all of mankind bear witness that He is their creator and only true God worthy of worship. He said, "That was In case you (mankind) should say on the day of Resurrection, "Verily we were unaware of all this." That is to say, we had no idea that You Allah, were our God. No one told us that we were only supposed to worship You alone. Allah went on to explain That it was also In case you should say, 'Certainly It was our ancestors who made partners (With Allah) and we are only their descendants; will You then destroy us for what those liars did?" Thus, every child is born with a natural belief in Allah and an inborn inclination to worship Him alone called in Arabic the "Fitrah".

If the child were left alone, he would worship Allah in his own way, but all children are affected by those things around them, seen or unseen.

The Prophet (PBUH) reported that Allah said, "I created my servants in the right religion but devils made them go astray". The Prophet (PBUH) also said, "Each child is born in a state of "Fitrah", then his parents make him a Jew, Christian or a Zoroastrian, the way an animal gives birth to a normal offspring. Have you noticed any that were born mutilated?"

So, just as the child submits to the physical laws which Allah has put in nature, his soul also submits naturally to the fact that Allah is his Lord and Creator. But, his parents try to make him follow their own way and the child is not strong enough in the early stages of his life to resist or oppose the will of his parents. The religion which the child follows at this stage is one of custom and upbringing and Allah does not hold him to account or punish him for this religion.

Throughout people's lives from childhood until the time they die, signs are shown to them in all regions of the earth and in their own souls, until it becomes clear that there is only one true God (Allah). If the people are honest with themselves, reject their false gods and seek Allah, the way will be made easy for them but if they continually reject Allah's signs and continue to worship creation, the more difficult it will be for them to escape. For example, in the South Eastern region of the Amazon jungle in Brazil, South America, a primitive tribe erected a new hut to house their main idol Skwatch, representing the supreme God of all creation. The homage to the God, and while he was in prostration to what he had been taught was his Creator and Sustainer, a mangy old flea-ridden dog walked into the hut. The young man looked up in time to see the dog lift its hind leg and pass urine on the idol. Outraged, the youth chased the dog out of the temple, but when his rage died down he realized that the idol could not be the Lord of the universe. Allah must be elsewhere, he now had a choice to act on his knowledge and seek Allah, or to dishonestly go along with the false beliefs of his tribe. As strange as it may seem, that was a sign from Allah for that young man. It contained within its divine guidance that what he was worshipping was false.

Prophets were sent, as was earlier mentioned, to every nation and tribe to support man's natural belief in Allah and man's inborn inclination to worship Him as well as to reinforce the divine truth in the daily signs revealed by Allah. Although, in most cases, much of the prophets' teachings became distorted, portions remained which point out right and wrong. For example, the ten commandments of the Torah, their confirmation in the Gospels and the existence of laws against murder, stealing and adultery in most societies.

Consequently, every soul will be held to account for its belief in Allah and its acceptance of the religion of Islam; the total submission to the will of Allah.

We pray to Allah, the exalted, to keep us on the right path to which He has guided us, and to bestow on us a blessing from Him, He is indeed the Most Merciful. Praise and gratitude be to Allah, the Lord of the worlds, and peace and blessings be on prophet Muhammed, his Family, his companions, and those who rightly follow them.

CHAPTER 15

INTRODUCTION TO THE QUR'AN

Praise be to Allah, the Cherisher and Sustainer of the worlds. Who has said in His Noble Book:

"There has come to you from Allah Light and a Perspicuous Book." (5.15) And may peace and blessings be upon the Seal of the Prophets, Muhammad, who has said that:

"The best among you is he who learned the Qur'an and then taught it." (Narrated by the six except Muslim)

May the peace and blessings of Allah be upon him, his family and all his Companions. The Glorious Qur'an is the Book of Allah, the Wise and Worthy of all Praise, Who has promised to safeguard it from any violations in its purity. It becomes incumbent upon each and every person who seeks the dignity of this world and the bliss of the Hereafter to regulate his life according to it, to implement its commandments and to pay homage to the magnificence of the One Who revealed it. This can be an easy task for those favoured with guidance from Allah, especially those blessed by an understanding of Arabic, the language of the divine communication. But for those not acquainted with Arabic, their ignorance is a barrier between them and this source of guidance and illumination. A translation of the message of Allah is thus a task not to be taken lightly or performed superficially.

Before we begin to study the Qur'an, we must realise that unlike all other writings, this is a unique book with a supreme author, an eternal message and a universal relevance. Its contents are not confined to a particular theme or style, but contain the foundations for an entire system of life, covering a whole spectrum of issues, which range from specific articles of faith and commandments to general moral teachings, rights and obligations, crime and punishment, personal and public law, and a host of other private and social concerns. These issues are discussed in a variety of ways, such as direct stipulations, reminders of Allah's favours on His creation, admonitions and rebukes. Stories of past communities are narrated, followed by the lessons to be learned from their actions and subsequent fates.

The Qur'an enjoys a number of characteristics unique to it alone, some of which are as follows:

● It is the actual Word of Allah; not created but revealed for the benefit of all mankind.

● "Blessed is He Who sent down the Criterion to His servant, that it may be An admonition to all creatures." (25.1)

● It is complete and comprehensive. The Almighty says: "Nothing have We omitted from the Book." (6.38)
In another place we read:
"And We have sent down to thee the Book explaining all things." (16.89)

● It is a theoretical and a practical Book, not only moralizing but also defining specifically the permissible and the forbidden. The importance of understanding the message of the Qur'an is undeniable, but simply reciting it with the intention of seeking Allah's pleasure and reward is also an act of worship and meritorious in itself. Allah Almighty says:

● "So take what the Prophet gives you, and refrain from what he prohibits you." (59.7)

● Allah has perfected His religion for all mankind with the revelation of this Book. He says:

● "This day have I perfected your religion for you, completed My favor upon you and have chosen for you Islam as your religion." (5.3)

● It is Allah's eternal miracle revealed to the Prophet Muhammad for all succeeding generations. In response to those who doubt the authorship of the Qur'an, Allah Almighty has challenged the most articulate Arabs to produce a whole book, ten chapters or even one solitary chapter which can be remotely comparable to the Qur'an. But to this day, no one has succeeded in meeting the challenge of the Almighty. The critics of the Qur'an have been struck dumb by its ineffable eloquence and surpassing beauty.

"Say, if the whole of mankind and jinns were to gather together to produce the like of this Qur'an, they could not produce the like thereof; even if they backed-up each other with help and support." (17.88)

The Almighty also says:

"Or they may say: 'He forged it.' Say: 'Bring ye then ten chapters forged, like unto it and call (to your aid) whom so ever ye can other than Allah, if ye speak the truth.'" (11.13)

And again:

"Or do they say: 'He forged if? Say: 'Bring then a chapter like! Unto it and call (to your aid) anyone ye can besides Allah, if it be ye speak the truth.'" (10.38)

● It has been revealed to re-establish the sincere worship of Allah alone, without association of any partners with Him.

"This is a Book with verses basic or fundamental (of established meaning), further explained in detail, from One Who is Wise and Well-Aware. (It teaches) that you should worship none but Allah." (11.1-2).

"And they have been commanded no more than this: to worship Allah, offering Him sincere devotion, being true in faith, to establish regular prayer and to give Zakat, and that is the religion Right and Straight." (98.5)

● It contains a complete code which provides for all areas of life, whether spiritual, intellectual, political, social or economic. It is a code which has no boundaries of time, place or nation:

"Verity this Qur'an doth guide to that which is most right." (17.9)

● Allah Almighty has taken upon Himself the duty of preserving the Qur'an for ever in its entirety, as He says:

"We have without doubt sent down the Message, and We will assuredly guard it (from corruption)." (15.9)

So well has it been preserved, both in memory and in writing, that the Arabic text we have today is identical to the text as it was revealed to the Prophet. Not even a single letter has yielded to corruption during the passage of the centuries. And so it will remain for ever, by the consent of Allah. In the Name of Allah, the Most Compassionate, the Most Merciful.

WAY TO THE QUR'AN

The Qur'an is the word of the Ever-living God; it has been sent down to guide man for all times to come. No book can be like it. As you come to the Qur'an, Allah speaks to you. To read the Qur'an is to hear Him, even to converse with Him, and to walk in His ways. It is the encounter of life with the Life-giver. 'God - there is no god but He, the Ever-living, the Self-subsisting (by whom all subsist). He has sent down upon you the Book with the Truth..... as a guidance unto mankind.....' (Al Imran 3: 2-3).

For those who heard it for the first time from the lips of the Prophet, blessings and peace be on him, the Qur'an was a living reality. They had absolutely no doubt that, through him, Allah was speaking to them. Their hearts and minds were therefore seized by it. Their eyes overflowed with tears and their bodies shivered. They found each word of it deeply relevant to their concerns and experiences, and integrated it fully into their lives. They were completely transformed by it both as individuals and as a corporate body - into a totally new, alive and life-giving entity. Those who grazed sheep, herded camels and traded petty merchandise became the leaders of mankind.

Today we have the same Qur'an with us. Millions of copies of it are in circulation. Day and night, it is ceaselessly recited. In homes, in mosques, and from pulpits. Voluminous exegetical works exist expounding its meaning. Words pour out incessantly to explain its teachings and to exhort us to live by it. Yet eyes remain dry, hearts remain unmoved, minds remain untouched, lives remain unchanged. Ignominy and degradation appear to have become the lot of the followers of the Qur'an. Why? Because we no longer read the Qur'an as a living reality. It is a sacred book, but it tells us something of the past only, concerning Muslims and Kaafirs, Jews and Christians, the faithful and the hypocrites, who 'once upon a time used to be'.

Can the Qur'an, again, be a living, relevant force, as powerful for us now, 1400 years away, as it was then? This is the most crucial question that we must answer if we wish to shape our destiny afresh under the guidance of the Qur'an.

There appear, however, to be some difficulties. Not least of which has to do with the fact that the Qur'an was revealed at a certain point in time. Since then we have travelled a long way, made gigantic leaps in technological know-how, and seen considerable social changes take place in human society. Moreover, most of the followers of the irfaan today do not know Arabic, and many who do have a little idea of the 'living' language of the Qur'an. They cannot be expected to absorb its idiom and metaphor, so essential to exploring and absorbing the depths of the Qur'anic meaning.

Yet its guidance, by its own claim, has an eternal relevance for all people, being the word of the Eternal God.

For the truth of this claim, it seems to me, it must be possible for us to receive, experience, and understand the Qur'an as its first recipients did, at least in some measure and to some degree. We seem to almost have a right to this possibility of receiving God's guidance in its fullness and with all its riches and joys. In other words, despite the historical incidence of the revelation in a particular language at a particular time and place, we should be capable of receiving the Qur'an now (because its message is eternal), capable of making its message as much a real part of our lives as it was for the first believers and with the same urgent and profound relevance for all our present concerns and experiences.

But how do we do this? To put it very forthrightly, only by entering the world of the Qur'an as if Allah were speaking to us through it now and today, and by fulfilling the necessary conditions for such an encounter.

Firstly, then, we must realize what the Qur'an as the word of God is and means to us, and bring all the reverence, love, longing, and will to act that this realization demands. Secondly, we must read it as it asks to be read, as Allah's Messenger instructed us, as he and his Companions read it. Thirdly, we must bring each word of the Qur'an to bear upon our own realities and concerns by transcending the barriers of time, culture and change.

For its first addressees, the Qur'an was a contemporary event. Its language and style, its eloquence and rationale, its idiom and metaphor, its symbols and parables, its moments and events were all rooted in their own setting. These people were both witnesses to and, in a sense, participants in the whole act of revelation as it unfolded over a period of their own time. We do not have the same privilege; yet, in some measure, the same ought to be true for us.

By understanding and obeying the Qur'an in our own setting, we will find it, as far as possible, as much a contemporary event for ourselves as it was then. For the essence of man has not changed, it is immutable. Only man's externalities the forms, the modes, the technologies - have changed. The pagans of Mecca may be no more, nor the Jews of Yathrib, nor the Christians of Najran, nor even the 'faithful' and the 'unfaithful' of the community at Medina; but the same characters exist all around us. We are human beings exactly as the first recipients were, even though many find it extremely difficult to grapple with the deep implications of this very simple truth. Once you realize these truths and follow them, once you come to the Qur'an as the first believers did, it may reveal to you as it did to them, make partners of you as it did of them. And only then, instead of being a mere revered book, a sacred fossil, or a source of magic-like blessing, it will change into a mighty force, impinging, stirring, moving and guiding us to deeper and higher achievements, just as it did before.

The New World that Awaits

As you come to the Qur'an, you come to a new world. No other venture in your life can be so momentous and crucial, so blissful and rewarding, as your journey to and through the Qur'an.

It is a journey that will take you through the endless joys and riches of the words that your Creator and Lord has sent to you and all mankind. Here you will find a world of untold treasures of knowledge and wisdom to guide you on the pathways of life, to mould your thoughts and actions. In it you will find deep insights to enrich you and guide you along the right course. From it you will receive a radiant light to illuminate the deeper reaches of your soul. Here you will encounter profound emotions, a warmth to melt your heart and bring tears running down your cheeks.

It is crucial for you because, as you travel through the Qur'an, at every step you will be summoned to choose, and to commit to Allah. To read the Qur'an is nothing less than to live the Qur'an willingly, sincerely, devotedly, and totally. The outcome of your entire life depends on how you heed the call given by God. The journey is therefore decisive for your existence, for mankind, for the future of human civilization.

A hundred new worlds lie in its verses.
Whole centuries are involved in its moments.

Know, then, that it is the Qur'an, and only the Qur'an, which can lead you on and on to success and glory in this world and in the world-to-come.

What is the Qur'an?

It is beyond man's power to comprehend, or to describe, the greatness and importance of what the Qur'an holds for him. Yet, to begin with, you must have some idea of what it is and what it means to you, such that you are inspired to immerse the whole of your self in the Qur'an, in total commitment, complete dedication and ceaseless pursuit, as it demands.

The Qur'an is Allah's greatest blessing for you. It is the fulfilment of His promise to Adam and his descendants:

"There shall come to you guidance from Me, and whosoever follows My guidance no fear shall be on them, neither shall they sorrow" (al-Baqarah 2: 38).

It is the only weapon to help your frail existence as you struggle against the forces of evil and temptation in this-world. It is the only means to overpower your fear and anxiety. It is the only 'light' (nur), as you grope in the darkness, with which to find your way to success and salvation. It is the only healing (shifaa) for your inner sicknesses, as well as the social ills that may surround you. It is the constant reminder (dhikr) of your true nature and destiny, of your station, your duties, your rewards, your perils.

It was brought down by one who is powerful and trustworthy in the heavens - the angel Jibra'il. Its first abode was that pure and sublime heart, the like of which man has never had - the heart of the Prophet Muhammad, peace be on him.

More than anything, it is the only way to come nearer and closer to your Creator. It tells you of Him, of His attributes, of how He rules over the cosmos and history, of how He relates

Himself to you, and how you should relate to Him, to yourself, to your fellow men and to-every other existence.

·The rewards that await you here are surely many, increasing manifold in the Hereafter, but what awaits you at the end of the road, promises Allah in the Hadith quds, 'the eye has seen not, nor the ear heard, nor the heart of man ever conceived', and, adds Abu Hurayrah: read if you wish [in al-Sajdah 32: 17]: 'No human being can imagine what joys are being kept hidden for them in reward for all that they did' (Bukhari, Muslim).

Most important to remember is that what you read in the Qur'an is the word of Allah, the Lord of the worlds, which He has conveyed to you in a human language, only because of His mercy and care and providence for you. The Most-merciful, He has taught the Qur'an' (al-Rahman 55: 1-2). 'A mercy from your Lord' (al-Dukhan 44: 6). The majesty of the Qur'an, too, is so overpowering that no human being can comprehend it. So much so that, says Allah: If We had sent down this Qur'an upon a mountain, you would have seen it humbled, split asunder out of the fear of Allah' (al-Hashr 59: 20).

This act of Divine mercy and majesty is enough to awe and overwhelm you, to inspire you to ever-greater heights of gratitude, yearning and endeavour to enter the world of the Qur'an. Indeed, no treasure is more valuable and precious for you than the Qur'an, as Allah says of His generosity:

O men! There has come to you an exhortation from your Lord, healing for what is in the hearts, and a guidance, and a mercy for believers. Say: In [this] bounty of Allah, and in His mercy - in it let them rejoice. It is better than whatever they amass (Yunus 10:574).

Hazards and Perils

Rejoice you must, in the mercy and blessing and generosity of Allah. Seek you must, for the treasures that await your search herein. But the Qur'an opens its doors only to those who knock with a sense of yearning, a sincerity of purpose and an exclusive attention that befit its importance and majesty. And only those are allowed to gather its treasures, while they walk through it, who are prepared to abandon themselves completely to its guidance and do their utmost to absorb it.

It may quite possibly happen therefore that you may read the Qur'an endlessly, turn its pages laboriously, recite its words beautifully, study it most scholarly, and still fail to make an encounter with it that enriches and transforms your whole person. For, all those who read the Qur'an do not profit from it as they should. Some remain unblessed; some are even cursed.

The journey has its own hazards, as it must, just as it has its own precious and limitless rewards. Many never turn to it, though the Book always lies near at hand, and many are turned away from its gates. Many read it often, but come back empty-handed; while many others who read it never really enter its world. Some do not find, but are lost. They fail to hear God even among His own words; instead, they hear their own voices or those other than God's. Still others, though they hear God, fail to find inside themselves the will, the resolve and the courage to respond and live by His call. Some lose even what they had and, instead of collecting priceless gems, they return with back-breaking loads of stones which will hurt them for ever and ever.

What a tragic misfortune it would be if you came to the Qur'an and went away empty-handed - soul untouched, heart unmoved, life unchanged; 'they went out as they came in'. The Qur'an's blessings are limitless, but the measure of your taking from it depends entirely upon the capacity and the suitability of the receptacle you bring to it. So, at the very outset, make yourself more deeply aware of what the Qur'an means to you and what it demands of you; and make a solemn determination to recite the Qur'an in an appropriate manner, so that you may be counted among 'Those whom We have given the Book, they recite it as it ought to be recited; it is they who believe in it' (al-Baqarah 2: 121).

Tilawah

Tilawah is the word that the Qur'an uses to describe the act of its reading. No single word in English can convey its full meaning. 'To follow' is closest to its primary meaning. To read is only secondary, for in reading too, words follow each other, one closely behind the other, in an orderly and meaningful sequence. If one word does not follow the other, or if the sequence and order is not observed, the meaning is destroyed.

So, primarily, tilawah means, move closely behind, to go forward, to flow in a sequence, to go in pursuit, to take as a guide, leader, master, a model, to accept the authority, to espouse the cause, to act upon, walk after, practise a way of life, to understand, to follow the train of thought - or to follow. Reading the Qur'an, understanding the Qur'an, following the Qur'an - that is how those who have any right to claim faith in it relate themselves to it.

Tilawah or recitation is an act in which your whole person, soul, heart, mind, tongue and body participates. In short your whole existence becomes involved. In reading the Qur'an, mind and body, reason and feeling lose their distinction; they become fused. As the tongue recites and words flow from the lips, the mind ponders, the heart reflects, the soul absorbs, tears well up in the eyes, the heart quakes and trembles, the skin shivers and softens just as the heart does, there no longer remains any duality between the two, even your hair may stand on end. And 'so he walks in a light from his Lord... that is God's guidance, whereby He guides whomsoever He will' (al-Zumar 39: 22-3).

To read the Qur'an thus, as it deserves to be read, is not a light task; but nor is it too difficult or impossible. Otherwise the Qur'an could not have been meant for laymen like us, nor could it be the mercy and the guidance that it surely is. But obviously it does entail much travail of heart and mind, soul and intellect, spirit and body, and requires that certain conditions be observed and obligations be fulfilled - some inwardly, some outwardly. You should know them all, now, and endeavour to observe them before you enter the glorious world of the Qur'an.

Only then will you reap the full harvest of blessings that await you in the Qur'an. Only then will the Qur'an open its doors to you. Only then will it let you dwell inside it and dwell inside you. Nine months spent in the womb of your mother have transformed a drop of water into 'you' - hearing, seeing and thinking. Can you imagine what a lifetime spent with the Qur'an - seeking, hearing, seeing, thinking, striving - can do for you? It can make you into an entirely new 'being' - before whom even angels will feel proud to kneel.

Ascending at every step taken within the Qur'an and every moment spent therein, you will reach towering heights. You will be gripped by the power and beauty that breathe and move within the Qur'an.

From Abdullah Ibn 'Amr Ibn al-'As: The Prophet, Allah's blessings and peace be on him, said, 'The companion of the Qur'an will be told: recite and ascend, ascend with facility as you used to recite with facility in the world. Your final abode is the height you reach at the last verse you recite' (Abd Da'ud, Tirmidhi, Ahmad, Nasa'i).

In the Name of Allah, the Most Compassionate, the Most Merciful.

WHO WROTE THE HOLY QUR'AN

Qur'an, in Arabic, could only have been written by ONE of 3 possible sources:

1. The Arabs
2. Mohammad (peace be upon him)
3. Allah (GOD)

Besides the above mentioned sources, Qur'an couldn't possibly have been written by ANYONE else.

(NOTE: The first part is not meant to be a rigorous proof, it is something to ponder upon. However, the second part, about Mohammad [pbuh] wrote it contains more extensive proof.)

No other source is possible, because Qur'an is written in pure, rich, and poetic Arabic, which was not known to anyone other than the above mentioned sources, at that time. The Arabic language was at its peak in expression, richness, vocabulary, artistic, and poetic value during the time the Qur'an was being revealed. Anyone speaking the classical Arabic (the Arabic of Qur'an at the time it was revealed) would argue that a non-Arab entity couldn't possibly have written such an extensive and brilliant piece of literature in the Arabic language. Qur'an could only have been written by an Arabic speaking entity. An entity, who's knowledge, style, vocabulary, grammar, and way of expression was so powerful that it impacted the entire Arabian peninsula, the east, the west, and continues to impact people all over the globe today! At no other time, in the history of Arabic language, had it ever achieved its peak in expression, literature, and development, than the time of Arabia during the 6th Century, the time when Qur'an was being revealed.

At no other time in the history of Arabic language had the language ever achieved its highest potential than the time of Arabia during the 6th Century, the time when Qur'an was being revealed. The language reached its peak in richness, artistic value, and poetry, during that time. With the Arabic language at its peak, and the best of Arabic writers, poets present in Arabia, it is impossible that a non-Arabic speaking entity would write a book like Qur'an and have such a dynamite impact on the Arabs!

So only an Arabic speaking entity could have write Qur'an. With that in mind, we're left with three choices:

1.   The Arabs wrote it.
2.   Mohammad (peace be upon him) wrote it.
3.   Allah (GOD) wrote it.

Let us examine the three choices one by one:

(1)   Arabs wrote it ? ─────────

What Qur'an teaches goes DIRECTLY against the pagan Arab culture, religion, and gods, that existed before the Qur'an was revealed. Qur'an condemns idol worshipping, but the Arabs, loved their idol gods, and worshipped them regularly. Qur'an raised the status of women; the Arabs treated women next to animals. The Arabs would never write something that goes against their most important belief of idol worshipping. Qur'an goes against most of the social habits (such as backbiting, slandering, name calling, etc.) which the Arabs were heavily indulged into. For example, the Arabs would call insulting nicknames such as Abu Jahal (the father of ignorance). Qur'an condemns and prohibits taking interest on money, whereas, the Arabs freely levied heavy interest rates in loans and businesses. Qur'an condemns and prohibits alcohol drinking, whereas, the Arabs consumed alcohol freely. The Qur'an condemns and prohibits gambling, whereas, the Arabs were some of the worst gamblers. The Arabs would never write something so comprehensively against just about all of their customs and culture and religious beliefs, as the Qur'an is.

During the time of the Holy Prophet (pbuh), the Arabs would indulge in all the social habits that the Qur'an condemns and prohibits. How can Arabs then write something that would negate their entire society's norms and ideologies ?

Did a group of Arabs or an individual Arab write Qur'an? Perhaps a rebel Arab beduoin, or a society's misfit, or someone with different ideals and norms decided one day to write Qur'an? The answer to these questions is also 'no'. Because, if we read Qur'an, we notice that there is no author! No individual has his/tier name written on the cover of Qur'an! Anytime an individual writes a book, he/she writes his/her name on the cover. The author's name always appears on his/her book, and there is always an author who is credited for writing that book. No one in the history of the world has EVER claimed to have written the Qur'an, nor anyone's name ever appeared in front of the Qur'an as being the 'author'. This is the only book in the world without an author. No one in the world has ever been accused of writing the Holy Qur'an, except the Prophet Mohammad (peace be upon him), by non-Muslims.

Qur'an has no author, and no group or individual in Arabia ever claimed to have written it, nor any group or an individual recited, taught, and explained Qur'an except the Prophet Mohammad (pbuh) and his followers. The Prophet Mohammad (peace be upon him) was the only Arabian who first practiced, explained, and preached Qur'an, and ended up making a lot of Arab tribes his enemies. Any historian, Muslim or non-Muslim would argue that the only possible source of Qur'an can be the Prophet Mohammad (pbuh), the man responsible to recite it, teach it, and explain it to the people of Arabia. In fact, many historians today still think that only Mohammad (pbuh) could possibly have written it. This leads one to conclude that the Prophet (pbuh) must have written it!

(2) Mohammad (pbuh) wrote it ? ──────────

First, he was illiterate!! How can an illiterate person come up with such a rich, poetic, intellectual, and inspiring text that it rocked the entire Arabia?

Mohammad (pbuh) never went to school ! No one taught him. He had no teacher of any kind in any subjects. How can he have the knowledge of all the science, astronomy, oceanography, etc. that is contained in the Qur'an ? (For example, the mention of ocean currents, stars, earth, moon, sun and their fixed paths in Soorah Rahman; and many other scientific statements that are found in Qur'an, that I cannot state in this short article) When the Qur'an was revealed, the Arabic language was at its peak in richness, poetic value, literature, etc. The Qur'an came and challenged the best literature in Arabic, the best poetry in Arabic of the time. Mohammad (pbuh) being illiterate could not possibly have come up with something so immaculate that it even exceeded the best of poetry, and literature in Arabic at the time of the language's PEAK of development. Arabic language had never been so rich in expression, poetic value, vocabulary, and variety in literature, as it was in the time of the writing of the Qur'an. At a time like this, the Qur'an came and exceeded the best of Arabic in all aspects of the language: poetry, literature, expression, etc. Any classical Arabic speaker would appreciate the unbeaten, unchallenged, and unmatched beauty of the language of the Qur'an.

An illiterate man is simply not capable of writing such a book.

Mohammad (pbuh) had no reason to come up with something like the Qur'an and cause the entire society of Arabia to become his enemy. Why would he do something like that? Why would he write something going against almost all of the norms of the society, and lose his family, relatives, friends, and other loved ones, and not to mention all the wealth he lost ?

The Qur'an was revealed over a period of 23 years! A very long time! Is it possible for someone to maintain the same exact style of Arabic speech, as demonstrated in the Qur'an, for over 23 years?

Also, what the Prophet Mohammad (saaw) used to say is recorded in what we call his hadeeth (sunnah). If we look at the Arabic style of the hadeeth, and compare it with the style of Qur'an, we can clearly see that they are clearly DIFFERENT, and DISTINGUISHABLE Arabic styles. The prophet (saaw) spoke in public. It does not make sense that a man has two UNIQUE, Distinguishable, and completely different styles of speech in public. Yet another reason why Mohammad (saaw) couldn't possibly have written the Qur'an.

Here's what our famous Muslim Scholar, Ahmad Deedat said in an article under the heading. Was the Qur'an written or inspired:

"Behold! The angels said: "0 Mary! O God has chosen you and purified you - Chosen you above the women of all nations." Qur'an-3:42

"Chosen you above the women of all nations." Such an honour is not to be found given to Mary even in the Christian Bible!

Knowing full-well, and believing as we do, that the whole Qur'an is the veritable Word of God, we will nevertheless agree, for the sake of argument, with the enemies of Muhammed (pbuh) for a moment, that he wrote it. We can now expect some cooperation from the unbeliever.

Ask him, "Have you any qualms in agreeing that Muhammed (pbuh) was an Arab?" Only an opinionated fool will hesitate to agree. In that case there is no sense in pursuing any discussion. Cut short the talk. Close the book! With the man of reason, we proceed. "That this Arab, in the first instance, was addressing other Arabs. He was not talking to Indian Muslims, Chinese Muslims, or Nigerian Muslims. He was addressing his own people —the Arabs. Whether they agreed with him or not, he told them in the most sublime form - words that were seared into the hearts and minds of his listeners that Mary the mother of Jesus—A JEWESS—was chosen above the women of all nations. Not his own mother, nor his wife nor his daughter, nor any other Arab woman, but a Jewess! Can one explain this? Because to everyone his own mother or wife, or daughter would come before other women.

Why would the Prophet of Islam honour a woman from his opposition! and a jewess at that! belonging to a race which had been looking down upon his people for three thousand years? Just as they still look down upon their Arab brethren today.

SARAH AND HAGAR: The Jews get their cock-eyed racism from their Holy Book, where they are told their father, Abraham, had two wives—Sarah and Hagar. They say that they are the children of Abraham through Sarah, his legitimate wife; that their Arab brethren have descended through Hagar, a "bondswoman", and that as such, the Arabs are inferior breed.

Will anyone please explain the anomaly as to why Muhammed (pbuh) (if he is the author) chose this Jewess for such honour? The

answer is simple - HE HAD NO CHOICE - he had no right to
speak of his own desire. "IT IS NO LESS THAN AN
INSPIRATION SENT DOWN TO HIM." (Qur'an, 53:4).

SURA MARYAM: There is a Chapter in the Holy Qur'an,
named Sura Maryam "Chapter Mary" (XIX) named in honour
of Mary, the mother of Jesus Christ (pbuh); again, such an honour
is not to be found given to Mary in the Christian Bible. Out of
the 66 books of the Protestants and 73 of the Roman Catholics,
not one is named after Mary or her son. You will find books
named after Matthew, Mark, Luke, John, Peter, Paul and two
score more obscure names, but not a single one is that of Jesus
or Mary!

If Muhammad (pbuh) was the author of the Holy Qur'an,
then he would not have failed to include in it with MARYAM,
the mother of Jesus, his own mother - AMINA, his dear wife -
KHADIJA, or his beloved daughter - FATIMA. But No! No! this
can never be. The Qur'an is not his handiwork!

Another Muslim writes:

I was reading about the charge that the prophet, Mohammed
(pbuh), has written the Qur'an himself. Before you go any further
in reading this post, please ask yourself whether you are an honest
truth seeker or just another argumentative person, if the former,
continue, otherwise, save your time and jump to the next post.

Islam is based on faith that is supported by a number of
strong miracles such as knowing what events to take place ahead
of time or coming up with supernatural deeds in front of people.
The holy Qur'an has these signs and much more. First, The holy
Qur'an predicted many events to take place ahead of the time
of the revelation of that verse; for example, predicting the destruction
of Persian empire at a time where the later had a monumental
victory over Rome. If the prophet, as some people claim, has
written the Qur'an, then he would have put his future in real
jeopardy (50% chance) since neither satellite photos nor on-ground
intelligence personnel were available to him at the revelation time.
Further, numerous details about many natural phenomena were
detailed in the Qur'an and, until recently, they were proven by
experts to be amazingly accurate. For example of the physical
development of the fetus inside the womb along with timing given

by many verses matches exactly what leading authorities in Embryology are claiming to be recent discoveries. Moreover, verses that gives descriptions about the creation of the universe and the function of mountains in balancing earth and many other descriptions/explanations arc available to be read and to be understood. If the prophet was the author, wouldn't he be prone to make weak inferences similar to those who claim that earth is square and whoever says otherwise should be killed ?

The prophet also has demonstrated many supernatural miracles not by his own power, but by the power of the creator. He went to Jerusalem back in one night and gave a detailed description of the carnival that was travelling on that route and also specific accident happened to them at that night (in those days, it takes a month or so for a round-trip). In another occasion, he provided water for an entire army from a small plate between his hands. There are many other miracles that require serious truth seeker to read about and to think about it.

From the above, it reasonable to conclude that the Qur'an is not the PROPHET CREATION. HE HAD NO WAY TO PREDICT ALL THESE EVENTS AND TO BE RIGHT ALL THE TIME, ESPECIALLY WHEN KNOWING THAT THE PROPHET HIMSELF WAS ILLITERATE !!!

Embryology and Life Sciences in Qur'an.

"The Developing Human. Clinically Oriented Embryology" K.L. Moore.

The work by Prof. Keith Moore is probably the most detailed study of the subject. Prof. Keith Moore is Professor and Chairman of the Department of Anatomy, University of Toronto.

His books on anatomy and on embryology are used at many medical school as standard instruction books. The Yale Medical school uses both his books. The Yale Bookstore phone number for Medical books is: (203) 772-2081. Their general information number is (203) 432-4771. (New Haven, Connecticut).

He is *the* authority on embryology. I strongly recommend the latest edition of the latter book as it mentions how accurately the Qur'an describes embryo development. Prof. Moore has said:

"It has been a great pleasure for me to help clarify statements in the Qur'an about human development. It is clear to me that these statements must have come to Muhammed from God or Allah because almost all of this knowledge was not discovered until many centuries later. This proves to me that Mohammed must have been a messenger of God or Allah."

Prof. Marshal Johnson, Professor and Chairman of the Department of Anatomy and Director of the Daniel Baugh Institute, Thomas Jefferson University, Philadelphia. He says:

"The Qur'an describes not only the development of external form but emphasizes also the internal stages – the stages inside the embryo of its creation and development, emphasizing major events recognized by contemporary science.... If I were to transpose myself into that era, knowing what I know today and describing things, I could not describe the things that were described. I see no evidence to refute the concept that this individual Mohammed had to be developing this information from some place, so I see nothing in conflict with the concept that Divine Intervention was involved...."

That leaves us to our third option: **God wrote it** ! May Allah Guide Us All to Straight Path. Ameen.

Qur'an: Chapter 4, Verse 82:

"Do they not consider (ponder) on the Qur'an ? If it had been from anyone except Allah, they would surely have found in it much discrepancy (contradictions)."

Still unsure or doubtful ? Qur'an is the word of Allah. Allah challenges to His creations: Chapter 2, Verses 23 & 24.

2: 23. "And if you are in doubt as to what We have revealed to our servant. Then produce a Chapter like thereunto; And call your witnesses or helpers besides Allah, If you are true."

2: 24. "But if you cannot, and surely you cannot. Then fear the fire Whose fuel is men and stones. Which is prepared for those who reject."

In the Name of Allah, the Most Compassionate, the Most Merciful.

THE COLLECTION OF THE QUR'AN

The manner in which the Qur'an was collected is among the issues that have been used by those who maintain the belief in tahrif (alteration) to prove that there has been tahrif [in the sense of the corruption of the text] as well as taghyir (change) in the Qur'an, and that the very manner of the Qur'an's collection would, in the normal course of events, involve this corruption and change in it. Hence, it is imperative that the discussion should be undertaken in order to complete the treatment of the subject regarding the protection of the Qur'an from corruption and its freedom from omission or any alteration.

The source of this error [about tahrif] is the claim that the Qur'an was collected under Abu Bakr's order, following the slaying of seventy reciters of the Qur'an at the battle of Bi'r Mauna, and of four hundred persons at the battle of Yamama. Fearing that the Qur'an would be lost and would disappear from the people, 'Umar and Zayd b. Thabit undertook to collect it from fragments written on palm branches, flat stones, and pieces of wood, and from the breasts of the people [who had memorized it], provided that two witnesses would testify that what they [reported] was part of the Qur'an. All this has been suggested in a number of accounts. Ordinarily, it is expected that some of it would be lost to those who assumed the responsibility for this task, except if they were infallible [and divinely protected from forgetting]. This can be witnessed among those who undertake to collect the poetry of one or more poets, when this poetry is scattered, 'this rule is inevitable and arises from habit. The least that we can expect is that alteration has occurred, for it is possible to fail in the effort to find two witnesses on some [revelation] that was heard from the Prophet (peace be upon him and his progeny). Hence, there can be no certainty that omission did not occur.

CHAPTER 16

CHRONOLOGY

6TH CENTURY (500-599) C.E.

545 : Birth of Abdullah, the Holy Prophet's father.

571 : Birth of the Holy Prophet. Year of the Elephant. Invasion of Makkah by Abraha the Viceroy of Yemen, his retreat.

577 : The Holy Prophet visits Madina with his mother. Death of his mother.

580 : Death of Abdul Muttalib, the grandfather of the Holy Prophet.

583 : The Holy Prophet's journey to Syria in the company of his uncle Abu Talib. His meeting with the monk Bahiraat Bisra who foretells of his prophethood.

586 : The Holy Prophet participates in the war of Fijar.

591 : The Holy Prophet becomes an active member of "Hilful Fudul", a league for the relief of the distressed.

594 : The Holy Prophet becomes the Manager of the business of Lady Khadija, and leads her trade caravan to Syria and back.

595 : The Holy Prophet marries Hadrat Khadija. Seventh century

7TH CENTURY (600-699) C.E.

605 : The Holy Prophet arbitrates in a dispute among the Quraish about the placing of the Black Stone in the Kaaba.

610   :   The first revelation in the cave at Mt. Hira. The Holy
            Prophet is commissioned as the Messenger of God.

613   :   Declaration at Mt. Sara inviting the general public to
            Islam.

614   :   Invitation to the Hashimites to accept Islam.

615   :   Persecution of the Muslims by the Quraish. A party of
            Muslims leaves for Abyssinia.

616   :   Second Hijrah to Abysinnia.

617   :   Social boycott of the Hashimites and the Holy Prophet
            by the Quraish. The Hashimites are shut up in a glen
            outside Makkah.

619   :   Lifting of the boycott. Deaths of Abu Talib and Hadrat
            Khadija. Year of sorrow.

620   :   Journey to Taif. Ascension to the heavens.

621   :   Second pledge at Aqaba. The Holy Prophet and the
            Muslims migrate to Yathrib.

623   :   Nakhla expedition.

624   :   Battle of Badr. Expulsion of the Bani Qainuqa Jews
            from Madina.

625   :   Battle of Uhud. Massacre of 70 Muslims at Bir Mauna.
            Expulsion of Banu Nadir Jews from Madina. Second
            expedition of Badr.

626   :   Expedition of Banu Mustaliq.

627   :   Battle of the Trench. Expulsion of Banu Quraiza Jews.

628   :   Truce of Hudaibiya. Expedition to Khyber. The Holy
            Prophet addresses letters to various heads of states.

629   :   The Holy Prophet performs the pilgrimage at Makkah.
            Expedition to Muta (Romans).

630   :   Conquest of Makkah. Battles of Hunsin, Auras, and
            Taif.

631   :   Expedition to Tabuk. Year of Deputations.

632   :   Farewell pilgrimage at Makkah.

632 : Death of the Holy Prophet. Election of Hadrat Abu Bakr as the Caliph. Usamah leads expedition to Syria. Battles of Zu Qissa and Abraq. Battles of Buzakha, Zafar and Naqra. Campaigns against Bani Tamim and Musailima, the Liar.

633 : Campaigns in Bahrain, Oman, Mahrah Yemen, and Hadramaut. Raids in Iraq. Battles of Kazima, Mazar, Walaja, Ulleis, Hirah, Anbar, Ein at tamr, Daumatul Jandal and Firaz.

634 : Battles of Basra, Damascus and Ajnadin. Death of Hadrat Abu Bakr. Hadrat Umar Farooq becomes the Caliph. Battles of Namaraq and Saqatia.

635 : Battle of Bridge. Battle of Buwaib. Conquest of Damascus. Battle of Fahl.

636 : Battle of Yermuk. Battle of Qadsiyia. Conquest of Madain.

637 : Conquest of Syria. Fall of Jerusalem. Battle of Jalula.

638 : Conquest of Jazirah.

639 : Conquest of Khuizistan. Advance into Egypt.

640 : Capture of the post of Caesaria in Syria. Conquest of Shustar and Jande Sabur in Persia. Battle of Babylon in Egypt.

641 : Battle of Nihawand. Conquest of Alexandria in Egypt.

642 : Battle of Rayy in Persia. Conquest of Egypt. Foundation of Fustat.

643 : Conquest of Azarbaijan and Tabaristan (Russia).

644 : Conquest of Fars, Kerman, Sistan, Mekran and Kharan. Martyrdom of Hadrat Umar. Hadrat Othman becomes the Caliph.

645 : Campaigns in Fats.

646 : Campaigns in Khurasan, Armeain and Asia Minor.

647 : Campaigns in North Africa. Conquest of the island of Cypress.

648   :   Campaigns against the Byzantines.

651   :   Naval battle of the Masts against the Byzantines.

652   :   Discontentment and disaffection against the rule of Hadrat Othman.

656   :   Martyrdom of Hadrat Othman. Hadrat Ali becomes the Caliph. Battle of the Camel.

657   :   Hadrat Ali shifts the capital from Madina to Kufa. Battle of Siffin. Arbitration proceedings at Daumaut ul Jandal.

658   :   Battle of Nahrawan.

659   :   Conquest of Egypt by Mu'awiyah.

660   :   Hadrat Ali recaptures Hijaz and Yemen from Mu'awiyah. Mu'awiyah declares himself as the Caliph at Damascus.

661   :   Martyrdom of Hadrat Ali. Accession of Hadrat Hasan and his abdication. Mu'awiyah becomes the sole Caliph.

662   :   Khawarij revolts.

666   :   Raid of Sicily.

670   :   Advance in North Africa. Uqba b Nafe founds the town of Qairowan in Tunisia. Conquest of Kabul.

672   :   Capture of the island of Rhodes. Campaigns in Khurasan.

674   :   The Muslims cross the Oxus. Bukhara becomes a vassal state.

677   :   Occupation of Samarkand and Tirmiz. Siege of Constantinople.

680   :   Death of Muawiyah. Accession of Yazid. Tragedy of Kerbala and martyrdom of Hadrat Hussain.

682   :   In North Africa Uqba b Nafe marches to the Atlantic, is ambushed and killed at Biskra. The Muslims evacuate Qairowan and withdraw to Burqa.

683   :   Death of Yazid. Accession of Mu'awiyah II.

684 : Abdullah b Zubair declares himself as the Caliph at 'Makkah. Marwan I becomes the Caliph' at Damascus. Battle of Marj Rahat.

685 : Death of Marwan I. Abdul Malik becomes the Caliph at Damascus. Battle of Ain ul Wada.

686 : Mukhtar declares himself as the Caliph at Kufa.

687 : Battle of Kufa between the forces of Mukhtar and Abdullah b Zubair. Mukhtar killed.

691 : Battle of Deir ul Jaliq. Kufa falls to Abdul Malik.

692 : The fall of Makkah. Death of Abdullah b Zubair. Abdul Malik becomes the sole Caliph.

695 : Khawarij revolts in Jazira and Ahwaz. Battle of the Karun. Campaigns against Kahina in North Africa. The Muslims once again withdraw to Barqa. The Muslims advance in Transoxiana and occupy Kish.

8TH CENTURY (700-799) C.E

700 : Campaigns against the Berbers in North Africa.

702 : Ashath's rebellion in Iraq, battle of Deir ul Jamira.

705 : Death of Abdul Malik. Accession of Walid I as Caliph.

711 : Conquest of Spain, Sind and Transoxiana.

712 : The Muslims advance in Spain, Sind and Transoxiana.

713 : Conquest of Multan.

715 : Death of Walid I. Accession of Sulaiman.

716 : Invasion of Constantinople.

717 : Death of Sulaiman. Accession of Umar b Abdul Aziz.

720 : Death of Umar b Abdul Aziz. Accession of Yazid II,

724 : Death of Yazid II. Accession of Hisham.

725 : The Muslims occupy Nimes in France.

732 : The battle of Tours in France.

737 : The Muslims meet reverse at Avignon in France.

740 : Shia revolt under Zaid b All. Berber revolt in North Africa. Battle of the Nobles.

741 : Battle of Bagdoura in North Africa.

742 : The Muslim rule restored in Qiarowan.

743 : Death of Hisham. Accession of Walid II. Shia revolt in Khurasan under Yahya b Zaid.

744 : Deposition of Walid II. Accession of Yazid III and his death. Accession of Ibrahim and his overthrow. Battle of Ain al Jurr. Accession of Marwan II.

745 : Kufa and Mosul occupied by the Khawarjites.

746 : Battle of Rupar Thutha, Kufa and Mosul occupied by Marwan II.

747 : Revolt of Abu Muslim in Khurasan.

748 : Battle of Rayy.

749 : Battles of Isfahan and Nihawand. Capture of Kufa by the Abbasids. As Saffah becomes the Abbasid Caliph at Kufa.

750 : Battle of Zab, Fall of Damascus. End of the Urnayyads.

751 : Conquest of Wasit by the Abbasid. Murder of the Minister Abu Salama.

754 : Death of As Saffah. Accession of Mansur as the Caliph.

755 : Revolt of Abdullah b All. Murder of Abu Muslim. Sunbadh revolt in Khurasan.

756 : Abdul Rahman founds the Umayyad state in Spain.

762 : Shia revolt under Muhammad (Nafs uz Zakia) and Ibrahim.

763 : Foundation of Baghdad. Defeat of the Abbasids in Spain.

767 : Khariji state set up by lbn Madrar at Sijilmasa. Ustad Sees revolt in Khurasan.

772 : Battle of Janbi in North Africa. Rustamid. State set up in Morocco.

775 : Death or the Abbasid Caliph Mansur, Accession of Mahdi.

777 : Battle of Saragossa in Spain.

785 : Death of the Caliph Mahdi. Accession of Hadi.

786 : Death of Hadi. Accession of Harun ur Rashid.

788 : Idrisid state set up in the Maghrib. Death of Abdul Rahman of Spain, and accession of Hisham.

792 : Invasion of South France.

796 : Death of Hisham in Spain; accession of al Hakarn.

799 : Suppression of the revolt of the Khazars. Ninth century.

9TH CENTURY (800-899) C.E.

800 : The Aghlabid rule is established in North Africa.

803 : Downfall of the Barmakids. Execution of Jafar Barmki.

805 : Campaigns against the Byzantines. Capture of the islands of Rhodes and Cypress.

809 : Death of Harun ur Rashid. Accession of Amin.

814 : Civil war between Amin and Mamun. Amin killed and Mamun becomes the Caliph.

815 : Shia revolt under Ibn Tuba Tabs.

816 : Shia revolt in Makkah; Harsama quells the revolt. In Spain the Umayyads capture the island of Corsica.

817 : Harsama killed.

818 : The Umayyads of Spain capture the islands of Izira, Majorica, and Sardinia.

819 : Mamun comes to Baghdad.

820 : Tahir establishes the rule of the Tahirids in Khurasan.

822 : Death of Al Hakarn in Spain; accession of Abdul Rahman. II.

823 : Death of Tahir in Khurasan. Accession of Talha and his deposition. Accession of Abdullah b Tahir.

827 : Mamun declares the Mutazila creed as the state religion.

833 : Death of Mamun. Accession of Mutasim.

836   :   Mutasim shifts the capital to Samarra.

837   :   Revolt of the Jats.

838   :   Revolt of Babek in Azarbaijan suppressed.

839   :   Revolt of Maziar in Tabaristan. The Muslims occupy South Italy. Capture of the city of Messina in Sicily.

842   :   Death of Mutasim, accession of Wasiq.

843   :   Revolts of the Arabs.

847   :   Death of Wasiq, accession of Mutawakkil.

850   :   Mutawakkil restores orthodoxy.

849   :   Death of the Tahirid ruler Abdullah b Tahir; accession of Tahir II.

852   :   Death of Abdur Rahman II of Spain;, accession of Muhammad I.

856   :   Umar b Abdul Aziz founds the Habbarid rule in Sind.

858   :   Mutawakkil founds the town of Jafariya.

860   :   Ahmad founds the Samanid rule in Transoxiana.

861   :   Murder of the Abbasid Caliph Mutawakkil; accession of Muntasir.

862   :   Muntasir poisoned to death; accession of Mutasin.

864   :   Zaidi state established in Tabaristan by Hasan b Zaid.

866   :   Mutasim flies from Samarra, his deposition and accession of Mutaaz.

867   :   Yaqub b Layth founds the Saffarid rule in Sistan.

868   :   Ahmad b Tulun founds the Tulunid rule in Egypt.

869   :   The Abbasid Caliph Mutaaz forced to abdicate, his death and accession of Muhtadi.

870   :   Turks revolt against Muhtadi, his death and accession of Mutamid.

873   :   Tahirid rule extinguished.

874   :   Zanj revolt in South Iraq. Death of the Samanid ruler Ahmad, accession of Nasr.

877	:	Death of Yaqubb Layth in Sistan, accession of Amr b Layth.
885	:	Death of Ahmad b Tulun in Egypt, accession of Khamar-wiyiah.
866	:	Death of Muhammad I the Umayyad ruler of Spain, accession of Munzir. Death of Abdullah b Umar the Habbari ruler of Sind.
888	:	Death of Munzir the Umayyad ruler of Spain, accession of Abbullah.
891	:	The Qarmatian state established at Bahrain.
892	:	Death of the Samanid ruler Nasr, accession of Ismail.
894	:	The Rustamids become the vassals of Spain.
896	:	Death of the Tulunid ruler Khamarwiyiah; accession of Abul Asakir Jaish.
897	:	Assassination of Abul Asakir Jaish; accession of Abu Musa Harun.
898	:	Qarmatians sack Basra.

10TH CENTURY (900-999) C.E

902	:	Death of the Abbasid Caliph Muktafi; death of the Saffarid ruler Amr.
903	:	Assassination of the Qarmatian ruler Abu Said; accession of Abu Tahir.
905	:	Abdullah b Hamdan founds the Hamdanid rule in Mosul and Jazira. End of the Tulunid rule in Egypt.
907	:	Death of the Abbasid Caliph Muktafi; accession of Muqtadir.
908	:	End of the Saffarid rule, annexation of their territories by the Samanids.
909	:	Ubaidullah overthrows the Aghlablds and founds the Fatimid rule in North Africa.
912	:	Death of the Umayyad Amir Abdullah in Spain, accession of Abdur Rahman III.

913 : Assassination of the Samanid ruler Ahmad II, accession of Nasr II.

928 : Mardawij b Ziyar founds the Ziyarid rule in Tabaristan.

929 : Qarmatians sack Makkah and carry away the Black Stone from the Holy Kaaba. In Spain, Abdur Rahman III declares himself as the Caliph.

931 : Deposition and restoration of the Abbasid Caliph Muqtadir. Death of the Qarmatian ruler Abu Tahir; accession of Abu Mansur.

932 : Death of the Abbasid Caliph Muqtadir; accession of Al Qahir.

934 : Deposition of the Abbasid Caliph Al Qahir; accession of Ar Radi. Death of the Fatimid Caliph Ubaidullah ; accession of Al Qaim.

935 : Assassination of the Ziyarid ruler Mardawij; accession of Washimgir. Death of Hamdanid ruler Abdullah b Hamdan accession of Nasir ud Daula.

936 : By coup Ibn Raiq becomes the Amir ul Umara.

938 : By another coup power at Baghdad is captured by Bajkam.

940 : Death of the Abbasid Caliph Ar Radi, accession of Muttaqi.

941 : Assassination of Bajkam, capture of power by Kurtakin.

942 : Ibn Raiq recaptures power.

943 : Al Baeidi captures power. The Abbasid Caliph Muttaqi is forced to seek refuge with the Hamdanids. Sail ud Daula captures power at Baghdad and the Caliph returns to 'Baghdad. Power is captured by Tuzun and Sail ud Daula retires' to Mosul. Death of the Samanid ruler Nasr II accession of Nuh

944 : Muttaqi is blinded and deposed, accession of Mustakafi.

945 : Death of Tuzun. Shirzad becomes Amir ul Umra. The Buwayhids capture power. Deposition of the Abbasid Caliph Mustakafi.

946 : Death of the Fatimid Caliph Al Qaim, accession of Mansur. Death of the Ikhshid ruler Muhammad b Tughj, accession of Abul Qasim Ungur.

951 : The Qarnaatiana restore the Black Stone to the Holy Kaaba.

954 : Death of the Sasanid ruler Nuh, accession of Abdul Malik.

961 : Death of the Samanid ruler Abdul Malik, accession of Manauf. Alptgin founds the rule of the Ghazanavids. Death of the Umayyad Caliph Abdul Rahman III in Spain; accession of Hakam. Death of the Ikhshid ruler Ungur accession of Abul Hasan Ali.

965 : Death of the Qarmatian ruler Abu Mansur; accession of Hasan Azam. Assassination of the Ikhshid ruler Abul Hasan Ali; power captured by Malik Kafur.

967 : Death of the Buwayhid Sultan Muiz ud Daula, accession of Bakhtiar. Death of the Hamdanid ruler Sail ud Daula.

968 : Byzantines occupy Aleppo. Death of the Ikhshid ruler Malik Kafur; accession of Abul Fawaris.

969 : The Fatimids conquer Egypt.

972 : Buluggin b Ziri founds the rule of the Zirids Algeria.

973 : Shia Sunni disturbances in Baghdad; power captured in Baghdad by the Turkish General Subuktgin.

974 : Abdication of the Abbasid Caliph Al Muttih; accession of At Taii.

975 : Death of the Turk General Subuktgin. Death of the Fatimid Caliph Al Muizz.

976 : The Buwayhid Sultan Izz ud Daula recaptures power with the help of his cousin Azud ud Daula. Death of the Samanid ruler Mansur, accession of Nuh II, in Spain death of the Umayyad Caliph Hakam, accession of Hisham II.

978 : Death of the Buwayhid Sultan Izz ud Daula, power captured by Azud ud Daula. The Hamdanids overthrown by the Buwayhids.

979   :   Subkutgin becomes the Amir of Ghazni.

981   :   End of the Qarmatian rule at Bahrain.

982   :   Death of the Buwayhid Sultan Azud ud Daula; accession of Samsara ud Daula.

984   :   Death of the Zirid ruler Buluggin, accession of Mansur.

986   :   The Buwyhid Sultan Samsara ud Daula overthrown by Sharaf ud Daula.

989   :   Death of the Buwayhid Sultan Sharaf ud Daula, accession of Baha ud Daula.

991   :   Deposition of the Abbasid Caliph At Tail, accession of Al Qadir.

996   :   Death of the Zirid ruler Mansur, accession of Nasir ud Daula Badis.

997   :   Death of the Samanid ruler Nuh II, accession of Mansur II.

998   :   Death of the Samanid ruler Mansur II, accession of Abdul Malik II. Mahmud becomes the Amir of Ghazni.

999   :   End of the Samanids.

11TH CENTURY (1000-1099) C.E.

1001   :   Mahmud Ghazanavi defeats the Hindu Shahis.

1004   :   Mahmud captures Bhatiya.

1005   :   Mahmud captures Multan and Ghur.

1008   :   Mahmud defeats the Rajput confederacy.

1010   :   Abdication of Hisham II in Spain, accession of Muhammad.

1011   :   In Spain Muhammad is overthrown by Sulaiman.

1012   :   In Spain power is captured by Bani Hamud. Death of the Buwayhid Baha ud Daula, accession of Sultan ud Daula.

1016   :   Death of the Zirrid ruler Nasir ud Daula Badis, accession of Al Muizz.

1018 : In Spain power is captured by Abdul Rahman IV.

1019 : Conquest of the Punjab by Mahmud Ghazanavi.

1020 : The Buwayhid Sultan ud Daula is Overthrown by Musharaf ud Daula, Death of the Fatimid Caliph Al Hakim, accession of Al Zahir.

1024 : In Spain assassination of Abdul Rahman IV, accession of Mustafi.

1025 : Death of the Buwayhid Mushgraf ud Daula, accession of Jalal ud Daula.

1029 : In Spain death of Mustafi, accession of Hisham III.

1030 : Death of Mahmud Ghazanavi.

1031 : In Spain deposition of Hisham III, and end of the Umayyad rule. Death of the Abbasid Caliph Al Qadir, accession of Al Qaim.

1036 : Death of the Fatimid Caliph Al Zahir, accession of Mustansir. Tughril Beg is crowned as the king of the Seljuks.

1040 : Battle of Dandanqan, the Seljuks defeat the Ghazanavids. Deposition of Masud the Ghazanavid Sultan, accession of Muhammad. Al Moravids come to power in North Africa.

1041 : The Ghazanavid Sultan Muhammad is overthrown by Maudud.

1044 : Death of the Buwayhid Jalal ud Daula, accession of Abu Kalijar.

1046 : Basasiri captures power in Baghdad.

1047 : The Zirids in North Africa repudiate allegiance to the Fatimid and transfer allegiance to the Abbasids.

1048 : Death of the Buwayhid Abu Kalijar, accession of Malik ur Rahim.

1050 : Yusuf b Tashfin comes to power in the Maghrib.

1055 : Tughril Beg overthrows the Buwayhids.

1057 : Basasiri recaptures power in Baghdad, deposes Al Qaim and offers allegiance to the Fatimid Caliph.

1059 : Tughril Beg recaptures power in Baghdad, al Qaim is restored as the Caliph.

1060 : Ibrahim becomes the Sultan of Ghazni. Yusuf b Tashfin founds the city of Marrakesh. The Zirids abandon their capital Ashir and establish their capital at Bougie.

1062 : Death of the Zirid ruler Al Muizz, accession of Tamin.

1063 : Death of the Seljuk Sultan Tughril Beg, accession of Alp Arsalan.

1071 : Battle of Manzikert, the Byzantine emperor taken captive by the Seljuks.

1073 : Death of Alp Arsalan, accession of Malik Shah.

1077 : Death of the Abbasid Caliph Al Qaim, accession of Al Muqtadi.

1082 : The Al Moravids conquer Algeria.

1086 : Battle of Zallakha. The Al Moravids defeat the Christians in Spain. Death of the Rum Sejuk Sultan Sulaiman, accession of Kilij Arsalan.

1091 : The Normans conquer the island of Sicily; end of the Muslim rule.

1092 : Death of the Seljuk Sultan Malik Shah, accession of Mahmud.

1094 : Death of Mahmud; accession of Barkiaruk. Death of the Abbasid Caliph Al Muqtadi, accession of Mustahzir.

1095 : The first crusade.

1099 : The crusaders capture Jerusalem.

12TH CENTURY (1100-1199) C.E

1101 : Death of the Fatimid Caliph Al Mustaali, accession of Al Aamir.

1105 : Death of the Seljuk Sultan Barkiaruk, accession of Muhammad.

1106 : Death of the Al Motavid Yusuf b Tashfin.

1107 : Death of the Rum Seljuk Sultan Kilij Arsalan, succession of Malik Shah.

1108 : Death of the Zirid ruler Tamin, accession of Yahya.

1116 : Death of the Rum Seljuk Sultan Malik Shah, accession of Rukn ud Din Masud.

1118 : Death of the Seljuk Sultan Muhammad; accession of Mahmud II. Death of the Abbasid Caliph Mustahzir, accession of Mustarshid. In Spain the Christians capture Saragossa.

1121 : Death of the Fatimid Caliph Al Aamir, accession of Al Hafiz.

1127 : Imad ud Din Zangi establishes the Zangi rule In Mosul.

1128 : Death of the Khawarzam Shah Qutb ud Din Muhammad; accession of Atsiz.

1130 : Death of the Seljuk Sultan Mahmud II; accession of Tughril Beg II.

1134 : Assassination of the Abbasid Caliph Mustarshid; accession of Al Rashid. Death of the Seljuk Sultan Tughril Beg II, accession of Masud.

1135 : Deposition of the Abbasid Caliph Al Rashid, accession of Al Muktafi.

1144 : Imad ud Din Zangi captures Edessa from the Christians, second crusade.

1146 : Death of Imad ud Din Zangi, accession of Nur ud Din Zangi.

1147 : In the Maghrib Al Moravids overthrown by the Al Mohads under Abul Mumin.

1148 : End of the Zirid rule in North Africa.

1149 : Death of the Fatimid Caliph Al Hafiz, accession of Al Zafar.

1152 : Death of the Seljuk Sultan Masud, accession of Malik Shah II. Hamadid rule extinguished in North Africa.

1153 : Death of the Seljuk Sultan Malik Shah II, accession of Muhammad II.

1154 : Death of the Fatimid Caliph Al Zafar, accession of Al Faiz.

1156 : Death of the Rum Seljuk Sultan Rukn ud Din Masid, accession of Arsalan II.

1159 : Death of the Seljuk Sultan Muhammad II, accession of Gulaiman.

1160 : Death of the Abbasid Caliph Al Mukta, accession of Al Mustanjid. Death of the Fatimid Caliph Al Faiz, accession of Al Azzid.

1161 : Death of the Seljuk Sulaiman, accession of Arsalan Shah.

1163 : Death of the Al Mohad ruler Abul Mumin, accession of Abu Yaqub Yusuf.

1170 : Death of the Abbasid Caliph Mustanjid, accession of Al Mustazii.

1171 : Death of the Fatimid Caliph Al Azzid. End of the Fatimids. Salah ud Din founds the Ayyubid dynasty in Egypt.

1172 : Death of the Khawarzam Shah Arsalan, accession of Sultan Shah.

1173 : The Khawarzam Shah Sultan Shah is overthrown by Tukush Shah.

1174 : Salah ud Din annexes Syria.

1175 : The Ghurids defeat the Guzz Turks and occupy Ghazni.

1176 : Death of the Seljuk Sultan Arsalan Shah, accession of Tughril Beg III.

1179 : Death of the Abbasid Caliph Al Mustazaii, accession of Al Nasir. Shahab ud Din Ghuri captures Peshawar.

1185 : Death of the Al Mohad ruler Abu Yaqub Yusuf, accession of Abu Yusuf Yaqub.

1186 : The Ghurids overthrow the Ghaznavids in the Punjab.

1187 : Salah ud Din wrests Jerusalem from the Christians, third crusade.

1191 : Battle of Tarain between the Rajputs and the Ghurids.

1193 : Death of Salah ud Din; accession of Al Aziz. Second battle of Tarain.

1194 : Occupation of Delhi by the Muslims. End of the Seljuk rule.

1199 : Death of the Khawarzam Shah Tukush Shah; accession of Ala ud Din. Death of the Al Mohad ruler Abu Yusuf Yaqub; accession of Muhammad Nasir. Conquest of Northern India and Bengal by the Ghurids.

13TH CENTURY (1200-1299) C.E.

1202 : Death of the Ghurid Sultan Ghias ud Din; accession of Mahmud.

1204 : Shahab ud Din Ghuri defeated by the Ghuzz Turks.

1206 : Death of Shahab ud Din Ghuri. Qutb ud Din Aibik crowned king in Lahore.

1210 : Assassination of the Ghurid Sultan Mahmud, accession of Sam. Death of Qutb ud Din Aibak, accession of Aram Shah in India.

1211 : End of the Ghurid rule, their territories annexed by the Khawarzam Shahs. In India Aram Shah overthrown by Iltutmish.

1212 : Battle of Al Uqab in Spain, end of the Al Mohad rule in Spain. The Al Mohads suffer defeat by the Christians in Spain at the Al-Uqba. The Al Mohad Sultan An Nasir escapes to Morocco where he dies soon after. Accession of his son Yusuf who takes over title of Al Mustansir.

1214 : In North Africa death of the Al Mohad ruler Al Nasir, accession of Al Mustansir. The Banu Marin under their leader Abdul Haq occupy the north eastern part of Morocco.

1216 : The Banu Marin under their leader Abdul Haq occupy north eastern part of Morocco. The Al Mohads suffer defeat by the Marinids at the battle of Nakur. The Banu Marin defeat the Al Mobads at the battle of Nakur.

1217 : The Marinids suffer defeat in the battle fought on the banks of the Sibu river. Abdul Haq is killed and the Marinids evacuate Morocco. In the battle of Sibu the Marinids suffer defeat; their leader Abdul Haq is killed and they evacuate Morocco.

1218 : Death of the Ayyubid ruler Al Adil, accession of Al
          Kamil. The Marinids return to Morocco under their
          leader Othman and occupy Fez.

1220 : Death of the Khawarzam Shah Ala ud Din, accession
          of Jalal ud Din Mangbarni.

1222 : Death of the Zangi ruler Nasir ud Din Mahmud, power
          captured by Badr ud Din Lulu.

1223 : Death of the Al Mohad ruler Muntasir, accession of
          Abdul Wahid. Death of Yusuf Al Mustansir, accession
          of Abdul Wahid in Morocco. In Spain a brother of
          Yusuf declares his independence and assumes the title
          of Al Adil. In Spain Abu Muhammad overthrows Al
          Adil. Al Adil escapes to Morocco and overthrows
          Abdul Wahid.

1224 : Death of the Al Mohad ruler Abdul Wahid, accession
          of Abdullah Adil.

1225 : Death of the Abbasid Caliph Al Nasir, accession of Al
          Mustansir.

1227 : Death of the Al Mohad ruler Abdullah Adil, accession
          of Mustasim. Assassination of Al Adil, accession of his
          son Yahya who assumes the throne under the name of
          Al Mustasim.

1229 : Death of the Al Mohad ruler Mustasim, accession of
          Idris. The Ayyubid Al Kamil restores Jerusalem to the
          Christians. Abu Muhammad dies in Spain and is
          succeeded by Al Mamun. Al Mamun invades Morocco
          with Christian help. Yahya is defeated and power is
          captured by Al Mamun. He denies the Mahdiship of
          Ibn Tumarat.

1230 : End of the Khawarzam Shah rule.

1232 : Death of the Al Mohad ruler Idris, accession, of Abdul
          Wahid II. Assassination of Al Mamun; accession of his
          son Ar-Rashid.

1234 : Death of the Ayyubid ruler Al Kamil, accession of Al
          Adil.

1236 : Death of Delhi Sultan Iltutmish. Accession of Rukn ud Din Feroz Shah.

1237 : Accession of Razia Sultana as Delhi Sultan.

1240 : Death of Ar-Rashid; accession of his son Abu Said.

1241 : Death of Razia Sultana, accession of Bahram Shah.

1242 : Death of Bahram Shah, accession of Ala ud Din Masud Shah as Delhi Sultan. Death of the Al Mohad rules Abdul Wahid, accession of Abu Hasan. Death of the Abbasid Caliph Mustansir, accession of Mustasim.

1244 : The Al Mohads defeat the Marinids at the battle of Abu Bayash. The Marinids evacuate Morocco.

1245 : The Muslims reconquer Jerusalem.

1246 : Death of the Delhi Sultan Ala ud Din Masud Shah, accession of Nasir ud Din Mahmud Shah.

1248 : Death of the Al Mohad ruler Abul Hasan, accession of Omar Murtaza. Abu Said attacks Tlemsen, but is ambushed and killed; accession of his son Murtada.

1250 : The Marinids return to Morocco, and occupy a greater part thereof.

1258 : The Mongols sack Baghdad. Death of the Abbasid Caliph Mustasim. End of the Abbasid rule. Fall of Baghdad, end of the Abbasid caliphate. The Mongol Il-Khans under Halaku establish their rule in Iran and Iraq with the capital at Maragah. Berek Khan the Muslim chief of the Golden Horde protests against the treatment meted out to the Abbasid Caliph and withdraw his Contingent from Baghdad.

1259 : Abu Abdullah the Hafsid ruler declares himself as the Caliph and assumes the name of Al Mustamir.

1260 : Battle of Ayn Jalut in Syria. The Mongols are defeated by the Mamluks of Egypt, and the spell of the invincibility of the Mongols is broken. Baybars becomes the Mamluk Sultan.

1262 : Death of Bahauddin Zikriya in Multan who is credited with the introduction of the Suhrawardi Sufi order in the Indo-Pakistan sub-continent.

1265 : Death of Halaku. Death of Fariduddin Ganj Shakkar the Chishti saint of the Indo-Pakistan sub-continent.

1266 : Death of Berek Khan the first ruler of the Golden Horde to be converted to Islam. The eighth crusade. The crusaders invade Tunisia. Failure of the crusade.

1267 : Malik ul Salih establishes the first Muslim state of Samudra Pasai in Indonesia. Murtada seeks the help of the Christians, and the Spaniards invade Morocco. The Marinids drive away the Spaniards from Morocco. Assassination of Murtada; accession of Abu Dabbas.

1269 : Abu Dabbas is overthrown by the Marinida, End of the Al Mohads. End of the rule of the Al Mohads in Morocco, the Marinids come to power in Morocco under Abu Yaqub.

1272 : Death of Muhammad I the founder of the state of Granada. Yaghmurason invades Morocco but meets a reverse at the battle.

1273 : Death of Alaluddin Rumi.

1274 : Death of Nasiruddin Tusi. The Marinids wrest Sijilmasa from the Zayenids. Ninth crusade under Edward I of England. The crusade ends in fiasco and Edward returns to England.

7277 : Death of Baybars.

1280 : Battle of Hims.

1283 : Death of Yaghmurasan. Accession of his son Othman.

1285 : Tunisis splits in Tunis and Bougie.

1286 : Death of Ghiasuddin Balban. Death of Abu Yusuf Yaqub. Bughra Khan declares his independence in Bengal under the name of Nasiruddin.

1290 : End of the slave dynasty Jalaluddin Khilji comes into power. Othman embarks on a career of conquest and by 1290 C.E. most of the Central Maghreb is conquered by the Zayanids.

1291 : Saadi.

1296 : Alauddin Ghazan converted to Islam.

1299 : Mongols invade Syria. The Marinids besiege Tiemsen the capital of the Zayanids.

14TH CENTURY (1300-1399) C.E.

1301 : In Bengal, Death of Ruknuddin the king of Bengal, succeeded by brother Shamsuddin Firuz.

1302 : In Granada, Death of Muhammad II; succession of Muhammad III.

1304 : In the Mongols II Khans empire. Death of Ghazan, succession of his brother Khudabanda Ul Jaytu. In Algeria, Death of Othman, succession of his son Abu Zayan Muhammad.

1305 : In the Khiljis empire, Alauddin Khilji conquers Rajputana.

1306 : In the Chughills empire. Death of Dava, succession of his son Kunjuk.

1307 : In the Marinids empire. Assassination of the Marinid Sultan Abu Yaqub Yusuf; accession of Abu Thabit

1308 : In the Chughills empire. Deposition of Kunjuk, power captured by Taliku, In Algeria, Death of Abu Zayan Muhammad, succession of his brother Abu Hamuw Musa. In the Marinids empire, Abu Thabit overthrown by Abu Rabeah Sulaiman.

1309 : In the Chughills empire. Assassination of Taliku, accession of Kubak. In Granada, Muhammad III overthrown by his uncle Abul Juyush Nasr.

1310 : In the Chughills empire, Kubak overthrown by his brother Isan Buga. In the Marinids empire, Abu Rabeah Sulaiman overthrown by Abu Said Othman. In the Khiljis empire, Alauddin conquers Deccan.

1312 : In Tunisia, In Tunis Abul Baqa is overthrown by Al Lihiani.

1313 : In the Mongols II Khans empire. Invasion of Syria, the Mongols repulsed. In the Golden Horde empire. Death of Toktu, accession of his nephew Uzbeg.

1314 : In Kashmir, Rainchan an adventurer from Baltistan overthrows Sinha Deva the Raja of Kashmir. Rainchan is converted to Islam and adopts the name of Sadrud Din. In Granada, Abul Juyush overthrown by his nephew Abul Wahid Ismail.

1315 : In Tunisia, War between Bougie and Tunis, Lihani defeated and killed. Abu Bakr becomes the ruler of Bougie and Tunis.

1316 : In the Mongols II Khans empire. Death of Khudabanda Ul Jaytu, succession of Abu Said. In the Khiljis empire. Death of Alauddin, accession of Shahabuddin Umar, usurpation of power by Malik Kafur, a Hindu convert.

1318 : In the Khiljis empire. Assassination of Malik Kafur, deposition of Shahabuddin Umar, accession of Qutbuddin Mubarak. In the Chughills empire, Isan Buga overthrown by Kubak.

1320 : In the Khiljis empire. Assassination of Qutbuddin Mubarak, usurpation of power by Khusro Khan a Hindu convert. Khusro Khan overthrown by Ghazi Malik. End of the rule of Khiljis. In Tunisia, Abu Bakr expelled from Tunis by Abu Imran. In the Tughluqs empire, Ghazi Malik founds the rule of the Tughluq dynasty.

1321 : In the Chughills empire. Death of Kubak, succession of Hebbishsi who is overthrown by Dava Temur.

1322 : In the Chughills empire, Dava Temur overthrown by Tarmashirin, who is converted to Islam. In Bengal, Death of Shamsuddin Firuz. The kingdom divided into two parts. Ghiasuddin Bahadur became the ruler of East Bengal with the capital at Sonargaon, Shahabuddin became the ruler of West Bengal with the capital at Lakhnauti.

1324 : In Bengal, Shahabuddin dies and is succeeded by his brother Nasiruddin.

1325 : In the Tughluqs empire, Death of Ghazi Malik (Ghiasuddin Tughluq); accession of his son Muhammad Tughluq. In Granada, Assassination of Abul Wahid Ismail, succession of his son Muhammad IV. Assassination of Muhammad IV. Accession of his brother Abul Hallaj Yusuf. In the Samudra Pasai empire.

Death of Malik al Tahir I, accession of Malik al Tahir II. In Bengal, with the help of Ghiasuddin Tughluq, Nasiruddin overthrows. Ghiasuddin Bahadur and himself become's the ruler of United Bengal.

1326 : In the Ottoman Turks empire. Death of Othman, succession of Orkhan. Orkhan conquers Bursa and makes it his capital.

1327 : In the Ottoman Turks empire. The Turks capture the city of Nicaea.

1329 : In the Tughluqs empire, Muhammad Tughluq shifts the capital from Delhi to Daulatabad in Deccan.

1330 : In the Chughills empire, Death of Tramashirin, succession of Changshahi. Amir Hussain establishes the rule of the Jalayar dynasty at Baghdad. In Tunisia, Abu Bakr overthrows Abu Imran and the state is again united, under him. In Bengal, Muhammad b Tughluq reverses the policy of his father and restores Ghiasuddin Bahadur to the throne of Sonargeon.

1331 : In the Marinids empire, Death of Abu Said Othman, secession of Abul Hasan. In Bengal, Annexation of Bengal by the Tughluqs.

1335 : In the Mongols II Khans empire. Death of Abu Said, power captured by Arpa Koun. In the Chughills empire. Assassination of Changshahi, accession of Burun.

1336 : In the Mongols II Khans empire, Arpa defeated and killed, succeeded by Musa. Birth of Amir Temur, In the Jalayar empire. Death of Amir Hussain, succession of Hasan Buzurg. In the Ottoman Turks empire. The Turks annex the state of Karasi. In Bengal, The Tughluq Governor at Sonargeon assassinated by armour bearer who captured power and declared his independence assuming the name of Fakhruddin Mubarak Shah.

1337 : In the Mongols II Khans empire. The rule of Musa overthrown, Muhammad becomes the Sultan. In the Sarbadaran empire, on the disintegration of the II-Khan rule, Abdur Razaq a military adventurer establishes an independent principality in Khurasan with the capital at Sabzwar. In the Muzaffarids empire, On the disintegration of the II Khan rule Mubarazud Din Muhammad established the rule of the Muzaffarid dynasty. In the Ottoman Turks empire, The Turks capture the city of Nicomedia. In Algeria, Algeria is occupied by Marinids.

1338 : In the Mongols II Khans empire, Muhammad overthrown, succession of Sati Beg. Sati Beg marries Sulaiman who becomes the co-ruler.

1339 : In Kashmir, Death of Sadrud Din, throne captured by a Hindu Udyana Deva. In the Chughills empire, Deposition of Burun, accession of Isun Temur. In Bengal, The Tughluq Governor at Lakhnauti-Qadr Khan assassinated and power is captured by the army commander-in-chief who declares his independence and assumes the title of Alauddin Ali Shah.

1340 : In the Muzaffarids empire. The Muzaffarids conquer Kirman. In the Chughills empire. Deposition of Isun Temur, accession of Muhammad.

1341 : In the Golden Horde empire. Death of Uzbeg, succession of his son Tini Beg.

1342 : In the Golden Horde empire, Tini Beg overthrown by his brother Jani Beg.

1343 : In the Chughills empire, Muhammad overthrown, power captured by Kazan. In Bengal, Ilyas an officer of Alauddin murders his patron and captures the throne of West Bengal.

1344 : In the Mongols II Khans empire. Deposition of Sulaiman, succession of Anusherwan.

1345 : In the Samudra Pasai empire. Death of Malik al Tahir II, accession of Tahir III. His rule lasted throughout the fourteenth century. In Bengal, Ilyas captures East Bengal and under him Bengal is again united. He establishes his capital at Gaur.

1346 : In the Chughills empire, Deposition of Kazan, accession of Hayan Kuli. In Tunisia, Death of Abu Bakr, succession of his son Fadal. In Kashmir, Death of Udyana Deva, throne captured by Shah Mirza who assumed the name of Shah Mir, and rounded the rule of Shah Mir dynasty.

1347 : The Marinids capture Tunisia. In the Bahmanids empire, Hasan Gangu declares his independence and establishes a state in Deccan with the capital at Gulbarga.

1349 : In Kashmir, Death of Shah Mir, accession of his son Jamsbed. In Algeria, The Zayanids under Abu Said Othman recapture Algeria.

1350 : In the Sarbadaran empire, Revolt against Abdur Razaq. Power captured by Amir Masud. In Tunisia, Deposition of Fadal, succession of his brother Abu Ishaq. In Kashmir, Jamshed overthrown by his step brother Alauddin Ali Sher.

1351 : In the Marinids empire, Death of Abul Hasan, succession of Abu Inan. In the Tughluqs empire. Death of Muhammad Tughluq accession of Firuz Shah Tughluq.

1352 : In Algeria, The Marinids again capture Algeria. Abu Said Othman is taken captive and killed.

1353 : End of the Mongol II Khan rule, In the Ottoman Turks empire, The Turks acquire the fortress of Tympa on the European side of the Hollespoint. In the Muzaffarids empire. The Muzaffarids conquer Shiraz and establish their capital there.

1354 : In the Muzaffarids empire, The Muzaffarids annex Isfahan. In Granada, Assassination of Abu Hallaj Yusuf, succession of his son Muhammad V.

1356 : In the Jalayar empire, Death of Hasan Buzurg, succession of his son Owaia.

1357 : In the Golden Horde empire, Death of Jani Beg, succession of Kulpa.

1358 : In the Bahmanids empire, Death of Hasan Gangu, accession of his son Muhammad Shah. In the Muzaffarids empire. Death of Mubarazuddin Muhammad; accession of Shah Shuja. In the Marinids empire. Assassination of Abu Inan, succession of Abu Bakr Said. In Bengal, Death of Ilyas, succession of his son Sikandar Shah.

1359 : In the Ottoman Turks empire, Death of Orkhan, succession of Murad. In the Muzaffarids empire. Shah Shuja deposed by his brother Shah Mahmud. In Tunisia, Abul Abbas a nephew of Abu Ishaq revolts and establishes his rule in Bougie. In Algeria, The Zayanids under Abu Hamuw II recapture Algeria. In the Marinids empire, Abu Bakr Said overthrown by Abu Salim Ibrahim. In Granada, Muhammad V loses the throne in palace revolution, succeeded by Ismail.

1360 : In the Muzaffarids empire, Death of Shah Mahmud. Shah Shuja recaptures power. In the Chughills empire, Power captured by Tughluq Temur. In Granada, Ismail overthrown by his brother-in-law Abu Said.

1361 : In the Ottoman Turks empire, Murad conquers a part of Thrace and establishes his capital at Demolika in Thrace. In the Golden Horde empire, Kulpa overthrown by his brother Nauroz. In the Marinids empire, Abu Salim Ibrahim overthrown by Abu Umar. Abu Umar overthrown by Abu Zayyan.

1362 : In the Golden Horde empire, State of anarchy. During 20 years as many as 14 rulers came to the throne and made their exit. In Granada, Abu Said overthrown by Muhammad V who comes to rule for the second time. In Kashmir, Death of Alauddin Ali Sher, succeeded by his brother Shahabuddin.

1365 : In the Ottoman Turks empire, The Turks defeat the Christians at the battle of Matiza, the Byzantine ruler becomes a vassal of the Turks.

1366 : In the Marinids empire, Assassination of Abu Zayyan, succession of Abu Faris Abdul Aziz.

1369 : Power captured by Amir Temur. End of the rule of the Chughills. Amir Temur captures power in Transoxiana. In Tunisia, Death of Abu Ishaq. Succession of his son Abu Baqa Khalid.

1370 : In Tunisia, Abu Baqa overthrown by Abul Abbas under whom the state is reunited. In the Sarbadaran empire, Death of Amir Masud, succession of Muhammad Temur.

1371 : In the Ottoman Turks empire, Invasion of Bulgaria, Bulgarian territory upto the Balkans annexed by the Turks.

1372 : In the Marinids empire, Death of Abu Faris, succession of Abu Muhammad.

1374 : In the Marinids empire, Abu Muhammad overthrown by Abul Abbas.

1375 : In the Sarbadaran empire. Deposition of Muhammad Temur, power captured by Shamsuddin. In the Jalayar empire, Death of Owais, succession by his son Hussain.

1376 : In Kashmir, Death of Shahabuddin, succeeded by his brother Qutbuddin.

1377 : In the Bahmanids empire, Death of Muhammad Shah, succeeded by his son Mujahid.

1378 : In the Bahmanids empire, Mujahid assassinated, throne captured by his uncle Daud.

1379 : Turkomans of the Black Sheep empire, Bairam Khawaja found the independent principality of the Turkomans of the Black Sheep and established his capital at Van in Armenia. In the Bahmanids empire. Assassination of Daud; accession of Muhammad Khan.

1380 : In the Golden Horde empire, Power is captured by Toktamish, a prince of the White Horde of Siberia. In Amir Temur's empire, Amir Temur crosses the Oxus and conquers Khurasan and Herat. Amir Temur invades Persia and subjugates the Muzaffarids and Mazandaran.

1381 : In Amir Temur's empire. Annexation of Seestan, capture of Qandhar.

1384 : In Amir Temur's empire, Conquest of Astrabad, Mazandaran, Rayy and Sultaniyah. In the Muzaffarids empire, Death of Shah Shuja, accession of his son Zainul Abdin. In the Marinids empire, Abul Abbas overthrown by Mustansir. Turkomans of the Black Sheep empire. Death of Bairam Khawaja, succession of Qara Muhammad.

1386 : In Amir Temur's empire. Annexation of Azarbaijan, Georgea overrun. Subjugation of Gilan and Shirvan.

Turkomans of the Black Sheep defeated. In the Marinids empire, Death of Mustansir, succession of Muhammad.

1387 : In the Marinids empire, Muhammad overthrown by Abul Abbas who comes to power for the second time.

1388 : In Algeria, Death of Abu Hamuw II, succession of Abu Tashfin. In the Tughluqs empire. Death of Firuz Shah Tughluq, succeeded by his grandson Ghiasuddin Tughluq II.

1389 : In the Muzaffarids empire, Death of the poet Hafiz Shirazi. In the Tughluqs empire, Death of Ghiasuddin Tughluq II, accession: of Abu Bakr Tughluq Shah. Turkomans of the Black Sheep empire. Death of Qara Muhammad, succession of Qara Yusuf.

1390 : In the Tughluqs empire, Abu Bakr overthrow by Nasiruddin Tughluq. In Bengal, Death of Sikandar Shah, accession of his son Ghiasud. In the Burji Mamluks empire, The rule of the Burji Mamluks rounded by Saifuddin Barquq.

1391 : In Amir Temur's empire. Annexation of Fars. In the Muzaffarids empire, Annexation of the Muzaffarids by Amir Temur. In Granada, Death of Muhammad V, succession of his son Abu Hallaj Yusuf II.

1392 : In the Jalayar empire, Death of Hussain, succession of his son Ahmad. In Granada, Death of Abu Hallaj ; succession of Muhammad VI.

1393 : Amir Temur defeats Tiktomish, the ruler of the Golden Horde. Capture of the Jalayar dominions by Amir Temur. In the Marinids empire. Death of Abul Abbas; succession of Abu Faris II.

1394 : Amir Temur defeats the Duke of Moscow. In the Tughluqs empire. Death of Nasiruddin Tughluq, accession of Alauddin Sikandar Shah. In Kashmir, Death of Qutbuddin. Turkomans of the White Sheep empire, Qara Othman established the rule of the White Sheep Turkomans in Diyarbekr.

1395 : In the Golden Horde empire, Amir Temur defeated Toktamish and razes Serai to the ground. End of the rule of the Golden Horde. Annexation of Iraq by Amir Temur. In the Tughluqs empire. Death of Sikandar Shah. Accession of Muhammad Shah.

1396 : In the Amir Temur's empire. Destruction of Sarai, end of the rule of the Golden Horde. In the Sarbadaran empire, Principality annexed by Amir Temur.

1397 : In the Bahmanids empire. Death of Muhammad Khan.

1398 : In the Amir Temur's empire, Campaign in India. In the Marinids empire. Death of Abu Faris II. In the Tughluqs empire. Invasion of Amir Timur, Mahmud Shah escapes from the capital. In Morocco, Death of the Marinid Sultan Abu Paris II: succession of his son Abu Said Othman.

1399 : In the Amir Temur's empire, Campaign in Iraq and Syria. In the Burji Mamluks empire, Death of Saifuddin Barquq, succession of his son Nasiruddin in Faraj.

15TH CENTURY (1400-1499) C.E.

1400 : In the Burji Mamluks empire, The Mamluks lost Syria which was occupied by Amir Timur.

1401 : In the Golden Horde empire, Death of Timur Qutluq, the ruler, installed by Amir Timur. Accession of Shadi Beg.

1402 : In the Ottoman Turks empire, Defeat of Bayazid at the battle of Ankara, taken captive Amir Timur.

1403 : In the Ottoman Turks empire, Muhammad I, the son of Bayazid ascended the throne.

1405 : In the Timurids empire. Death of Amir Timur, succession of his son Shah Rukh.

1407 : In the Golden Horde empire. Deposition of Shadi Beg, installation of Faulad Khan by the king maker Edigu.

1410 : In the Golden Horde empire. Deposition of Faulad Khan, installation of Timur.

1412 : In the Golden Horde empire, Deposition of Timur, installation of Jalaluddin. In the Burji Mamluks empire. Death of Nasiruddin Faraj, succession of Al Muayyad.

1413 : In the Golden Horde empire, Deposition of Jalaluddin, installation of Karim Bardo.

1414 : In the Golden Horde empire, Deposition of Karim Bardo, installation of Kubak Khan.

1416 : In the Golden Horde empire. Deposition of Kubak Khan, installation of Jahar Balrawi. Deposition of Jahar Balrawi, installation of Chaighray.

1419 : In the Golden Horde empire, Death of Edigu, overthrown of Chaighray, power captured by Ulugh Muhammad.

1420 : In the Golden Horde empire, Ulugh Muhammad overthrown by Daulat Bairawi. Turkomans of the Black Sheep empire, Death of Qara Yusuf; succession of his son Qara Iskandar. In Morocco, Assassination of Abu Said Othman; succession of his infant son Abdul Haq.

1421 : In the Ottoman Turks empire, Death of Muhammad I; accession of his son Murad II. In the Burji Mamluks empire, Death of Al Muayyad, succession of Muzaffar Ahmad. Muzaffar Ahmad overthrown by Amir Saifuddin Tata, Death of Saifuddin Tata, succession of his son Muhammad. Muhammad overthrown by Amir Barsbay.

1424 : In the Golden Horde empire. Death of Daulat Bairawi, succession of Berk. In Algeria, The Halsida of Tunisia occupy Algeria. This state of affairs continued throughout the fifteenth century.

1425 : In the Uzbegs empire, Abul Khayr, a prince of the house of Uzbeg declare his independence in the western part of Siberia.

1427 : In the Golden Horde empire, Berk overthrown by Ulugh Muhammad who captured power for the second time.

1430 : In the Uzbegs empire, Abul Khayr occupies Khawarazm.

1434 : Turkomans of the Black Sheep empire, Deposition of Qara Ikandar; installation of his brother Jahan Shah. Turkomans of the White Sheep empire. Death of Qara

Othman, succession of his son Ali Beg. In Tunisia, Death of Abul Faris after a rule of forty years, succession of his son Abu Abdullah Muhammad.

1435 : In Tunisia, Deposition of Abu Abdullah Muhammad, power captured by Abu Umar Othman.

1438 : In the Burji Mamluks empire, Death of Barsbay, accession of his minor son Jamaluddin Yusuf; Yusuf overthrown and power captured by the Chief Minister Saifuddin Gakmuk. Turkomans of the White Sheep empire, Ali Beg overthrown by his brother Hamza.

1439 : In the Golden Horde empire, Ulugh Muhammad withdrew from Sarai and found the principality of Qazan. Said Ahmad came to power in Sarai.

1440 : Turkomans of the White Sheep empire, Hamza overthrown by Jahangir a son of Ali Beg.

1441 : *in* the Golden Horde empire, Crimea seceded from Sarai.

1446 : In the Timurids empire. Death of Shah Rukh, succession of Ulugh Beg. In the Ottoman Turks empire. Second battle of Kossova resulting in the victory of the Turks. Serbia annexed to Turkey and Bosnia became its vassal.

1447 : In the Golden Horde empire, Astra Khan seceded from Sarai.

1449 : In the Uzbegs empire, Abul Khayr captures Farghana. In the Timurids empire, Death of Ulugh Beg, succession of Abdul Latif.

1450 : In the Timurids empire, Assassination of Abdul Latif, accession of Abu Said.

1451 : In the Ottoman Turks empire, Death of Murad II; accession of his son Muhammad II.

1453 : In the Ottoman Turks empire. Capture of Constantinople by the Turks. Turkomans of the White Sheep empire. Death of Jahangir; accession of his son Uzun Hasan. In the Burji Mamluks empire. Death of Gakmuk. succession of his son Fakhruddin Othman.

Othman overthrown by the Mamluk General Saifuddin Inal.

1454 : In the Ottoman Turks empire, Attack against Wallachia, Wallachia became a vassal state of Turkey.

1456 : In the Ottoman Turks empire. Annexation of Serbia.

1461 : In the Ottoman Turks empire. Annexation of Bosnia and Herzogovina. In the Burji Marnluks empire. Death of Saifuddin Inal, succession of his son Shahabuddin Ahmad. Shahabuddin Ahmad overthrown by the Mamluk General Saifuddin Khushqadam.

1462 : In the Ottoman Turks empire. Annexation of Albania.

1465 : In the Golden Horde empire. Death of Said Ahmad, succession of his son Khan Ahmad. In Morocco, Assassination of Abdul Haq. End of the Marinid rule. Power snatched by Sharif Muhammad al Jati.

1467 : Turkomans of the Black Sheep empire. Death of Jahan Shah, end of the rule of the Black Sheep Turkoman rule. Turkomans of the White Sheep empire, Jahan Shah of the Black Sheep attacked the White Sheep. Jahan Shah was defeated and the Black Sheep territories annexed by the White Sheep. In the Burji Mamluks empire. Death of Khushqadam, accession of his son Saifuddin Yel Bey. Deposition of Yel Bey, power captured by the Mamluk General Temur Bugha.

1468 : In the Uzbegs empire. Death of Abul Khayr, succession of his son Haidar Sultan. Turkomans of the White Sheep empire, Uzun Hasan defeated the Timurids at the battle of Qarabagh whereby the White Sheep became the masters of Persia and Khurasan. In the Burji Mamluks empire. Deposition of Femur Bugha, power captured by the Mamluk General Qait Bay.

1469 : In the Timurids empire. Death of Abu Said, disintegration of the Timurid state. In Khurasan Hussain Baygara came to power and he ruled during the remaining years of the fifteenth century.

1472 : In Morocco, Sharif Muhammad al Jati overthrown by the Wattisid chief Muhammad al Shaikh who establishes the rule of the Wattisid dynasty.

1473 : In the Ottoman Turks empire. War against Persia; Persians defeated.

1475 : In the Ottoman Turks empire. Annexation of Crimea. War against Venice. Tukey became the master of the Aegean Sea.

1478 : Turkomans of the White Sheep empire. Death of Uzun Hasan, succession of his son Khalil.

1479 : Turkomans of the White Sheep empire, Khalil overthrown by his uncle Yaqub.

1480 : In the Golden Horde empire. Assassination of Khan Ahmad, succession of his son Said Ahmad II.

1481 : In the Golden Horde empire. Said Ahmad II overthrown by his brother Murtada. In the Ottoman Turks empire, Death of Muhammad II, accession of Bayazid II.

1488 : In the Uzbegs empire. Death of Haider Sultan, succession of his nephew Shaybani Khan. In Tunisia, Death of Abu Umar Othman after a rule of 52 years, succession of Abu Zikriya Yahya.

1489 : In Tunisia, Abu Zikriya Yahya overthrown by Abul Mumin.

1490 : In Tunisia, Abul Mumin overthrown, power recaptured by Abu Yahya.

1493 : Turkomans of the White Sheep empire. Death of Yaqub. accession of his son Bayangir.

1495 : Turkomans of the White Sheep empire, Bayangir overthown by his cousin Rustam.

1496 : In the Burji Marnluks empire. Abdication of Qait Bay, succession of his son Nasir Muhammad.

1497 : Turkomans of the White Sheep empire, Rustam overthrown by Ahmad. Anarchy and fragmentation.

1498 : In the Burji Mamluks empire. Deposition of Nasir Muhammad, power captured by Zahir Kanauh.

1499 : In the Uzbegs empire, Shayhani Khan conquered Transoxiana. In the Golden Horde empire. Death of Murtada, succession of Said Ahmad III. In the Ottoman

Turks empire. The Turks defeated the Venetian fleet
in the battle of Lepanto.

16TH CENTURY (1500-1599) C.E.

1500 : In the Burji Mamluks empire, Zahir Kanauh overthrown
by Ashraf Gan Balat.

1501 : Isamil I establishes the Safavid dynasty in Persia, and
the Twelve-Imam Shi'ism becomes the state religion.

1507 : The Portuguese under d'Albuquerque establish
strongholds in the Persian Gulf.

1508 : Turkomans of the White Sheep empire. End of the
White Sheep dynasty and the annexation of their
territories by the Safawids.

1511 : D'Albuquerque conquers Malacca from the Muslims.

1517 : The Ottoman Sultan Selim Yavuz ("the Grim") defeats
the Mamluks and conquers Egypt.

1520 : The reign of Sulayman the Magnificent begins.

1526 : Louis of Hungary dies at the Battle of Mohacs.

1526 : The Battle of Panipat in India, and the Moghul conquest;
Babur makes his capital at Delhi and Agra.

1528 : The Ottomans take Buda in Hungary.

1529 : Unsuccessful Ottoman siege of Vienna.

1550 : The architect Sinan builds the Suleymaniye mosque in
Istanbul.

1550 : The rise of the Muslim kingdom of Atjeh in Sumatra.

1550 : Islam spreads to Java, the Moluccas, and Borneo.

1556 : The death of Sulayman the Magnificent.

1568 : Alpujarra uprising of the Moriscos (Muslims forcibly
converted to Catholicism) in Spain.

1571 : The Ottomans are defeated at the naval Battle of
Lepanto, and their dominance in the Mediterranean is
brought to a close.

1578 : The Battle of the Three Kings at Qasr al-Kabir in
Morocco. King Sebastian of Portugal is killed.

1588 : Reign of Safavid Sultan Shah Abbas I begins.

1591 : Mustaili Ismailis split into Sulaymanis and Daudis.

17TH CENTURY (1600-1699) C.E.

1600 : Sind annexed by the Mughals. End of the Arghun rule in Sind.

1601 : Khandesh annexed by the Mughals.

1603 : Battle of Urmiyah. Turks suffer defeat. Persia occupies Tabriz, Mesopotamia. Mosul and Diyarbekr. Death of Muhammad III, Sultan of Turkey, accession of Ahmad I. In Morocco al Shaikh died.

1604 : In Indonesia death of Alauddin Rayat Shah, Sultan of Acheh, accession of Ali Rayat Shah III.

1605 : Death of the Mughal emperor Akbar; accession of Jahangir.

1607 : Annexation of Ahmadnagar by the Mughals.

1609 : Annexation of Bidar by the Mughals.

1611 : Kuch Behar subjugated by the Mughals.

1612 : Kamrup annexed by the Mughals.

1617 : Death of Ahmad I, Sultan of Turkey, accession of Mustafa; Deposition of Mustafa: accession of Othman II.

1618 : Tipperah annexed by the Mughals.

1620 : In Turkey deposition of Mustafa, accession of Othman II.

1622 : In Turkey Mustafa recaptured power.

1625 : In Turkey deposition of Mustafa, accession of Murad IV.

1627 : Death of the Mughal emperor Jahangir, accession of Shah Jahan.

1628 : Reign of Safavid Sultan Shah Abbas I comes to an end.

1629 : In Persia death of Shah Abbas; accession of grandson Safi.

1631 : Death of Mumtaz Mahal, wife of Mughal Emperor Shah Jahan and the lady of Taj Mahal, Agra.

1637 : Death of Iskandar Muda in Indonesia; accession of Iskandar II.

1640 : Death of Otthman Sultan Murad IV, accession of his brother Ibrahim.

1641 : Turks capture Azov. In Indonesia death of Iskandar II; accession of the Queen Tajul Alam.

1642 : In Persia death of Shah Safi, accession of Shah Abbas II.

1648 : In Turkey Ibrahim deposed; accession of Muhammad IV.

1656 : Muhammad Kuiprilli becomes the Grand Minister in Turkey.

1658 : Deposition of the Mughal emperor Shah Jahan, accession of Aurangzeb.

1661 : Death of Muhammad Kuiprilli, accession of his son Ahmad Kuiprilli.

1667 : Death of Shah Abbas II; accession of Shah Sulaiman.

1675 : Execution of the Sikh Guru Tegh Bahadur. In Indonesia death of the queen Tajul Alam, accession of the queen Nur ul Alam.

1676 : Death of the Grand Wazir of Turkey Ahmad Kuiprilli, succession by Kara Mustafa.

1678 : In Indonesia death of the queen Nur ul Alam, accession of the queen Inayat Zakia.

1680 : Death of Marhatta chieftain Shivaji.

1682 : Assam annexed by the Mughals. Aurangzeb shifts the capital to Aurangabad in the Deccan.

1683 : The Turks lift the siege of Vienna and retreat. Kara Mustafa the Grand Wazir executed for the failure of the expedition.

1686 : Annexation of Bijapur by the Mughals.

1687 : Golkunda annexed by the Mughals. Second battle of Mohads. Defeat of the Turks by Austria. Deposition of Muhammad IV. Accession of Sulaiman II.

1688 : In Indonesia death of queen Inayat Zakia, accession of the queen Kamalah.

1690 : Death of the Ottoman Sultan Sulaiman II, accession of Ahmad II.

1692 : Death of the Turk Sultan Ahmad II, accession of Mustafa II.

1694 : In Persia death of Shah Safi, accession of Shah Hussain.

1699 : In Indonesia death of Queen Kamalah.

18TH CENTURY (1700-1799) C.E.

1700 : Murshid Quli Khan declares the independence of Bengal and establishes his capital at Murshidabad.

1703 : Ahmad III becomes the Ottoman Sultan. Birth of Shah Wali Ullah. Birth of the religious reformer Muhammad b Abdul Wahab.

1707 : Death of the Mughal emperor Aurangzeb, accession of his son Bahadur Shah.

1711 : War between Turkey and Russia. Russia defeated at the battle of Pruth.

1712 : Death of the Mughal emperor Bahadur Shah, accession of Jahandar Shah.

1713 : Jahandar Shah overthrown by his nephew Farrukh Siyar.

1718 : In the war against Austria, Turkey suffers defeat. By the treaty of Passarowich Turkey loses Hungary.

1719 : Deposition of the Mughal emperor Farrukh Siyar Muhammad Shah ascends the throne. In Sind the Kalhoras came to power under Nur Muhammad Kalhora.

1722 : Saadat Khan found the independent state of Oudh. Battle of Gulnabad between the Afghans and the Persians. The Persians were defeated and the Afghans under Shah Mahmud became the masters of a greater part of Persia. Shah Hussain taken captive, accession of Shah Tahmasp II.

1730 : Zanzibar freed from Portugese rule and occupied by Oreart.

1747 : Ahmad Shah Durrani established Afghan rule in Afghanistan.

1752 : Death of Shah Abdul Latif Bhitai, writer of Sassi Pannu, Sohni Mahinwal and Umer Marvo.

1752 : Ahmed Shah Durrani captured Punjab, Kashmir and Sind.

1761 : Death of Shah Waliullah Dehiavi.

1761 : Battle of Panipat. Ahmad Shah Durrani came to India at the invitation of Shah Waliullah Dehlavi and smashed rising Maratha power in the battle of Panipat.

1764 : Conversion to Islam of Areadi Gaya, ruler of Futa Bandu State in West Sudan.

1773 : Death of Ahmad Shah Durrani.

1783 : End of Kalhora rule in Sind.

1797 : Death of Muhammad Khan Qachar, king of Persia.

1797 : Russia occupied Daghestan.

1799 : Ranjit Singh declared himself Maharajah of Punjab defeating Afghans.

1799 : Khoqand declared independent Islamic State.

19TH CENTURY (1800-1899) C.E.

1803 : Shah Abdul Aziz ibn Saud assassinated by a Shia fanatic. Shah Shuja proclaimed as King of Afghanistan.

1804 : Othman Dan Fodio established Islamic State of Sokoto in Central Sudan.

1805 : Ibn Saud captured Madinah defeating the Turk garrison.

1805 : Faraizi movement launched in Bengal. Muhammad Ali appointed Pasha of Egypt by the Turks.

1806 : Khanate of Khiva came into limelight under the rule of Muhammad Rahim Khan.

1807 : Darqawi sect revolted against Turkish domination. Tunisia repudiated suzerainty of Algeria.

1811 : Birth of Ali Muhammad Bab founder of Bab movement.

1811 : British occupied Indonesia.

1812 : Madina fell to Egyptians.

1813 : Makkah and Taif captured by Egyptian forces and Saudis expelled from Hijaz.

1814 : Iran executed treaty of alliance with the British known as Definitive Treaty.

1814 : Death of Ibn Saud II.

1814 : King Othman of Tunisia assassinated by his cousin Mahmud.

1816 : British withdrew from Indonesia restoring it to the Dutch.

1822 : Death of Maulay Ismail in Morocco.

1827 : Malaya became a preserve of the British according to Angio-Netherland treaty in 1824.

1828 : Russia declared war against Turkey.

1829 : Treaty of Adrianople.

1830 : French forces landed near Algiers and occupied Algeria ending 313 years rule of Turks.

1831 : Syed Ahmad Barelvi and Shah Ismail leaders of Jihad movement in India fell fighting the Sikhs in Balakot.

1832 : Turks defeated in the battle of Konia by Egyptian forces.

1832 : Sayyid Said, King of Oman, shifted his capital to Zanzibar.

1834 : Abdul Qadir recognised as ruler of the area under his control by the French.

1839 : Defeat of Turkey by the Egyptians in the battle of Nisibin.

1840 : Quadruple Alliance by the European powers to force Egypt to relinquish Syria.

1840 : British frees occupied Aden.

1841 : State of Adamawa established by Adams adjacent to Nigeria.

1842 : Amir Abdul Qadir, ousted from Algeria by the French, crossed over to Morocco.

1842 : Shah Shuja assassinated ending the Durrani rule in Afghanistan.

1847 : Amir Abdul Qadir surrendred to France under the condition of safe conduct to a Muslim country of his choice but France violated its pledge and sent him as a captive to France.

1849 : Death of Muhammad Ali Pasha.

1850 : Ali Muhammad Bab arrested and executed by Iranian government. Qurratui Ain Tabira, a renowned poetess and staunch advocate of Babism also shot dead.

1852 : Release of Amir Abdul Qadir by Napolean III. He settled in Turkey.

1853 : Khiva annexed by Russia.

1857 : British captured Delhi and eliminated Mughal rule in India after 332 years. Last Mughal Emperor Bahadur Shah Zafar was exiled to Rangoon in Burma. This was also the end of 1000 years of Muslim rule over India.

1859 : Imam Shamil laid down arms before Russian forces and the Islamic State of Daghestan became a Russian province.

1860 : Maulay Muhammad defeated by Spain.

1861 : Death of Sultan Abdul-Majid of Turkey.

1862 : Faraizi movement fizzled out after the death of Dadu Miyan.

1865 : Khoqand State liquidated by Russia.

1869 : Jamaluddin Afghani exiled from Afghanistan. He proceeded to Egypt.

1871 : Tunisia recognised suzerainty of Turkey through a Firman.

1876 : Britain purchased shares of Khediv Ismail in the Suez canal and got involved in Egyptian affairs.

1878 : Turkey handed over Cyprus to Britain.

1878 : Adrianople fell to Russia.

1879 : Jamaluddin Afghani exiled from Egypt.

1879 : Treaty of Berlin. Turkey lost 4/5th of its territory in Europe.

1881 : France invaded Tunisia and the Bey acknowledged supremacy of France as a result of the treaty of Bardo.

1881 : Muhammad Ahmad declared himself Mahdi in northern Sudan.

1882 : Egypt came under British military occupation.

1883 : Death of Amir Abdul Qadir in Damascus.

1885 : Muhammad Ahmad declared free Government of Sudan under his rule.

1885 : Death of Mahdi Sudani five months after the occupation of Khartum.

1890 : End of Banbara State.

1895 : Afghanistan got Wakhan corridor by an understanding with Russia and British India making Afghan border touch China.

1895 : Mirza Ghulam Ahmad of Qadian claimed prophethood.

1897 : State of Bagirimi occupied by the French.

1899 : Fall of Mahdi State occupied by the British and the Egyptians jointly.

20TH CENTURY (1900-1992) C.E

1901 : Ibn Saud (Abd al-Aziz) captures Riyad.

1901 : French forces occupy Morocco.

1904 : Morocco becomes a French protectorate under the Conference of Algeciras.

1904 : The Presian constitution is promoted.

1905 : The beginning of the Salafiyyah movement in Paris with its main sphere of influence in Egypt.

1907 : The beginning of the Young Turks movement in Turkey.

1912 : The beginning of the Muhammadiyyah reform movement in Indonesia.

1914 : Under Ottoman rule, secret Arab nationalist societies are formed.

1914 : World War I.

1916 : Arab revolt against Ottoman (Turkish) rule. Lawrence of Arabia leads attacks on the Hijaz Railway.

1918 : Armistice signed with Ottomans on October 30.

1918 : World War I ends on November 11.

1918 : Syria and Damascus become a French protectorate.

1921 : Abd Allah bin Husayn is made King of Transjordan. His father was the Sharif of Mecca.

1921 : Faysal bin Husayn is made King of Iraq. His father was the Sharif of Mecca.

1921 : Abd al-Karim leads a revolt against colonial rule in Moroccan Rif and declares the "Republic of the Rif".

1922 : Mustafa Kemal abolishes the Turkish Sultanate.

1924 : The Turkish Caliphate is abolished.

1924 : King Abd al-Aziz conquers Mecca and Medina, which leads to the unification of the Kingdoms of Najd and Hijaz.

1925 : Reza Khan seizes the government in Persia and establishes the Pahlavi dynasty.

1926 : Abd al-Aziz (Ibn Saud) assumes title of King of Najd and Hijaz.

1927 : Death of Zaghlul, an Egyptian nationalist leader.

1928 : Turkey is declared a secular state.

1928 : Hasan al-Banna founds the Muslim Brotherhood.

1932 : Iraq granted independence by League of Nations.

1934 : War between King Abd al-Aziz and Imam Yahya of the Yemen.

1934 : Peace treaty of Ta'if.

1934 : Asir becomes part of Saudi Arabia.

1935 : Iran becomes the official name of Persia.

1936 : Increased Jewish immigration provokes widespread Arab-Jewish fighting in Palestine.

1939 : World War II.

1941 : British and Russian forces invade Iran and Reza Shah is forced to abdicate in favor of his son Mohammad Reza Shah in Iran.

1943 : Beginning of Zionist terrorist campaign in Palestine.

1945 : End of World War II.

1946 : Jordan, Lebanon, and Syria are granted independence from Britain and France.

1947 : Creation of Pakistan from Muslim Majority area in India.

1948 : Creation of state of Israel. Arab armies suffer defeat in war with Israel.

1949 : Hasan al-Banna, leader of the Muslim Brotherhood, is assassinated.

1951 : Libya becomes independent.

1952 : King Faruq of Egypt forced to abdicate.

1953 : General Zahedi leads coup against Musaddeq, Shah returns to power.

1953 : Death of King Abd al-Aziz (Ibn Saud) of Saudi Arabia.

1953 : The foundation stone is laid to enlarge the Prophet's mosque in Medina.

1956 : Morocco becomes independent.

1956 : Tunisia becomes independent.

1957 : The Bey of Tunisia is deposed, and Bourguiba becomes president.

1957 : Enlargement of the Haram in Mecca begins.

1962 : Algeria becomes independent.

1962 : Death of Zaydi Imam of Yemen (Ahmad). Crown Prince Bahr succeeds him and takes the title Imam Mansur Bi-Llah Muhammad.

1965 : Malcom X is assassinated.

1968 : The enlargement of the Haram in Mecca is completed.

1969 : King Idris of Libya is ousted by a coup led by Colonel Qadhdhafi.

1973 : King Zahir Shah of Afghanistan is overthrown.

1975 : Death of Elijah Mohammad, leader of Nation of Islam among African Americans in North America.

1975 : Wallace Warith Deen Mohammad assumes leadership of Nation of Islam and shifts movement toward Islamic Orthodoxy renaming it American Muslim Mission.

1978 : Imam Musa Sadr is apparently assassinated after he disappears on a trip to Libya. He was the religious leader of the Lebanese Twelve-imam Shi'ites. He promoted the resurgence of Shi'ites in Lebanon and set the foundation of Amal.

1979 : The Shah leaves Iran on January 15, thus bringing the Pahlavi dynasty to an end.

1979 : On I Muharram AH 1400/21 November, the first day of the 15th Islamic century, fanatics led by students of the Theological University of Medina attempt to promote one of their group as Mahdi and thus fulfill a certain prophetic Hadith: "A man of the people of Medina will go forth, fleeing to Mecca, and certain of the people of Mecca will come to him and will lead him forth against his will and swear fealty to him between the rukn (Black Stone corner of the Kabah) and the Maqam Ibrahim." They hold the Haram of Mecca against the army for two weeks. Sixty-three of the 300 fanatics are captured alive, the mosque is recovered, and the conspirators are all put to death.

1980 : Beginning of the Iran-Iraq war.

1989 : Iran-Iraq comes to an end with much loss of life.

1990 : Military annexation of Kuwait by Iraq, under Ba'athist leader Saddam Hussain, is reversed in 1991 by a coalition of United States-led forces.

April 18, 1993 : President Ishaq Khan dismisses Sharif Government.

October 19, 1993 : Benazir Bhutto becomes Prime Minister for the second time after winning general elections.

November 13, 1993 : Farooq Leghari, a Bhutto nominee, is elected President.

January 1994 : Peace talks with India break down over Kashmir.

November 5, 1996 : President Farooq Leghari sacks Bhutto, dissolves Parliament and calls elections for February 3.

February 3, 1997 : Sharif's Pakistan Muslim League party wins general elections by landslide margin.

February 17, 1997 : Sharif becomes Prime Minister for the second time.

March 28, 1997 : Pakistan and India resume peace talks at foreign secretary level for the first time since 1994.

December 2, 1997 : President Farooq Leghari resigns after a six-month legal battle to have Sharif investigated for misuse of power during his first Premiership.

May 28, 1998 : Pakistan conducts five nuclear tests in response to India's tests earlier in the month.

August 4, 1998 : Guerrillas in India's Kashmir region kill 19 people as cross-border firing by the Indian and Pakistani armies runs into its sixth day.

October 18, 1998 : Pakistan and India end their first peace talks in a year with agreement to meet again next February in New Delhi.

April 15, 1999 : Former Pakistan Prime Minister Benazir Bhutto and her husband are sentenced in absentia to a five-year jail term on charges of corruption.

June-July 1999   : Weeks of border skirmishes erupt between
                      Pakistan and India over Muslim militant
                      infiltrators who seized hilltop position on
                      the Indian side of the Line of Control.

July 12, 1999   : Pakistan orders the Muslim Militant infiltra-
                      tors to withdraw from Kashmir, ending the
                      standoff with India.

October 12, 1999   : Sharif overthrown in military coup.

October 14, 1999   : Parliament building sealed.

October 4, 1999   : Parliament building sealed.

October 15, 1999   : Pakistan comes under army rules.

APPENDIX

STATISTICS

Population : 144,616,639 (July 2001 est.)

Age structure : *0-14 years :* 40.47% (male 30,131,400; female 28,391,891)

15-64 years: 55.42% (male 40,977,543; female 39,164,663)

65 years and over: 4.11% (male 2,918,872; female 3,032,270) (2001 est.)

Population growth rate : 2.11% (2001 est.)

Birth rate : 31.21 births/1,000 population (2001 est.)

Death rate : 9.26 deaths/1,000 population (2001 est.)

Net Migration rate : -0.84 migrant(s)/1,000 population (2001 est.)

Sex ratio : *at birth* : 1.05 male(s)/female
under 15 years : 1.06 male(s)/female
15-64 years : 1.05 male(s)/female
65 years and over : 0.96 male(s)/female
total population : 1.05 male(s)/female (2001 est.)

Infant mortality rate : 80.5 deaths/1,000 live births (2001 est.)

Life expectancy at birth : *total population:* 61.45 years
male : 60.61 years
female : 62.32 years (2001 est.)

Total fertility : 4.41 children born/woman (2001 est.)
rate

HIV/AIDS - adult :   0.1% (1999 est.)
prevalence rate

HIV/AIDs - : 74,000 (1999 est.)
people living
with HIV/AIDs

HIV/AIDS - : 6,500 (1999 est.)
deaths :

Nationality : *noun:* Pakistani (s)
                  adjective : Pakistani

Ethnic groups : Punjabi, Sindhi, Pashtun (Pathan), Baloch,
                     Muhajir (immigrants from India at the time
                     of partition and their descendants).

Religions : Muslim 97% (Sunni 77%, Shi'a 20%), Christian,
                 Hindu, and other 3%.

Languages : Punjabi 48%, Sindhi 12%, Siraiki (a Punjabi
                 variant) 10%, Pashtu 8%, Urdu (official) 8%,
                 Balochi 3%, Hindko 2%, Brahui 1%, English
                 (official and lingua franca of Pakistani elite
                 and most government ministries), Buru-
                 shaski, and other 8%.

Literacy : *definition :* age 15 and over can read and
                write.
                Total population : 42.7%
                male : 55.3 %
                female : 29% (1998).

Location : Southern Asia, bordering the Arabian Sea,
                between India on the east and Iran and
                Afghanistan on the west and China in the
                north.

Geographic : 30 00 N, 70 00 E
coordinates

Map references	: Asia

Area	: *total* : 803,940 sq km *land* : 778,720 sq km water : 25,220 sq km

Area - comparative	: slightly less than twice the size of California.

Land boundaries	: *total* : 6,774 km *border countries*: Afghanistan 2,430 km, China 523 km, India 2,912 km, Iran 909 km

Coastline	: 1,046 km

Maritime claims	: *contiguous zone* : 24 NM *continental shelf* : 200 NM or to the edge of the continental margin *exclusive economic zone* : 200 NM *territorial sea* : 12 NM

Climate	: mostly hot, dry desert; temperate in northwest; arctic in north

Terrain	: flat Indus plain in east; mountains in north and northwest; Balochistan plateau in west

Elevation extremes	: *lowest point* : Indian Ocean 0 m *highest point* : K2 (Mt. Godwin-Austen) 8,611 m

Natural resources	: land, extensive natural gas reserves, limited petroleum, poor quality coal, iron ore, copper, salt, limestone

Land use	: *arable land* : 27% *permanent crops* : 1% *permanent pastures* : 6% *forests and woodland* : 5% *other* : 61% (1993 est.)

Irrigated land	: 171,100 sq km (1993 est.)

Natural hazards	: frequent earthquakes, occasionally severe especially in north and west; flooding along the Indus after heavy rains (July and August)

Environment - : water pollution from raw sewage, industrial
current issues   wastes, and agricultural runoff, limited
                      natural fresh water resources a majority of
                      the population does not have access to
                      potable water, deforestation; soil erosion;
                      desertification.

Environment - : *party to* : Biodiversity, Climate Change,
international   Desertification, Endangered Species, Environ-
agreements   mental Modification, Hazardous Wastes,
                     Law of the Sea, Marine Dumping, Ozone
                     Layer Protection, Ship Pollution, Wetlands.

                     signed, but not ratified : Marine Life Conser-
                     vation, Nuclear Test Ban.

Geography - : controls Khyber Pass and Bolan Pass,
note   traditional invasion routes between Central
                  Asia and the Indian Subcontinent.

GOVERNMENT

Country name : *conventional long form :* Islamic Republic of
                   Pakistan.
                   conventional short form : Pakistan
                   former : West Pakistan

Government : federal republic
type

Capital : Islamabad

Administrative : 4 provinces, 1 territory*, and 1 capital
divisions   territory**, Balochistan, Federally Adminis-
                     tered Tribal Areas*, Islamabad Capital
                     Territory**, North-West Frontier Province,
                     Punjab, Sindh.

                     note : the Pakistani-administered portion of
                     the disputed Jammu and Kashmir region
                     includes PoK and the Northern Areas.

Independence : 14 August, 1947 (from UK)

National : Republic Day, 23 March (1956)
holiday

Constitution	:	10 April 1973, suspended 5 July 1977, restored with amendments 30 December 1985, suspended 15 October 1999.
Legal system	:	based on English common law with provisions to accommodate Pakistan's status as an Islamic state; accepts compulsory ICJ jurisdiction, with reservations.
Suffrage	:	21 years of age; universal; separate electorats and reserved parliamentary seats for non-Muslims.
Executive branch	:	*note :* following a military takeover on 12 October 1999, Chief of Army Staff and Chairman of the Joint Chiefs of Staff Committee, Gen. Pervez MUSHARRAF suspended Pakistan's constitution and assumed the additional title of Chief Executive; exercising the powers of the head of the government, he appointed an eight-member National Security Council to function as Pakistan's supreme governing body; President Mohammad Rafiq TARAR remains the ceremonial chief of state; on 12 May 2000, Pakistan's Supreme Court unanimously validated the October 1999 coup and granted MUSHARRAF executive and legislative authority for three years from the coup date.

chief of state: President Mohammad Rafiq TARAR (since 31 December 1997).

head of government : Chief Executive Gen. Pervez MUSHARRAF (since 12 October 1999).

cabinet : Cabinet appointed by .the chief executive.

elections : president elected by Parliament for a five-year term; election last held 31 December 1997 (next to be held NA 2002); following legislative elections, the leader of the majority party or leader of a majority coalition is usually elected Prime Minister - by the National Assembly; election last held 3 February 1997 (next to be held NA); note - Gen. Pervez MUSHARRAF overthrew the government of Prime Minister Mohammad Nawaz SHARIF in the military takeover of 12 October 1999; in May 2000, the Supreme Court validated the October 1999 coup and set a three-year limit in office for Chief Executive MUSHARRAF.

election results : Rafiq TARAR elected president; percent of Parliament and provincial vote -NA%; results are for the last election for Prime Minister prior to the military takeover of 12 October 1999- Mohammad Nawaz SHARIF elected Prime Minister: percent of National Assembly vote - NA%

Legislative branch

: *note -* Gen. Pervez MUSHARRAF dissolved Parliament following the military takeover of 12 October 1999; bicameral Parliament or Majlis-e-Shoora consists of the Senate (87 members indirectly elected by provincial assemblies to serve six-year terms; one-third of the members up for election every two years) and the National Assembly (217 seats - 10 represent non- Muslims; members elected by popular vote to serve five-year terms).

elections : Senate - last held 12 March 1997 (next to be held NA); National Assembly - last held 3 February 1997 (next to be held NA); note - no timetable has yet been given for elections following the military takeover.

election results : Senate-percent of vote by party - NA%; seats by party- PML/N 30, PPP

17, ANP 7, MQM/A 6, JWP 5, BNP 4, JUI/F 2, PML/J 2, BNM/M 1, PKMAP 1, TJP 1, independents 6, vacant 5; National Assembly - percent of vote by party- NA%; seats by party - PML/N 137, PPP 18, MQM/A 12, ANP 10, BNP 3, JWP 2, JUI/F 2, PPP/SB 1, NPP 1, independents 21, minorities 10; note - Gen. Pervez MUSHARRAF dismissed Parliament 15 October 1999.

Judicial branch : Supreme Court (justices appointed by the president); Federal Islamic or Shari'a Court.

Political parties : *note:* Gen. Pervez MUSHARRAF dissolved
and leaders Parliament following the military takeover of 12 October 1999, however, political parties have been allowed to operate: Awami National Party or ANP [Wali KHAN]; Balochistan National Movement/Hayee Group or BNM/H [Dr. HAYEE Baluch]; Baluch National Party, or BNP [Sardar Akhtar MENGAL], Jamhoori Watan Party or JWP [Akbar Khan BUGTI] Jamiat-al-Hadith or JAH (Sajid MIR]; Jamiat Ulema-i-Islam, Fazlur Rehman faction or JUI/F [Fazlur REHMAN]; Jamiat Ulema-i- Pakistan, Niazi faction or JUP/NI [Abdul Sattar Khan NIAZI]; Millat Party [Farooq LEGHARI]; Milli Yakjheti Council or MYC is an umbrella organization which includes Jamaat-i-lslami or Ji [Qazi Hussain AHMED], Jamiat Ulema-i-Islam, Sami-ul-Haq faction or JUI/S [Sami ul-HAQ], Tehrik-I-Jafria Pakistan or TJP [Allama Sajid NAQVI], and Jamiat Ulema-i-Pakistan, Noorani faction or JUP/NO [Shah Ahmad NOORANI]; Mutahida Qaumi Movement, Altaf faction or MQM/A [Altaf HUSSAIN]; National People's Party or NPP [Ghulam Mustapha JATOI]; Pakhtun Khwa Milli Awami Party

or PKMAP [Mahmood Khan ACHAKZAI]: Pakhtun Quami Party or PQP [Mohammed AFZAL Khan]; Pakistan Awami Tehrik or PAT [Tahir ul QADRI]; Pakistan Muslim League, Functional Group or PML/F [Pir PAGARO]; Pakistan Muslim League, Junejo faction or PML/J [Hamid Nasir CHATTHA]; Pakistan Muslim League, Nawaz Sharif faction or PML/N [Nawaz SHARIF]; Pakistan National Party or PNP [Hasil BIZENJO]: Pakistan People's Party or PPP [Benazir BHUTTO]: Pakistan People's Party/Shaheed Bhutto or PPP/SB [Ghinva BHUTTO]; Pakistan Tehrik-e-Insaaf or PTI [Sman KHAN] *note:* political alliances in Pakistan can shift frequently.

Political pressure groups and leaders : military remains important political force; ulema (clergy), landowners, industrialists and small merchants also influential

International organization participation : AsDB,C(suspended),CCC,CP, ECO, ESCAP, FAO, G-19, G-24, G-77, IAEA, IBRD, ICAO, ICC, ICFTU, ICRM, IDA, IDB, IFAD, IFC, IFRCS, IHO, ILO, IMF, IMO, Inmarsat, Intelsat, Interpol, IOC, IOM, ISO, ITU, MINURSO, MONUC, NAM, OAS (observer), OIC, OPCW, PCA, SAARC, UN, UNAMSIL, UNCTAD, UNESCO, UNHCR, UNIDO, UNIKOM, UNMIBH, UNMIK, UNMOP, UNOMIG, UNTAET, UPU, WCL, WFTU, WHO, WIPO, WMO, WToO, WTrO.

Flag description : Green with a vertical white, band (symbolizing the role of religious minorities) on the hoist side; a large white crescent and star are centered in the green field; the crescent; star, and color green are traditional symbols of Islam.

ECONOMY

Economy-overview

: Pakistan is a poor, heavily populated country, suffering from internal political disputes, lack of foreign investment, and a costly confrontation with neighboring India: Pakistan's economic outlook continues to be marred by its weak foreign exchange position, which relies on international creditors for hard currency inflows. The MUSHARRAF government wilt face an estimated $21 billion in foreign debt coming due in 2000-03, despite having rescheduled nearly $2 billion in debt with Paris Club members. Foreign loans and grants provide approximately 2.5% of government revenue, but debt service obligations total-nearly 50% of government expenditure. Although Pakistan successfully negotiated a $600 million IMF Stand-By Arrangement, future loan installments will be jeopardized if Pakistan misses critical IMF benchmarks on revenue collection and the fiscal deficit. MUSHARRAF has complied largely with IMF recommendations to raise petroleum prices, widen the tax net, privatize public sector assets,: and improve the balance of trade. However, Pakistan's economic prospects remain uncertain; too little has changed despite the new administration's intentions. Foreign exchange reserves hover at roughly $1 billion, GDP growth hinges on crop performance, the import bill has been hammered by high oil prices, and both foreign and domestic investors remain wary of committing to projects in Pakistan.

GDP

: Purchasing power parity— $282 billion (2000 est.)

GDP-real   : 4.8% (2000 est.)
growth rate

GDP-per capita : Purchasing power parity–$2,000 (2000 est.)

GDP-   : *agriculture:* 25.4%
composition by   *industry:* 24.9%
sector   *services:* 49.7% (1999 est.)

Population below : 40% (2000 est.)
poverty line

Household   : *lowest 10% :* 4.1%
income or
consumption   *highest 10%* 27.7% (1996).
by percentage
share

Inflation rate   : 5.2% (2000 est.)
(consumer
prices)

Labor force   : 40 million
                       note: extensive export of labor, mostly to
                       the Middle East, and use of child labor
                       (2000 est.)

Labor force -   : agriculture 44%, industry 17%, services 39%
by occupation   (1999 est.)

Unemployment : 6% (FY99/00 est.)
rate

Budget   : *revenues:* $8.9 billion

                       expenditures: $11.6 billion, including capital
                       expenditures of $NA (FY00/01 est.)

Industries   : textiles, food processing, beverages,
                       construction materials, clothing, paper
                       products, shrimp

Industrial   : 3.8% (1999 est.)
production
growth rate

Electricity-production	: 62.078 billion kWh (1999)
Electricity - production by source	: *fossil fuel:* 63.38% *hydro:* 36.51% *nuclear:* 0.11% *other:* 0% (1999)
Electricity-consumption	: 57.732 billion kWh (1999)
Electricity-exports	: 0 kWh (1999)
Electricity-imports	: 0 kWh (1999)
Agriculture - products	: Cotton, wheat, rice, sugarcane, fruits, vegetables; milk, beef, mutton, eggs
Exports	: $8.6 billion (f.o.b., FY99/00)
Exports - commodities	: textiles (garments, cotton cloth, and yarn), rice, other agricultural products
Exports - partners	: US 24%, Hong Kong 7%, UK 7%, Germany 6%, UAE 6% (FY99/00)
Imports	: $9.6 billion (f.o.b., FY99/00)
Imports - commodities	: machinery, petroleum, petroleum products, chemicals, transportation equipment, edible oils, grains, pulses, flour
Imports - partners	: Saudi Arabia 8%, UAE 8%, US 6%, Japan 6%, Malaysia 4% (FY99/00)
Debt - external	: $38 billion (2000 est.)
Economic aid - recipient	: $2 billion (FY99/00)
Currency	: Pakistani rupee (PKR)
Currency code	: PKR

Exchange rates : Pakistani rupees per US dollar—59.152
(January 2001), 52.814 (2000), 49.118 (1999),
44.943 (1998), 40.918 (1997), 35.909 (1996)

Fiscal year   : 1 July - 30 June

COMMUNICATIONS

Telephones -   : 2.861 million (March 1999)
main lines in
use

Telephones-   : 158,000(1998)
mobile cellular

Telephone   : *General assessment :* The domestic system is
system   mediocre, but improving; service is adequate
                    for government and business use, in part
                    because major businesses have established
                    their own private systems; since 1988, the
                    government has promoted investment in
                    the national telecommunications system on
                    a priority basis, significantly increasing
                    network capacity; despite major improve-
                    ments in trunk and urban systems, tele-
                    communication services are still not readily
                    available to the majority of the rural
                    population

                    domestic: microwave radio relay, coaxial
                    cable, fiber-optic cable, cellular, and satellite
                    networks

                    international: satellite earth stations - 3 Intelsat
                    (1 Atlantic Ocean and 2 Indian Ocean); 3
                    operational international gateway exchanges
                    (1 at Karachi and 2 at Islamabad): microwave
                    radio relay to neighboring countries (1999)

Radio broadcast : AM 27, FM 1, shortwave 21 (1998)
stations

Radios   : 13.5 million (1997)

Television broadcast stations	:	22 (plus seven low-power repeaters) (1997)
Televisions	:	3.1 million (1997)
Internet country code	:	pk
Internet Service Providers (ISPs)	:	30(2000)
Internet users	:	1.2 million (2000)

TRANSPORTATION

Railways	:	*total:* 8,163 km *broad gauge:* 7,718 km 1.676-m gauge (293 km electrified; 1,037 km double track) *narrowgauge:* 445 km 1.000-m gauge (1996 est.) (2000)
Highways	:	*total:* 247,811 km *paved:* 141,252 km (including 339 km of expressways) *unpaved:* 106,559 km (1998)
Waterways	:	none
Pipelines	:	crude oil 250 km; petroleum products 885 km; natural gas 4,044 km (1987)
Ports and harbors	:	Karachi, Port Muhammad bin Qasim
Merchant marine	:	*total:* 17 ships (1,000 GRT or over) totalling 240,605 GRT/367,040 DWT *ships by type:* cargo 13, container 3, petroleum tanker 1 (2000 est.)
Airports	:	117 (2000 est.)
Airports-with paved runways	:	*total:* 82 *over 3,047m:* 12 *2,438 to 3,047 m:* 21 *1,524 to 2,437 m:* 32 *914 to 1,523 m:* 14 *under 914 m:* 3 (2000 est.)

Airports - with : *total:* 35
unpaved   *1,524 to 2,437m;* 7
runways   *914 to 1,523m;* 11
                         under 914m: 17 (2000 est.)

Heliports   : 8(2000 est.)

MILITARY

Military   : Army, Navy, Air Force, Civil Armed Forces,
branches   National Guard

Military   : 17 years of age
manpower -
military age

Military   : *males age 15-49:* 35,770,928 (2001 est.)
manpower -
availability

Military   : *males age 15-49:* 21,897,366 (2001 est.)
manpower - fit
for military
service

Military   : *males:* 1,657,723 (2001 est.)
manpower -
reaching military
age annually

Military   : $2.435 billion (FY99/00)
expenditures -
dollar figure

Military   : 3.9% (FY99/00)
expenditures -
per cent of GDP

FESTIVALS AND EVENTS

Ramadan

Muslims around the world are once again anticipating the arrival of the holiest month of the year. During Ramadan, the ninth month of the Islamic calendar, Muslims all over the world unite in a period of fasting and spiritual reflection, renewal and family bonds.

Basant

The Festival of Kites, is said to be originated in India. It has been said as an Indian hobby, but in the cities of Punjab such as Lahore, Faisalabad and Rawalpindi, basant is the time when skies are filled with kites of all colors.

Christmas Day

25th December, 2000

December 25th is a public holiday in Pakistan, but it is in memory of Jinnah, the founder of Pakistan. In Christian homes, cards and gifts are exchanged, new clothes are worn and friends houses are visited. In the villages of Urdu and Punjabi, it is called Bara Din, the Big Day. The villagers wear bright clothes because it is a happy occasion. People embrace and greet each other with 'Bara Din Mubarrak Ho', 'the blessing of Christmas on you'.

INDEX